George Gallup in Hollywood

FILM AND CULTURE

John Belton, General Editor

• Susan Ohmer •

GEORGE GALLUP

in

HOLLYWOOD

Columbia University Press

New York

COLUMBIA UNIVERSITY PRESS

Publishers Since 1893

New York   Chichester, West Sussex

Copyright © 2006 Columbia University Press

Library of Congress Cataloging-in-Publication Data

Ohmer, Susan.
George Gallup in Hollywood / Susan Ohmer.
p. cm.— (Film and culture)
Includes bibliographical references and index.
ISBN 0-231-12132-6 (cloth : alk. paper) —
ISBN 0-231-12133-4 (pbk. : alk. paper)
1. Motion picture audiences—United States—Research—History—
20th century.   2. Gallup, George, 1901–   I. Title.   II. Series.
PN1995.9.A8046   2006
791.4307'2—dc22   2006019332

Columbia University Press books are printed on permanent
and durable acid-free paper.

Printed in the United States of America

c 10 9 8 7 6 5 4 3 2 1
p 10 9 8 7 6 5 4 3 2 1

The author wishes to thank the following:

The Harry Ransom Humanities Research Center, the University of Texas
at Austin, for permission to cite material from the David O. Selznick and John
Hay Whitney Papers, and to publish advertisements for *Gone with the Wind*;

The Oral History Collection of Columbia University, for permission to cite
material from "The Reminiscences of George Horace Gallup" and "The Reminiscences of Eugene Meyer";

The University Archives, University of Iowa Libraries, Iowa City, Iowa, for
permission to use material from the Kent Collection of photographs;

The Rockefeller Archive Center, for permission to cite material from the
Nelson Rockefeller Papers, folders 675 and 681, box 90, Record Group II, 2C,
Rockefeller Family Archives, Tarrytown, New York.

To Don and Larry,
who saw me through this project

Contents

List of Illustrations   ix
Acknowledgments   xi

1 What Do Audiences Want?   1

2 Guesswork Eliminated   13

3 The Laws That Determine Interest   31

4 America Speaks   51

5 Piggybacking on the Past   77

6 Singles and Doubles   91

7 Boy Meets Facts at RKO   121

8 David O. Selznick Presents:
Audience Research and the Independent Producer   163

9 Gallup Meets Goofy:
Audience Research at the Walt Disney Studio   193

10 Like, Dislike, Like Very Much   215

Abbreviations Used and Collections Consulted   231
Notes   233
Index   277

List of Illustrations

FIGURE 1.1 Early movie house interior with audience and piano player (c. 1913)   3

FIGURE 2.1 George Gallup at the University of Iowa in the mid-1920s   24

FIGURE 2.2 Gallup's novel method (1928) for measuring reader interest in the newspaper   26

FIGURE 2.3 Comic-strip ad for Grape-Nuts   29

FIGURE 3.1 Gallup's 1932 study for Liberty magazine makes Gallup famous in the advertising industry   37

FIGURE 4.1 Gallup interviewer questioning a voter   64

FIGURE 5.1 The Hollywood branch of the Audience Research Institute at Hollywood and Vine (1941)   80

FIGURE 6.1 Press release by Gallup showing Hollywood's influence on popular reading tastes (1939)   95

FIGURE 6.2 The Double Feature Poll (July 1940)   107

FIGURE 7.1 Orson Welles with reporters on the day after the "War of the Worlds" broadcast in October 1938   143

FIGURE 7.2 Lucille Ball, Desi Arnaz, and Ann Miller in Too Many Girls (1940)   150

FIGURE 7.3 Jan Wiley and Ginger Rogers in a scene from RKO's Kitty Foyle
(1940)   156

FIGURE 8.1 Gallup's research influenced the exhibition and promotion
of Gone with the Wind   179

FIGURE 8.2 On the basis of Gallup's research, David O. Selznick decided
to copy the visual style of the book's cover in ads for the film.   180

FIGURE 8.3 MGM ads developed for the second anniversary release
of Gone with the Wind   186

FIGURE 9.1 Walt Disney, Deems Taylor, and conductor Leopold Stokowski
discuss plans for Fantasia (1940).   199

Acknowledgments

Academia offers many pleasures, and the greatest of these may be having colleagues with whom one can share ideas. It makes me very happy to be able to thank the many people and institutions that sustained me while I wrote this book.

My research has benefited from generous financial support. The Institute for Scholarship in the Liberal Arts at the University of Notre Dame provided summer grants and travel funds that enabled me to devote time to this project and to present my research at conferences. I thank Chris Fox, Julia Douthwaite, and Cindy Bergeman for their assistance. Mark Roche, Dean of the College of Arts and Letters at Notre Dame, also made research funds available to me. Several archives awarded grants that made it possible for me to examine materials in their collections. I am grateful for a J. Walter Thompson Research Grant from the Hartman Center of Duke University; a Dorot Fellowship from the Harry Ransom Humanities Research Center of the University of Texas-Austin; and an Everett Helm Visiting Fellowship from the Lilly Library at Indiana University. At New York University, a Graduate Arts and Sciences Dean's Dissertation Fellowship and the Jay Leyda Memorial Teaching Fellowship made it possible to get this project off the ground. Thank you all very much.

In the course of doing my research I enjoyed the assistance and conversation of many people. Alec Gallup, George Gallup, Jr., and Sara Van Allen took the time to share their thoughts about George Gallup's work in Hollywood.

Tom Simonet exemplified collegiality when he sent me notes of his interviews with Gallup and Paul Perry. I would also like to thank the late Don Cahalan for sharing his memories of the Audience Research Institute (ARI), and Kendall O'Connor, Card Walker, Harry Tytle, and George Heinemann for giving me their perspectives on how the Disney studio regarded Gallup's work. At Young & Rubicam, John Rindlaub told me of Gallup's speeches about his work in film, and Maureen Pine helped me find evidence of his advertising studies from the 1930s. In gathering information about the early days of the Gallup organization, I drew on the expertise of Lois Timms-Ferrara at the Roper Center for Public Opinion Research at the University of Connecticut at Storrs, who found creative ways to dig up buried treasures. David Smith and Paula Sigman made the extensive files at the Disney studio available to me. Thomas Staley, Charles Bell, and Pat Fox of the Ransom Center worked tirelessly to help me find material in the Selznick collection. Ellen Gartrell and Jacqueline Reid worked marvels in the Special Collections department at Duke. At the University of Iowa, I appreciate the willingness of the Special Collections staff to unearth bulky volumes of the *Daily Iowan*. The Interlibrary Loan Department at Notre Dame made my life much easier. Thank you, Ken Kinslow. My able and hard-working research assistant Jessica Lienau showed endless patience in finding Gallup material.

This book first took shape in the Department of Cinema Studies at New York University, and both the manuscript and I benefited greatly from the suggestions of faculty and students there. Robert Sklar took the time to encourage someone who loved archives, and inspired me to imagine a future based on that kind of research. Bill Simon read this work with such interest and attention that he convinced me that someone else might, too. Robert Stam helped shape my theoretical framework with wit and sensitivity. Janet Staiger led me to see how an industrial approach to film studies could yield rewarding insights. My writing and analysis benefited as well from classes and discussions with the brilliant Annette Michelson and the ever-generous Bill Everson. I would like also to thank friends who shared their ideas and reminded me that we were all in this together: John Hagen, Shelley Stamp, Ben Singer, Steve Elworth, Melinda Barlow, Art Simon, Harold Stadler, Ella Shohat, Giuliana Bruno, Leger Grindon, and Susan Ryan. John Belton offered several helpful suggestions that shaped the manuscript in its early form.

At the University of Michigan, I enjoyed opportunities to explore various aspects of this work with colleagues in the Film and Video Studies program. Thank you, Gaylyn Studlar, Bill Paul, and Frank Beaver. It was very helpful, too, to walk down the hall and discuss polling with colleagues in Communication Arts. I am grateful to Vincent Price, Mike Traugott, Susan Douglas, Kristin Harrison, Nick Valentine and Miriam Metzger for sharing their considerable knowledge of polling methods with me. At Notre Dame, I thank Jim Collins, Chris Becker, Wendy Arons, Jessica Chalmers, Aaron Magnan-Park, Tom Guglielmo, Peter Holland, Mark Pilkinton, Greg Sterling, Bob Schmuhl, Ben Giamo, Ava Preacher and Coleen Hoover for their interest and support. My work has also benefited from the encouragement and example of Matthew Bernstein, Miriam Hansen, Richard Maltby, Mark Langer, Michael Curtin, Thomas Doherty, Virginia Wright Wexman, and Michele Hilmes.

As this project moved through the publishing process, I was fortunate to receive encouragement and helpful advice from Susan Herbst, Charles Musser, Karen Riggs, James Carey, and an anonymous reviewer. Don Crafton and Karen Backstein read every line of the manuscript and offered suggestions that improved it. Any remaining faults are due solely to me. Roy Thomas's careful copyediting whipped the manuscript into shape. No one could ask for an editor with more patience and tact than Jennifer Crewe. Working with her has been one of the most enjoyable parts of this experience.

Big projects take shape in small pieces, and the comfort and support provided by friends and family make the process easier. I was fortunate to share the joys and challenges of this project with Karen Backstein and Catherine Benamou. Karen helped me untie what seemed like impossible knots at crucial moments, and Catherine's late-night phone calls of commiseration reminded me of what collegiality is all about. Kay Taylor Hightower helped ease the burdens of authorship with trips to the theater, opera, and ballet. Ann Levy provided a model of entrepreneurship that inspired me to keep going. Heidi Ardizzone, Cheri Gray, Pam Robertson Wojcik, Amy Sarch, Joe Shiroky, Sheri Alpert, and Meredith Gill illustrated how much fun collaboration can be. I am deeply grateful as well to Mirella Affron for her encouragement at a key moment.

I would also like to thank my parents, Charles and Bobbe Ohmer, and my six brothers—Chuck, Dave, John, Mike, Mark, and Richard—for always asking how the book was going, and for wanting to read it. Their sincere interest and genial questions led me to think about how to make history more accessible.

Finally, I want to thank Larry Miller and Don Crafton, without whose support and encouragement this book would not have been written. Larry cheered the project from its beginning, and Don saw it through to the end. Thank you both for believing it could be done. This book is dedicated to you.

George Gallup in Hollywood

1

What Do Audiences Want?

Early in the twentieth century, Adolph Zukor operated a luxury motion picture theater in New York City. Named the Crystal Hall for the glass staircase at its entrance, the theater was located at Broadway and 14th Street, a busy shopping and theater district. Zukor, a Hungarian immigrant who had worked as a furrier on the Lower East Side before he became a film exhibitor, wanted to know more about what his customers enjoyed in this new form of entertainment. In his autobiography *The Public Is Never Wrong*, he described how he went about studying audiences' reactions:

> In the Crystal Hall it was my custom to take a seat about six rows from the front. . . . I spent a good deal of time watching the faces of the audience, even turning around to do so. . . . With a little experience I could see, hear and "feel" the reaction to each melodrama and comedy. Boredom was registered—even without comments or groans—as clearly as laughter demonstrated pleasure.[1]

Nearly one hundred years later, the industry measures our reactions to films primarily by numbers—and the larger the better. Box office grosses for films that opened over the weekend are available on Monday morning, providing a quick indication of whether the public liked or disliked Hollywood's most recent offerings. In an effort to anticipate our reactions, many studios hold test screenings in advance of a film's release. At these sessions, audiences who have been selected according to age and gender receive questionnaires that ask them to evaluate a film's cast, plot, director, and title. Depending on the survey, opinions can be expressed either as numbers or letter grades, yielding a score that sums up a film's appeal. Comments from these test screenings often determine how much money a studio will spend to market a film, and can result in an excited "buzz" about a project or whispers of its early demise.

From the era before film studios that Zukor described, to the multimedia conglomerates of today, the film industry has been driven by the question, "What do audiences want?" The industry's unceasing efforts to answer this question underscore how important audiences are: our likes and dislikes determine whether films make money and whether the companies that produce them stay in business. Though the reasons for studying audience's reactions remain the same, how this is done has changed dramatically over time, as these two experiences illustrate. Zukor's vivid description of being able to "see, hear, and 'feel'" audiences' reactions evokes an era when producers sat down and watched films along with the public (fig. 1.1). These personal experiences encouraged Zukor and other pioneers to believe they had a direct pipeline to audiences' feelings, and could, over time, develop an almost intuitive sense of what people liked. Though today's market researchers may also sit in the theater with an audience, they rely more often on information gathered from surveys. While Zukor assessed audiences' general reactions, questionnaires today ask for comments on specific elements of a film that are thought to affect ticket purchases. Marketing firms use this information to construct posters, trailers, and advertisements that emphasize qualities audiences say they enjoy. Questionnaires also provide more specific information than Zukor could glean. Where Zukor saw simply a mass of ticket buyers, contemporary market researchers break viewers into distinct socioeconomic groups. This information allows studios to target films more precisely to particular segments of the audience.

Within the trajectory formed by Zukor's on-the-spot observations and the more scientific methods of today, the decade of the 1940s marks a critical juncture. Before then, directors, producers, and exhibitors relied primarily on their own observations, on fan mail, or on reports in trade papers for indications of how audiences felt about a film. Though there were some informal studies of public opinion during the 1920s and 1930s, it was not until the 1940s that the industry began to employ what were considered to be more scientific methods for studying viewers' responses, using carefully designed questionnaires and population samples. These new methods reflected the emergence of national opinion polls in the United States and the development of more sophisticated techniques of empirical research in print and broadcasting media. Most of the techniques market researchers use today to analyze films and their viewers originated during the 1940s.

FIGURE 1.1 Early movie house interior with audience and piano player (c. 1913). A Keystone film is shown on the screen. Many Hollywood moguls of the 1940s who felt they didn't need scientific research to tell them what audiences wanted had begun their careers watching films in theaters like this one.   (*Courtesy Corbis*)

How these techniques developed, and why Hollywood began to use them, is the subject of this book.

The central force in this process was George Gallup, the man whose name has become synonymous with opinion polling. The Gallup Organization has measured Americans' reactions to candidates in every presidential election since 1936, and journalists continue to cite its findings as definitive evidence of public opinion. The company's regular surveys on education provide data for policymakers in universities and government agencies, and its studies of popular attitudes toward religion have launched national debates about Americans' values and beliefs. Despite some famous blunders, such as the 1948 election, when Gallup incorrectly predicted that Thomas Dewey would defeat Harry Truman, polls carrying his name are seen as authoritative sources of information about public opinion on a wide range of subjects.

Though George Gallup is best known for his political surveys, he spent most of his career in advertising. After completing his Ph.D. at the University of Iowa, he carried out readership studies for newspapers and magazines, and gradually focused his research on advertising. His innovative methods drew the attention of several New York agencies, and in 1932, Young & Rubicam hired him to be its director of research, in charge of print and broadcast studies. With the agency's support, Gallup established the polling service that bears his name, in time for the 1936 presidential election. In 1940, after his political poll had become solidly established, Gallup founded the Audience Research Institute (ARI) with the idea of adapting the techniques used in advertising and political polling to study film audiences. By the end of the 1940s, ARI had conducted literally thousands of surveys for more than a dozen clients. The institute strove to isolate every factor that might influence viewers' responses, from a film's title, narrative, and cast through its advertising and publicity. Its findings affected films ranging from *Gone with the Wind* to Walt Disney's cartoons, and shaped the careers of many stars and producers. In their scope and comprehensiveness, ARI's studies represent the first full-scale effort at empirical market research in Hollywood.

Gallup's career was remarkably linear: one project led to another, and people whom he met in one field became points of entry into another. Tracking his journey from graduate work in psychology, to advertising, to political surveys allows us to see how these ways of studying human behavior influenced his approach to film. Gallup was not alone in making the transition from advertising to political surveys. Two other researchers, Elmo Roper and Archibald Crossley, also used techniques drawn from advertising to study voters' responses during the 1936 presidential election, but Gallup publicized these new methods more vigorously. His interviews in popular magazines and frequent speeches to business and community groups made him the symbol for these new "scientific" techniques.

In the late 1930s, opinion polling emerged as a major force in U.S. politics and culture. Newspapers began to report the results of election surveys as a regular feature, and business magazines commissioned studies of consumer attitudes on such disparate subjects as automobiles, vacations, cigarettes, and drinking. Polling became an object of fascination. Popular magazines and academic journals analyzed the methods and implications of opinion research in great detail. When Gallup and others argued for the importance of these new techniques, they criticized earlier ways of studying public opinion. These discussions of the flaws and failures of earlier work illuminate the assumptions that governed the newer methods. By examining the formation of new methods of opinion research in politics during this period and the disputes they engendered, we can understand how social and economic forces in Depression America structured this developing field of applied research. It was during the 1936 election that opinion polling, as we know it today, with carefully constructed questionnaires and population samples, made a dramatic entrance into the political arena.

Gallup's work in Hollywood also emerged during a period of intense activity in media research. The Payne Fund Studies of the early 1930s, Paul Lazarsfeld's work on radio in the 1940s, and Hadley Cantril's study of reactions to Orson Welles's "War of the Worlds" broadcast (1940) mark significant milestones in the history of communication research. In contrast to these projects, which were funded by academic or philanthropic organizations, Gallup's work was frankly commercial, commissioned by companies that wanted to increase the profitability of their newspapers, magazines, radio programs, or films. By tracing the dissemination of his influence throughout the studio system, we can locate the specific forces that shaped his research and learn what was at stake in these initial forays into the unknown territory of American taste.

The Audience and the System

Film theorists have distinguished between two words that are commonly used to refer to viewers—*spectators* and *audiences*. Theorists who analyze the "spectator" focus on the subconscious or unconscious levels of our responses to films, the processes of absorption, voyeurism, and desire that are evoked as we watch stars on a large screen in the dark. As Annette Kuhn notes, this model of spectatorship as "a set of psychic relations" ignores the social implications of filmgoing. "It is the social act of going to the cinema . . . that makes the individual cinemagoer part of an audience." The audience, according to Kuhn, "is a group of people who buy tickets at the box office . . . people who can be surveyed, counted and categorized according to age, sex, and socioeconomic status."[2] It is the activity of the "audience" that most concerns the industry. Film and television producers may speculate about the internal psychological processes of the "spectator," but they can easily observe the external movements of "audiences" into and out of theaters. Of course, these two processes are linked—presumably, one leads to the other—but the actions of the audience in buying tickets is what most concerns Hollywood.

Most discussions of the viewer in film studies have proceeded from a psychoanalytic or cognitive model, not a sociological one.[3] Many theorists working within these frameworks reject empirical research as a representation of audience activity because they feel that it does not sufficiently account for the complexities of our experiences.[4] Gallup's work in Hollywood recognized the challenges involved in analyzing how we respond to films, and looking at it enables us to see how one key researcher formulated some of the methods used today. Recent work in television studies by Virginia Nightingale and others suggests that there are ways to use social science data more creatively in understanding our responses.[5] In contrast to the blanket dismissal of quantitative research on the part of some film theorists, I suggest that writings on the cultural study of quantification and the sociology of knowledge offer methods of analysis that are attentive to the deeper implications of this work. The approach I will outline is particularly relevant to Gallup, since his polls took shape at a time when the assumptions and techniques involved in empirical research were being debated openly.

Historically, the kind of audience research Gallup conducted was a relatively recent redefinition of public opinion. Public opinion is not a concept with a fixed and eternal meaning, but a discursive formation whose structures and functions change and are changed by social, cultural, and political practices. Concepts of both "the public" and "opinion" reflect processes at work within a particular culture and historical period. Since the eighteenth century, when antiroyalist forces in France posited the existence of a "public opinion" that opposed the king, many different political and social groups have evoked it as a rhetorical figure to support their views.[6] The concept of the "public" has become more inclusive since that era, as the democratic movements of the nineteenth and twentieth centuries increased the number of groups who are represented within that rubric. Similarly, the idea of "opinion" has connoted varying degrees of emotion and reason, depending upon the social context in which it was discussed. The public's opinions can be seen as the result of thoughtful deliberation, as in many philosophies of democracy, or as the result of anger and repression, as in the aftermath of the French Revolution.[7]

In the words of Ien Ang, one quality that distinguishes modern formulations of public opinion is that they have "fallen into professional hands."[8] Since the mid-twentieth century many forms of public opinion, such as polls and market research, are "institutionally produced," that is, they embody an institution's idea of what constitutes opinion. Ang draws on the work of Michel Foucault to argue that modern forms of public opinion represent a regime of knowledge that embodies specific power relations.[9] What distinguishes public opinion studies in the twentieth century is their use of quantitative forms. In *Numbered Voices*, Susan Herbst reviews the different ways that people have expressed their opinions on politics over the past several centuries and notes that in the modern era forms of opinion that are taken as significant are those that represent our ideas in terms of numbers and percentages. In previous historical periods, by contrast, people expressed their attitudes toward power by organizing protest marches, staging strikes, holding town meetings, and sending the king to the guillotine.[10] Since the mid-1930s, when Gallup and others developed scientific polling, our views on politics have been routinely summarized as percentages for and against a particular candidate or issue. Similarly, our behavior in the marketplace is also described in terms of patterns of consumption. Knowing what large numbers of people buy is considered to be an accurate index of our preferences.

This modern desire to express opinions in quantitative terms represents an epistemological shift within the history of public opinion that has significant repercussions for Gallup's work and for media research today. Herbst and Ang refer to James Beniger's study *The Control Revolution* (1986), which surveys the ways that science, politics, and business have increased the level of rationalization and standardization within modern life.[11] Beniger examines developments in fields as diverse as communication, transportation, finance, and science to show how modern societies attempt to control production, the flow of information, and the structure of bureaucracies. Gallup's work in advertising, media research, political polling, and film creates a framework in which to study how these processes develop across various cultural fields.

When opinions are expressed as numbers, they are easier to count and manage. Numbers connote a sense of control and foster the illusion that the multiplicity of experience can be contained, which is why, as Mary Poovey argues, "numbers have come to epitomize the modern fact."[12] Twentieth-century opinion polls and market research represent the most recent example of this trend, but the pattern originated in the eighteenth century. Patricia Cline Cohen has explored how people in that period introduced quantitative frameworks into everyday existence:

> They began to see quantities where, before, men thought of qualities. The body politic could be thought of as a population, death could be comprehended as a mortality rate. Even . . . temperature became an ascertainable number of degrees. . . . This new propensity to measure and count meant that certain kinds of experience hitherto considered to be wholly subjective became amenable to objective description through the use of numbers.[13]

Cline draws attention to the cultural and epistemological significance of counting, noting that in a world of flux and turbulence like the Enlightenment, "quantification must have seemed an alluring way to impose order."[14] Quantification implies control, and in Depression America, when Gallup began working, we see this same pattern recur. Warren Susman notes the significance of polling for the 1930s:

> Americans had "empirical" evidence of how they felt and thought regarding the major issues of the day and generally shared attitudes and beliefs. It was easier now to find the core of values and opinions that united Americans, the symbols

that tied them together, that helped define the American way. . . . The polls themselves became a force, an instrument of significance, not only for the discovery
and molding of dominant cultural patterns, but also for their reinforcement.[15]

Twentieth-century culture valorizes statistical knowledge; it is, as Ang and
Foucault note, a "discourse invested with truth value."[16] When scientific,
quantitative discourse is taken as the most accurate representation of public
opinion, however, other forms of expression are displaced. Institutions that
track public opinion in the spheres of politics or media select characteristics
of viewers and texts that are important to them. In the case of market research
in film, factors such as age, class, and race become relevant insofar as they
contribute to the box office. Opinion polls are rarely open-ended or designed
to accommodate many kinds of audience response. Pierre Bourdieu and others have drawn attention to the fact that opinion polls, and we could say by extension audience research, are not complete and accurate representations of
the range of human experiences and beliefs. The questions asked in an opinion survey may not really concern the people questioned, and their answers
will be interpreted according to the needs of the institution doing the study.[17]

In attempting to sum up our views, to provide a comprehensive account
of public opinion, quantitative research often leaves something out. What is
displaced, according to Ang, is the complexity and contingency of everyday
life, whether it is media usage or the process of choosing the next president.[18]
The definition of public opinion is always tentative and provisional, and subject to revision. A total summation of audience behavior is "never completely
achieved, and has to be continuously pursued."[19]

A fundamental premise of this book is that empirical evidence is a construction, a numerical representation of reactions and behaviors. Rather than
"read off" the information Gallup presented, I consider how the information
in polls was gathered, categorized, interpreted, and deployed. Numbers are
not taken at face value, but are examined for the assumptions, influences,
structures of power, and ideologies they encode. Quantitative research is not
just raw data but a discourse that provides a way of defining, understanding,
exploring, and sometimes managing the unpredictable elements of human
psychology. Like market researchers today, and many scholars of film reception, ARI believed that our reactions to films are linked to our age, class,
gender, and place of residence. However, while film historians today seek to
uncover the specifics of film reception and focus on the uniqueness of individuals or social groups, ARI, on the contrary, aimed to speak for a national
mass audience of filmgoers. Its connection with Gallup, and the polls that
purported to speak for a nation of voters, gave credence to that stance for
many in Hollywood.[20]

In stressing that audience research is a construction, I will also examine the institutional and ideological forces that molded Gallup's work in film. The cultural status of Gallup's film work waxed and waned according to the status of his political polls. ARI's research illustrates how film viewing came to be linked with other forms of consumption in American culture, and how audiences' desires were defined within the parameters of commercial studio production. Audience research positions both films and film viewers as products to be studied and molded.

The next two chapters survey Gallup's media research before he began working in Hollywood. When he described his methods to the film industry, Gallup often referred to his prior research, and his film studies shared many of the methods and assumptions of his earlier work. Gallup's studies of newspaper and magazine readers established his pragmatic orientation, and focused on the practical problems confronting business executives. Like his later film research, these early studies strove to pinpoint specific factors influencing audience response and drew attention to class and gender differences. Contemporary discussions of Gallup's media research praised his rigorous methods and ability to gain access to subconscious desires.

Gallup's primary claim to fame, however, was the polling service he initiated in 1936. Chapter 4 discusses the origin of the Gallup Poll and assesses its impact on American culture of the 1930s. Gallup's brilliant strategy for launching his poll during the 1936 election stands as a landmark in the history of survey research. He drew national attention when he predicted the outcome of the election months in advance and when he published articles and made speeches introducing the public to the concept of opinion polls. The 1936 election irrevocably established opinion polling as part of American culture, as the public became fascinated with the notion that one could measure the views of a large number of people by asking questions of a few. This chapter illuminates how "Gallup" became a brand name in American culture, one already familiar to the studio executives he met in Hollywood.

A primary reason for the ready acceptance of Gallup's work in Hollywood was his cultural status as an expert on opinion polling. My analysis will look at how concepts of authority and expertise are constructed, in order to assess how notions of "objectivity" and "science" gained credence during the mid-1930s. This period marks a major shift in cultural discussions of public opinion, what it is and how it can be measured. It is the era in which polls came to replace many other expressions of public opinion in the social arena. In part because they present numbers that carry an aura of precision, polls have come to be considered definitive indices of public opinion. My discussion reconstructs the debates about the new "scientific" approach to studying opinion during the period when polls originated, to see how experts took over the task of representing public opinion.

Gallup was not the only member of the Audience Research Institute, and in fact it could be argued that his many professional responsibilities during this period would have precluded a close involvement with the day-to-day work of the institute. Chapter 5 uncovers the financial and administrative connections between Gallup's film research and his work in advertising and political polling. Gallup used his political polls to carry out preliminary surveys for his film company, and found many of ARI's staff there as well, including David Ogilvy, who wrote many of the institute's early reports and later founded his own advertising agency. This chapter reveals the creative ways that Gallup financed a new venture in film in the midst of the Depression, and this while he was still employed at Young & Rubicam.

After completing these smaller, private studies, ARI went public with its survey work in a project dealing with double features, the subject of heated debate within the film industry. ARI encountered mixed reactions in Hollywood with this survey. The moguls, producers who had been making movies for decades, resented this intrusion from an outsider who purported to understand audiences better than they did. By contrast, independent producers and studio executives trained in sales and marketing appreciated the significance of ARI's work. Chapter 6 looks at how Gallup launched his film research service with the double features poll and how the economic and industrial tensions that were simmering in Hollywood in 1940 exploded in its wake.

Chapter 7 examines ARI's work for its first client, RKO Radio Pictures, with whom it had an exclusive contract from the spring of 1940 through the summer of 1942. The chapter details the kinds of information Gallup and Ogilvy presented to the company about the public and how this research affected stars, scripts, and advertising campaigns. Ogilvy's descriptions of the public sometimes make their reactions more audible, while at other times his voice is louder than theirs. Letters and memos from various administrative levels in the company reveal dramatically different reactions to this work, depending upon the executive's background or beliefs about filmmaking.

In contrast to chapter 7, which analyzes how market research functioned within a major studio, chapters 8 and 9 evaluate the studies that ARI conducted for two independent producers, David O. Selznick and Walt Disney. Independent producers established their own production companies outside of the major studios, in order to maintain more control over their films, retain a larger share of the profits, and sometimes push the boundaries of conventional norms of storytelling. However, independents were not completely free of the majors, as they relied on the same creative personnel and system of divided labor as the larger studios. Independents also needed the majors to finance their films and to distribute them once they were completed. In the 1940s, relations between the independents and the studios were often contentious: the two groups needed each other, yet their goals were not always congruent. Gallup's research for Selznick and Disney illustrates how market research could give independents more leverage with the major studios—or conversely, provide a means through which the majors could exercise control over them.

During World War II there was a lull in commercial opinion polling, though the military and government greatly increased their use of survey research. Chapter 10 offers an overview of ARI's work after World War II and analyzes how Hollywood's response to Gallup at that time reflected shifts in the film industry's economic and structural conditions. Studios that were not interested in research before the war saw its potential at the end of the decade. Though some used audience research as part of preproduction planning, most used Gallup to develop advertising and marketing campaigns tailored to particular audiences. By 1950, market research had become so widespread in Hollywood that MGM analyst Leo Handel was able to compile a catalog of methods and techniques in *Hollywood Looks at Its Audience*.[21]

During the 1940s, exhibitors, actors, and even viewers challenged the hegemony of the studio system. Audience research became one of the battlegrounds for these disputes about control and authority. As actors and writers saw it, statistical research muzzled innovation. Survey questions usually asked viewers to imagine performers in familiar roles, rather than new ones, and so reinforced existing star images. Questions about new films referred to established popular genres, which perpetuated these narrative forms. Actors and screenwriters argued that it was difficult to develop new forms of action or characterization when surveys only measured audiences' responses to existing ones. Exhibitors, for their part, resented the idea of scientific research taking the place of their own firsthand accounts of local viewers. Even some members of the audience complained about the way they were represented in surveys and organized their own studies to counter Gallup's.

The development and use of audience research during the 1940s illustrate how this seemingly neutral data can serve as an index of tensions within the industry. Discursive constructions of public opinion became a force field in which anxieties about power and control were manifested. In speaking of the audiences who went to the cinema, producers, directors, writers, actors, and exhibitors attempted to assert their authority over film production and reception. Audiences in turn fought for control over how their desires and interests were represented. In the 1940s, discourses about film audiences become a means to understand and manage change and uncertainty within the industry as a whole. The raw material provided by statistics and surveys were symptoms of larger industrial and ideological pressures emerging at this time. The book concludes by examining the controversies about market research in the wake of the 1948 election and assesses the continuing impact of Gallup's work today.

Gallup's Audience Research Institute essentially introduced market research to Hollywood, yet its work is not well known in media studies today. This book provides a comprehensive study of the company, its origins and methods, the controversies it engendered, and its enduring impact. For film studies, this history brings to light an unknown part of Hollywood's past and shows how we might find room for a critical analysis of market research within reception studies. Within the fields of American Studies, marketing, and public opinion, Gallup's film research illustrates how seemingly disparate endeavors can be connected creatively. Many of these techniques survive in different forms today. By rediscovering the debates that took place when they began, we can better understand what is at stake in market research, and become more cognizant of the way it represents us.

2

●●●●●●●●●●

Guesswork Eliminated

In American popular culture, Iowa has attained an almost metaphorical
significance as a place that exemplifies traditional values that are rooted
in the farm and the prairie. Hollywood, too, has recognized the state's
symbolic possibilities and has used it as the setting or inspiration for such
diverse films as *State Fair* (1933 and 1945), *The Best Years of Our Lives* (1946),
The Music Man (1962), and *The Bridges of Madison County* (1995).[1] For
Gallup, Iowa served as a touchstone against which to measure many later
experiences. Born and raised in Jefferson, he displayed an entrepreneurial
spirit that later enabled him to begin the Gallup Poll in the midst of the
Depression. His experiences growing up in a family that prized independent
thinking inspired a commitment to intellectual life and an impulse to question authority, even if it meant telling Hollywood executives that he knew
more about their audiences than they did. Gallup earned his undergraduate
and graduate degrees in Iowa City, at the University of Iowa, where he developed a passion for journalism and established a network of friends with
whom he would work throughout his career. As a college student in the 1920s
who was actively involved in campus life, he formed a sense of how popular
culture offered new ways of imagining oneself and one's relationships to others. Through his academic research, Gallup explored contemporary trends
in scientific management and applied psychology that provided the intellectual and methodological foundations for his later research in film. As both

his emotional and intellectual center, Iowa was crucial in forming Gallup's outlook on his life and work.

Prairie Grass Roots

In *Prairie Grass Roots*, his history of Gallup's hometown, Thomas Morain describes the period in which Gallup grew up as one of rapid change in Iowa due to technological innovations in transportation and agriculture that created widespread economic prosperity. In 1901, when Gallup was born, Jefferson was a small town of less than 3,000, but its location on the Raccoon River about sixty miles northwest of Des Moines provided many advantages. The town was a county seat and transportation hub, criss-crossed by numerous train lines that carried Iowa grain and livestock to the east and brought back finished goods in return. The central part of the state also benefited from the massive increase in the amount of land that was brought under cultivation during the late nineteenth century. Gallup's father made money buying and selling land as prices rose rapidly in the state between 1900 and 1919. By the time of Gallup's birth, Iowa's reputation and symbolic significance as the corn and hog capital of the country had been secured.[2]

Gallup's ancestors had migrated to the area from New England after the Civil War and had brought with them a keen interest in politics and culture. Though Iowans had been supporting the Republican Party since after the Civil War, Gallup's own family showed more varied political sentiments. His grandfather was a staunch Republican who had fought for the Union during the Civil War, while his uncle ran for local office on the Democratic ticket. Gallup's father, on the other hand, considered himself an independent and detested Theodore Roosevelt, the Republican president whom most of Jefferson supported.[3] Gallup's belief in perseverance, hard work, and the inherent dignity of the common man mirrored the values professed by fellow Iowan, Herbert Hoover, whose national career began during Gallup's youth. Though Gallup insisted that he did not belong to any political party when he became a pollster, Democratic politicians believed he favored the Republicans, and it was through Republican friends that he first met studio executives in Hollywood.

Even the house he grew up in embodied the independence that Gallup prized in his family. The Gallups lived on the edge of town, in an octagonal house that his father had designed and built to catch more of the sun's rays. George Gallup senior held a series of jobs, as a farmer and teacher, but his son remembered him as being more of a philosopher or scholar who lived almost entirely in the world of ideas. "Problems of everyday life never concerned him very much," his son said later.[4] George senior encouraged his children to be independent and to question the status quo; George junior recalled that his father "would refuse to do anything in an orthodox way."[5] His family owned a large library of over one thousand books that the parents encouraged their children to read. In later interviews Gallup said he felt proud of his father's independence and intellectual curiosity and believed that this background encouraged him to think creatively and to challenge conventional wisdom.[6]

Though Gallup's father didn't spend much time in the business world, he encouraged his sons to learn about it. While they were still in grade school, his father gave him and his older brother a herd of dairy cows to raise. In return for taking care of the animals, they were allowed to keep the money they earned selling milk. During this time Iowa was becoming a dairy center for the country, so Gallup's small business benefited from this broader trend.[7] By high school, Gallup was earning enough money to pay for all the equipment for the football and basketball teams, which at that time did not receive money from the school for their supplies.[8] Perhaps because of these early experiences, Gallup developed a talent for spotting opportunities to make money, an entrepreneurial flair that served him well in later business ventures.[9]

A Place of Fantasy and Spectacle

In the fall of 1919, Gallup enrolled at the University of Iowa. College enrollments were booming in the 1920s throughout the United States, and Iowa was no exception. The university had grown slowly since its founding in 1847, but during the 1920s the number of students who earned undergraduate degrees there tripled.[10] Gallup's chief passion as a student was his work on the campus newspaper, the *Daily Iowan*. Journalism was not an official major during Gallup's years at Iowa, though the university now has an endowed chair named after him, but Gallup worked on the paper throughout his undergraduate years, acting as managing editor in his junior year and then as editor-in-chief when he was a senior. Under his leadership, the paper expanded beyond the campus to serve all of Iowa City, by adding local news and information from the Associated Press wire services. The physical size of the paper expanded as well; Gallup made it wider and longer to allow more room for news and feature articles, including a full page devoted to sports. To finance this expansion, he recruited more advertising from local merchants, which enabled him to reduce prices and increase circulation.[11]

The pages of the *Daily Iowan* present a vivid picture of student life during this period. News of social activities predominates, including parties at fraternities and sororities, homecoming, and even celebratory oxen roasts that were held during football season. Many students at the university during the 1920s also experienced significant financial hardships, as the *Daily Iowan* documented. After World War I the economic boom that buoyed Gallup's childhood ended abruptly. The federal government eliminated subsidies it had paid Iowa farmers to maintain production during the war, and food exports overseas declined. The price of farmland plummeted, and farmers who had bought land and equipment on credit suffered severe financial hardships.[12] The *Daily Iowan* estimated that between one-quarter and one-fifth of undergraduates worked full or part time to pay their expenses. For his part, Gallup started a towel concession in the university gym to earn money.[13]

American novels of the 1920s, such as F. Scott Fitzgerald's *This Side of Paradise*, depict college students as enjoying carefree lives that revolve around parties and dances. Iowa students experienced more financial pressures than Fitzgerald's Princeton comrades, yet the pages of the *Daily Iowan* teem with ads for teashops, dances, and clothing stores. Many ads acknowledged the financial limitations under which students lived, by advertising the latest fashions at reasonable cost. Killian's Department Store offered Poiret twill suits and Canton Crepe frocks for good prices, while the Armstrong Clothing Company offered men suits that displayed the "English tendency" favored by "eastern college men."[14] The ads created an image of fantasy and luxury while offering ways to make this lifestyle affordable and attainable.

Among the ads that populated the *Daily Iowan*, those for film screenings stand out. Of the four pages that usually made up each issue, ads for current films often took up one quarter to one half of a page and sometimes a full page. Many consisted of detailed line drawings that portrayed scenes in a film or its stars. Harold Lloyd and Charlie Chaplin, Gloria Swanson and Pola Negri appeared often, as did the films of Cecil B. DeMille and D. W. Griffith. Since Iowa City theaters such as the Strand and the Englert changed their programs every few days, as did many theaters of the time, the pages of the *Daily Iowan* displayed an ever-changing array of images. Film theaters emerged as spaces of fantasy and spectacle and often continued this effect through live stage shows and musical accompaniment.[15]

It was during the 1920s that Hollywood's self-promotion kicked into high gear.[16] In this period Hollywood became a cultural space as well as a geographical place, one that engaged the imaginations of much of the country. The notion of "stardom" that originated during the 1910s gathered force, and with it the idea that stars might serve as ego ideals for their audiences or as projections of their viewers' fantasies.[17] Film ads in the *Daily Iowan* sketched a world of glamour and daring, where women were sultry and seductive, men suave and debonair. A large ad for Anna Q. Nilsson's *What Women Will Do*

(1921) invited viewers to share her life as she "smuggled opium, dodged the police; wore spangles in a cabaret; and thrilled pleasure seekers by her dive from a flying trapeze."[18] For male viewers, an ad for the six-reeler *Burn 'Em Up Barnes* presented Johnny "Torchy" Hines "as the star of a rollicking, racing romance Full of Speed, Laughs and Thrills."[19]

According to Morain, these films inspired imitation, or at least dreams of imitation, in many Iowans. "Local clothing and hairstyles followed Hollywood leads, even to the point where girls yearned for very slinky gowns that hugged the body."[20] On campus, both the content and design of the *Daily Iowan* fostered a connection between films and the purchase of consumer goods, especially clothing. Clothing ads appeared right next to ads for the latest film releases, and images of film stars were sandwiched between sketches of models in overcoats and new frocks. At a time when college was taking on increased importance as a place of socialization for adolescents, the campus newspaper disseminated images of the cinema that encouraged teens to imagine their lives in relation to the stars on screen, and to view the purchase of products as a means of living out these fantasies.

The impact of films went beyond inspiring viewers to new heights of consumption, however. Gaylyn Studlar has suggested that films of the 1920s created a space in which viewers could work out new models of behavior in the wake of a rapidly changing world. For men becoming adults in the wake of World War I, caught between "the contrary demands of modernism and antimodernism, urbanization and agrarian ideals, women's changing social roles and the desire for traditional gender arrangements," action-oriented stars such as Douglas Fairbanks or Tom Mix offered new ways to revivify masculinity.[21] For women, the cinema provided "a secure setting for indulging in a fantasy of mutual romance and sexual interest."[22] The prominence of these ads in the *Daily Iowan*—ads that Gallup himself brought in—suggests that films were a popular form of leisure entertainment among students. The visual contrasts and juxtapositions these film ads create with the other ads and articles in the paper mirrored the way cinema itself provided an imaginative space where students could deal with the complexities of their moment in history.

Applied Psychology

Though journalism absorbed much of Gallup's time outside the classroom, his academic training at the university was in psychology. Gallup earned his bachelor's degree, master's, and doctorate in that field, at a time when psychology was expanding dramatically both as a profession and as a force in

American society. The number of people in the United States who earned doctorates in psychology doubled between 1920 and 1930, and many of them went to work in government and business in addition to academia.[23] Many who had helped the government during World War I to classify new recruits found jobs after the war in emerging industries such as retailing, communication, and automobile manufacturing, where new theories of industrial psychology were changing relations between employers and employees. The faculty and program at Iowa were part of these broader social trends, and through his work there Gallup became engaged with contemporary intellectual debates about the possibility and value of measuring human behavior, ideas that shaped his approach to film later.

To analyze an audience's reactions to film implies that human behavior can be observed empirically, and that these observations can be analyzed or quantified in some way. Yet this seemingly simple proposition hides profound assumptions. Before 1900, most books on psychology were written by philosophers or theologians who rejected the notion that one could study feelings or attitudes with the same methods used to study chemical reactions. As historian Otto Klemm wrote, in words that would have resonated later with many Hollywood producers, "There is something in the very nature of mental processes . . . which resists the attempt to subject them to scientific treatment. . . . The facts of consciousness are not data which are discovered like a rare mineral or which can be observed like an unfamiliar phenomenon in nature." [24] Yet by the end of the nineteenth century, some scientists had begun to argue that mental processes had a physical basis. A key figure in this discussion was Wilhelm Wundt, a German scientist who redirected the focus of psychology from metaphysical inquiries about the nature of consciousness to an approach that explored the physical link between the mind and the body. In 1879 Wundt founded the world's first laboratory for experimental psychology in Leipzig, Germany, and began to study physical elements of perception, such as reaction time, in a controlled environment. Wundt did not think that human reactions could be reduced simply to mechanical impulses, but he believed that psychology should pay more attention to the physical roots of behavior. [25]

Wundt's laboratory became a mecca for students from all over the world. Some who studied with him returned to the United States to launch the first university programs in psychology. They included James McKeen Cattell, who became the first professor of psychology in America; G. Stanley Hall, who taught psychology at Johns Hopkins; Walter Dill Scott, the first professor of applied psychology at the Carnegie Institute of Technology in 1915; and Hugo Münsterberg, the industrial psychologist and film theorist who joined the Harvard faculty. What distinguished these psychologists from their European counterparts was a desire to apply psychological methods to problems facing government and business. As one historian put it, the American version of the German approach was resolutely practical and frankly commercial.

Many of these psychologists worked with the U.S. government during World War I to evaluate new recruits. They administered group intelligence tests to soldiers and assigned them to particular tasks based on the results. After the war these psychologists established consulting firms to provide similar services to private businesses. These firms included the Scott Company, established in 1919, and the Psychological Corporation, which Cattell founded in 1921.[26] Scott, Cattell, and others joined a rapidly expanding business sector where companies were adopting Frederick Winslow Taylor's theories of scientific management. "Taylorism" studied the work process to determine the most efficient means to carry out each step of a production process, but psychologists argued that employers also needed to pay attention to workers, and their selection, motivation, and training. If people differed in their abilities, as intelligence tests proved, then they were probably better suited for some jobs rather than others.[27]

Psychologists believed they could help employers place workers in the right job for their skills. To do so, they developed standardized tests that employers could use to measure the intelligence, dexterity, motor skills, and personality traits of prospective employees. Companies ranging from Macy's to H. J. Heinz to Equitable Life Assurance hired psychologists to evaluate their personnel practices and rationalize their hiring processes.[28] As Donald Napoli described, "by promising to bring the personalities of their workers and clients within the realm of human understanding and control, applied psychology offered managers an important tool in further rationalizing their operations."[29]

The psychology program at Iowa is linked directly to these broader trends in the field. George Patrick established the university's program in 1887, after finishing his Ph.D. at Johns Hopkins, where he studied with Wundt's former student G. Stanley Hall. Patrick taught Wundt's theories at Iowa and set up the university's first experimental psychology lab in 1890.[30] In 1897, Carl Seashore joined the faculty and remained at Iowa for the next fifty years. During Gallup's time at the university, Seashore served as dean of the Graduate School and head of the psychology department, where he was Gallup's teacher and mentor. In a later interview, Gallup called Seashore "a great personal friend" and one of the professors who had a lasting influence on his life and career.[31]

Like Gallup, Seashore was an Iowa native who had grown up on a farm. After college he went off to graduate school at Yale, where he became disenchanted with the philosophical approaches to psychology advocated by William James and decided that a scientific laboratory was the best place to study human behavior. When he joined the faculty at Iowa, Seashore assumed responsibility for the experimental laboratory and directed it during the entire time that Gallup was a student. His book *Elemental Experiments in Psychology* (1908) was used in basic psychology courses at the university during Gallup's time there, and in 1923, during Gallup's senior year, he published a survey of contemporary approaches in the field that drew on material he taught in the university's principal course in psychology. The course syllabus included in the book indicates that Gallup received a solid grounding in both dominant and emerging theories in psychology at the time, including the work of William James and John Dewey, John Broadus Watson's behaviorism, and experimental and industrial psychology.[32]

Like his colleagues in the east, Seashore became interested in developing methods to measure aptitude. He was part of the task force that classified Army recruits during World War I, and afterwards he started a program at Iowa to administer placement exams to incoming freshmen. Seashore advocated using quantitative exams to determine who should go to college and to place students into the appropriate courses for their level of ability. His research and that of other faculty he recruited led to the development of the American College Testing program (the ACT tests) that made Iowa into a nationally known testing center. Within the university, Seashore also collaborated with colleagues in the medical and dental schools to develop aptitude tests that could be used to judge someone's fitness for these professions.[33] During his half century at the university, Seashore gained a national reputation as a proponent of using quantitative tests to measure behavior and aptitude, and it is this approach that Gallup followed in his own research.

The Killian Scale

The research Gallup completed while he was a graduate student at Iowa was a logical outgrowth of these broader trends in psychology. For his master's degree, he built on the courses he had taken with Seashore in psychological measurement to investigate a topic of interest to industrial psychologists: salesmanship. Gallup's graduate thesis looks at traits that business executives thought were essential for a successful retail salesperson and presents a new method for measuring them consistently. Salesmanship had become a hot topic among psychologists in the 1920s because salesclerks played a pivotal role in the distribution of goods to a mass market. As Susan Porter Benson demonstrates in her fascinating history *Counter Cultures*, the emergence of department stores in the late nineteenth century meant that more people bought ready-made goods instead of producing what they needed themselves, and salesclerks were their point of contact with these retail emporiums.[34] Taylor himself believed that the selection of salesclerks was a crucial issue in the postwar period, and several universities had begun to study the subject. The Carnegie Institute of Technology in Pittsburgh created a Bureau of Salesmanship Research in 1918, and Harvard and New York University offered courses on retailing to business students.[35] Gallup's choice of topic reflected, all at the same time, trends in academic research, a pressing issue in business, and a career development opportunity.

Gallup began by critiquing the prevailing methods for measuring a salesperson's aptitude, including the work done by Dill Scott and others. His thesis bibliography includes many references to Scott's writings and Münsterberg's, as well as other works in contemporary industrial psychology. He noted that the tests industrial psychologists used to evaluate job candidates measured their skill in intellectual tasks, such as association, computation, logic, and picture completion, but did not focus on qualities more directly related to sales ability. Psychologists recognized that character traits such as honesty or an outgoing personality were important in retailing, but no one had found a way to measure these qualities quickly and easily in the context of an employment interview. Gallup tried to define some of the personality traits that would be useful in a sales situation and to develop a way of measuring them objectively so employers would be able to screen job candidates more easily. [36]

For assistance he turned to Killian's Department Store, which had been one of the chief advertisers in the *Daily Iowan* when he was recruiting ads. The store's educational director, the person in charge of training salespeople, allowed Gallup to test his hypotheses on Killian's employees. Gallup administered some of the commonly used tests to the staff and compared the results with the sales manager's own evaluation of the employee and the clerk's sales record.[37] The results supported his hypothesis that "success in department store selling rested primarily upon personality traits and not upon interests, abilities, or personal history," the traits measured in existing tests. Gallup then invented his own testing instrument, which he called the "Killian Graphic Scale," that defined what he thought were the key personality traits involved in sales. He also listed concrete ways that an employer could gauge these traits. For example, an ability to relate to customers was crucial for a salesperson. Gallup argued that managers could assess this trait by looking at such specifics as a clerk's sales-talk vocabulary, ability to adapt to the buyer, and dexterity in performing product demonstrations. The Killian Graphic Scale enabled managers to evaluate each of these behaviors along a continuum, so that if an employer were looking at a salesperson's attitude toward his or her job, the manager could note whether the employee "knocked" the store, showed a "passive loyalty," or spoke as "a booster."[38] The Killian Graphic

Scale went beyond conventional tests that measured intellectual ability or mental alertness and focused on more general character traits that were important in sales work. Gallup's method was attractive because it seemed to reduce the ambiguity involved in judging performance by using objective criteria instead of subjective impressions.[39]

Gallup's work was symptomatic of a larger development within psychology at that time. The emphasis on objectivity over subjectivity, and the idea that quantitative measures of behavior were superior to subjective ones, is a hallmark of what historian Dorothy Ross calls "scientism." Ross argues that this shift to quantitative measures within the social sciences during the 1920s served to establish a new discourse of professionalism. As psychologists moved into the business world and began to research areas in which they themselves lacked firsthand experience, they used statistics and a specialized vocabulary to give their findings an aura of expertise.[40] Ross's description of how a concept of "expertise" takes shape applies as well to Gallup's move into advertising in the 1930s, the introduction of his political polls, and his work in Hollywood. In each case, Gallup challenged what he saw as subjective and intuitive approaches to human behavior among industry insiders, and argued that scientific methods and quantitative measurements would yield more accurate information.

Though applied psychologists employed the discourses of science, the issues they investigated and the solutions they proposed were not completely neutral. In the words of historian Loren Baritz, industrial psychologists were "servants of power." [41] Their task was to facilitate business operations, not to question how work was organized. As Napoli describes them, social scientists were "architects of adjustment": they facilitated the adjustment of workers to jobs and managers to the demands of expanding industry.[42] It is this approach that infuses Gallup's film research in the 1940s. He carried out research for film producers, not stars or writers, and framed his questions to meet the needs of studio executives. Gallup's focus on the practical problems confronting business executives developed out of his own experiences as an entrepreneur and his academic training in applied psychology at Iowa. His graduate work linked him to broader intellectual movements that valorized the scientific measurement of human behavior and use of quantitative means to describe personality traits.

Guesswork Eliminated

The trend toward professionalization and the increased use of empirical evidence that shaped psychology during the 1910s and 1920s can be seen in the field of journalism as well. Newspaper and magazine publishers began gathering demographic information about their subscribers during the 1920s both for their own use and to demonstrate to advertisers what kinds of customers they could reach. In universities, journalism became established as an academic program and a profession that required specialized preparation. Schools began to hire faculty from the social sciences who were trained in quantitative methods, and they in turn educated students to look at the events around them dispassionately and to record and analyze their observations. The notion of "objectivity" that began to emerge in the nineteenth century took hold in many universities, and reporters came to believe it was their job to present a neutral view of developing events.[43]

In Iowa City, the University of Iowa established a School of Journalism in the 1920s where Gallup taught while he was a graduate student (fig. 2.1). There he became involved in several activities that aimed to advance journalism as a profession. He was one of the founders of Quill and Scroll, the national honor society for high school journalists, and served as a judge in its annual competition for student newswriters and photographers from around the country. He and his colleagues also edited a book that described how school newspapers could place themselves on a more businesslike footing by studying their readers' interests scientifically and by paying strict attention to finances.[44]

When the time came to write his doctoral dissertation, Gallup found a topic that combined both his training in psychology and his interest in journalism. Dissertations are usually seen as the culmination of one's graduate work, but in Gallup's case the method he developed in his thesis made him famous and established a methodology that guided much of his later research. The idea for Gallup's dissertation grew out of a job he held in 1922, the summer before his senior year, when he conducted readership studies for the *St. Louis Globe Democrat*. To find out what people liked in the paper, Gallup and his assistants went door to door asking subscribers which sections they read. Most people said they read news items—foreign news, editorials, political coverage—but almost no one reported that they read more popular sections such as the comics. Gallup found it hard to believe that people only read news columns, and decided that asking them to remember what they read might not yield a complete picture of their interests.[45] Out of this experience grew the idea for his doctoral thesis, "An Objective Method for Determining Reader Interest in the Content of a Newspaper."[46]

The method Gallup proposed was designed to tell editors about the strengths and weaknesses of specific elements in their papers. Newspapers already kept track of circulation, but Gallup pointed out that there was a difference between circulation and readership. Knowing a paper's subscriber

FIGURE 2.1 George Gallup (*standing, left*) taught journalism and advertising at the University of Iowa in the mid-1920s. His experiences there formed the basis for much of his later work.   (*Kent Collection, University Archives, University of Iowa Libraries, Iowa City, Iowa*)

base did not indicate how many people actually read an issue, or which features they enjoyed. Gallup criticized the strategies editors at the time were using to determine what readers liked. Some relied on letters readers sent, while others felt they knew from personal experience what readers wanted. In Gallup's view, this was simply "guesswork." Just as he argued in his master's thesis that sales managers relied too much on personal impressions, he asserted that newspaper editors relied too much on instinct in deciding what readers enjoyed. Intuition, he felt, might have been useful "a generation ago," when each social or ethnic group had its own newspaper and editors belonged to the same community as their readers. But the consolidation of many newspapers in the 1920s meant that editors could not assume readers shared their views.[47] Later, in Hollywood, Gallup would make similar arguments to the film industry, saying that box office returns did not indicate which specific elements of a film that viewers enjoyed, and that older moguls who felt a personal affinity with the audience might be out of touch with contemporary interests. In both cases, arguments for the value of scientific methodology were framed as part of a discourse on modernity which drew contrasts between "a generation ago" and today and argued for the value of empirical studies in analyzing a more complex world.

To carry out his research, Gallup worked with the *Des Moines Register & Tribune*, a paper whose recent history mirrored the trends in journalism he discussed. Its publisher, Gardner Cowles, Sr., had purchased the *Register* in 1903 with his partner Harvey Ingham, but in 1927 began to shift control of the paper to his two sons. John Cowles became vice president and general manager of the paper in 1924, and Gardner Cowles, Jr., nicknamed "Mike," worked as a reporter and city editor before becoming managing editor in 1929, at the age of 26. Mike Cowles had met Gallup on one of his trips to Iowa City and was impressed with his efforts to modernize the *Daily Iowan*. When Gallup proposed to study reader interest in newspapers for his dissertation, Cowles put the resources of the *Register & Tribune* at his disposal. Cowles allowed the interviewers to represent themselves as members of the paper's research department and printed special editions of the paper for them. He also gave Gallup names of subscribers in Des Moines and several towns and farm areas nearby.[48]

The new, more objective method Gallup proposed was intended to resolve problems with existing approaches. Drawing on his experiences in St. Louis, Gallup decided that it was useless to ask people directly what they read, because they might not remember, or they might mention what they usually read, rather than what they had actually noticed in a particular issue. Interviews and questionnaires also made people self-conscious, he felt. Rather than be honest about what they enjoyed, people might exaggerate their interest in news and minimize their pleasure in lighter fare. To get around these obstacles, Gallup and his student assistants visited people in their homes with a clean copy of a paper that had already been published and asked people to go through it, page by page, and point out everything they had looked at, including the ads. He also asked people how much of an article they had read—the headline, first paragraph, or more—and carefully marked every column, article, or ad they selected. After counting the features chosen he presented the results in the form of tables and graphs (fig. 2.2).

The results of Gallup's research astounded everyone. First, he found that subscribers to the *Register & Tribune* read only about 15 percent of the paper. And in contrast to what people had said in previous studies, hardly anyone read the news. Instead, the most popular feature proved to be the picture page, followed closely by the comics. Sports columns, advice to the lovelorn, and even obituaries garnered more attention than analyses of major political and social issues. Gallup also detected significant gender differences in readers' responses. Women paid more attention to birth notices and health columns and read continuing serials, whereas men favored the weather report and relished political cartoons. There were significant differences between classes as well. The reading habits of major executives and small business

NEWSPAPER READING

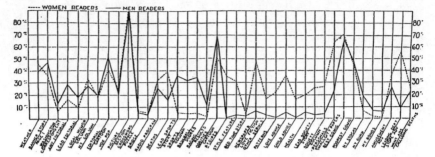

FIGURE 2.2 Gallup's novel method for measuring reader interest in the newspaper provided the first empirical evidence that more people read the comics and the picture page than news or editorial features. This 1928 study suggested new ways of reaching people's hidden interests. *(Courtesy Advertising & Selling, March 1932: 50)*

owners were similar to each other's, but different from those of skilled workers and manual laborers.[49]

Intuitively, many of these findings seem right: many people would rather read advice columns over breakfast than delve into an extended analysis of current events. To Gallup, these findings "proved" that his new objective method could get at hidden recesses of human consciousness. As he wrote later, "the very high percentages found in the instance of items which are considered 'low-brow' and the low percentages for things 'high-brow' offer common sense proof of the truthfulness of the reader when confronted by the situation developed by this method."[50] During the period when tabloid newspapers such as the *New York Daily News* became endemic in large eastern cities and attracted criticism for their focus on sin, sex, and scandal, Gallup provided statistical evidence to show that readers in the rest of the country shared the same interest in these topics. As advertising historian Roland Marchand put it, Gallup's research "seemed to demonstrate that the 'tabloid mind' was neither a class phenomenon nor confined to the urban masses. . . . Midwestern Iowans had tastes similar to those of the tabloid readers of polyglot New York City."[51]

Gallup's results suggested that he had uncovered something secret about human behavior, interests that people might not admit to if they were asked directly. And it was precisely this sense of getting at something hidden that attracted interest in his work. After seeing the results of his research, Mike

Cowles asked Gallup to come to Des Moines in 1929 to head a new department of journalism at Drake University. Cowles also invited him to sit in on editorial meetings at the paper and to suggest ways that the staff could use his research.[52] For the next two years Gallup taught, consulted at the paper, and carried out research studies for several other newspapers. His work began to influence practices in journalism and in other fields.

One aspect of Gallup's work that interested Cowles was his finding that 90 percent of newspaper readers looked at the picture page. In the 1920s many papers included a special rotogravure section in their Sunday editions that consisted of one or more pages of photos. Usually they were isolated stills that were not grouped or placed in sequences. On the basis of Gallup's research, Mike Cowles experimented with grouping images on the *Sunday - Register*'s picture page to construct a narrative, in the same way that images might be sequenced in a film. The *Sunday Register* published a pictorial history of World War I that was tremendously successful and that Cowles syndicated to other papers. The *Register* also published sequences of photos taken at local sporting events to capture reader interest. These photo sequences and pictorial histories increased the paper's circulation even in the midst of the Depression and enhanced its prestige in the newspaper world.[53] Gallup's research, and Mike Cowles' creative use of it, heightened awareness of the power of visual images to lure readers' attention.

In addition to editors, companies that advertised in the papers also took notice of Gallup's work. In April 1931, William Randolph Hearst was looking for a way to make the 16-page comic section in his *American Weekly* pay for itself. He and Hawley Turner, the executive editor of Hearst's "Comic Weekly," wanted to sell the comics page as a sales medium. In making his pitch to advertisers, Turner cited Gallup's research, noting his findings that "more adults read the best comic strip on an average day than the front page banner story. . . . Bankers, University presidents, professors, doctors . . . read comic strips as avidly as truck drivers and day laborers." Hearst's newspapers offered space in the comics section for ads that were designed to look like cartoon strips.[54]

In May 1931, General Foods and its advertising agency, Young & Rubicam, decided to try comic-strip advertising for Grape-Nuts cereal, which had not been selling well. Young & Rubicam developed ads that featured two cartoon characters named "Egbert Energy" and "Suburban Joe," who touted the cereal's benefits to their friends and acquaintances. These ads used humor, suspense, and situations involving children to wrap the commercial message in a soft sell (fig. 2.3). In one ad, a young girl tantalized her friends by telling them she has something surprising in the bag she carried, "a remarkably strengthening food" that contains "carbohydrates, and proteins, and phosphorus and iron." When they cannot stand the suspense any longer and demand to see what it is, she pulled out a box of Grape-Nuts.[55]

These comic-strip ads were tremendously successful and sales of the cereal increased immediately. Within two months, Grape-Nuts shipments reached their highest level in eight years. This was especially impressive because cereal consumption was declining in 1931, and Grape-Nuts was the most expensive ready-to-eat cereal on the market. The campaign had an equally dramatic impact on newspaper publishers. Within one year, forty-three other papers announced that they would also accept advertising in their comics sections. Within six years, the annual expenditure on continuity strip ads by national advertisers jumped from less than $1,000 to $16.5 million.[56]

Market researchers during the 1930s considered the Grape-Nuts campaign to be a landmark in advertising history. Textbooks for the next twenty years cited it as a model.[57] A key reason for this excitement was that Gallup proposed a scientific method for bringing to light subconscious desires. His method for studying newspaper readers' true interests seemed to promise a way to access emotions that had previously escaped advertising's reach. This reaction to his work can be explained by changes within the field of marketing during this period. Up through the mid-1920s, markets were seen as organized and logical systems that could be managed and controlled. As American industry succeeded in increasing production, however, imbalances between supply and demand appeared. Business leaders began to believe that they needed to create demand, not just wait for it to appear, and they looked to psychologists to assist in this process. In this period, one advertising historian notes, advertising techniques changed from treating customers as people who made rational decisions, to treating them as if they were whimsical creatures who could be reached only through appeals to their impulses.[58]

Comic-strip ads in particular were seen as an ideal way to pull the reader into advertising and bypass possible negative reactions. "If the reader could be made to smile or laugh, or if he could be induced to read copy which entertained him and thus . . . avoid the controversial issues which might have given rise to his suspicions," wrote Otis Pease, "he was considered a more likely target for successful persuasion."[59] It was expected that the entertainment in the ad would arouse the reader's imagination and sustain it through a sales pitch. In comic strip ads, "the two are so intertwined that the reader's response to the first readily transfers itself to the second." [60] The Grape-Nuts campaign represented an exemplary instance of this new marketing strategy. Copywriters marveled at the way the comic strip carried readers through the selling message. "You can see the possibility of leading the reader through a series of steps right up to the point of sale . . . and then having him go

FIGURE 2.3 As a result of Gallup's research, William Randolph Hearst offered space in the comics section of his newspapers for ads designed to look like comic strips. Shipments of Grape-Nuts reached their highest level in eight years after these ads began running.

(Courtesy Tide, May 1931: 52)

out to do the same thing in a sort of hypnotic trance."[61] General Foods was trying to sell this expensive cereal during the first years of the Depression, so it couldn't be promoted on the basis of cost. Young & Rubicam's comic-strip ads associated the product with childhood and having fun, times when people didn't worry about money.

Both Gallup's early work in Iowa and his later research in Hollywood sought to measure the ineffable: the secret of success in sales, what people noticed in the paper, the qualities of a popular film. In doing so he criticized the existing techniques used in each field for being imprecise and impressionistic, and advocated newer, "scientific" methods that represented people's reactions in quantitative terms. Although he recognized the difficulty of measuring emotion and behavior, Gallup nonetheless remained strongly committed to finding empirical techniques to study them.

Gallup's experiences growing up in Iowa left him with a lifelong love of the Midwest and a special feel for the people who lived there. After he had become well known as a pollster, an interviewer for the *New Yorker* suggested that Gallup's Iowa roots explained why he felt comfortable with the idea of sampling. "New Yorkers differ so much among themselves that the concept of the average American seems mythical," he wrote. "Dr. Gallup, however, understands that the average American exists, and, furthermore, he likes and respects him. He has even, from long association, come to resemble one."[62] Whether or not he resembled a New Yorker's vision of the average American, Gallup felt strongly that the voices of the people in the rest of the country needed to be heard, and this populist feeling inflected his later work in Hollywood. His time as a child and young adult in Iowa developed in him a commitment to learning more about the "common man" and the intellectual tools for doing so.

3

●●●●●●●●●●●

The Laws That Determine Interest

In the summer of 1931, as the Grape-Nuts comic-strip campaign was gathering steam, Gallup left Iowa to teach journalism and advertising at Northwestern University. The success of that campaign, along with the publication of a number of articles about his work, led to several new projects in which he applied the method from his dissertation to study magazines and then advertisements. As the Depression wore on, businesses clamored for evidence that the money they spent on advertising was being put to good use. Gallup's proven success at uncovering the public's interests attracted attention from several advertising agencies.

In spring 1932 Gallup accepted a position as director of research for the advertising agency Young & Rubicam. Its ambitious chief executive Raymond Rubicam wanted to propel the company to the front ranks of Madison Avenue and believed that systematic research would give the agency an edge. He hired Gallup to establish the first copy research department in the industry, to study the company's ads and devise ways to improve them. Gallup and his colleagues delved into the most basic components of print and broadcasting ads in the belief that it was possible to find the precise elements that attracted readers' and listeners' attention. His work treated advertisements as bundles of stimuli that could be manipulated to awaken half-conscious interests and desires, an approach that extended his earlier research on newspapers. The assumptions he made about the public's interests, and the methods he developed to gauge their responses, formed the building blocks for his research in Hollywood.

Let's Use Facts

If the 1920s was the "Advertising Decade," as historian Stephen Fox suggests, when agencies and their clients worked in happy symbiosis to promote the consumption of mass-produced goods, then the 1930s saw this mutually beneficial alliance come screeching to a halt.[1] Faced with a massive decline in sales, businesses drastically reduced their advertising budgets. Consumers, embittered by the broken promises of the giddy twenties, attacked advertising as deceitful and manipulative. And the federal government launched investigations into the truthfulness of advertising claims. Agencies, threatened from all sides, turned to empirical research to shore up their declining reputations and prove their value to clients and critics. In this climate of heightened anxiety, the advertising industry quickly seized on Gallup's work as a solution to some of its problems.

Many advertisements of the 1920s were designed to stimulate consumption by appealing to subconscious needs and desires. By the end of the decade, some commentators had come to view these tactics as manipulative and deceitful. In 1927 Stuart Chase and Frederick Schlink, an economist and an engineer, published an exposé of advertising practices, *Your Money's Worth*, which portrayed consumers as dazed and distracted, beset from all sides by the exaggerations and distortions of advertising claims.

> We buy not for the value of the product to meet our specific needs but because the story told on every billboard, every newspaper and magazine page, every shop window, every sky sign, every other letter we receive—is a pleasing, stimulating and romantic story. . . . But whether or not it is a fairy story we do not know save through the bitter and wasteful process of trial and error.[2]

Chase and Schlink's description of a public beset by competing claims on its attention echoes descriptions by sociologists of the period about the ways that modern life bombarded people with ideas and sensations. The book sold more than 100,000 copies and launched a nationwide consumer movement that eventually led Congress to give the Federal Trade Commission authority to regulate advertising.[3]

Adding to these attacks from outside, industry insiders also expressed disgust with what they saw as the field's cynicism and corruption. In *Through Many Windows* (1926), former copywriter Helen Woodward confessed that she and others had no idea why some ads worked and others didn't. "Some were failures and none of us exactly knew why. . . . Neither my clients nor myself were able to have any feeling of certainty about whether an advertisement was good or not. . . . It is like deciding in advance whether a play is going to succeed or not. Our whole conclusion after years of working at that kind of thing was that the longer we worked at it the less we knew about it."[4] James Rorty, who wrote advertising copy before becoming a freelance journalist, described the general strategy of advertisers in this way in *Our Master's Voice* (1934): "Figure out what they want, promise 'em everything, and blow hard."[5] Articles in popular magazines also satirized advertising as deceitful and a waste of money.[6] Reflecting the concerns of the troubled times, more magazine articles on consumers and their problems were published in 1933–34 alone than in the twenty-year period from 1900 to 1920.[7]

While advertising's critics questioned its motives, business executives questioned its value. Like many other parts of the economy, advertising suffered from the massive economic slowdown of the early 1930s. Many businesses did not have enough money to advertise their products and this, combined with growing doubts about advertising's effectiveness, caused a dramatic decline in the number of ads published. The amount of money spent on advertising in national magazines dropped by 50 percent between 1929 and 1933, with the largest year to year decline occurring in 1931–32, when money spent on magazine ads dropped 30 percent.[8] Not only did magazines publish fewer ads, they published fewer pages altogether. The *Saturday Evening Post* provides a vivid example. What is considered to be the high-water mark of national advertising occurred on December 6, 1929, when the *Post* published a 272 page issue that included 168 pages of ads. By contrast, its issue for July 2, 1932, contained only 25 pages of advertising out of a total of 76 pages. Even allowing for the seasonal differences between a Christmas issue and one aimed at summer readers, the decline in both editorial and advertising space is dramatic. Some newspapers could not attract enough advertising to stay in business: Pulitzer's *New York World* and Hearst's *New York American* stopped publishing partly for this reason.[9]

At the beginning of the Depression, many ad agencies resorted to desperate measures to draw attention to their clients' products. Historian Ralph Hower noted that "the shrieking headlines, gross exaggeration, and downright deceit" that characterized ads of the early 1930s "had no parallel except the patent-medicine advertising of the nineteenth century."[10] But as consumers organized and became more aware of themselves as active agents in the economic process, and as the government began to investigate advertising claims, ad agencies were forced to change their practices. Businesses began to demand that agencies prove that their methods brought results and were cost-effective. One full-page ad in *Advertising & Selling* quoted an archetypal client who insisted, "Let's not spend money on opinion . . . let's use the FACTS! When I spend cold hard cash for advertising I want to *know* that I'm reaching a lot of people with money to spend—and that I'm doing it economically."[11]

To answer this demand for "proof," and to counter the criticisms raised by consumer groups and government investigations, agencies in the 1930s began to beef up their research services and to hire experts with advanced degrees in psychology and statistics. Though some agencies, most notably J. Walter Thompson, employed psychologists during the 1920s, the practice did not become more prevalent until the Depression. Advertisers hoped that by using empirical methods they could shore up their declining reputations and boost confidence in their work among business executives. As Hower noted, agencies "had to retrench on the one hand and improve service on the other. Thus it was no accident that substantial gains were made after 1930 in the application of scientific methods to the analysis of markets and advertising results."[12] It was in this environment that Gallup's research gained attention.

Something New and Important

During July and August 1931, before he began teaching at Northwestern, Gallup received a commission from Bernarr Macfadden, the new owner of *Liberty* magazine. Macfadden had become a millionaire by publishing such popular fare as *True Story* and *True Romances* and purchased *Liberty* in April 1931 to elevate his public profile and boost his chances at obtaining political office. Since *Liberty* had been losing money, he wanted to prove to advertisers that his magazine could reach customers, so he hired Gallup to compare its readers to those of three other national weeklies—the *Saturday Evening Post*, *Collier's*, and the *Literary Digest*.[13]

Using the method pioneered in his dissertation, Gallup sent interviewers to visit 15,000 homes in six cities, to ask people from various economic groups which parts of each magazine they had read. The study focused on the editorial features in the magazines, but interviewers also asked people which ads they had noticed or read. The investigators marked each section that readers had seen, read in part, or read completely, and included every editorial feature of any size, and every ad, from a full-page spread to a small column at the back.[14] Gallup found that *Liberty*, with its concisely written articles and vibrant color illustrations, attracted the most interest. Publishers of the other magazines used in the study complained that it was easier for people to remember what they read in *Liberty* than in thicker publications such as the

Saturday Evening Post, but the Association of National Advertisers certified Gallup's results.[15]

The *Liberty* study came to be regarded as a landmark of reader recognition surveys because it marked the first time that anyone had conducted a national survey comparing the readership of major weekly magazines. The idea of asking people directly what they read struck many as novel.[16] Marketing textbooks throughout the 1930s discussed this work, and advertising agencies took notice. [17] J. Walter Thompson, the leading agency on Madison Avenue, devoted an entire staff meeting in November 1931 to the report.[18] Publishers, agencies, and their corporate clients wanted to know more about this new method for finding out what people actually read in their magazines.

Although the report mentioned which ads people noticed, advertising was not its main interest. In 1932, however, *Liberty* commissioned a follow-up study that focused exclusively on this area. Gallup's earlier report found that some ads attracted more attention than others, and this second study was designed to learn why.[19] Using the same method employed in his earlier work, Gallup sent a staff of interviewers with recent copies of the four magazines to people's homes and asked them to point out all the editorial features and advertisements they had read. Gallup then classified the ads according to the subject and size of their headlines; whether they used photographs or drawings as illustrations; emphasized the product itself or user's experiences of it; and the kinds of emotional appeals they made to the reader, whether to a desire for ambition, health, novelty, efficiency, or sex. Researchers correlated responses to each ad with the gender of each participant.[20] As with his study of newspaper readership, the results stunned publishers and advertisers alike.

Gallup's advertising study for *Liberty* was the first time that anyone looked at the readership for individual ads.[21] Industry insiders were astonished by how much the response to an ad could differ, depending upon its size, graphic design, or location in a magazine.[22] The report included dozens of charts that documented how reader interest varied with different kinds of headlines, typography, illustrations, or because of an ad's position on the page. In his discussion Gallup drew attention to the gender differences that emerged. Both men and women enjoyed looking at illustrations, he noted, but women liked photographs of people best, while men preferred drawings of products. Both groups responded to headlines that described someone's experiences with a product, but women noticed them three times more often than men. Gallup suggested that advertisers who wanted to reach women should show someone's experience with a product, preferably through photographs, and those aimed at men should stress a product's quality, using drawings.[23] His analysis treats these differences as obvious and expected, as if they were inherent in human nature.[24]

In March 1932, *Liberty* prepared a report summarizing Gallup's conclusions and sent it to one thousand people in the advertising industry.[25] Macfadden also placed full-page ads in *Advertising Age* every other week from October 1931 through June 1932 that featured testimonials from corporate executives who claimed that Gallup's research had persuaded them to advertise in *Liberty* instead of other magazines.[26] This combination of pertinent research and unrivaled promotion by the client who commissioned it made Gallup a legend in the advertising world. Articles reviewing his findings exploded into print in early 1932 in publications such as *Printer's Ink*, *Tide*, and *Advertising & Selling* (fig. 3.1). In January 1932 the American Association of Schools and Departments of Journalism invited Gallup to discuss his work at its annual convention, and *Editor & Publisher* used the talk as the basis for a three-part series on his work. These articles highlighted Gallup's academic credentials and professional experience, referring to "Professor" Gallup, the "famed investigator" from Northwestern. They praised his "scientific" research and use of "fact-finding methods" that one journalist claimed would "set people straight."[27]

"Before the print was even dry" on the *Editor & Publisher* article, according to Gallup, Lever Brothers invited him to come to Boston to evaluate their advertising for Lux soap.[28] Lever had introduced the soap in 1925 after their research determined that women wanted a cake of soap that smelled and looked expensive but that only cost a dime. At that time the most luxurious soaps were manufactured in France and could cost as much as one dollar, so Lever detected a niche. Its nicely scented and affordable Lux Toilet Soap became an immediate hit among women of all classes.[29] The company and its advertising agency J. Walter Thompson devoted considerable resources to studying women's responses and to crafting ad campaigns based on them. Thompson hit upon the idea of using testimonials, a popular advertising method of the period, in the belief that women would be more likely to try the product if someone they trusted recommended it. Some Lux ads featured the woman next door, while others presented society ladies who testified to its virtues. Even before Gallup provided scientific evidence of the value of testimonials, Thompson was using them in its ads.

Several years after introducing Lux, Thompson decided to feature Hollywood actresses in these testimonials. The agency asked a representative from *Photoplay* magazine to go to Hollywood and distribute free samples of the soap to several dozen directors and several hundred actresses. Thompson wanted to be able to claim that Lux was Hollywood's favorite soap, so its agent went door to door checking dressing rooms to be sure that only Lux

FIGURE 3.1 Gallup's 1932 study for *Liberty* magazine marked the first time anyone had analyzed the readership for individual ads. The magazine promoted his research widely and made Gallup famous within the advertising industry.

(*Courtesy Advertising & Selling [February 1932]: 70*)

was available. *Photoplay*'s skillful negotiations with studio executives, and the unlimited free samples Thompson distributed, persuaded over 400 actresses to lend their name to the product. Lever launched the ads in January 1928, and within one month sales increased over 1,000 percent in Los Angeles.[30]

To track the effectiveness of its campaign, Thompson used a variety of methods, such as sending representatives to women's homes to ask what they thought of the soap; mailing questionnaires to social groups and clubs;

and including a coupon for a free sample in the ads. Interviews and questionnaires told the agency how women felt about the product and how they used it, while the mail-in coupons allowed them to assess which ads gained the greatest number of responses.[31] Beginning in February 1933, however, the agency began a new kind of study, which it called "Gallup tests." Thompson hired Gallup to check whether people noticed and read the ads in newspapers, using his well-known method of going through the paper page by page. He noted each woman's degree of interest in each ad, whether she "glanced" at it or showed "sustained interest," and compared responses to ads of different sizes. For each one he determined whether the response was "normal" for ads of that size or below normal.[32] The Gallup tests for Lux soap were notable in their detail and precision and, like his earlier newspaper and magazine studies, they appeared to capture the moment of reading. The Lux tests also marked the first time that Gallup studied the public's reactions to Hollywood stars.

That Thompson labeled these studies "Gallup" tests suggests that, by mid-1932, Gallup had become almost a brand name in advertising research. *Liberty* continued to refer to "the Gallup method" in its advertising even after other people took over the studies.[33] In early 1932 Gallup made several trips to New York to meet with executives, and during one such visit met with Raymond Rubicam, one of the founders of Young & Rubicam, the agency that had developed the comic-strip advertising for Grape-Nuts.[34] Rubicam realized that Gallup's methods represented "something new and important" in advertising. "For the first time, some of the guesswork might be stripped from advertising. Now it might be possible to measure . . . the important factors that make advertising successful." [35] Gallup felt that Rubicam understood the importance of research, and when Rubicam offered him the opportunity to establish the first full-fledged Copy Research Department on Madison Avenue, he jumped at the chance. "Raymond Rubicam was far more interested intellectually in how advertising works than the other people I talked to," Gallup recalled later, "and he offered me the complete freedom that I didn't think was possible in the business world."[36]

Though he had intended to stay for only a few years and then return to teaching, Gallup remained with the agency for fifteen years, until 1947. Documents of his work from the agency's archives afford an in-depth understanding of the issues he addressed, the methodologies he developed, and the recommendations he made to the company. Gallup continued to work for Young & Rubicam almost the entire time he was in Hollywood, and the research methods and personal contacts he developed at the agency were fundamental to his work in film.

Proven Facts and Honest Comparisons

For over a decade Young & Rubicam had forged a corporate image and an ethos that perfectly suited Gallup's training and aspirations. The agency's decision to hire him marked an important milestone in its quest for leadership in the advertising field. John Orr Young and Raymond Rubicam established their company in Philadelphia in 1923 and moved their offices to New York three years later. Over the next two decades its client list came to include many well-known U.S. brands, such as Gulf Oil, Jell-O, Sanka, Grape-Nuts, Borden's evaporated milk, Packard cars, and Arrow shirts. Young & Rubicam earned a permanent place in advertising history when one of its copywriters thought of naming Borden's trademark cow "Elsie." The agency's clients also sponsored a number of popular radio programs, featuring such stars as Jack Benny, Kate Smith, Fred Allen, Arthur Godfrey, Helen Hayes, and Dinah Shore.[37]

When Young left the agency a few years after its launch, Rubicam took charge and soon became its public symbol. A former copywriter himself, Rubicam became famous for inventing the slogan "The Instrument of the Immortals" to describe Steinway pianos.[38] According to one source, he had "the loyalty of his agency to the point of devotion," and even his colleagues in the rest of the industry admired his integrity and commitment to quality. [39] In the midst of the Depression, he nurtured a distinctive style. As Stephen Fox describes: "At a time of grim hard selling, Rubicam favored stylish, indirect persuasion, well crafted and visually attractive, that even used humor to make its pitch."[40] Rubicam believed that advertising should be unobtrusive and speak directly to the customer. "The way to sell is to get read first, and the way to get read is to say more about the reader and less about yourself and your product. Mirror the reader to himself; then show him afterwards how your product fits his needs."[41] In order to talk more intelligently to the customer, it was necessary to know more about him or her. Like Gallup, Rubicam felt that copywriters should not rely on their own experiences to understand their customers, but should use research to gather information.[42]

The decision to hire Gallup illustrated Rubicam's determination to advance the company from its position behind industry leader J. Walter Thompson. Thompson recognized that hiring Gallup was a bold move. "I say—watch Rubicam. He is a great salesman, he is alert, and he is always trying something, and he's always learning. He has just hired Dr. Gallup . . . and soon you will find Rubicam copy is Gallup-tested."[43] After Gallup was hired, Young & Rubicam circulated memos summarizing his newspaper work and research for *Liberty*. The documents portrayed Gallup as a national authority whose record of success would stimulate new ideas. Gallup's first assignment with Young & Rubicam was to apply the method he used in the *Liberty* study to analyze the advertising and editorial content in seven women's magazines. The agency wanted to know how each compared in terms of reader interest, so that it could determine which would be the most effective vehicle for their clients. Young & Rubicam also asked Gallup to identify the specific features of its ads that attracted readers' attention, such as their typeface, headline, color, size, or position on the page, and compare them with ads from other agencies.[44]

Young & Rubicam hoped to apply Gallup's research findings to all its accounts. "The final result of all this testing should be to give us . . . generalizations which can guide us in the preparation of copy."[45] It was also hoped that his studies would have a predictive value, that they would "discover to us new trends in the public's reading appetite and advertising predilections—trends which a client of ours can take advantage of in their early stages."[46] The memos made clear what was at stake in Gallup's work, arguing that only with "proven facts and honest comparisons can we expect to build new and convincing ideas, so necessary in these highly critical, highly competitive times."[47] Rubicam hoped that the firm's association with Gallup would strengthen its competitive edge and enhance profits.

Not By Reason Alone

What distinguished Young & Rubicam from other advertising agencies in the 1930s was its decision to make copy-testing the central component of its research. The agency was the first to use reading and noting scores as a guide to creative effort.[48] In the Lux campaign, J. Walter Thompson knew which ads gained more attention, but could only speculate about the exact features that had attracted readers' interest. Gallup and his colleagues at Young & Rubicam tried to analyze the components of an ad down to the smallest unit in order to pinpoint the elements that inspired people to make a purchase. If they could identify these elements, then it should be possible to design similar ads that would be equally successful.[49]

One of the theorists whose work influenced Gallup when he studied psychology at Iowa was Walter Dill Scott, whose books were enjoying a revival in 1931. A fundamental theory of Scott's work was that ads appealed to people on a sensory level, not a rational one. "We can not depend on people's imagination or memory or reasoning alone in making an appeal."[50] Scott believed that whether people paid attention to ads depended not only on the verbal appeals they used but also on specific design elements such as the ad's color, size, shape, and position on a page. These elements, he believed, could exercise an effect on viewers comparable to the process of hypnosis and induce them to want to buy something. According to Scott, it was possible to increase interest in an ad by manipulating various components of it to make sure it was noticed and remembered.[51]

Gallup and his colleagues conducted extensive tests with different kinds of layouts and typography to see how they affected readers. One area of research examined how people's interest varied in relation to the shape of an ad or its position on a page. Young & Rubicam found evidence to support a popular belief that ads appearing "above the fold" in a newspaper attracted more attention than those appearing below the fold. Gallup and his staff also determined that ads placed on the right-hand page of a newspaper did not attract enough attention to warrant paying the higher cost of that popular position. Studies about the effects of different layouts were matched in detail by research into different kinds of typography. Before Gallup began working at the agency, Young & Rubicam had followed the accepted practice of presenting advertising in blocks of text that required close reading. At Gallup's urging, the agency began experimenting with texts that were broken up into smaller units and that used asterisks, italics, or boldface to highlight important ideas. Young & Rubicam's designers also began using more white space within the ads, to make them easier to read and to break up the monolithic appearance of the copy. The research department disseminated these findings to copywriters and the art department, and Gallup had the full support of the agency's art director, who was always ready to experiment with new layouts or illustrations.[52]

These manipulations of the visual appearance of an ad were designed to overcome readers' lack of interest and lure them into reading a sales pitch before they realized what was happening. An ideal ad, in Gallup's view, was one that looked so much like the rest of the paper or magazine that readers couldn't tell them apart. In one memo Gallup praised an issue of *Life* in which some of the ads were built around groups of photos, with a minimal amount of text. These ads, he pointed out, looked just like the rest of the magazine, and readers paid more attention to them because the layout did not broadcast their identity. As a result of this research, Young & Rubicam clients who had not used photos before began to do so.[53]

Building on Gallup's studies about advertising appeals for *Liberty* magazine, Young & Rubicam argued that in order to sell a product, ads should depict readers' everyday problems and explain how the product could help. Ideally, ads should create a vivid scenario—for example, through the use of demonstrations, or before and after pictures, to illustrate how the product could solve the problem.[54] This, too, reflected the influence of Walter Dill Scott, who argued that ads should "find a means for picturing or representing the article in use, so clear, vivid, and unambiguous that it will catch the reader's attention strongly, and make an intense impression by reason of its seeming realness or actuality."[55] As examples, Gallup often pointed to Young & Rubicam's ads for Packard, which featured a drawing of a young boy sitting on a fence and gazing at the car, with a caption that read, "When he grows up, that's what he wants." The ad created a visual and narrative context in which the viewer could fantasize for a moment that the car was his, and suggested that possessing it was the fulfillment of a childhood dream. Another ad used an image of the Venus de Milo to raise the question of what to do when drinking coffee kept you awake. In the ad the statue, usually seen in an upright position, was shown lying on its side, and the caption read, "Drink Sanka and Sleep." By presenting a familiar object in an unfamiliar pose, the ad awakened readers' curiosity and created an indelible impression that would be associated with the product in the future. Presumably readers would think of Sanka the next time they found themselves drinking coffee late in the day. Both ads avoided a "reason why" approach based on words and used images instead to attract attention.[56]

Gallup and Young & Rubicam followed a similar strategy for radio advertising. Advertising had been a source of controversy within American radio since the first broadcasts in the 1910s, as Susan Smulyan documents in *Selling Radio*. One critic felt that advertising "would become an Old Man of the Sea—practically impossible to shake off."[57] As Smulyan describes, and as we know today, this prophecy has come to pass, since commercials are the way that radio in the United States pays for its programming. Businesses with products to sell dealt with this resentment by finding ways to advertise indirectly.

One way to make advertising less obvious was to embed the commercial in the program in such a way that it slipped into the listener's mind and circumvented conscious awareness. This was done through "integrated" commercials, in which the commercial message became part of the entertainment, by sounding like the rest of the nonadvertising text.[58] Integrated radio commercials functioned in the same way as the comic-strip ads for Grape-Nuts, by softening the boundaries between ads and entertainment. Gallup's research inspired the agency to create commercials in this format. As he described:

> We have found in the case of radio programs that people pay more attention to commercials when they are woven into the fabric of the program. When there is an abrupt change—when an announcer gives a straight commercial—many listeners tune out mentally. When the commercials are fitted into the show— when they are introduced in an interesting way—listeners are more likely to pay attention to them.[59]

An example of this kind of commercial can be found in Young & Rubicam's first big hit, *The Jack Benny Show*, which was sponsored by Jell-O. Instead of using direct advertising that positioned the commercials in a separate space, Benny sprinkled references to the product throughout the show, using humor to soften the repetition. For example, in one 1934 broadcast, a segue from one segment to another punned on the word "hello" when Benny said, "Jell-O again. This is Jack Benny speaking." Young & Rubicam ran a full-page ad in *Fortune* in February 1937 describing the extensive preparation that went into the program.[60] At a time when sponsors hired the stars, wrote the scripts, and allocated time between the program and its commercials, the ad explained how Young & Rubicam's writers inserted Jell-O commercials after the script was finished so that they would be an integral part of the show. Jack Benny and the rest of the cast are shown rehearsing in the company of agency staffers. *Variety* awarded Young & Rubicam a special citation in 1940 for its pioneering work on integrated commercials.[61]

Young & Rubicam assumed that viewers had to be lured or seduced into noticing ads, and that their resistance could be overcome by blurring the boundaries between the ad and the material around it.[62] By carefully placing a newspaper or magazine ad in a particular location, and varying its written and graphic elements, an advertiser could overcome readers' lack of interest. The components of an ad were designed to get attention and create interest, and then the written text could make the sales pitch. The belief that one could analyze an ad to find the fundamental components that influenced readers is also the basis of Gallup's work in Hollywood, where he tried to define the precise elements of a film that stimulated audiences' interest. He argued that aspects such as a film's title, stars, subject, or genre evoked associations that could in themselves create positive or negative reactions from audiences. Just like advertisers in the 1930s, studio executives faced with the economic and legal challenges in Hollywood in the 1940s found the precision and scientific aura of Gallup's research appealing.

Traffic Patterns and Cost Per Thousand

Gallup and Young & Rubicam's study of readership patterns enabled them to correlate reader interest with specific textual components. A memo written in 1935 asserted that, "By analysis, we can tell to a great extent what makes an ad click or what can hurt it, from the standpoint of makeup, position, etc."[63] As part of its research, Young & Rubicam also measured what percentage of an ad people read, that is, whether they just noticed it or whether they read part or all of it. The agency also measured reader "traffic" through each section of a publication and calculated noting and reading scores in relation to the overall traffic for that section. A well-read ad had more value in a section that attracted a lot of readers or "traffic" than if it was in a section without many readers.[64]

As these studies accumulated, the agency began to calculate average "noting and reading" scores for ads of comparable size and color. Then Young & Rubicam took the scores from earlier ads and compared them to later ones, to determine whether new ads performed above or below the "par" values for previous ones.[65] The agency also compared the "par" values for its ads with those from other agencies to determine how its work measured up against the competition. In a memo from August 1937, for example, Gallup noted that Young & Rubicam's full-page magazine ads had an average readership of 14 percent compared with an average of 9 percent for ads produced by other companies. Gallup then used these numbers to establish performance benchmarks for the agency. For instance, he announced that, instead of a 14 percent "notice rate," the company should aim for a 20 percent rate.[66] The idea of using averages as benchmarks reemerges when Gallup works at the Disney studio in the late 1940s, in studies that assign a numerical rating to the enjoyment people experienced while watching cartoons. As in his work at Young & Rubicam, the studies at Disney also served to establish performance benchmarks for employees.

Young & Rubicam displayed a similar precision in measuring radio programs. The early 1930s was a period of great turmoil in radio audience measurement. Before that time there was little formal research on the composition or interests of radio audiences. Stations who wanted to know more about their listeners offered free prizes if people would write to them, and used this information to construct "coverage maps" that showed what cities and towns they were reaching. This information told them the range of their signal and the locations of some of their listeners, but not much else. There was also no way to compare audiences for one show against those for another.[67]

At first, companies that advertised on the radio accepted that it was difficult to know exactly whom they were reaching. But as the Depression went on, each form of mass media needed to prove what kinds of sales it could generate. Newspapers and magazines had circulation figures, but there was nothing comparable in radio. To meet the demand for reliable evidence, the Association of National Advertisers and the American Association of Advertising Agencies commissioned Archibald Crossley to conduct regular and continuous studies of radio audiences. Crossley founded the Cooperative Analysis of Broadcasting (CAB) in March 1930 to provide the organizations that bought time on radio, the sponsors and their advertising agencies, with information about the audiences they reached.[68]

Crossley used a technique known as telephone recall, where interviewers telephoned people and asked what program they had heard during a previous time period. At first the CAB asked people what programs they had listened to during the prior 24-hour period, then it began calling throughout the day to ask what listeners remembered about the preceding few hours. Nearly all these calls reached listeners in the thirty-three cities served by CBS and the two NBC networks. These methods led to two criticisms of the CAB's work: that it relied on people to remember what they had listened to, and that it did not include listeners in the entire United States. The fact that the CAB used telephones made its work possible, but it also meant that its surveys excluded people who could not afford them during the Depression.[69] The method also tended to favor programs whose stars were already well known, whose names people would remember, rather than emerging performers.

Gallup and Young & Rubicam introduced a new way to measure radio audiences. In 1931, before he joined Young & Rubicam and while he was teaching at Drake, Gallup had developed what became known as the coincidental method. With this approach, interviewers went house to house asking people what program they were listening to at that moment and who sponsored it. This method overcame one of the objections to the CAB's recall method, since listeners didn't have to remember what they had listened to in the past; they only had to state what they were listening to at the moment of the interview. As he had done with his newspaper research, Gallup formulated a method that bypassed memory and the changes memories can bring, to capture the experience of reception at the moment it occurred.[70]

Many people in broadcasting immediately appreciated the advantages of the coincidental method: it provided immediate results that were more accurate than the ones obtained through telephone recall. After Young & Rubicam hired Gallup, it made this technique the basis for all its telephone surveys in the 1930s and 1940s. Other rating services also adopted this strategy, including the "Hooperatings" that began in 1938 and that became the standard for radio audience measurements into the 1950s. Even the CAB switched to the coincidental method in 1941. Gallup's method became the benchmark against which other radio audience measurements were judged.[71]

Just as he had with his first newspaper study, Gallup used his new method of radio research to puncture existing myths. He found that radio audiences were smaller than advertisers and the CAB claimed, and that hardly anyone knew who sponsored their favorite programs. Gallup made other changes that improved the quality of information the agency had to work with, compared with what the CAB provided. His audience sample encompassed a greater variety of geographical regions, not just the large metropolitan areas measured by the CAB, and the agency used personal interviews and telephone calls to reach a broader demographic group.[72] The same concerns will reappear in his first major survey for Hollywood, on audience reactions to double features, where he challenges the film industry's numbers on attendance and argues that he can do a better job than Hollywood of reaching a cross-section of the American public.

Cost was the driving factor in all of Young & Rubicam's research. Just as space was a commodity in print media, time was the commodity for sale in radio.[73] The agency calculated that there were sixteen hours in a day when people weren't sleeping and that were available for broadcasts. Since programs were generally fifteen minutes long during the 1930s, each 16-hour day was divided into 15-minute segments, making available 64 segments a day and 448 segments per week. Theoretically, each of these segments was available for sponsored broadcasts, but they did not all have the same value. Young & Rubicam's Station Relations Department had charts graphing the number of radio sets in use for every 15-minute period for every day of the week, and detailed graphs of responses to specific programs. These enabled the agency to determine which nights were best for the radio programs it sponsored, and which hours of each night had the most sets in use. Young & Rubicam could assess the "cost per listener reached," "cost per thousand families," and "cost per thousand identifiers" for advertising messages, providing an exact measure of sales effectiveness.[74] Later, Gallup would estimate the potential audience for a film and enable Disney and others to assess the cost for reaching members of different groups.

One criticism of the telephone coincidental method that was often heard in the 1930s was that it did not indicate the "flow" of audiences from one program to another, or their reactions at different moments during a program.[75] The coincidental method provided a snapshot view of one moment of reception, but did not indicate anything about the moments before or after the interview. To answer questions about reactions to programs over time, Young & Rubicam developed what it called a "bits and pieces" study of radio programs, to evaluate different features and strengthen weak spots within individual shows.[76] Its research department set up listening groups in people's homes and asked their opinions on different shows and segments within them. Some of these groups used a "voting machine" that enabled listeners to turn a dial along a 180-degree axis to indicate their degree of like or dislike for a program or personality. With this device, Young & Rubicam could track the increase or diminution of interest as a program unfolded, information that could also be used to place ads. These groups, which today would be called focus groups, helped the agency discover radio personalities who were moving up in popularity, like Fred Allen and Arthur Godfrey.[77] Gallup used a similar device to monitor people's reactions to films when he worked in Hollywood, and producers such as David O. Selznick used the information it provided to edit sequences of films where audiences lost interest.

Gallup and Young & Rubicam changed the way advertising was done throughout the industry. Gallup's idea that blocks of advertising copy should be broken up became standard industry practice within five years. In one memo, Gallup noted that nearly two-thirds of all the ads published in *Good Housekeeping* in 1932 used large blocks of copy, while by 1937 the same percentage of ads was broken into smaller units and used livelier copy—practices that Young & Rubicam had initiated based on his research. Other agencies also developed more ads that used images rather than words, a style Gallup advocated.[78] In addition to changing the industry's methods, Gallup also fulfilled Rubicam's goal of moving Young & Rubicam to the forefront of the field. Billings almost doubled from 1935 to 1937, from $12 million to $22 million, and within a few years Young & Rubicam had the largest volume of any agency in the United States.[79] In 1936 an industry-wide committee awarded Gallup a medal for his "distinguished contribution" to advertising research and at the same time gave Young & Rubicam an award for excellence in copy research—the area Gallup directed.[80] Throughout his life Raymond Rubicam said that his decision to hire Gallup was one of his greatest professional accomplishments.[81]

The Laws That Determine Interest

Gallup's success reinforced the belief that his research uncovered basic truths about human nature. As research data accumulated, Young & Rubicam came to believe that "there *are* certain laws that determine the interest of an advertisement—and how many readers that advertisement will attract."[82] Sigurd Larmon, the agency's president after Raymond Rubicam retired, asserted that

> Things that have interested people over and over again in the past will interest them over and over again in the future. By studying these recurrents over a long enough period of time, categories of likes and dislikes may be established. Thus, a great many advertising practices can be divided into sheep and goats. By avoiding the goats, the overall interest in advertising can be heightened. . . . By cataloging a wide range of products, and charting the relative interest inherent in each, we know how much harder we have to work to get attention for a cake of soap than for a jar of beauty cream.[83]

The precision with which Gallup analyzed both audiences and texts, and the success Young & Rubicam enjoyed when it implemented his findings, reinforced the idea that the agency had found a more reliable way to win the public's attention and its clients' trust.

Gallup's career on Madison Avenue began at a time when advertising agencies had become acutely aware of how difficult it was to reach the public, and when their clients were demanding that they prove their value. Advertisers latched onto Gallup's work because his new, more precise methods seemed to offer a way to reach previously inaccessible areas of human nature. His work portrayed people as being unaware of their emotions and easily reached through narratives or images that engaged their attention before they realized what was happening. Young & Rubicam's success at reaching customers led the agency to conclude that Gallup's findings revealed universal truths about people, their interests, and their reactions.

Gallup portrayed his research methods as "modern," "scientific," and "objective," in contrast to the "hunches" and "guesswork" agencies had relied on in the past. His method of textual analysis dissected ads in minute detail in order to understand why they did or did not work. His research reports translated the complexities of media texts and audiences' reactions to them into useful and manageable data. The charts, memos, and numerical scores created an illusion that the unpredictability of human behavior could at least be monitored, if not controlled.

Broadcast historian Donald Hurwitz has described radio research of the 1930s in terms that can be used to summarize market research in general at this time, including Gallup's work for Young & Rubicam. Hurwitz argues that market research during this period supplied broadcasters and advertisers with "an edifice of rational procedures" by "paring down the variety and complexity" of human response to a more manageable level. "By enumerating the fluid audience and making it appear fixed and static, ratings helped translate . . . differences into demographic descriptions . . . which managers then could preempt on behalf of the mass market." Audiences who had been "discrete, atomized psychological units" were endowed with the qualities of "uniform, averaged groups."[84] This new scientific discourse reflects the movement of psychologists out of academia and into business, and the infiltration of new modes of analysis into areas of culture that had not been the object of empirical research before. In the Depression, this new discourse of empiricism seemed to offer some stability in a shifting and uncertain world.

In the mid-1930s, radio agencies launched a concerted effort to bring film stars to the airwaves, and some, including Young & Rubicam, opened offices in Hollywood. Gallup's work at the agency gave him the research experience and professional contacts that made it possible for him to work in Hollywood. There were many advertising executives who were interested in motion pictures, however, and what made Gallup stand out were his political polls. The next chapter explores the origin and development of these surveys. Though they dealt mainly with political issues, the Gallup polls were not totally separate from his market research because they shared research techniques and even staff. Political polling emerged during the Depression as an outgrowth of the work already being done in advertising. Like advertisers, political polltakers also emphasized the scientific and objective qualities of their work. Gallup's own promotion of polling, and the massive publicity he received in the press, created the context for his film research. When Gallup came to Madison Avenue, he was well known; after the success of his 1936 election surveys, he became a household word.

4

America Speaks

The year 1936 marks a watershed in election polling. In addition to the work being done in advertising, the Psychological Corporation, the organization founded after World War I to explore commercial applications for psychology, was conducting a continuous series of nationwide surveys to assess American attitudes toward the New Deal, the first ongoing, systematic study of public opinion.[1] Paul Cherington and Elmo Roper initiated a quarterly poll in *Fortune* magazine that included questions about the candidates during the months before the election. Archibald Crossley, the head of radio's Cooperative Analysis of Broadcasting (CAB), moved beyond radio research to measure people's views on politics. Market research and political polls used similar techniques—standardized questionnaires, face-to-face interviews, and population samples that represented larger demographic groups—and researchers moved back and forth between these two realms.[2] But of all these researchers, it was Gallup who emerged as the acclaimed representative of what *Business Week* called "one of this season's major new industries."[3]

Among all these groups, it was Gallup who promoted polling by making his surveys the basis for a syndicated column that appeared week after week in the *Washington Post*. It was Gallup who publicly challenged the reigning poll of the day, the *Literary Digest*, in what amounted to a duel of methodologies. In one of the riskiest and most audacious gambles ever undertaken in the history of opinion polling, Gallup made an all-or-nothing bet that put his career on the line: he challenged the *Digest*'s confident prediction that Alf Landon would defeat Franklin Roosevelt in the presidential election. Gallup's success positioned him as a spokesperson for America, and his speeches and articles galvanized interest in opinion polling among politicians, business executives, and Hollywood producers. Within a few months after the 1936 election most of the country knew about the Gallup Poll. It was his success in this election that inspired one of Selznick's associates to say, "A story including the name 'Gallup' means a hell of a lot."[4]

Polling, like advertising research, constructs a representation of public opinion that translates the multiple and chaotic forms of human beliefs into neat packages of numbers. Polls make opinions accessible and manageable to politicians and businesses, and this was one of the reasons that Gallup's work appealed to these groups. But Gallup's work did not just involve interpreting numbers. He brought to his research a fierce commitment to make the people behind those numbers visible to those in power. As a native of Iowa who had expatriated to New York, he felt that many people in positions of power really didn't know what "the common man" thought about the issues of the day. One reason for Gallup's success may have been that he combined a populist belief in everyday people with an understanding of the goals and priorities of business executives. At the same time, his claims to represent "the people" did not always convince other observers of the era, who argued that polls could, by their very nature, direct our attention in certain ways, and that ways of composing samples could disenfranchise certain groups. The quick absorption of polls into contemporary political discourse led some to question how well they represented Americans, and whether they might have oversimplified the complex and tumultuous events of the Depression.

Analyzing the origins and reception of Gallup's political polls helps us to understand his work in Hollywood in several ways. From a methodological standpoint, many of the techniques Gallup used to study filmgoers derived from his political polls as well as his advertising research: the use of population samples, the attention to demographic variables, the awareness of age and gender differences. Going further, Gallup actually used his political polls to ask the public questions about films; surveys that asked people if they voted for Roosevelt also asked for the names of their favorite film stars. Gallup examined the demographic information he gathered about the voting population to construct a representation of the filmgoing population as well. The rhetoric he used to promote his polls, that they were more objective and scientific, repeats the arguments he made to newspaper editors when he urged them to stop relying on guesswork and personal experience and use facts, and anticipates his arguments to studio executives in Hollywood. Finally, by analyzing the range of reactions to his political polls, we can better understand the contradictory responses his work received from the film industry, responses that, like the reactions to his polls, illuminate controversies within Depression culture as a whole.

The Miniature Electorate

Gallup recalled in later interviews that the idea to poll public opinion was "in the air" in the early 1930s, yet it was developments in his own family that galvanized his interest. In 1926 Gallup's father-in-law ran as the Democratic candidate for governor in Iowa, but he had a heart attack at the end of the campaign. In 1932, Iowa's governor put Gallup's mother-in-law on the ticket as secretary of state. Although no Democrat had won a major office in Iowa since the Civil War, the Roosevelt landslide of 1932 carried her to victory. The dramatic surge of Democratic support in Iowa and the rest of the country intrigued Gallup, and he decided to apply some of the research methods used in advertising to examine voters' behavior.[5]

Advertising agencies used census data to compile information about consumers. Gallup drew on government surveys to compile voting records for every county since 1836 and compared these records with the results of each presidential election. Thus he was able to assemble a list of "barometer areas" that consistently voted the way the rest of the country did. In late 1933, he mailed ballots to inhabitants of these cities and towns whom he had selected to represent the general population in that region and used their responses to predict the results of the 1934 congressional elections. The responses from these carefully selected participants matched election results in many areas to within 1 percent.[6]

To fund this research, Gallup turned to Harold Anderson, a college friend who had edited Northwestern's student newspaper when Gallup served as editor of the *Daily Iowan*. After college Anderson became the head of the Publisher's Syndicate, an organization that marketed editorial features and comic strips to newspapers across the country. Gallup and Anderson developed the idea of writing a column based on survey research that could be syndicated.[7] They would ask Americans their views on major issues of the day and report these findings as a regular news feature. On the basis of these preliminary studies, the Publisher's Syndicate gave Gallup a contract for a weekly column based on information derived from his research and, in the fall of 1935, Gallup formally established the American Institute of Public Opinion (AIPO) to carry out and publicize this work.[8] Gallup would use this same method of financing, in which an ancillary product (the column) subsidized the primary research activity (polling) when he began his motion picture research. In Hollywood he offered continuing studies of stars and of the public's awareness of advertising campaigns as a subscription service, and they in turn funded his other film research.

From the beginning, Gallup took great pains to position AIPO as independent and politically neutral. Early press releases described it as "a fact-finding organization that has no affiliation with any political party or with any economic group."[9] In a speech six months after AIPO was formed, Gallup said further, "The Institute of Public Opinion is not a pressure group; it is not trying to *influence* public opinion. Its sole function is to *report* it."[10] As Gallup saw it, AIPO's use of scientific techniques to measure public opinion proved its objectivity. Though he eventually stopped using barometer areas and conducted personal interviews instead of mailing ballots, two other components—sampling and demographic quotas—remained as cornerstones of his methods.

Sampling is based on the theory that one can measure the beliefs and attitudes of a large population by examining a subset of that group. This is possible, however, only if the subset has been chosen in such a way that it reflects key characteristics of the larger population. This principle is well known in medicine and agriculture, where researchers take portions of a bacterial culture or a crop of vegetables to gain information about the rest of the material.[11] Gallup used one form of sampling in his 1934 studies, when he measured voters' opinions using specific counties and towns to represent the rest of America, based on the extent to which their voting practices matched those of the country as a whole.[12] The issue with sampling, of course, is how one determines who is included in the subset. Researchers in the 1930s believed that people's opinions were related to specific social factors, such as their place of residence, age, gender, income, and education. These were the primary demographic quotas used in advertising and in radio audience measurement; Gallup's research at Young & Rubicam studied opinions in relation to these variables.[13] This was also the practice in the 1936 election polls: Roper, Crossley, and Gallup all assumed that many of the characteristics that influenced consumer behavior also influenced voting.

AIPO constructed its population samples on two levels. First, Gallup and his staff divided the country into geographical regions, such as New England or the South. Within these regions, they selected cities, towns, and rural areas whose voting practices closely matched the final percentages in the three previous elections. This stratified sampling developed a list of specific towns where voters would be asked for their views. Once these areas were chosen, AIPO selected individuals within them whose demographic characteristics matched those of the voters in the rest of the state. It chose people on the basis of age, income, race, gender, political affiliation, and how they voted in the 1932 election. Each group received the same proportion of ballots as it cast in the 1932 election, and the number of votes from each state was proportionate to its population and electoral vote. AIPO mailed three-quarters of its ballots and sent interviewers to question people who it found did not respond to mail inquiries. [14]

Gallup described this approach in one of his weekly columns in the *Washington Post*. Since Illinois, for example, had 6 percent of the U.S. population in 1935, 6 percent of a survey's ballots came from there. Seven out of ten people in Illinois lived in urban areas, so the same number of ballots needed to come from people in those areas. One voter out of eight in the state was on relief, and one in ten had come of age since the 1932 election, so AIPO used these same percentages in its balloting. Some 56 percent of Illinois' voters were Democrats and 42 percent Republicans, and AIPO duplicated these affiliations in its own votes.[15] None of these quotas were integrated. That is, AIPO did not ask its interviewers to find urban female Democrats, just females and urban residents and Democrats. A woman who fit this description would count once in each category. Interviewers had to be careful to keep track of the quotas they were expected to reach. If they hadn't met some of their quotas by the end of the week, they might find themselves looking for a wealthy woman aged 18 to 24 who lived on a farm.[16]

In many articles about its methods, AIPO emphasized that it made a special effort to reach people from lower-income groups and those who lived on farms and in small towns. AIPO interviewed people who were on relief in person, since Gallup's 1934 surveys had revealed that people from this socioeconomic group did not or could not respond to written requests for their opinions.[17] Cherington and Roper's polls for *Fortune*, by contrast, focused on urban residents and constructed samples that included 10 percent well-to-do voters and 30 percent upper-middle class.[18] Since they were measuring people's interests in travel and luxury goods for the executives who read *Fortune*, this kind of sample was appropriate, however.

In addition to reaching people from lower-income groups and rural areas, AIPO also focused on young adults who had become old enough to vote since the 1932 election. Its demographic categories for the 1936 election included ages 17–20 and 21–24, which allowed AIPO to track how the age of the voting population was shifting. AIPO surveys were sensitive to variations in political philosophies as well. Voters who supported socialism were allowed to choose this as a category, instead of being confined to the traditional Republican and Democratic affiliations.[19] One group whose voice was not heard, however, was African-Americans. AIPO's surveys were designed to measure the views of voters, and since blacks were not allowed to vote in many southern states, they were not included in election surveys in those areas.[20]

Its sensitivity to class and philosophical differences distinguished AIPO's polls from others of the time.[21] In his columns for the *Washington Post*, Gallup described AIPO's sample as a "miniature electorate" and its surveys as "a national election on a small scale."[22] Other essays in the paper described survey participants as "the great mass of citizens . . . a cross section of farmers, bankers, bakers, lawyers, clerks, bootblacks and all other classes of persons."[23] The headline for a column published on October 20, 1935, asked: "Does the Forgotten Man Still Feel Forgotten? He Answers for Himself in the Weekly Poll."[24] AIPO borrowed the famous phrase from Roosevelt's inaugural address to position itself as a new spokesperson for America. Gallup also asked interviewers to write down people's comments in their own words, and AIPO's news releases quote them often. The colorful and distinctive language voters use fleshes out the more abstract charts of numbers. Gallup's commitment to providing a voice for Americans formed the basis of his later arguments that polls were a force for democracy.

A Smooth-Running Machine

Another quality that distinguished Gallup from other researchers of the time was his early appreciation of the synergies that could be created between pollsters and the press. Gallup's was the only election poll that appeared in the *Washington Post*. Elmo Roper's polls appeared quarterly in *Fortune*, and Archibald Crossley's reports in William Randolph Hearst's papers, but the *Washington Post* carried AIPO's surveys on the first page of its "News and Features" section every week beginning in October 1935. This special position kept Gallup's name in front of government leaders and gave him a highly visible platform from which to launch his reputation and challenge his rivals. The kinds of questions AIPO asked also kept its surveys in front of the public: they included trend questions that measured attitudes toward FDR and the New Deal at regular intervals.[25] These set up a continuing narrative in the paper that promoted AIPO as a valuable source of information in a time of political upheaval.

Today the *Washington Post* probably remains most closely associated with Katharine Graham, but it was her father, Eugene Meyer, who purchased the paper in June 1933, when it was in receivership and losing $1.3 million a year. Meyer came to Washington after earning a fortune on Wall Street by investing in copper, autos, oil, and railroads.[26] After he took control of the paper, Meyer launched a campaign to increase circulation and advertising, and sought advice from other publishers, including Gardner Cowles, who had funded Gallup's dissertation at Iowa, and Carl Ackerman, dean of the Graduate School of Journalism at Columbia, where Gallup taught part time from 1935 through 1937. At their recommendation, Meyer asked Gallup for advice about editorial and staff changes at the *Post*.[27] The two men met shortly after Gallup began his experiments in the 1934 congressional election, and Gallup asked Meyer if the publisher would be interested in a poll about crucial issues of the day. Meyer was familiar with the idea of sampling from his early experiences as a mining engineer, and thought that surveys would give politicians more accurate information than they could get from their mail or from pressure groups.[28] He promised to give Gallup's column a prominent place in the Sunday paper and even hired a blimp to fly over Washington to advertise its first appearance on October 20, 1935.[29]

Meyer's decision to publish AIPO's findings in the *Post* connected Gallup's surveys with a long tradition of polls in American newspapers going back to the *Harrisburg Pennsylvanian*, which announced in the summer of 1824 that Andrew Jackson was ahead of John Quincy Adams in what became a controversial presidential election. Most of these newspaper surveys took place around election time and focused on their local communities. These "straw polls" measured people's opinions informally, without using statistical techniques. Some papers sent reporters out on the street to question people; others published ballots in the paper and asked readers to vote by sending them in. These papers took pride in speaking for their communities and felt a responsibility to their readers to be fair and accurate. By the early twentieth century, many large regional papers and some magazines were publishing these straw polls, including the *St. Louis Dispatch* and the *Chicago Record-Herald*, for which Gallup had conducted readership studies. When he established AIPO, Gallup hired Claude Robinson, a recent Columbia graduate, to serve as its Associate Director. Robinson had written a history of straw polls for his doctoral dissertation, and his research gave Gallup comprehensive information about these earlier forms of polling.[30]

When he began AIPO and his regular newspaper column, "America Speaks," Gallup challenged the hegemony of local papers and questioned whether they had the authority to speak for all Americans. Just as in his earlier studies of newspaper readership, Gallup suggested that traditional ways of gauging public opinion, such as straw polls, were inadequate to represent the heterogeneity of the American people. In his weekly columns, Gallup argued for the modern and scientific quality of his approach, and stressed that his surveys would provide a more reliable indication of where Americans stood on Roosevelt and his policies.[31] To prove it, he launched an attack against the leading magazine poll of the day, the *Literary Digest*.

By the mid-1930s the *Literary Digest* had become the largest and most famous straw poll in the country. It had correctly predicted the winner of every presidential race since 1916 and had called the popular vote to within less than 1 percent during the 1932 presidential election. The most famous characteristic of the *Digest* poll was its size. At first the magazine published a question form in its pages and asked readers to send it in. Then the *Digest* began mailing these "ballots" to subscribers and people whose names it obtained from telephone directories, auto registration lists, and other public documents. It is estimated that between 1916 and 1932 the *Digest* mailed about 350 million ballots to people drawn from these "tel-auto" lists. During the 1932 election alone it distributed twenty million mail ballots. The sheer size of the *Digest* poll constituted its claim to veracity, and it seemed infallible to the journalists, politicians, and members of the public who read it.[32]

The *Digest* launched its 1936 election poll in an article that highlighted its record and the massive effort required to process these millions of ballots:

THE DIGEST's smooth-running machine moves with the swift precision of thirty years' experience to reduce guesswork to hard facts. . . . This week, 500 pens scratched out more than a quarter of a million addresses a day. Every day, in a great room high above motor-ribboned Fourth Avenue, in New York, 400 workers deftly slid a million pieces of printed matter—enough to pave forty city blocks—into the addressed envelops [*sic*]. Every hour, in THE DIGEST'S own Post Office Substation, three chattering postage metering machines sealed and stamped white oblongs; skilled postal employees flipped them into bulging mailsacks; fleet DIGEST trucks sped them to express mail-trains. . . . Next week, the first answers from those ten million will begin the incoming tide of marked ballots, to be *triple-checked*, verified, *five times* cross-classified and totaled.[33]

In addition to describing the enormous energy that went into mailing and tabulating its ballots, the *Digest's* publicity emphasized the reach and scope of its search. For the 1936 election the magazine obtained lists of people from phone books, club rosters, city directories, lists of registered voters, and government occupational data. In some communities it simply blanketed the area and balloted everyone in town. Altogether the magazine mailed ten million ballots, and the *Digest* reported these returns week by week as they accumulated, a strategy that created a sense of breathless anticipation. Articles in the weeks leading up to the election exclaimed: "*Digest* Poll Machinery Speeding Up" . . . "*Digest's* First Hundred Thousand" . . . "Half-Million" . . . "*Digest* Poll Passes Million Mark." The numbers sounded like a countdown and enhanced the impression that Americans were rushing to return their ballots. The *Digest* reported responses by state, so it could track the Electoral College vote, but did not mention age, gender, or income. In fact, only 2.4 million ballots were returned, or 24 percent of the number that was sent out, but the idea that more than a million people were voting in this nationally advertised campaign seemed impressive enough.[34]

Gallup had analyzed the *Digest's* readership as part of his research for the *Liberty* magazine project, and Robinson had made a detailed study of its methods in his dissertation and subsequent book, so AIPO knew a great deal about its competitor. Robinson found that in the 1924 and 1928 elections, the *Digest* predicted that the victor would win by a larger majority than he actually did. Had the elections been closer, the *Digest* would have been wrong on the Electoral College vote. In fact, the *Digest* was correct in its percentages only in the 1932 election, when it predicted FDR's margin of victory to within a fraction of 1 percent. During the 1920s, according to Robinson's calculations, its predictions were off by an average of 12 percent, but since it called the winner, no one objected.[35]

Robinson observed that the *Digest* consistently overestimated the strength of the Republican vote, and he theorized that this was because the magazine used its own subscription list and the tel-auto lists. *Digest* subscribers consisted mainly of people from middle- and upper-income groups, with a large preponderance of doctors, lawyers, and other professionals, which skewed its demographic base toward Republicans. Its use of tel-auto lists also presented problems. Most people couldn't afford cars during the Depression, so many of the names on these lists were probably wealthy people who would vote Republican. The lists were also biased in terms of age and gender, because many families registered their phones and cars in the name of the male head of the family. Since the *Digest* relied on mail ballots, it could expect to receive higher returns from educated people who were accustomed to communicating by mail, and this would further skew their results in favor of Republicans.[36]

Even before the election, the *Digest* had its own evidence that its methods were biased toward Republicans. A poll it conducted in January 1936 found that 63 percent of the poll's participants opposed Roosevelt's New Deal, which clearly did not represent the people who had voted him into office in 1932.[37] As Robinson pointed out, the magazine could have corrected for this by weighting votes, but the editors did not do so.[38] Gallup, on the other hand, realized from his 1934 studies that class differences had increased during the Depression, and he surmised that they were going to play a major role in the 1936 election. The *Digest* assumed that a large enough sample would cover any contingency, but AIPO and others noted that it wouldn't matter how many people were counted if the pool included mainly Republicans and people from upper-income groups.[39]

After Gallup had thoroughly analyzed every aspect of the *Digest's* procedures, he publicly challenged the magazine to a competition. Gallup predicted what the *Digest* would announce in November, by measuring the same socio-economic groups who responded to its mail ballots. In other words, Gallup sampled the *Digest*'s own sample by selecting a group that mirrored the characteristics of its poll.[40] In his first "America Speaks" column on Sunday, July 12, 1936, Gallup announced what the *Digest* would conclude before its poll even got under way. He recalled later:

> We thought the best way to meet the challenge and to get some recognition was to come out flatly in the middle of the summer and say they were going to be wrong; their system wouldn't work this year. Since we were in a sense as expert as they were in that system and we could sample the same people that they had sampled in the same way, we knew that we had the answer.[41]

Gallup's bold gambit was not quite the gamble it appeared to be, as he had evidence to support his prediction. But to add fuel to the fire, he offered a money-back guarantee to the subscribers of his syndicated column if his election forecast was wrong—a move that could have bankrupted AIPO just when it was getting started.[42]

In his first column for the *Post*, Gallup predicted that, come November, the *Digest* would find that 56 percent of the public favored Alf Landon and 44 percent supported Roosevelt. AIPO's own surveys at this point indicated that the reverse would be true, that 52 percent of the public would vote for Roosevelt and 48 percent for Landon. Gallup publicized these findings in large charts and explained his methods in detail: the use of samples, the demographic characteristics he measured, and why AIPO interviewed lower-income Americans in person. Related articles exposed the class bias of the *Digest*'s mailing lists and argued that class differences would be crucial to the 1936 election.[43]

The *Literary Digest* did not take AIPO's attacks lightly. Its editor, Wilfred J. Funk, chastised Gallup for having the gall to predict what his poll would find three months in advance. Funk wrote, "We've been through many poll battles. We've been buffeted by the gales of claims and counter-claims. But never before has any one foretold what our poll was going to show before it was even started."[44] Since AIPO published monthly reports on the election and weekly columns on current issues, its surveys gained more and more attention. Subscriptions to Gallup's syndicated column "America Speaks" increased by nearly 50 percent that fall, and the Sunday *New York Times* published a lengthy article explaining to readers what this new technique of sampling was all about.[45] Hadley Cantril's analysis was a model of clarity and would have helped thousands of *Times* readers understand the issues at stake in the battle between traditional straw polls and quota samples. Cantril also depicted Gallup's techniques as scientific, thereby positioning AIPO's work as modern and innovative.[46]

AIPO's methods themselves contained a built-in form of suspense. The institute's use of weekly and biweekly samples enabled it to measure how opinions changed over time.[47] With the *Digest* poll, 71 percent of the people who received ballots mailed them within one week, so it was in effect a snapshot of one moment in time, one that ignored the last several months of campaigning.[48] AIPO's methodology generated suspense: how would opinions shift this week? The race also built interest in the *Post*, which offered readers a "1936 Election Scorecard" where they could write down the results of each AIPO election poll.[49] The contest between AIPO and the *Digest* stimulated interest in Gallup's work and promoted the *Washington Post* at the same time.

Because of Gallup's challenge to the *Literary Digest*, the 1936 election also became a test of polling methods, a David and Goliath contest between the massive and famous *Digest* poll and the newer, more nimble AIPO surveys. AIPO kept the focus on its methodology all the way up to the election. A headline in the *Post* on October 4 argued that, "Election Will Show If Sampling Method Is Accurate," and Gallup's last column on the Sunday before the election asserted that, "Voting Tuesday to Test Clashing Poll Methods."[50] Two days before voters cast their election ballots, AIPO and the *Digest* were in opposite camps: the *Digest* was predicting that Landon would win with 57 percent of the vote, while AIPO calculated that FDR would be victorious with 54 percent. Gallup's final newspaper column also revealed how much the tension had increased. AIPO filled its usual page in the *Post* with descriptions of its methods and even included a discussion of Jacob Bernoulli's probability theory. On that Sunday, however, AIPO knew it was right about one thing: the *Digest*'s forecast was what AIPO had said it would be, back in July.

Journalists in the 1930s pointed out how much criticism Gallup endured for daring to defy the *Digest*. *Newsweek* claimed that he was "heaped with abuse," and even papers that subscribed to "America Speaks" sometimes published Gallup's column on an inside page and put news releases from its rivals up front. One story reported that Gallup's wife took him on a trip to Florida to escape the tension.[51] When Election Day was over, however, AIPO was victorious: Roosevelt received 61 percent of the total vote, and the *Digest* was wrong by 14 percent, the greatest error in the history of national polling.

"Is Our Face Red!"

The *New York Times* index for 1936 lists two columns of names under the heading "Presidential Campaign of 1936—Polls." Some names are familiar, such as the League of Women Voters, while other surveys are unique, having been conducted at hotels or filling stations where reporters had stopped on the road.[52] Most of these polls predicted a victory for Franklin Roosevelt, though Landon led among farmers and newspaper editors. Yet the 1936 presidential election stands in survey history as a monument to the battle between Gallup and the *Digest*.

Of the three pollsters who defined themselves through their use of scientific techniques—Gallup, Roper, and Crossley—Gallup became the most famous, even though Roper and Crossley were more accurate. Gallup predicted that Roosevelt would win by 53.8 percent, when he in fact won by 60.7 percent. Elmo Roper called the election within a closer percentage than AIPO, 61.7 percent, using only 3,500 personal interviews, and Archibald Crossley predicted that 53.9 percent of American voters would support FDR, which matched Gallup's prediction. Roper, however, did not make an explicit projection for the election. In the October 1936 issue of *Fortune*, the last one published before the election, Roper said only that FDR had about a 60 percent approval rating, and that 69.2 percent of the people surveyed thought he would win.[53] If one takes this approval rating as a prediction, then Roper's estimate was closer than Gallup's; but Roper did not measure how people planned to vote, just who they thought would win. It was suggested later that *Fortune*'s editors refused to believe Roper's numbers and decided not to publish a prediction because its publisher, Henry Luce, opposed FDR.[54] Crossley's results were also suppressed: his survey information was published in Hearst's newspapers, and Hearst, who hated Roosevelt, was afraid that polls showing him in the lead would create a bandwagon effect.[55] Gallup was the only pollster who stated publicly and often that FDR would win the election and who disseminated this prediction in his own syndicated newspaper column.

The *Digest*'s failure raised significant methodological issues for researchers in the 1930s. Several articles at the time, and more since, have analyzed the reasons behind the *Digest*'s failure and have pointed to two causes—sample bias and response bias. As we've seen, the *Digest*'s sample was skewed in favor of older Republican men. This was also true in the 1932 election, but in 1932 even Republicans voted for Roosevelt to express their disgust with Hoover, and many mailed in the *Digest* forms as a way to register their protests.[56] In 1936, however, the preponderance of older Republican men on the *Digest*'s mailing list did not accurately represent a voting population that included many voters who recently had come of age and many who had grown poorer.

The second reason behind the *Digest*'s failure was the response bias in its survey, the fact that only 2.4 million people out of 10 million returned their ballots. AIPO tested this hypothesis in a May 1937 survey that asked Americans whether they had received a *Digest* ballot; whether they returned it; if they changed their minds after mailing it; for whom they finally voted; and whether or not they owned a car or telephone. The study found that two and a half times as many Roosevelt supporters as Landon supporters failed to return their ballots.[57] Peverill Squire, who analyzed this data, estimated that of the *Digest*'s 18 percent gap, 11 percent could be attributed to sample bias and 7 percent to the low response rate of certain groups.[58]

The *Digest* conceded the merits of this last argument in "What Went Wrong with the Polls?" an editorial published two weeks after the election in an issue whose cover exclaimed: "Is Our Face Red!"[59] The *Digest* claimed that it didn't overlook "the have-nots" because in some cities, like Chicago, it polled every third registered voter. The editorial also noted that FDR received plenty of support from people from its readers' social classes. The *Digest* acknowledged, however, that the 24 percent reply rate for its survey, and the preponderance of Republicans on its rolls, probably explained its error. Even Wilfred J. Funk, the editor who had attacked Gallup for his early prediction, admitted on the day after the election that the *Digest* poll did not cover a representative sample of the population.[60]

The competition between the *Digest* and AIPO changed both organizations after the election. The *Literary Digest* ceased publication less than a year after Roosevelt's victory, though not only because of its election embarrassment. The magazine had experienced financial difficulties before the poll began, which was why it mailed ten million ballots instead of the twenty million it had sent out in 1932. Even though AIPO had predicted Roosevelt's victory, it was off by 7 percent, so Gallup reevaluated his methods. The institute decided to discontinue mail ballots and to use face-to-face interviews exclusively (fig. 4.1). Gallup also realized that it was necessary to continue polling up to the day of the election. It had stopped ten days before the November vote, and this may have explained the error in the percentages it gave for Roosevelt.[61] Despite these limitations, AIPO's victory led politicians and business executives to conclude that small, carefully distributed samples could be a valuable tool for studying public opinion.[62] Although Gallup's results were not much better than other pollsters, his publicity about AIPO's philosophy and methods kept his work before the public.

What We Think

Even though he underestimated the extent of FDR's victory, Gallup's startling success in the 1936 election made his polls famous literally overnight.

FIGURE 4.1 Gallup interviewer questioning a voter. The 1936 presidential election marked the first use of scientific polls. Gallup's successful challenge of the *Literary Digest*'s election forecast made his name a household word.   (*Courtesy Corbis*)

Even interviewers from rival polling firms began to tell people they worked for Gallup, because his name guaranteed entry into people's homes.[63] At a time when public opinion seemed to be shifting and indeterminate, and when many in power were afraid of the directions it could take, AIPO's scientific techniques seemed to offer a way to make sense of these changes.

Gallup's regular columns continued to highlight the scientific basis of his research. On the Sunday after the election, the *Post* published an article explaining "How Scientific Poll Forecast Unprecedented Roosevelt Landslide." The article explained AIPO's methods in detail and emphasized again that "a continuous scientific poll may forecast how 45,000,000 people will vote by sampling the opinion of a cross section of 100,000 to 200,000."[64] The successful pollsters immediately began looking for ways to tie their methods to other, potentially more profitable, fields. Both Gallup and Archibald Crossley gave speeches after the election in which they stressed that the techniques used in political polling were applicable to market research. The *New York Times* reported that business executives were already exploring the possibility of using research modeled after the polls to study reactions to their new products.[65] The idea of surveying a small group in order to understand a larger population fascinated many, the *Times* wrote.

> To business men, as well as to those in market research lines, the value of proper "sampling" in getting a cross-section of consumer reaction on political or marketing questions has been highlighted by the accuracy of the Gallup and Crossley surveys and by the wide margin of error by which *The Literary Digest* straw vote failed. . . . The lessons learned in the straw balloting will prove particularly valuable to big business interests who will use similar market surveys to determine public reactions to contemplated changes in business policies.[66]

In addition to opening up new avenues of research in business, Gallup's polls also changed the way journalists thought of their work. Newspaper publishers had been among Landon's greatest supporters; the *New York Times* estimated that only 40 percent of the nation's papers supported Roosevelt in the 1936 election.[67] Some commentators argued that his victory proved papers had lost touch with their readers and no longer functioned as the voice of their communities. In some cases editors' preferences for Landon may have led them to suppress evidence of FDR's popularity that appeared in Gallup's research. Papers known to favor Republicans, such as the *Los Angeles Times*, often put articles about the *Digest* polls in a more visible position than news of Gallup's surveys. After the election, some papers reexamined their use of polls and the ways they covered elections.[68]

Having a ready source of information on public opinion also expanded the definition of "news." Gallup pointed out that the polls themselves could become a source of news and could provide starting points for more in-depth stories.[69] Eugene Meyer, the *Washington Post* publisher, argued that AIPO's success had changed the very definition of journalism:

> It takes all four to bring the complete story: news coverage, pictures, editorial analysis, and American reactions as shown in the Gallup polls. In other words, the polls have changed journalism, just as the organization of press associations did, just as the advent of half-tone photo-engravings did, just as the rise of the columnists and commentators did. The reporting of opinion as well as of events has become a part of modern journalism.[70]

Within a few years, the press began to treat Gallup's surveys as indicators of what "we" really thought. An article in the September 1939 issue of *Harper's,* for example, asserted that AIPO had "consolidated the babble of one hundred and thirty million American voters into one voice," and used its

66 • AMERICA SPEAKS

findings to discuss "What We Think About Foreign Affairs."[71] The symbiotic
connection between polls and the press that we take for granted today became solidified in the wake of Gallup's success.

In addition to journalists, politicians in the late 1930s also came to accept AIPO's surveys as an index of U.S. public opinion. The *New York Times*
began running articles discussing whether or not the public as represented
in the Gallup Poll supported legislation Congress was considering, such as
the WPA and government health insurance.[72] The *Congressional Digest* also
cited Gallup's surveys as evidence of how Americans felt.[73] The success of
Gallup's election polls changed Franklin Roosevelt's own use of polling data.
As Richard Steele documents, through most of the 1930s FDR obtained information about public opinion from a variety of sources. He subscribed to a
clipping service that monitored 350 newspapers and 43 magazines, and read
summaries provided by various government agencies of press reaction to
specific pieces of legislation. The White House mailroom counted the views
people expressed in letters to the president and forwarded this information
to FDR.[74] Roosevelt also worked with Emil Hurja, a former newspaper editor and congressional aide, who had combined information from straw polls
with reports from Democratic precincts and caucuses to help plan the 1932
campaign.[75] After 1940, FDR began to rely almost exclusively on polls. Staff
members and friends clipped them from newspapers, and pollsters themselves often sent him advance copies. Roosevelt also commissioned surveys
from Hadley Cantril, the Princeton professor who explained Gallup's methodology in the *New York Times*.[76] Roosevelt saw polls as a way to find out
what concerns he needed to address to increase support for his programs.[77]
We often assume that more recent presidents, such as John F. Kennedy and
Bill Clinton, were the first to rely heavily on polls, but this trend developed
in the 1930s, as an extension of market research, the work of social scientists,
and of course, from Gallup's astonishing election prediction and the publicity he generated.

The Pulse of Democracy

Another reason why AIPO's surveys became so famous is that after the 1936
election, Gallup launched a national campaign to educate the public about
polling. He gave speech after speech to political groups, journalists, teachers,
and business executives in which he promoted the idea that polls were "the
pulse of democracy." Many of these speeches were privately printed and later
excerpted in magazine articles.[78] In 1940, Gallup also coauthored a book, *The
Pulse of Democracy*, which provided a passionate and articulate discussion of

AIPO's philosophy and research strategies.[79] These speeches and writings made him better known than any other figure in American polling.

Gallup, in the words of Irving Crespi, "believed in the collective wisdom of ordinary people and distrusted political intellectuals and experts."[80] He liked to cite Theodore Roosevelt's statement that "the majority of the plain people will day in and day out make fewer mistakes in governing themselves than any smaller body of men will make in trying to govern them."[81] This belief in the fundamental value of popular opinion links Gallup to a long line of political philosophers that extends back to Aristotle and includes Jean-Jacques Rousseau, Jeremy Bentham, and John Dewey.[82] Since ancient Greece, philosophers have debated whether masses of people were more ignorant or more enlightened than the constituent individuals who composed them. While Plato believed that masses were ignorant, Aristotle was among the first to argue that the combined views of many could compensate for the limitations of a few.[83] In the eighteenth century, during the French Revolution, antimonarchist forces, including Rousseau, argued that public opinion was the "Queen of the World" and could be strong enough to restrain the tyranny of kings.[84] In the nineteenth century, Jeremy Bentham in England avowed that public opinion "comprised all the wisdom and all the justice of a nation."[85] Like Bentham, Gallup's views took shape at a time when the ideal of political participation was threatened by economic turmoil, but his articles and speeches affirmed a fundamental commitment to democracy.

In Gallup's opinion, the American people were often ahead of their representatives in government. "We are only beginning to realize some of the possibilities of consulting the people on scores of vital issues affecting them and obtaining their guidance—as to fundamental values—on the issues of the day."[86] This belief that people can sometimes govern themselves better than their leaders could stood in sharp contrast to the views of some of Gallup's contemporaries, who felt that people didn't have enough information to make decisions about politics and should leave government affairs in the hands of experts.[87] In contrast to Gallup's praise of democracy, demagogues such as Huey Long and Father Coughlin were haranguing FDR on the radio. What politics needed, Gallup believed, was a way to ascertain the public's views in a timely fashion, independently of self-proclaimed spokespeople, so that government officials could take their opinions into account while legislation was still being debated.

As several historians have noted, Gallup believed that the New England town meeting represented the ideal form of political participation because people could express their views directly on issues affecting their communities.[88] In modern life, however, town meetings were impractical, and few Americans could express their thoughts directly to their elected representatives. Gallup

believed that polls could be this mechanism for self-expression. Public opinion polls, in his view, "provide a swift and efficient method by which legislators, educators, experts, and editors, as well as ordinary citizens throughout
the length and breadth of the country, can have a more reliable measure of
the pulse of democracy."[89] Polls "make the masses articulate."[90] They "make
a distinct contribution to the science of government by recording the views
of the nation on an issue at any desired time. Congress or the Administration
need not guess in the future regarding the will of the people."[91] AIPO's polls
could reveal the public's views on specific questions because they were carried
out on a regular basis and dealt with current issues. They provided "continuous nation-wide referendums" and a "week-to-week audit of public opinion"
on breaking issues.[92] Gallup often pointed out that when people voted for a
candidate, they did not necessarily agree with him or her on every issue. Polls
could give a better indication of where the public stood.[93]

Gallup also thought that polls could provide a counterweight to the pressure exerted on legislators by special interests groups who claimed to represent the public for their own interests. Polling, he believed, could provide
scientific evidence to support or refute these claims.[94] One example of this
use of polling occurred during a congressional debate about an embargo during World War II. The bill's supporters flooded Congress with telegrams,
and William Randolph Hearst printed ballots in his newspapers for people
to send in to indicate their support. But the congressional committee that
was debating the legislation threw out this "evidence" of public opinion after
the polls conducted by Gallup and Roper demonstrated that most Americans
were against the embargo.[95] Gallup also saw polls as a force against totali-
tarianism. He distinguished between true expressions of public opinion in
polls and pseudo-expressions such as the 1936 Nazi Nuremberg rallies. "The
artificial creation of an apparent majority, whether in a vote which allows no
freedom of choice, or in the organized enthusiasm of a popular rally supervised by the secret police, provides a poor index of public opinion."[96]

Polls could also bridge some of the social and economic differences that
tore other countries apart during the 1930s. *The Pulse of Democracy* offers a
ringing affirmation of AIPO's ability to break through divisions in American
culture. Through the work of "the shock troops of public-opinion research,"
AIPO obtained a panoptic view of society, moving from "a third-floor tene-
ment" in New York to "a smart Park Avenue apartment." Institute interviewers "talk to the prominent industrialist who runs a huge factory employing
thousands of employees, just as they talk to the old lady who silently mops
his office when everyone else has gone home."[97] Gallup believed that polls
offered a way to understand and perhaps mediate the potentially divisive
aspects of American culture in the 1930s. Through surveys, public opinion,

which had brought down kings, could be channeled into more acceptable frameworks that would enable democratic institutions to continue functioning in a time of crisis.

America Speaks?

Though Gallup often said that his polls provided objective, scientific evidence of Americans' views on political and social issues, others were not so sure. Almost as soon as AIPO had proven its utility in the 1936 election, some journalists, politicians, and even social scientists began to question Gallup's claims to objectivity. Some argued that the way AIPO worded questions reflected inherent biases and could channel people's answers in particular directions. Others noted that the act of talking to an interviewer could in itself make people self-conscious about their responses and affect what they said. In looking at how AIPO reported its findings in graphs and charts, one might also examine how the choice of headlines and illustrations emphasized some findings more than others.

In the 1930s, academic researchers were acutely aware of the possibilities for multiple interpretations within surveys. Many books and articles discussed the implications of word choice and question construction, for example.[98] Journalists sympathized with the challenges that pollsters faced in writing survey questions, yet they offered thoughtful critiques of AIPO's methods. James Wechsler, writing in the *Nation* in 1940, noted that the AIPO staffers who wrote survey questions ranged from "left Democrat to right Republican" and that they tried hard to find "a vantage point above the battle where questions can be formulated in a spirit of peace and neutrality." At the same time, he provided several examples of how AIPO's surveys emphasized opposition to relief programs and labor unions. He cited an April 1938 survey that asked: "In your opinion which will do more to get us out of the depression—increased public spending for relief and public works or helping business by reducing taxes?" To which 79 percent of respondents said, "helping business." Wechsler notes: "Was it a fair question? 'Helping business' has affirmative overtones; 'spending' is almost an epithet. Moreover, liberals argue that 'spending' would 'help business' while the stimulus of 'reduced taxes' might prove negligible. Actually the questions accepted a Wall Street diagnosis of our ills." He finds a similar pro-business slant in AIPO's questions about labor unions:

> More recently the institute queried: "Do you think that labor unions should be regulated to a greater extent by the federal government?" An overwhelming

majority said yes. Such a poll could be used as evidence of popular clamor for federal curbs on labor unions. What would have happened if the question had posed specific federal restrictions instead of the general, amiable concept of "regulation"?[99]

Wechsler's sense that AIPO stressed the negative aspects of relief and of labor unions found support in a study that Arthur Kornhauser published in *Public Opinion Quarterly* about polls AIPO conducted between 1940 and 1945. Kornhauser found that AIPO asked twice as many questions about labor unions as *Fortune* did, and that three quarters of its questions stressed the negative aspects of unions, compared to about one-third of the questions asked in other polls.

> The most common themes have to do with what is *wrong* with unions, what restrictive measures are required, what the public thinks about wartime strikes, make-work rules, undemocratic union practices, and similar points with respect to which labor is under attack. By contrast, the essential functions and positive accomplishments of unions in protecting and improving the lot of working people are only rarely mentioned.[100]

Kornhauser also notes that the questions AIPO repeated across multiple surveys were almost all negative, which he says "serve to reiterate and reinforce in the public's thinking points against unions which are already condemned."[101]

Other studies found that AIPO's choice of interviewers may have influenced Americans' responses to this question. Daniel Katz conducted an experiment where he sent five of AIPO's regular interviewers, who were usually white, middle-class, and college-educated, out to interview people, along with four working-class people who were trained to act as interviewers as part of the experiment. Katz found dramatic differences in the responses they received. People who talked to Gallup's regular interviewers expressed more support for business and less for labor, while people who talked to the working-class interviewers expressed much stronger support for the unions. The regular AIPO interviewers not only found fewer people who were pro-labor, the ones they did find did not talk as freely as the pro-labor people who met the working-class interviewers. When Katz asked the AIPO interviewers to fill out the questionnaire themselves, he learned that they tended to be more conservative than their working-class colleagues. Katz concluded that one reason AIPO consistently underrepresented Democratic support for Roosevelt is that pro-union voters may have hesitated to reveal their thoughts to AIPO's interviewers.[102]

AIPO's surveys also revealed a distinct bias against Franklin Roosevelt that was apparent from the beginning of its surveys for the 1936 election. Although its polls indicated again and again that FDR would be voted back into office, AIPO repeatedly cast doubt on this possibility. The headline for its *Washington Post* column on June 7, 1936, read "F.D.R. Gains Again in Poll But Is Still Below His 1932 Strength," even though the statistics below it showed that 55.8 percent of voters supported him.[103] A month later, AIPO noted that Landon was ahead in electoral votes, even if Roosevelt was leading in the popular vote.[104] When AIPO published the results of its monthly trend polls about FDR's popularity, it presented these findings in the form of a line graph that showed the president's popularity descending noticeably. The majority of Americans always supported him, but the arrangement of the chart dramatized any fluctuation in their sentiments.[105] Even when three consecutive surveys indicated that FDR would be reelected, AIPO still did not relent. One subheading suggested wistfully that, "Much Can Still Happen to Change the Total."[106] After Roosevelt won by a landslide, AIPO asked, "Do you think the Republican party is dead? (If yes), how do you think it can be revived? (If no), do you think it will win in 1940?"[107]

One can explain the pro-business, anti-FDR bias that is apparent in these polls in several ways. Some journalists claimed that Gallup was a Republican and that he favored Landon in the 1936 election.[108] Gallup told others, however, that he did not vote after 1928 because he wanted to remain scrupulously neutral. Eugene Meyer, his prominent placing of Gallup's surveys in the *Washington Post* notwithstanding, openly supported Landon for president in 1936.[109] Since many of the newspapers that paid for Gallup's syndicated column were Republican, it was good business to ask them for question ideas. And when the *Literary Digest* was so certain that Landon would win, AIPO may have played up FDR's vulnerabilities as a way of hedging its bets. After the election, AIPO conducted two to three polls a week, while Gallup was still the full-time head of research at Young & Rubicam. One may also wonder how much his staff was responsible for some of the biases in question wording.[110] It should be noted that Gallup cooperated fully with both the Katz and Kornhauser studies that critiqued his methods, which highlights his continuing interest in methodological issues.

A Smooth and Even Uniformity

This discussion of the ideological implications of specific polls, and whether they were consciously or unconsciously influenced by mercantile considerations, leads to a discussion of the broader ramifications of survey methodology.

It is precisely the ability of polls to summarize opinion that raises questions about their limitations as a form of expression. In representing public opinion, one of the most significant elements of AIPO's work, and that of other commercial researchers in the 1936 election, was that they reported results as numbers. Susan Herbst has argued that this format represents an epistemological shift in the history of public opinion. People have expressed their opinions since ancient Greece through oratory, printing, petitions, strikes, crowd protests, letters to the editor, and finally, the sample survey, the twentieth-century avenue for expressing opinions.[111] What distinguishes the sample survey from these other forms of public opinion is its claim to objective validity. Unlike earlier forms of expression, pollsters claim to use scientific techniques to measure and categorize people's views. They channel multiple and contradictory ideas into what appear to be neatly structured frameworks. In Herbst's words, polls "condense" political opinions into "numerical symbols."[112] Viewpoints that may be vague and diffuse look clear and coherent when they are summarized in percentages and charts.

One drawback of this approach is that it fails to take into account the flux and change of social groups and their attitudes. James Boyce, a nineteenth-century English politician and historian whom Gallup often quoted, captured the effect of this condensation in his description of polls. Though this statement refers to the actual election polls where people vote, it applies equally to survey research:

> Bringing men up to the polls is like passing a steam roller over stones newly laid on a road: the angularities are pressed down, and an appearance of smooth and even uniformity is given which did not exist before. . . . Moreover, opinion, which may have been manifold till the polling, is thereafter generally two-fold only. There is a view which has triumphed and a view which has been vanquished.[113]

That polls create the illusion of a view which has triumphed and a view which has been vanquished points to another significant aspect of Gallup's work: polls such as his divide opinion into binary forms—either/or, agree/disagree. Leo Bogart points out that

> This model has the virtue of great simplicity, but it makes no sense, because conflicting and contradictory opinions may be held simultaneously and because they constantly jostle one another for dominance. . . . Human nature is too subtle, fragile and complex to be measured by a question which asks, "Do you agree or disagree?"[114]

Such questions may reflect our larger "belief systems," but they limit, according to Herbst, "the character and intensity of our political expressions."[115]

Gallup was not alone in the 1930s in recognizing that public opinion was shifting and contingent. Cantril, for instance, explored in detail the forces that affect it. His 1940 study of reactions to Orson Welles's "Invasion from Mars" broadcast found that psychological variables, such as people's attitudes toward religion and feelings of security, were just as important in determining their reactions to the broadcast as their age, gender and socio-economic class.[116] Paul Lazarsfeld's research on how people chose which candidate to support during the 1940 election found that opinion was shaped by a "two-step flow" of ideas from opinion leaders to larger numbers of people.[117] These researchers, as well as many others of the period, recognized that opinions could be influenced by psychological and interpersonal factors as well as by social ones.[118] Gallup certainly understood the importance of these elements, but his focus was not so much on the *process* of opinion formation as its *result*, and how to articulate these results to people in power. Gallup and the other commercial polltakers were more concerned with the instrumental value of their polls. Like his media research, Gallup's polls synthesized complex responses into a form that could be used by government and business.

Gallup probably did more than any other figure in this century to disseminate the idea that polls are accurate, reliable indicators of public opinion. He reiterated that "public opinion is something real that exists ready to be measured objectively . . . if you ask your questions of a valid cross-section of the general public, you have a valid measure of the public's thinking on that topic at that time."[119] Gallup's numerous speeches and articles circulated this image of public opinion as empirical fact to many business leaders and political groups. Yet in circulating his ideas, Gallup also revealed different ways that opinions can be represented and interpreted. One result of the methodological competition between Gallup and the *Literary Digest* is that it brought to light the processes by which opinion polls are formulated. John Durham Peters has argued that public opinion since the eighteenth century "has never existed apart from mediated representations, and thus has always had an important 'textual' or symbolically constructed component."[120] Gallup's discussion of his work in the *Washington Post* and in his speeches and articles highlighted this textual and symbolic dimension. By creating a dichotomy between "objective" and "scientific" construction in competition with the *Digest*'s traditional and intuitive one, he perhaps inadvertently acknowledged the possibility that there may not be one infallible method for representing the true complexity of public opinion.

The fact that polling methods and conclusions were subject to so much discussion and reinterpretation can be seen as proof that public opinion is not a fixed, stable entity but one that shifts with other cultural forces. A central argument in French theorist Pierre Bourdieu's writing is that "public opinion does not exist," it is a fiction, "an object to be molded." The function of polling "is perhaps to impose the illusion that a public opinion exists, and that it is simply the sum of a number of individual opinions."[121]

Despite their simplicity, numerical representations have several qualities that make them attractive to organizations in a complex, technologically oriented modern society. Numbers are concise and efficient, which makes them useful tools. Numbers can be categorized and manipulated more easily than other expressions of opinion, such as conversations or street demonstrations.[122] Because scientific polls seem more accurate, and because they provide information that can easily be manipulated, they have begun to replace other expressions of public opinion in the media. Journalists, advertising agencies, and market research firms cite survey information as concrete proof of public attitudes. Politicians constantly refer to polls to gauge where they stand and to learn what issues the public cares about. Presidential campaigns during the last several decades have built many of their platforms and advertising around issues that polls indicate are important to voters.[123] For politicians, surveys function as a form of public affirmation: "If a policymaker can show that the public is behind him or her," according to Herbst, "it becomes easier to continue on that course."[124]

As Peters notes, "Citizens do not themselves produce public opinion today; it must be generated through the machinery of polling. The power to constitute the public space, then, falls into the hands of the experts, not of the citizens."[125] As journalists, politicians, and advertisers circulate images of "the public," we become more self-conscious of ourselves.[126] The surveys we hear seem to be definitive and to have represented us so completely that, as Herbst argues, "they give the illusion that the public has already spoken in a definitive manner. When the polls are published, and presidents and policymakers claim that they will heed these polls, what more is there to say?"[127]

Herbst's statement brings us full circle in Gallup's work, as we see that in the process of "speaking for" America, polls have effectively supplanted other forms of political and social discourse. When scientific methods are valorized, other means of expressing opinions are lost. By translating the multiplicity and diversity of opinions into percentages and graphs, polls reify the subject of which they speak. All these issues reappear when Gallup goes to Hollywood. The methods of film research he proposes challenge conventional wisdom in the film industry and the ability of studio executives, trade papers, and theater owners to represent audiences' reactions. Some of his research was thought to favor the interests of the studios over those of ex-hibitors, directors, and performers, just as his political polls were thought to favor business over labor. Executives in the film industry's New York offices readily accepted his polls as an indicator of public interests, while local the-ater owners challenged their accuracy. The demographic information his film surveys present gave Hollywood a more detailed view of the public than it had ever had, and Gallup's methods enabled him to refine his analysis of film texts as well. Most of all, it was the reputation Gallup established as a result of his political polling that made his name one to conjure with in Hollywood.

5

Piggybacking on the Past

At the time of his successful election forecast, Gallup was working as the director of the American Institute of Public Opinion while holding a demanding position as director of research at Young & Rubicam. How did a top advertising executive who had established a suddenly famous polling service find time to carry out research in film? And how did he pay for the cost of interviewers, data processing, and research analysts during the Depression? Archival records from the late 1930s and interviews with Gallup and his associates reveal that it was Gallup's advertising work and his political polls that supported his early forays into motion picture research. Gallup's interest in Hollywood developed at the same time that the advertising industry as a whole began to collaborate more extensively with film studios, and when Young & Rubicam was expanding its own contacts in Hollywood. The agency provided financial and material support to Gallup through its West Coast office, and enabled him to meet Hollywood executives who would later commission research from him. As Don Cahalan, who worked with Gallup during this period, put it, Gallup found ways for his film work to "piggyback" on his other endeavors.[1]

In addition to the support he received from his advertising colleagues, Gallup built on the network of associates he had developed through his political polls. Gallup's stunning victory as an election forecaster was catalytic. He became a legend in some quarters, and his fame created an aura of success that attracted more interest. Through his contacts from political work Gallup met people who eventually formed the nucleus of his film research company. On a more practical level, Gallup also used AIPO and its regular surveys to gather demographic information about film audiences and to test methodological issues involved in film research. If, as Herbert Schiller has suggested, "the opinion poll is a social invention that cannot be considered apart from the institutional web in which it functions," then to assess Gallup's work in Hollywood we want to examine the nexus of relationships he created among his many endeavors.[2]

Sort of a Challenge

Gallup began thinking about how to do research in film in 1934 or 1935, after he had become established at Young & Rubicam, and while he was putting together the framework for his political polls. The methodological challenges of studying the public's reactions to films intrigued him, he said later. "It was sort of a researcher's dream because every aspect of it presented a new problem that no one had ever thought through, had ever done anything about."[3] It was one thing to measure attitudes toward advertisements or presidential candidates, but even more challenging to study reactions to popular entertainment. Many people didn't think it could work with film. "The people we ran into on occasion said . . . 'you can research politics and products and advertisements and all these other things, but . . . research has no place in the field of motion pictures.' So that was sort of a challenge."[4] Gallup's commitment to empirical research and his conviction that surveys could provide information of practical value also motivated him. "The creative people tend to think that it's impossible for fact-finders, such as I am, to get any information or help them in any way."[5]

In addition to the methodological hurdles it posed, film research seems to have awakened in Gallup the same populist convictions that had inspired his political polls. Gallup felt that Hollywood was out of touch with many Americans' interests, and that his surveys could provide a more accurate picture of what people were thinking, just as they had in politics. "I had the firm conviction that any product, any service, entertainment or anything else that had to reach millions of people had to be a proper subject of research. How could people sit in Hollywood and know how people who lived in New Jersey or Florida would be thinking?"[6] As in politics, Gallup saw film research as a way to make these voices audible to the executives who produced their entertainment.

Though Gallup's interest in film research grew out of personal convictions, his ideas took concrete form at a time when Young & Rubicam began producing radio programs in Hollywood. In the early 1930s, as Michele Hilmes has documented, film studios and radio stations began to explore mutually beneficial opportunities for promotion. RKO and Paramount publicized their new film releases by dramatizing them as radio broadcasts, and Warner Bros. invited the public to watch radio programs being produced at its Los Angeles station KFWB.[7] In February 1934, Young & Rubicam launched a behind-the-scenes program called *Forty-Five Minutes in Hollywood*, in which a *Photoplay* editor interviewed a film star about his or her upcoming release and a radio actor or actress reenacted scenes from the film. Other shows followed that featured Hollywood stars in radio adaptations, including *Silver Theater* (1937) and *The Screen Guild Theater* (1939), and by 1939 Young & Rubicam had become a leader in finding creative ways to promote films on the radio.[8] The agency sponsored a tie-in with the premiere of *Knute Rockne* in South Bend, Indiana, the home of Notre Dame, and developed ad campaigns for grocery stores that simultaneously promoted Jack Benny's new films, his radio show, and his sponsor, Jell-O. *Billboard* was so impressed with Young & Rubicam's ability to forge "tie-ups" among film studios, radio networks, and corporate sponsors that the magazine awarded the agency top prize in its Annual Exploitation Survey for three years in a row, from 1939 to 1941.[9]

In 1936, after the success of *Forty-Five Minutes from Hollywood*, Young & Rubicam signaled its commitment to the film industry by opening a branch office at 6253 Hollywood Boulevard, on the famed corner of Hollywood and Vine (fig. 5.1).[10] Several radio stations were located at that intersection during the 1930s, and many broadcasts of the period opened with the statement, "This program is being brought to you from Hollywood and Vine."[11] When Gallup formally launched the Audience Research Institute (ARI) in 1940, he established its West Coast headquarters in this Young & Rubicam office.

ARI and Young & Rubicam enjoyed a relationship of cozy reciprocity. In addition to lending its facilities, Young & Rubicam also offered Gallup administrative expertise: Raymond Rubicam served as ARI's chairman of the board, and Sigurd Larmon, who took over after Rubicam retired, also became an ARI director.[12] Rubicam and Larmon may have provided financial assistance as well. In an interview with media historian Thomas Simonet, Gallup mentioned that some of his advertising colleagues had "a small financial interest" in ARI.[13] David Ogilvy later described the company as "an undertaking owned jointly by Dr. Gallup and Young & Rubicam."[14] *Variety* reported in 1944 that Rubicam was the second largest shareholder after Gallup and that he had bought out Young & Rubicam's original share.[15] Since ARI was privately owned, there are no public records that would allow us to trace its financing, but these comments suggest that Gallup's colleagues

FIGURE 5.1 Gallup established the Hollywood branch of the Audience Research Institute at Hollywood and Vine, shown here at night in 1941.   (*Courtesy Corbis*)

at Young & Rubicam provided some of the financial backing he needed to begin this new venture.

In addition to providing more direct forms of support, Young & Rubicam offered Gallup "most favored nation" opportunities to meet others who could assist his film research. Agency executives discussed Gallup's polls along with his advertising work with prominent business executives, including John Hay Whitney, one of the wealthiest men in the United States at that time.[16] Whitney was an active patron of the arts during the 1930s and backed David O. Selznick's productions of films in Technicolor. He also became one of the first investors to commission film research from Gallup. Young & Rubicam executives also promoted Gallup's work when they met with Hollywood producers to discuss their advertising campaigns. Sigurd Larmon, for example, visited David Selznick in December 1940 to discuss whether Young & Rubicam might handle the advertising for his films. His follow-up letter mentioned Gallup's film research and spoke positively about his political polls. He even sent Selznick a copy of AIPO's news release for that week.[17] Gallup, in turn, promoted Young & Rubicam in his own dealings with Hollywood executives. In September 1940, Gallup persuaded Walter Wanger that radio would be a good medium in which to promote *Foreign Correspondent*, the Alfred Hitchcock film that he had produced. Gallup pointed out that Jack Benny, as well as Bob Hope and Bing Crosby, had promoted films on their radio shows, both of which were produced by Young & Rubicam. After this conversation, Wanger gave the go-ahead for a radio play version of *Foreign Correspondent*.[18]

It was also through Young & Rubicam that Gallup found his chief assistant at ARI, David Ogilvy. Ogilvy, later the founder of the Ogilvy and Mather advertising agency, was to become a legend of American advertising. His fame rests in part on a book he would write later, *Confessions of an Advertising Man*, a compendium of witticisms and practical advice that contains such famous remarks as "the consumer isn't a moron; she is your wife."[19] Ogilvy was born in London and attended Oxford. He spent a year working in the kitchen of a Paris hotel and then sold cooking stoves door-to-door around England. He was so successful that the firm asked him to write a training manual for its salesmen.[20] "The Theory & Practice of Selling the Aga Cooker" displayed the rhetorical flair that became Ogilvy's trademark, in such bon mots as: "The good salesman combines the tenacity of a bulldog with the manners of a spaniel." "If you have any charm, ooze it."[21]

In 1938 Ogilvy came to New York, at the age of 27, to learn American advertising methods, which he considered the best in the world. Later he recalls admiring the advertising campaigns of Young & Rubicam in particular. "When I looked at Young & Rubicam ads, or heard them on the radio, I sat in awe. Those Sanka coffee ads! I was completely swept away by it all!"[22] Gallup was similarly impressed when Ogilvy came to visit him at the ad agency. "In the process of building a staff to carry on research in [film], I was lucky enough to discover a young Britisher, David Ogilvy. David is one of the most talented persons I have ever known."[23]

Ogilvy became the assistant director of the Audience Research Institute in 1939, and he and Gallup traveled to Hollywood together to meet with producers and develop ideas for film research. He enjoyed the opportunity to hobnob with film personalities and became Gallup's right-hand man, accompanying him on trips to Hollywood and helping to develop new ideas for studies.[24] In interviews later in his life he recalled the thrill of meeting famous producers. "There was I, going to Hollywood all the time, and dealing with big shots like David Selznick and Sam Goldwyn. I was *dealing* with them; I had meetings with them, alone! I was on the telephone to them all the time."[25] Judging from the correspondence files at various studio archives, Ogilvy wrote most of the ARI reports that Hollywood producers read between late 1939 and September 1942, when he left to work in military intelligence.

It was Ogilvy who interpreted Gallup's methods and data to the film industry, in pithy commentaries that offered an amusing and sometimes sardonic look at American behavior. For the rest of his career he talked about the impact of Gallup's research on his own approach to advertising, saying that working for Gallup was "the luckiest break of my life."[26]

Another key member of Gallup's film research staff in the late 1930s was Barbara Miller Benson, his sister-in-law. Benson had organized and supervised the Reader Research Department at *McCall's* magazine and brought with her extensive experience in advertising and print media as well as a firm grasp of research methods. Ogilvy said later that Gallup installed her "to keep a professional eye on my shaky research procedures."[27] The two of them shared a fascination with cinema; a colleague recalled that Benson "loved films and every detail about them."[28] After Ogilvy resigned in 1942, Benson took over much of his correspondence with studio executives.

A Stream of Facts

Though Young & Rubicam provided the West Coast office for Gallup's film company, its East Coast base was at AIPO's offices in Princeton, where Gallup lived. One researcher who worked there at the time said that Gallup's film staff operated "out of a closet" in AIPO's second-floor walk-up on Nassau Street. The people doing film research worked "on sufferance," he recalled, in cubicles that were "cheek to jowl" with each other. ARI did not rent its own office space until Gallup signed his first contract with a Hollywood studio in 1940, a symptom of the frugality for which he was known.[29]

Besides using some of AIPO's office space for film research, Gallup also drew the rest of his film staff from the staff of his political polls. One of the first people he hired was Don Cahalan, who had joined AIPO in 1938, after completing his graduate work at the University of Iowa. At Iowa he had studied journalism and psychology with one of Gallup's former professors, Norman Meier, and wrote his master's thesis on the failure of the 1936 *Literary Digest* poll.[30] As Cahalan described it, Meier called Gallup and put Cahalan on the phone to talk about his *Digest* work. Gallup hired him to work on political surveys for the 1938 gubernatorial and congressional races, and Cahalan began doing film research when the election was over in late November.[31] Cahalan, in turn, was responsible for hiring another member of Gallup's film research staff, Paul Sheatsley. Sheatsley, a Princeton graduate, was editing a weekly newspaper in New Jersey when he began working as an AIPO interviewer. His exceptionally good data impressed Cahalan, who hired him in the spring of 1939 to supervise the interviewers for Gallup's film surveys.[32]

In addition to drawing personnel from his political polls, Gallup's film work also benefited from the prestige of his election surveys. Although Gallup insisted that AIPO and ARI were separate organizations, many of his actions reminded producers that he was involved in both.[33] During World War II, Gallup often circulated advance announcements of his political polls to clients in Hollywood. In September 1942, for example, he sent David Selznick a copy of a 14-page booklet entitled "An Analysis of American Public Opinion Regarding the War" that he had also distributed to Franklin Roosevelt and to officials in the Office of War Information. The booklet analyzed why Americans felt confused about U.S. involvement in Europe and recommended ways for the government and press to increase support for the war.[34] Having access to the same material that the president was reading would have heightened producers' sense that, through AIPO, they were connected with people even more powerful than themselves.

Both Gallup and Ogilvy drew analogies between politics and filmmaking that clearly were designed to flatter their clients. In June 1942, Ogilvy wrote Selznick a letter in which he compared ARI's film research to the inside information that military officials received. "Our function in the Hollywood set-up should be the same as that of the Intelligence Department in the Army set-up. Just as Intelligence keeps a stream of facts flowing across the desks of General Marshall and his staff, so we must strive to keep a stream of facts flowing across the desks of our clients in the motion picture industry."[35] Similarly, when Selznick wrote Gallup to complain about the way the California Republican State Finance Committee spent money, Gallup responded that spending money to support unpopular candidates was like trying to sell the public a picture it didn't want to see.[36] Though in his public comments Gallup stressed that his film company and his political polls were separate and distinct endeavors, his private communications with film executives reminded them that the two were in fact connected.

Gallup's political polls provided synergy for ARI: having a regular survey mechanism meant that he could ask the public about many different issues, including questions related to film. Even before he signed his first contract with a Hollywood studio, and before he founded ARI as a separate company, Gallup used his regular AIPO surveys to gather demographic information about the people who went to the cinema, and to ask their opinions on various film-related topics. Not only did interviewers ask people for their views on the New Deal, they also asked how often people went to the cinema and who were their favorite stars. That Gallup used AIPO to piggyback his film research suggests that his political surveys functioned both to gather information about politics and to launch other lines of research that grew into separate companies. The very first questions about film that appeared in an AIPO survey illustrate this point.

"Do You Go to the Movies?"

When Gallup started his political polls, he was able to use voter registration lists and census data from local and national government offices to develop a profile of American voters. Once he knew the demographic composition of the voting population, he and his staff constructed a sampling frame that ensured each group was represented in the surveys according to its presence in the voting population. When he began doing research in film, there were no comparable sources of information about film audiences. Hollywood kept records about average ticket prices and box office grosses, but these numbers were proprietary and assumed to be inflated. Trade papers had published a few local studies, but these were mainly based on interviews or postcards that people filled out when they came to the theater; they did not use scientific sampling. When Gallup began conducting film research, there were no national surveys that used sampling techniques to define the demographic makeup of the entire U.S. film audience.

Before he could begin asking people what they liked and disliked about films, then, Gallup had to determine which people to ask. This was the rationale for asking the nationwide cross-section of people who responded to his political polls about their moviegoing habits. The first film-related questions appear on an AIPO survey carried out during the first week of December 1936, one month after Roosevelt's reelection. The survey asked 1,949 adults nationwide, "Do you go to the movies?" "About how often?" "Who is your favorite man star?" "Who is your favorite woman star?" Though the names of these stars have not been archived, we know that 80 percent of the U.S. population said they went to the cinema.[37] This was not the first time that someone had asked the public how often they went to see a film. Elmo Roper posed the question in his poll for *Fortune* magazine in April 1936, which may have given Gallup the idea, but Roper did not ask the question on a regular basis, as AIPO did.[38] This question occurs nineteen times on AIPO surveys between the end of 1936 and the end of 1940; in 1937 alone AIPO asks about attendance nearly every month until August.

Just as political pollsters experimented with different ways of phrasing questions, AIPO explored different kinds of wording in order to measure how often people went to the cinema. For example, the survey completed during the week of December 16–21, 1936, asked, "Did you happen to go to the movies during the past *week*?" Fifty-seven percent said they had not. If the respondent said no, he or she was asked, "about how long is it since you have gone?" If he or she answered yes, the interviewer followed up by asking, "did you go more than once during the week?"[39] A poll conducted during the week of January 20–25, 1937, asked, "Did you happen to go to the movies during the past *month?*" and if respondents answered yes, they were asked how many times they "usually went during a month."[40] Some of these questions were dichotomous: they allowed respondents to answer only "yes" or "no." Others were open-ended, like the questions asking how many times someone went to the cinema; for these questions AIPO instructed interviewers to write down people's exact responses. For the December 16 survey, AIPO staffers used twenty-nine different time periods to code the data, and in January seventy-nine different time frames. Categories included "once every six months," "every two to three months," "once every month or two," "once every week or ten days," "once a week," "every two days," and "every day." Open-ended surveys are much more expensive and labor-intensive than surveys with dichotomous questions because handwritten answers have to be read and coded individually, while "yes" or "no" questions can be tabulated by mechanical counters. That questions about attendance appear so often, and in open-ended formats, indicates that this information was important to Gallup.

The frequency of these questions suggests that Gallup and his staff were trying to find a workable time frame that could sort out people who went to the cinema on a regular basis from those who did not. Gallup and his associates believed that there was no point in asking people who didn't go to see films very often what they liked or disliked. In their view, people who went to films often had a broader frame of reference with which to make a judgment and were contributing enough to the box office to make their opinions worth knowing. At the same time, Gallup believed that people who went to see films a lot might like everything and not be very discriminating in their tastes.[41] The question is, what period of time would include enough people who saw films, but eliminate those at either extreme, people who went too often or not at all. These two polls revealed that only 30 percent of the people surveyed had seen a film in the past week, but around 65 percent had been to the cinema in the past month.[42] On the basis of these polls, Gallup and his colleagues decided to use "once a month" as a working time frame.[43] Beginning in February 1937, surveys that included a question about film attendance usually phrased the question as "have you been to the movies in the past month?" AIPO continued to ask Americans about their attendance two or three times a year through 1947. These AIPO surveys were the means by which Gallup checked film attendance during most of the time he worked in Hollywood.

The surveys revealed other kinds of information that became significant in Gallup's later work in Hollywood. Interviewers uncovered a notable lack of interest in films among many Americans. Again and again surveys found that nearly one-quarter of respondents had not seen a film in three months. These answers gave Gallup an early indication that Hollywood might be exaggerating the number of people who went to see its films, a significant discovery whose impact will be discussed in the next chapter. AIPO's sensitivity to demographic groups also uncovered useful information. In his 1936 election polls, Gallup had made a point of including younger voters. The surveys that contained questions about attendance at films asked interviewers to speak to people in the following age groups: 17–20, 21–24, 25–34, 35–44, 45–54, and 55 and over. While everyone over 55 is lumped into one group, those under 35 merited three separate categories, underscoring the attention Gallup paid to younger viewers. This focus on teens and young adults revealed some surprising trends, as we shall see. Finally, the open-ended questions that asked people the name of their favorite film indicate that films that are now part of the canon of film studies were not the ones mentioned most often. The public's favorite film in 1937 was *Maytime*, which starred Jeanette MacDonald and Nelson Eddy, followed by *Lloyds of London*, with Freddie Bartholomew and Tyrone Power. Other recent films from the era that are now well known to fans and scholars, such as *The Thin Man*, *Camille*, *My Man Godfrey*, *Showboat*, and *Mr. Deeds Goes to Town*, were named as favorites by less than 2 percent of the people Gallup surveyed.[44]

Black and White and Color

That Gallup could use his political polls as a mechanism through which to launch his film research illustrates the benefits of the organizational and administrative links among his various endeavors. In January 1937, at the same time that he was trying to define the demographic composition of the U.S. film audience, Gallup carried out a study on public attitudes toward color films. The decision about whom to include, that was so important in his studies of attendance, takes on additional urgency in his surveys on color. These surveys illustrate how a poll's results can vary dramatically, depending on how it is constructed, and for whom.

Though color has been part of American cinema since its inception, the technology for creating it has undergone many changes since the early twentieth century, when each frame of film was painted by hand. By the mid-1930s, the Technicolor Corporation had developed two- and three-color processes that created a richer look. In the Depression, many producers could not afford to use them, particularly since the studios had spent millions of dollars converting to sound. Walt Disney was the first to employ Technicolor's new processes, through an exclusive agreement signed in 1932. Since Disney produced cartoons, Technicolor revised its agreement in 1933 to allow producers of live-action films to use its processes. In May 1933, Jock Whitney and his cousin Sonny bought a large block of stock in Technicolor and organized Pioneer Pictures for the purpose of making color films. Their first release was a live-action short, *La Cucaracha* (1934), a stunning illustration of the three-color process, which was followed by the features *Becky Sharp* (1935) and *The Dancing Pirate* (1936).[45]

Though *La Cucaracha* won an Oscar in 1934 for Best Comedy Short Subject, Pioneer's two features lost money. In October 1935, Whitney merged the company with Selznick International Pictures. This new company assumed Pioneer's contract to make Technicolor films and announced that its schedule of releases for 1936–37 would include four to six color films.[46] Color was controversial within Hollywood at that time: major stars such as Bette Davis and Claudette Colbert opposed it, but some studios were beginning to use it in high profile features, such as Warner Bros.' *The Adventures of Robin Hood* and Disney's first feature-length cartoon *Snow White and the Seven Dwarfs*.[47] Advertising agencies, too, were beginning to consider whether they should use color in the industrial films they made for clients.[48] Selznick's films became a showcase for Technicolor's possibilities, beginning with *The Garden of Allah*, released in November 1936, and then *Nothing Sacred* in 1937. Whitney felt that if Selznick's films succeeded, they might persuade the industry to try color and thereby increase the value of his stock.[49]

The Garden of Allah did well at the box office but did not bring in much profit to Selznick, because his distribution arrangement with United Artists prevented him from keeping much of the money.[50] To add to his financial burden, Selznick had purchased the screen rights to *Gone with the Wind* in July 1936 and had begun preproduction on the film. The lack of profits on *The Garden of Allah* and *Nothing Sacred* forced Whitney to put more money into Selznick International, and the development of *Gone with the Wind* would require even more.[51] It is during this time of financial strain at Selznick International, when the industry looked as if it might begin using Technicolor in more films, that Whitney contacted Gallup to inquire about retaining his services.

In January 1937, two months after the 1936 election, Whitney wrote Gallup to ask how he could learn about public attitudes toward color in motion pictures. Responding to this request from one of the richest men in America, Gallup offered to put AIPO's staff to work, "the same staff as now conducts the national polls." The surveys they agreed upon "would cover a cross-section of the American theatre-going public, with due weighting for the different strata of box-office prices paid and for the various frequencies of attendance at motion pictures."[52] On January 20, 1937, Whitney sent a telegram to his lawyer, John Wharton, saying that he was going to invest in a new company Gallup was forming.[53] That same week, January 20–25, AIPO asked Americans for the first time for their opinions regarding color films.

The survey asked people whether they would rather go to a movie in color, or rather go to see it if it was not in color.[54] AIPO repeated this question in February, and the responses were similar each time: 36–38 percent of the people surveyed said they preferred to see a movie that was not in color, 28–29 percent liked color, and 31–32 percent indicated no preference.[55] A third survey, conducted during the first week of March, also asked interviewers to get detailed reasons why people felt the way they did, though these responses have not been preserved.[56]

Not everyone was asked to answer these questions, however. All three surveys used a filter question, first asking respondents whether they had been to the movies in the past month. Only if they answered "yes" did interviewers continue with the question about color. Filter questions are used to separate informed opinions from uninformed opinions and improve the quality of data.[57] They make sure that respondents know something about the question that is being asked. In the earlier AIPO surveys about attendance, interviewers asked everyone for the names of their favorite male and female stars, even if they hadn't gone to the cinema in months. In the surveys about color, however, AIPO didn't ask people for their opinions unless they had gone to the cinema at least once during the previous month. In none of these polls did filmgoers express a clear preference for color—an outcome that would not have pleased Whitney. These results did, however, support what exhibitors were saying—that the public wanted "good stories with good cast names," and that color "is an added inducement only."[58]

In July 1937, AIPO experimented with dropping the filter question. Interviewers asked everyone, regardless of how often they went to the cinema, for their reactions to color, and got a strong negative response. The number of people who indicated they preferred color dropped from around 30 percent in earlier polls, to 24 percent.[59] This survey suggests that Gallup was casting about for a way to measure color in relation to attendance. It included a full page of instructions for interviewers. Instead of asking "did you happen to go to the movies during the past month," which had become the standard AIPO format, the survey went back to the open-ended format and asked, "When was the last time you went to the movies?" Interviewers were instructed to write down the exact response, and coders grouped the answers into fifty different categories. Everyone was asked about their attitudes toward color, including the 27 percent who said they went less than once a month. These people would have been excluded from the earlier surveys, which filtered them out if they did not go to the cinema at least once a month. When these infrequent filmgoers were included, the survey showed, they lowered the number of positive reactions toward color.

On August 11, 1937, John Wharton sent a telegram to David Selznick telling him that Gallup was conducting a survey on Technicolor but was not satisfied with the results.[60] That same week, August 11–16, AIPO asked the public about color again, using a different wording of the questions, and went back to using a filter question to screen out infrequent filmgoers. This time the survey asked, "If a movie in color was at one theater, and the same movie not in color was at another theater, which would you be more likely to go to?" When asked in these words, people who had been to the cinema at least once in the previous month expressed a more positive attitude toward color: 50 percent of them said that under those circumstances they would go to see the film in color.[61] It appears that Gallup was looking for this stronger positive response because AIPO didn't ask any more questions about color until more than a year later.[62]

We know from Wharton's telegram to Selznick that Gallup was not satisfied with the results of the earlier surveys, and the continual experiments with word choice and filter questions suggest that he was searching for a particular answer. A positive response to color would have served several purposes. Obviously, any evidence that the public preferred color films would have stimulated Hollywood's interest in using Technicolor and therefore increase the value of Whitney's stock. The fact that he and Wharton discussed these surveys with Selznick points to another possible reason why Gallup might have searched for a positive reaction. Selznick was in preproduction on Gone with the Wind in 1937, and its distributor MGM was not convinced that the film had to be in Technicolor. Selznick, however, felt strongly that Technicolor was needed to do justice to the material.[63] A survey proving that people wanted to see color films would have strengthened Selznick's case with MGM. In addition, earlier in 1937, Selznick told Whitney that he too was "very hot about personally getting into the Gallup company."[64] It is also possible that the questions on color were designed to show Selznick what survey research could do so that he would invest as well.

Was Gallup fine-tuning the questions? Or was he changing them to achieve a particular outcome? These surveys followed accepted procedures of the time in their use of filter questions and experiments with wording. Public Opinion Quarterly, the professional journal for researchers in this field, frequently published articles in this period about the implications of question wording and question order. Judged by the prevailing criteria, Gallup's efforts to reformulate questions and use different kinds of samples were fully in line with contemporary practice. All these polls are valid, methodologically, yet taken together they reveal that what appear to be "facts" can vary dramatically from survey to survey. Like the critics who found evidence of pro-Republican, antilabor biases in Gallup's political polls, one can also see that the way these surveys are constructed emphasizes some results more than others.

Returning to Schiller's argument that opinion polls cannot be considered separately from the institutional web in which they function, the links among Gallup's various lines of work, and the fact that he began his survey companies during the Depression, lead us to probe more deeply into the effect of these connections on the surveys themselves.[65] It was not unusual for poll-takers to seek private backing during this period; there were few government or university funds available for private research, and Gallup, Roper, and Crossley all funded their work by selling their analyses to commercial organizations. Gerald Lambert, the millionaire who invented Listerine's famous slogan "Always a bridesmaid, never a bride," paid for the surveys that Hadley Cantril carried out for Franklin Roosevelt during World War II. Whitney and Lambert knew each other and often socialized together.[66] It would not have been unusual or improper at this time to seek private funding. Yet the fact that Gallup speaks of forming a new company, at the same time he is carrying out research of great financial significance to his potential backer, demonstrates once again that these polls, though scientific, were not neutral. Gallup's next survey in Hollywood, about the public's attitudes toward double features, brings out this point more forcefully.

6

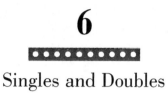

Singles and Doubles

By the end of the 1930s, when Gallup began working out methods to study films and film audiences, the Gallup Poll was flourishing. Since its debut in 1935, AIPO had sampled public opinion on more than nine hundred topics, ranging from sit-down strikes, the minimum wage, and capital punishment, to daylight savings time and the Prince of Wales.[1] The list of newspapers that subscribed to its syndicated column had increased by nearly 400 percent since the 1936 election and ranged from major metropolitan dailies such as the *New York Times*, *Atlanta Constitution*, and the *Boston Globe*, to local papers in Sheboygan (Wis.) and Elkhart (Ind.).[2] Polling had become endemic in American culture. One magazine noted that

> Business isn't run on hunches any more. Merchants and manufacturers aren't satisfied just to guess what the public wants. They really want to *know*. And that's why this new field of sampling public opinion has become a big business partner of Big Business. Advertising agencies, broadcasting companies, newspaper and magazine publishers, manufacturers of toothpastes, breakfast cereals, cigarettes, and cosmetics spend tremendous sums of money every year trying to get acquainted with Mr. and Mrs. Average American. . . . For the business man, every day is election day. And sales are the "votes" on which he lives.[3]

Though polling, and the Gallup Poll, were flourishing, Hollywood was not. The film industry was experiencing a box office slump and had become enmeshed in an antitrust suit with the federal government. Producers, exhibitors, and critics analyzed what was wrong with the industry and how to bring audiences back to the theaters. In the midst of these debates, Gallup presented his polls as an authoritative source of objective information. During the spring and summer of 1940, Samuel Goldwyn asked him to study one of the questions dividing Hollywood at that time: whether the public preferred to see single features or double bills when they went to the cinema. Gallup constructed a survey that would not only answer this question but also uncover other kinds of information about the public's preferences and behavior. Some of his findings astonished Hollywood and launched further debates about what the public wanted and, more important, who was entitled to speak for them. Gallup's double-feature poll revealed the tensions animating Hollywood at the height of the studio system and illustrates how empirical research can take on dramatically different meanings when viewed from conflicting perspectives.

Choosey Audiences and Inadequate Output

In popular memory, 1939 stands as a banner year in Hollywood. The last year of the decade marked the release of such enduring films as *Gone with the Wind, The Wizard of Oz, Stagecoach, Young Mr. Lincoln,* and *Ninotchka.* The year is so celebrated that the U.S. post office has issued a series of commemorative stamps to recognize its importance. Financially, however, the year was anything but stellar, and 1940 was even worse. Antitrust investigations in Washington, a sharp drop in domestic box office receipts, and the loss of foreign markets due to the war in Europe all combined to put financial pressure on the studios. These developments created the material conditions in which the debate about double features and audiences' reactions to them took place.

For most of the 1930s, the Justice Department investigated monopolistic practices in the film industry as part of the Roosevelt administration's antitrust efforts. In the summer of 1938, the department filed a lawsuit against eight studios, accusing them of using their affiliated theater chains to drive independent exhibitors out of business. The suit was scheduled to begin in June 1940 in federal court in New York, but adjourned before the first witness took the stand. Eventually the five major studios involved—RKO, Warner Bros., Twentieth Century-Fox, Paramount, and Loew's/MGM—settled out of court. In November 1940 they signed a consent decree that ended blind bidding and block booking, the two exhibition practices that the government alleged had unfairly hampered theater owners. The studios agreed to limit their advance bookings to blocks of five, instead of forcing theater owners to buy blocks of fifteen–twenty films at a time, and to preview films for exhibitors when they were offered for sale. They also agreed not to buy any more theaters for three years. The settlement was meant to redress the grievances theater owners had expressed and to diminish the economic power held by the studios.[4]

When studios could sell many films together in large blocks, there was less pressure on any one film to produce a profit. Under the terms of the settlement, individual films became much more important to each studio's bottom line. And it was easier to hide a failure in a block of twenty than in a block of five. The elimination of blind bidding also changed the economics of production. Studios now had to finish a picture before they could hold previews for theater owners, instead of screening rough cuts or providing a general description. This meant that a company could not make distribution deals until a film was finished, thus increasing the length of time it took to recoup costs.[5] This additional pressure occurred when box office admissions were already declining. The net earnings of the seven major studios fell 41.6 percent between 1937 and 1938 and another 11.4 percent between 1938 and 1939.[6] Variety noted that admissions for 1939 were below expectations and that the problem was considered "one of the toughest nuts the industry has ever been called upon to crack."[7]

Business magazines blamed the decline on changing popular preferences. Barron's claimed that "American audiences are much more 'choosey' than they used to be. They will wait in lines a mile long for the big hits—and stay away from the flops in droves."[8] Fortune's quarterly survey for August 1938 asked people to compare motion pictures to three other industries—automobiles, radio broadcasts, and air transportation—in terms of whether they "gave the public what it wants." Films came in dead last, with only 9.5 percent saying that motion pictures gave them what they wanted. In its analysis of the poll, Fortune blamed the slump in attendance on "the inadequacy of the output." "Let Hollywood look to its laurels," the magazine warned.[9] The general decline in the popularity of films also led Barron's to assert that Hollywood was losing its touch. "The industry is more dependent than ever on the miracle men who can turn out what the public wants. The trouble with this is that miracle men either lose the magic touch after a while or else eventually want such big money that there are only scanty pickings left over."[10]

These troubles on the domestic front were matched by events in other parts of the world. At the end of 1939, 30 to 40 percent of Hollywood's total income came from overseas, half from Great Britain alone. Like today, this overseas income represented the industry's profits; domestic revenues were usually just enough to cover expenses. Within a year, the war in Europe had significantly reduced Hollywood's foreign income. There were no revenues from theaters in the aggressor nations of Germany, Italy, and Japan or from the occupied countries of Poland and Czechoslovakia. Other countries that were under siege began limiting the amount of money that studios could convert into dollars, in order to keep these funds in their economies. In February 1940, currency restrictions reduced Hollywood's income from Great Britain by 50 percent, and in March, France placed a total embargo on exporting funds. In May 1940, during the same week that Gallup announced his survey on double features, Germany invaded Belgium and the Netherlands, and American film companies lost access to those markets as well.[11]

This combination of lost foreign revenue and declining attendance at American theaters created a dilemma for the industry. As *Variety* explained, exhibitors could not raise ticket prices because people couldn't afford to pay more, and they could not increase profits by holding films in theaters for longer periods of time because people wanted variety. Producers needed to cut costs, yet the changes in selling practices that were mandated by the antitrust decree meant that each picture had to stand on its own, a situation that encouraged more expensive productions.[12] Films were becoming more expensive to make at the same time that it was taking longer to recoup costs.

Some Kind of Black Magic

Though Gallup had corresponded about his work with John Hay Whitney and David O. Selznick, it was not until early 1939 that he made further public overtures to Hollywood. Once again, he used the regular AIPO surveys to ask the public for information that he then related to film. In October 1938, AIPO survey 136 asked Americans, "What is the most interesting book you have ever read?"[13] The way this question is worded does not suggest any link to film, but when Gallup interpreted the results in a press release and then in the *New York Times* a few months later, he stressed that the survey showed how much Hollywood had influenced the public's reading habits (fig. 6.1). Of the top twenty books, all but one had already been filmed or was in production—proving, he wrote, "the tremendous influence of Hollywood on reading tastes." According to Gallup's analysis of the survey data, many books owed their cultural lives to their film adaptations. "Hollywood did not create the original popularity of these books, but in giving them film treatment and a far greater audience the movies have unquestionably added to the circulation and endurance of the books themselves."[14] Some magazine columnists argued that the movie link was not as visible in the data as Gallup chose to make it, but his remarks were clearly designed to flatter the film industry and to highlight its impact on American culture.[15]

'Gone With Wind' Trails Bible in Public Interest

Nation-Wide Survey of Americans Shows Books That Have 'Interested' Them Most

By DR. GEORGE GALLUP
Director, American Institute of Public Opinion

NEW YORK, Jan. 14.—An exploratory survey by the American Institute of Public Opinion offers an answer today to the question:—

What books of all time have the greatest interest for contemporary Americans?

Though library charts and publishers' records show which books are in greatest demand with the book-reading and book-buying publics, very little has been known about the average American's book standards.

So to a selected cross-section of men and women in every State and every walk of life —farmers, chauffeurs, business men, telephone operators, relief-ers and their wives — the Institute put the question: "What is the most interesting book you have ever read?" The answers indicate today that:

1. The most popular single book on American bookshelves is the Bible.

2. Pressing the Bible closely at the present time is "Gone With the Wind," Margaret Mitchell's record-breaking novel of the South and the Civil War.

Nearly one person in five, of those having opinions, named the Bible. It was ranked first by men, by persons over thirty and by Southerners, Mid-Westerners and Westerners.

"Gone With the Wind" came first with women, with younger persons and with Easterners and New Englanders.

After the two leaders, the books most often mentioned are:

"Anthony Adverse," by Hervey Allen.

"The Citadel," by A. J. Cronin, a British author.

"How to Win Friends and Influence People," by Dale Carnegie.

"The Good Earth," by Pearl Buck, 1938 Nobel prize-winner for literature.

Best-Sellers And Classics

THE 1938 survey shows a pre-dominance of recent fiction "best-sellers," plus a strong representation of popular classics. Only one book in the first 20 was originally published between 1900 and 1930, that book being Jack London's "Call of the Wild," published in 1903.

The complete list of leaders is:

1. The Bible
2. Gone With the Wind
3. Anthony Adverse
4. The Citadel
5. How to Win Friends and Influence People
6. The Good Earth
7. Ben Hur
8. Northwest Passage
9. Little Women
10. A Tale of Two Cities
11. Les Miserables
12. Magnificent Obsession
13. Adventures of Tom Sawyer
14. Treasure Island
15. Count of Monte Cristo
16. Robinson Crusoe
17. Ivanhoe
18. The Green Light
19. David Copperfield
20. Call of the Wild

The survey shows that the Bible is much less popular with young people than with their parents and grandparents. The following table shows how the interest in the Bible declines with younger persons in the survey:

Age	% Naming Bible
Fifty and Over	37%
Forty-nine to Thirty	17%
Under Thirty	6%

Books Public Calls 'Most Interesting'

The following are the leaders in the American Institute of Public Opinion's survey of "most interesting" books:

1. The Bible.
2. Gone With the Wind, by Margaret Mitchell.
3. Anthony Adverse, by Hervey Allen.
4. The Citadel, by A. J. Cronin.
5. How to Win Friends and Influence People, by Dale Carnegie.
6. The Good Earth, by Pearl Buck.
7. Ben Hur, by General Lew Wallace.
8. Northwest Passage, by Kenneth Roberts.
9. Little Women, by Louisa May Alcott.
10. A Tale of Two Cities, by Charles Dickens.
11. Les Miserables, by Victor Hugo.
12. Magnificent Obsession, by Lloyd C. Douglas.
13. Adventures of Tom Sawyer, by Mark Twain.
14. Treasure Island, by Robert L. Stevenson.
15. Count of Monte Cristo, by Alexander Dumas.
16. Robinson Crusoe, by Daniel Defoe.
17. Ivanhoe, by Sir Walter Scott.
18. The Green Light, by Lloyd C. Douglas.
19. David Copperfield, by Charles Dickens.
20. Call of the Wild, by Jack London.

Influence of The 'Movies'

NEARLY all the leaders have been seized upon by Hollywood as motion picture material. Even the Bible has been screened in part, and "Gone With the Wind" has been "in casting" for more than two years.

"Anthony Adverse" was brought to the screen and became one of the leading box office pictures of 1935. "The Citadel," "The Good Earth," "Little Women" and "A Tale of Two Cities" have also been turned into outstanding pictures recently.

Hollywood is preparing a film version of Kenneth Roberts' "Northwest Passage" and has even purchased the title rights to Dale Carnegie's "How to Win Friends and Influence People."

Throughout the country six persons in every ten singled out some book or other in answer to the Institute's question, while the remainder declared "no special book occurred" to them or that they did little reading at all.

Women had less trouble in naming a book than men.

FIGURE 6.1 In 1939, Gallup began making overtures to the film industry. The press release he wrote for this survey highlighted Hollywood's influence on popular reading tastes.

(Public Opinion News Service, 1939)

Within a week, the Hollywood trade papers had picked up the news of Gallup's survey. A prominent story in the *Motion Picture Herald* on January 21, 1939, used his report to attack those who thought films should deal with pressing social issues. "The motion picture 'industry' is the show business, created and operated by showmen. These showmen are not and do not profess to be, educators, political leaders, economists, preachers of causes. They want to make money and enjoy success."[16] The article cited Gallup's research and pointed out that most Americans liked what Hollywood had given them. Like the advertising industry, the Hollywood trade press quoted "Dr." Gallup as an objective source of information that supported the film world's view of itself. The poll showed Hollywood that it had an ally in Gallup.

At the same time that he was analyzing this data, Gallup began a series of pilot studies in towns and cities around New Jersey. These studies were not part of AIPO's regular surveys and involved much smaller groups of people, often fifty or one hundred, instead of the samples of several thousand people that AIPO used. These pilot studies enabled Gallup and his staff to experiment with different kinds of questions and to learn more about what people looked for in films. They asked people how they decided which film to see. Was it by talking with friends, from advertisements, or watching previews? Some studies presented people with made-up titles to see what ideas the names evoked and which genres people preferred. These small-scale surveys took place from December 1938 through the summer of 1939 and indicate that Gallup was experimenting with different ways to investigate reactions to films. Many of the reports note that the data were inconclusive or that some questions proved to be unworkable, which suggests that he and his staff had not yet settled on the types of questions to be asked.[17]

Perhaps because he was still developing a more precise methodology, Gallup did not rush to begin work in Hollywood. In May 1939, Darryl F. Zanuck, head of production at Twentieth Century-Fox, wrote him that, "I have watched with interest the results that have been obtained by your surveys of public opinion, and feel that these methods and principles might be applied to the motion picture public with direct benefit to the production of screen plays."[18] It was not until early the following year that Gallup and Ogilvy traveled to Hollywood to meet with him. While they were in California, Gallup also met with Selznick's father-in-law, Louis B. Mayer, the head of MGM. Eugene Meyer, the *Washington Post* publisher who helped launch his political polls, introduced Gallup to his friend Mayer, whom he knew well through their work in Republican politics. Paramount also approached Gallup and Ogilvy about the possibility of asking the public for their reactions to films in its upcoming schedule.[19]

Gallup was able to meet these studio executives because of the associations he had forged in advertising and journalism. When trade papers mentioned him, though, they almost always referred to his political polls. The prospect of applying methods used in the Gallup Poll intrigued Hollywood. When Ogilvy discussed their work with reporters from the trade papers, some began to campaign for more scientific audience research.[20] Hollywood had conducted its own straw polls of exhibitors and patrons for years; hardly a month went by without the trade papers reporting that a magazine, social group, or interested observer had conducted a poll to find out what the public liked in film. In the few months before Gallup began negotiating with producers, for example, there were surveys by the *Ladies' Home Journal*, *Young America* magazine, and an eager fan that established his own monthly poll.[21] But in early 1940, some people in the industry began to feel that these informal queries were not enough.

In January 1940, *Variety* reported that the chief of theater publicity at Warner's had asked nearly one thousand families why people were not going to the cinema. According to *Variety*, the results were not considered satisfactory because they did not reveal the specific reasons for people's lack of interest. What was needed, *Variety* said, was a different kind of poll. "It is felt, however, that with a carefully worked out set of questions, put to a sufficient number of persons by experienced interviewers, such as those employed in the Gallup polls, a solution might really be found."[22]

A few months later the *Hollywood Reporter* took up the call. Editor W. R. Wilkerson asserted in his page one column that

There should be an organization set up in our business capable of accumulating the information that would be demanded, an organization that would be on call 52 weeks a year. . . . However, there is a question whether our company heads and their producers want this information, satisfied as they are that they are capable of making decisions for the ticket buyers. But the fact remains that, in ten years and with infinitely better product up and down the line, we have lost from 25,000,000 to 30,000,000 ticket sales every week, and that's not hay.[23]

The industry needed to overcome its reluctance and follow the lead of other forms of business, according to Wilkerson:

Other great industries, much smarter than our picture business, seek knowledge of their buyers. If their commodities are slipping, they strike out to find out WHY they are slipping. . . . But not our picture merchants. . . . But it shouldn't be. We should know why attendance has dropped during the past ten years, the past ten months or even ten days.

In Wilkerson's opinion, Gallup might be able to find out why films were failing with the public. "The taking of a Gallup poll or another similar authorization, is not too much for this business to stand. We can pay that kind of freight."[24] Edwin Silverman, president of the Essaness Theatres Corporation in Chicago, echoed his remarks, calling for the industry to hire a survey organization such as Gallup's. "The pictures are better now than they ever were; so, if we're losing money and audiences gradually, we ought to know definitely why."[25]

Though some in Hollywood respected Gallup's work because of his political polls, others doubted the usefulness of his research because they associated it with the advertising industry and with their competitors in radio. The westward movement of advertising executives in the mid- to late 1930s was not entirely welcome in Hollywood. *Variety* claimed that the demands of working in Hollywood had given some advertising executives nervous breakdowns.[26] Ad executives themselves felt shunned. One wrote that Hollywood viewed them "not only as 'the enemy' but also as 'upstart punks,' 'no status bums' and 'unwelcome invaders.'"[27] Some studio insiders felt that research methods that might work in the advertising-driven medium of radio had no place in the film industry.[28]

In a perceptive article entitled "Films, Radio Differ in Emotional Reaction to What 'Research' Implies," *Variety* explained why methods that worked in other media might not be as effective in film:

> Doorbell-ringing for the purpose of quizzing the public directly is more congenial to radio because of the advertising agency influence dominant in that field, and because the program sponsor is not, like the usual head of a film producing organization, a showman by training or instinct. On the contrary, the sponsor is usually an expert in merchandising, an amateur and an outsider in entertainment, as such. In entertainment he wants to be reassured by surveys, whereas the typical showman scorns surveys as silly little exercise for schoolboys.

Film executives would never feel comfortable with survey researchers, according to the article, because

> The film business values and prizes judgment, inspiration, the creative spark and thinks grosses react automatically. The crystal-gazer, complete with turban and surrounded by framed pictures of electric signs showing former successes cleaning up on Broadway, is a plausible and intelligent concept of showmanship in operation to the film man. Whereas it makes the radio sponsor, the advertising agency, the network tabulator shudder.[29]

In contrast to Wilkerson's effusive praise of Gallup as the solution to the industry's ills, *Variety* cited P. J. Wood, secretary of the Independent Theatre Owners of Ohio, who said, "the industry doesn't need a Doctor Gallup, a Doctor I.Q., or a Professor Quiz to tell what is wrong. It only needs to exercise a little good judgment by producing fewer pictures which, of itself, will, I believe, insure more pictures of quality."[30]

The opposing views expressed in these articles illuminate the broader context in which Gallup's work emerged in Hollywood. Some believed the industry would benefit from a scientific study by an outsider who would be free of the preconceived ideas that Hollywood held dear. Others felt that Hollywood had its own ways of finding out what people wanted in the cinema, and didn't need anyone to tell it what to do. Though *Variety* mocked the "showmen" and "crystal-gazers" of Hollywood, the article expressed the belief of many in the industry that they knew intuitively what kinds of films audiences wanted to see. This attitude helps explain why the moguls with whom he spoke, studio executives with long tenure in Hollywood, rejected Gallup's work. Twentieth Century-Fox and Paramount did not contract for his services, and despite the interests he shared with Eugene Meyer, neither did Louis B. Mayer. Gallup explained these results in generational terms:

> You see, in every field . . . when it goes from an art to a science, the old boys always hate to make the change, hate to accept the new, hate to admit that they don't have all the answers and feel they don't need any help from anyone. And this was generally true of all the people in Hollywood. The Warner Bros. and all the others who were well established couldn't see any possibility for research . . . we could never get along with some of the old boys, the Schencks and the Skourases and Louis Mayer and Warner Bros.—couldn't communicate with them at all; to them this was some kind of black magic that we were interested in doing.[31]

Gallup's remarks, and the tart dismissal of research in the *Variety* article, reflect the working of what Richard Maltby has called "the mythology of the moguls' unique abilities." As Maltby describes it:

> While everybody in the industry was concerned to 'give the public what it wants', only the moguls were seen to have the expertise to supply suitable products. Each success . . . strengthened their claim that their talents in selecting material and supervising its production supplied a vital element of stability to a business enterprise that had already been defined as inherently unstable. This in turn reinforced the security of their own positions, and provided the basis for

the further claim that their managerial expertise gave them a capacity denied others to predict public taste.[32]

Maltby regards this ideology as a defensive maneuver on the part of the moguls to protect their autonomy from the East Coast executives who were primarily concerned with profits. By suggesting that film production was unpredictable and even irrational, the moguls created a role for themselves as the people who were uniquely suited to manage the process.[33] The executives Gallup mentions—Mayer, Zanuck, and Jack Warner—were firmly ensconced in the film industry's hierarchy and saw no need to refer to sources other than their own judgment.

Maltby's analysis of the moguls' psychology points to another reason why these executives decided not to hire Gallup: despite the difficulties faced by the industry as a whole, their companies were in stronger financial shape than many other studios, so they may not have felt the need for outside advice. In 1939, Loew's/MGM's, Twentieth Century-Fox, Paramount, and Warner's received 95 percent of the net profits of the Big Seven studios. Thanks to *Gone with the Wind*, Loew's was the industry's biggest moneymaker, bringing in nearly half of Hollywood's entire net earnings. Paramount earned millions of dollars from its chain of theaters and did not rely as much on revenues from abroad, so its position was also strong. Warner Bros. had less than half the earnings of Fox, but still earned much more than RKO or Columbia. Though earnings for the film industry as a whole had declined in 1939, the studios that turned down Gallup's services were managing well.[34]

Looking beyond the ideologies of the film industry, one might also see another dynamic at work here, a conflict between different ways of knowing. Leo Rosten, a sociologist who was writing *Hollywood: The Movie Colony, the Movie Makers* during the same year that Gallup first visited Hollywood, described the moguls' source of knowledge in this way: "The movie makers work with hunches, not logic; they trade in impressions rather than analyses. It is natural that they court the intuitive and shun the systematic, for they are expert in the one and untutored in the other."[35] When Gallup introduced the possibility of studying the public scientifically, he questioned the adequacy of a culture that was based on personal experience, longevity, and intuition. Historian Gene Lyons has written more generally about what happens when social scientists meet groups whose culture is based on a different kind of epistemology:

> By its very nature, social science upsets the preconceptions and notions that give meaning to human experience. Knowledge about human nature tests and challenges taboos, ideologies, loyalties, all the assumptions upon which an individual or a group . . . has based his or its case, or even its raison d'être. . . .

Any group, public or private, that has a claim on public resources or an interest in maintaining the status quo, is bound to resist the systematic analysis of information that threatens the basis of its position.[36]

The discussion of Gallup's research in the trade papers framed his work as a source of information that was superior to the firsthand experiences of the moguls. Gallup is presented as an outside expert who can offer new methods that might supplant the time-honored ways that some in the industry had been using to gauge audiences' interests. Trade papers that tended to support independent producers and exhibitors, such as *Film Daily* and the *Hollywood Reporter*, welcomed his intervention. *Variety*, the chief industry organ, was more suspicious. Since many saw Gallup as challenging the Hollywood establishment, it is perhaps not surprising that the first person in Hollywood to ask him to initiate research was an independent producer who had fought many battles with the studio system and was looking for further ammunition to support his beliefs.

Of Sufficient Public Interest

Like Louis B. Mayer and the Warner brothers, Samuel Goldwyn was one of Hollywood's original founders. Unlike them, he had left the hierarchical structure of a studio to start his own production company. As an independent producer he brought to the screen such critically and financially successful films as *Dodsworth* (1936), *Stella Dallas* (1937), and *Wuthering Heights* (1939), and had worked with a roster of directors that included John Ford, Howard Hawks, King Vidor, and William Wyler.[37] In the early 1930s Goldwyn released an average of five films a year, but by the end of the decade his output had fallen to two annually. This decline in production meant that each film he made had to earn a profit. The antitrust settlement's elimination of blind bidding promised to hit him particularly hard. Since he was producing only a few films a year, and theater owners had to see them before deciding whether to rent them, he could run out of money before he needed to begin his next film. Larger studios such as MGM had more films in the pipeline and could keep revenues flowing; but for the independents, the antitrust decree could mean a cash flow crisis. In early 1940, Goldwyn was renegotiating his distribution deal with United Artists. When UA announced it intended to double-bill his next film *The Westerner*, which he feared would lower returns and reduce the film's importance, Goldwyn went into action.[38]

With all the challenges facing the film industry in 1940, Goldwyn believed that many of its problems, and his own difficulties, could be blamed on one thing—double features. The practice of showing two films on a program began during the 1910s in New England and spread to theaters around the country during the Depression. By 1937, 40 percent of theaters played them all the time. How this situation came about was the subject of heated debate. Producers and studio executives blamed exhibitors, claiming that duals began when theaters tried to attract more patrons by offering two films for the price of one. To meet the demand for product, studios began to crank out more low-budget films. Once this system became established, they could not afford to make fewer, more expensive films. Theater owners, however, blamed the studios for the prevalence of double features. Exhibitors claimed they had to show two films on a bill because the mass-produced films the studios sent them could not stand on their own. The fact that they had to buy films in large blocks also contributed to the rise of doubles, exhibitors argued. They had to buy more films than they needed to get the best ones, and once they had bought these large groups of films, they had to use them. They would much rather buy films individually or in smaller blocks, to see what they were getting.[39]

Even among theater owners, attitudes toward double bills varied. During the 1930s, double bills were one way that theaters that were independently owned could compete with the ones affiliated with the major studios. In areas where the affiliated theaters received the high quality "A" films from their parent studios, independents ran double bills to compete. In other cities the practice was reversed. Elsewhere, neighborhood houses used them to compete with downtown theaters that offered live stage shows; but as double bills became widespread, even those theaters began to run two films to replace the expensive live shows.[40]

As early as 1932, the *Harvard Business Review* reported that most producers, exhibitors, and distributors were in fact opposed to double bills, but felt that the other branches of the industry were more able to stop the practice.[41] Producers were not willing to invest in single features if they could only charge the same rental fees as for lower-budget double bills, and exhibitors didn't want to return to single-feature programs when audiences were accustomed to getting "two for the price of one" and when they were not convinced that there were enough high-quality single features to sustain a program. Studio executives insisted that if the public supported better pictures, they would be only too happy to supply them.[42]

As this debate suggests, disputes about double bills during the late 1930s reflected larger struggles for power and autonomy within the studio system. Theater owners viewed duals as evidence of their victimization at the hands of the studios, and as a strategy for extracting value from the material they were given. Double bills were a way to compete for authority in the vertically integrated film industry and to assert the importance of local preferences in the face of a national system. Studio executives argued that the voracious appetites of theaters limited the number of high-quality, high-budget films they could produce, yet they were afraid to challenge exhibitors who screened them, for fear that such an action might been seen as coercive by the Justice Department.

Double bills also hurt independent producers whose income came from individual films that they strove to make of high quality. Goldwyn had been a long-time opponent of double bills; the *Harvard Business Review* singled him out for the crusade he had been waging against the practice for most of the 1930s.[43] Goldwyn's attacks against double bills escalated in early 1940. In various articles he asserted that although Hollywood had produced 600 pictures in 1939, it did not really have "brains enough" to produce more than 200. Producers "are certainly not fooling anybody but themselves . . . when they call every picture released the best picture ever made." In his opinion, the answer was more high-quality, single films, which could be sold separately and played for longer periods of time—a situation that, obviously, favored independent producers who aimed to turn out just such films.[44] *Variety* headlined his prescription: "Sam Goldwyn Insists a Radical Revision of the Entire Pix Biz Structure Is Needed at This Time."[45]

Goldwyn wanted more ammunition to support his cause, and for that he turned to Gallup. In May 1940 he asked Gallup to bring the resources of his poll to bear on the issue by conducting a nationwide survey of public opinion regarding double features. Goldwyn offered to pay for the survey himself, but Gallup decided the topic was of sufficient public interest to be part of his regular polls. Gallup announced his intention to carry out the survey at a news conference on May 15. When reporters pointed out that the industry had already done many surveys on the subject, Gallup replied that AIPO's poll would be different from earlier studies because it would use a national cross-section of Americans, the same kind of sampling used in his political surveys. Gallup asserted that his organization, unlike Hollywood, was equipped to obtain "true facts" about public preferences, and that its findings would be impartial.[46]

The news that Gallup would conduct a national poll about this contentious subject made headlines in every Hollywood paper. *Film Daily* and the *Hollywood Reporter* announced the poll in front-page stories, and the *New York Times* discussed it in the "Film News of the Week" section. At the press conference Gallup hinted that his survey would not just explore attitudes toward "doubles," but would also find out why some people went to the movies and some did not, and how many people actually went to the cinema. Even before the poll began, he raised questions about the industry's attendance figures, saying that he doubted Hollywood's claim that 85 million people attended the cinema each week, and that the actual number was closer to 60 or 65 million.[47] The intense reaction to the poll before it even started showed there was more at stake than exhibition practices. The double-feature survey promised to be not just a study of attendance but a litmus test on public attitudes toward films in general, an explanation of why choosy audiences were turning away from Hollywood. This was heady stuff for the moguls.

As with his political polls and marketing surveys, Gallup claimed that he would bring modern scientific methods to this task. In so doing, he introduced a new kind of discourse on spectatorship, one that challenged the industry's belief that it could rely on intuitions, emotions, and personal experience. Just as he had argued that newspaper editors and the advertising industry should use facts instead of hunches to plan their work, he hoped to demonstrate to Hollywood that empirical research could improve productions and profits. This brash tactic echoed his challenge to the *Literary Digest* a few years earlier, though this public zeal was somewhat disingenuous: at the same time that he was announcing the double-features survey, Gallup had also signed a contract with RKO to carry out studies of its films.[48]

Singles and Doubles

Given the tensions that double features inflamed, it is not surprising that studios, theater owners, and the trade papers had all carried out straw polls on the subject. One prominent example was a survey conducted by Warner Bros. in April 1936, just as a bill banning block booking and blind bidding was being considered in Congress. The studio mailed questionnaires to 1,000 clubs and organizations, 2,000 newspapers, and 110 colleges and universities. Warners asked whether people preferred double bills or single features, and why. This survey was subject to a distinct class bias in its choice of respondents and sample bias because it relied on people to write back. As in the *Literary Digest* poll during the 1936 election, the people who participated in this study were college-educated members of organizations and civic groups. Since the study asked people to write back, it excluded anyone who was illiterate or felt uncomfortable replying by mail, had insufficient leisure time, or just did not care. Most of the respondents in this study disliked double bills and complained that watching two films gave them "fatigue and eyestrain." The few supporters of double features included a teenager who said they kept her friends off the streets, and a man who felt he could sleep better in theaters with longer programs.[49]

Shortly after Gallup announced his poll, *Variety* decided to conduct its own survey of exhibitors in 132 cities around the country. The paper released its findings over a period of several weeks in June 1940, and they generally anticipated the results of the AIPO poll. In the *Variety* study, both the public and exhibitors criticized double features but neither was willing to fight the trend. "John and Mary America" said they enjoyed getting two for the price of one. Kids under 20 also favored duals for the same reason. People who rarely went to the cinema said they liked double bills because they could catch up on what they had missed. Exhibitors told *Variety* they preferred single bills but felt the studios weren't producing enough good films to support a single-feature program.[50] Theater owners and filmgoers alike complained but continued to patronize double features, illustrating a split between their statements and their behavior that almost guaranteed further discussion.

Even before Gallup began his double-feature poll, trade papers had already published a great deal of information about attitudes toward double features. Like newspapers that conducted election surveys, Hollywood had its own tradition of straw polls. One might ask, then, how Gallup's poll differed from these surveys, and what kind of intervention it made within the prevailing industry discourses on this subject. As in other AIPO surveys, the answer lay in the way he conducted the poll and how he and others interpreted its results.

When AIPO began its well-publicized poll in July 1940, Gallup knew that Americans would say they preferred single features because he had already conducted two earlier surveys on the subject. In December 1937, AIPO asked the public: "Would you rather go to a movie showing a double feature (two full-length plays) or a single feature (one full-length play)?" Forty-five percent of the respondents said they preferred single features, 30 percent liked doubles, and 25 percent said that it did not matter or gave no answer. When this question was repeated a few weeks later, during the week of January 13–18, 1938, AIPO found a similar percentage of respondents saying they preferred singles (48 percent) over doubles (32 percent), while a smaller number said they had no opinion or did not answer (20 percent).[51] AIPO asked all respondents for their views, regardless of how often they went to the cinema. Thus, even before he began the "official" double-feature poll for Hollywood, Gallup knew the public favored single features over double bills, though not by a strong majority.

AIPO's double-feature poll took place during the week of July 13–18, 1940 (fig. 6.2). The survey form is extraordinary among AIPO polls because ten of the sixteen questions, or 60 percent of the survey, dealt with film-related issues, and several questions had multiple parts. The first six questions on the form asked about current social and political issues, such as whether the

United States should enter the war against Germany and Italy, while questions seven through sixteen focused on the key subject of the poll. Two questions asked about entertainment practices in general, whether respondents had spent the previous evening at home or away from home, and what they were doing: listening to the radio, dancing, playing cards, working, reading, going to the movies, and so on. Three questions asked about attendance. Interviewers asked everyone whether they happened to go to the movies yesterday, and in places where the poll was taken on Monday, whether they had gone to the movies on the previous Saturday. Each respondent was also asked how often he or she usually went to the movies.

Several questions asked for specific information about theaters that the respondent attended, e.g., "What theater did you attend the last time you went to the movies?" and "What was the approximate price of your admission?" Interviewers were instructed to write down the name of the theater and the city in which it was located, as well as the price of admission, to verify responses. The last questions of the series asked about double features in particular. Interviewers queried whether the most recent program people had seen included one or two full-length films, and whether there were theaters with each type of exhibition available to them. Two questions focused on the issues of greatest concern to Goldwyn and Hollywood. Question 14 stated: "Theater owners would like to know why people don't go to the movies more often. *In your own case*, what would you say are the main reasons why you don't go more often?" Question 15 asked: "Would you rather go to a theater showing one full-length picture, or two full-length pictures?"[52]

The large number of open-ended questions is unusual for an AIPO survey and indicates how important this information was. The institute asked its interviewers to write down word for word what people said when they explained why they did not go to the cinema more often, and why they preferred single or double bills. As in its earlier surveys on attendance and color, AIPO also tested alternative ways to word questions. An earlier form of the survey had asked: "Do you prefer single or double features?" Since Hollywood wanted to know what people went to see, not what they said they preferred, AIPO changed the question to ask which one they actually patronized.[53] The fact that the survey did not limit itself to double features, but asked about general preferences and attendance patterns, indicates that Gallup intended it to be a panoptic look at Americans' filmgoing practices.

There was, however, a potentially fatal flaw that resulted from asking movie-oriented questions as part of a political survey. AIPO polls were designed to sample the voting population, which was different from the filmgoing population. Filmgoers include children and teenagers, who would not have been counted in an AIPO poll. The demographic makeup of the filmgo-

DO NOT ASK PEOPLE UNDER 21 QUESTIONS 4, 5 or 6. (Space 4 under 21)
4. If President Roosevelt runs for a third term on the Democratic ticket against Wendell Willkie on the Republican ticket, how would you vote?

    ☐ Roosevelt 54%   ☐ Willkie 46%   ☐ Undecided

5. a. Do you remember FOR CERTAIN whether or not you voted in the 1936 Presidential election?

    ☐ Yes—Voted   ☐ No—didn't vote 15%   ☐ No—too young to vote 8%

  b. If "yes", ask: Did you vote for Lemke, Roosevelt, Thomas or Landon?

    ☐ Lemke   ☐ Roosevelt 68%   ☐ Thomas   ☐ Landon 52%

6. Suppose Roosevelt and Hull are the Democratic candidates for President and Vice-President—would you prefer to vote for them or for the Republican ticket of Willkie and McNary?

    ☐ Roosevelt and Hull 53%   ☐ Willkie and McNary 47%   ☐ Undecided

ASK EVERYONE.
7. Did you spend last evening at home or away from home?   ☐ Home   ☐ Away from home

8. How did you spend the evening?

☐ Radio	☐ Reading	☐ Movies	☐ Visiting	☐ Working
☐ Dancing	☐ Sports	☐ Cards	☐ Other games	☐ Housework
☐ All other (Please write in)				

9. Did you happen to go to the movies yesterday?   ☐ Yes   ☐ No

  Ask (a) ONLY IF INTERVIEW IS MADE ON MONDAY.

  a. Did you happen to go to the movies Saturday?   ☐ Yes   ☐ No

10. About how often do you usually go to the movies? _____

11. What theater did you attend the last time you went to the movies?

  Write in name of theater _____ City _____

  Interviewer: Check size of town where theater is located. ☐ Under 2500 ☐ 2500 to 5000

  ☐ 5000 to 10,000 ☐ 10,000 to 25,000 ☐ 25,000 to 100,000 ☐ Over 100,000

12. What was the approximate price of your admission? _____

13. Did the program you saw then include one full-length picture or two full-length pictures?

    ☐ One   ☐ Two

14. Theater owners would like to know why people don't go to the movies more often. In your own case, what would you say are the main reasons why you don't go more often?

_____

_____

15. Would you rather go to a theater showing one full-length picture, or two full-length pictures?

    ☐ One   ☐ Two   ☐ No difference

  Get full reasons _____

_____

16. Among the theaters which you could conveniently attend, are there some showing one full-length picture and some showing two full-length pictures?

    ☐ Yes   ☐ No

COMMENT _____

| ☐ Wealthy | ☐ AV | ☐ P | ☐ OR—WPA | ☐ Car 22 | ☐ Man 23 | ☐ Wh 2 |
| ☐ AV+ | ☐ P+ | ☐ OAA | ☐ OR—Home | ☐ No Car | ☐ Woman | ☐ Cl |

SPECIFIC OCCUPATION 27, 28, 29   ESTIMATE AGE 25, 26

STREET _____ CITY _____

FIGURE 6.2 The Double Feature Poll (July 1940)

(Roper Center for Public Opinion Research, University of Connecticut at Storrs)

ing audience differed from that of the voting population, too, in terms of income, education, age, and gender. The institute's challenge was how to construct a cross-section of American filmgoers in order to sample them. To do so, Gallup drew on the information he had obtained from his earlier studies of attendance. The pollster told interviewers exactly which groups to include in the double-feature poll. A special booklet instructed field personnel to obtain a good cross-section of ages in their locality and to make sure that approximately one-fourth of the respondents were between the ages of 15 and 24, and one-fifth between the ages of 25 and 34. This meant that 45 percent of the people who participated in this survey were under 35, a group that differed significantly from the voting population. Even children between the ages of six and twelve were included, though it is not clear how many.[54]

AIPO announced the results of this keenly anticipated poll on August 9, 1940, in its weekly release to newspapers. It was the first time an AIPO press release focused exclusively on film. The headline proclaimed that Americans wanted single features: 57 percent of the public opposed double bills, while 43 percent preferred them. The press release summarized the reasons behind these preferences in memorable, colloquial language. People who opposed double bills, the announcement noted, said that one of the films was usually poor; that sitting through two pictures was fatiguing and took too much time; and that "you generally think about a picture when you get home and a double feature gets you mixed up." Respondents who favored doubles said they gave more value for the money; that even if one picture was inferior, the other was likely to be good; and that double features provided the chance to "kill more time."

The press release analyzed the responses of various demographic groups. AIPO noted that double features were popular among people under 18 and among lower-income groups. Seventy-seven percent of children under 12 liked them, as did 58 percent of teenagers ages 12–17. People on relief favored double bills by 58 percent, whereas among those in the upper-income group, only 25 percent said they liked duals. Gallup drew attention to the implications of this age difference. "The importance of the younger age groups can be seen from the fact that more than 60 percent of all theater tickets bought in the nation each week . . . are purchased by persons under 30 years of age." Finally, Gallup noted that there were striking regional differences in public attitudes. People in New England, where double features began, preferred them more than any other group, while the central Eastern Seaboard and Rocky Mountain regions liked them least.[55]

In presenting the results of this poll, Gallup reported the numbers in a way that heightened the contrast between those who favored double features and those who opposed them. AIPO's two earlier polls in December 1937 and January 1938 also listed responses under the category of "no preference" or "no answer." The poll in August 1940, however, did not report any responses in these categories. During the 1930s, AIPO normally reported "no opinion" or "no answer" responses in two ways. The company listed these responses as a separate category, and also divided them proportionately into the other categories.[56] In his *A Guide to Public Opinion Polls*, Gallup explained the reasoning behind this practice. Only people who have opinions vote, since voting is a means of stating an opinion, he wrote. Eventually, people who are undecided will make up their minds on a subject, so it is reasonable to allocate their views to other categories. Whether or not one agrees with this argument, it was the case that AIPO typically reported results that eliminated the "no opinion" or "no answer" responses.[57]

The original codes and punch cards for this survey are no longer available, so it is not possible to reconstruct the exact results. But it is clear when we compare this AIPO poll with earlier ones that the company chose to eliminate any undecided opinions, thus heightening the contrast between the opposing sides in the dispute. The two earlier AIPO polls had found that although Americans liked single features more than double bills, single features did not have majority support. If the August poll had found the same results it would have been less dramatic. By eliding the "no opinion" responses, Gallup heightened the impact of this survey in a way that, intentionally or not, must have pleased Samuel Goldwyn.

The Lost 32 Million

Hollywood trade papers seized upon AIPO's report of its double-feature survey. *Variety, Film Daily*, the *Hollywood Reporter*, and the *Motion Picture Herald* ran front-page stories detailing the percentages that favored and shunned duals, and mulled over the demographic breakdown of responses by age, income, and geographical region. The *Los Angeles Times* also put the report on its front page. Even Wall Street made note of AIPO's conclusion that people preferred singles to double bills. *Poor's Survey* for August 1940 took these findings to mean that Hollywood could make more money if it produced more "A" films.[58] For Goldwyn, Gallup's report vindicated him and proved his contention that double bills hurt the industry. Before AIPO announced the results of its survey, Goldwyn persuaded Ogilvy to give him preliminary figures, and he published an article about them in the *Saturday Evening Post*. Goldwyn cited Gallup's statistics as proof that "Hollywood Is Sick." People opposed double bills by 3 to 1, he said, exaggerating the number that AIPO later released.[59]

Yet if we examine the results of Gallup's poll more closely, we find that very little of the information it provided was new to the industry. Earlier polls, including AIPO's, had already shown that many Americans preferred single features. *Fortune* had asked participants in its surveys about their attitudes toward double bills in July 1937, and found that only 21.7 percent liked them more than single features. Four months before the AIPO survey, in March 1940, a poll by *Cue* magazine, the predecessor of today's *New York* magazine, had also found a strong preference for single features. The differences among classes were no surprise either. *Fortune* found that poorer people liked duals for the same reason Gallup said: that they got more for their money. The *Harvard Business Review* noted in 1938 that theater managers took into account the incomes of people in their community when they selected films, so AIPO's discussion of class differences was not new either.[60] One thing that differentiated AIPO, though, was precisely that it was the "Gallup Poll," with its imprimatur of facticity and science.

The most striking fact that came out of the August 1940 survey was not even mentioned in AIPO's press release, but emerged in trade paper reports. AIPO found that weekly attendance in mid-July, when it conducted its poll, was not 85 million but about 53 million.[61] Furthermore, the *Hollywood Reporter* summarized, "an estimated total of 32,000,000 people, financially able to attend pictures frequently, actually go less than once a month."[62] According to *Variety*, this number was "considered by the film industry one of the most significant facts it has learned about itself in years."[63] Before Gallup, the Hays Office had been Hollywood's source for general attendance figures. In the course of conducting the poll, Gallup sent David Ogilvy to Washington to find out where the Commerce Department got its numbers on attendance. Ogilvy found that the government got its information from the Hays Office, and the Hays Office in turn quoted the Commerce Department as the source of its figures.[64] The AIPO poll broke this closed loop of self-created data and self-promoting distortion. The double-feature poll called into question the reliability not only of the industry's figures but those of the federal government.

Not surprisingly, the Hays Office challenged Gallup's figures. July was not a representative month, it said, because people stayed away from hot indoor theaters.[65] A few people in the industry, however, accepted Gallup's lower attendance figures. Rosten cited Gallup's number in his book because, he said, it was the only one based on systematic surveys.[66] Rosten, however, was trained in the social sciences and accepted the validity of empirical research. For the most part, however, the industry rejected the number of 53 million almost immediately. However, it seized on the idea that there was a "lost" audience of 32 million potential ticket buyers.

This selective attacking and embracing of Gallup's figures can be seen in two articles published in back-to-back issues of *Variety* in April 1942. On April 15, 1942, *Variety* reiterated the point that there were 30 million people who were able to go to see films but did not. The following week, in the

April 22 issue, the paper reported that attendance had increased 5 percent and now used 86 million as its base. The article on April 15, dealing with the lost 30 million, said nothing about the 86 million who usually attended, and the article on April 22, saying that 90 million people bought film tickets each week, said nothing about the lost 30 million.[67] If we put these articles together, it appears that the industry maintained two contradictory ideas: that 90 million people went each week, and that there were an additional 30 million viewers out there who could also go but didn't. If Hollywood really believed there were 90 million patrons, and another 30 million who might be patrons, nearly the entire population of the United States would have had to go to the cinema each week.

Further evidence that this number represented something more than an arithmetic figure can be found in other trade paper accounts. The two *Variety* articles cited above refer to the "lost audience" of 30 million people, not 32 million. The *New York Times* used 25 million instead. In one issue *Variety* even reported the statistic as 3,200,000.[68] It is clear when one tracks the coverage of this finding in the press that the precise number was not the issue; rather, what irked the industry was the lost revenue that number represented. What appears to be faulty arithmetic can be interpreted as a symptom of the tensions affecting Hollywood during this time. The idea of the "lost audience" haunted Hollywood's imagination even into the 1950s. Gallup's 32 million represented lost opportunities and lost revenues; their existence was proof that Hollywood wasn't doing enough to reach the public. As the *Hollywood Reporter* put it, "54,000,000 Tickets in July Week Against U.S. Figure of 85,000,000 Shows B.O. Flop."[69] These interpretations of the "lost 32 million" (or in this headline, 31 million) recast the double-feature debate into a contention that was not only about attendance but also about the quality of Hollywood films.

Mass Versus Class

The subsequent debate over what should be done to attract this missing 32 million back to the cinema reflected the structural and economic battles of the time. For exhibitors, the "lost 32 million" were a "vast, virtually untapped film attendance reservoir."[70] The Interstate Theatre Managers published a handbook of suggestions about how exhibitors could respond to Gallup's data, such as lowering prices for kids, having special attractions, and personally inviting customers to a film.[71] Others argued that the industry had to do a better job of advertising, and that people did not come to films because they didn't know about them. United Artists answered this call by crafting a

campaign for Alfred Hitchcock's *Foreign Correspondent* that was aimed spe-
cifically at "Gallup's 32,000,000 Who Don't Go to Pictures." The ad reminded viewers that United Artists specialized in single features for people with
"discriminating tastes."[72] The possibility of reaching the lost audience also
prompted RKO, Loew's, and Warners to adopt a "Nine O'Clock Plan" where-
by theaters screened the "A" feature on a double bill first, at 9:00 or 9:30, and
then showed the "B" film for anyone who wanted to see it. This plan pleased
fans of both single features and duals, since those who wanted to come early
and see the main feature could do so, while audiences who wanted to see
both films could stay.[73]

Much of the debate over this "lost" audience focused on which part of
that audience was likely to return. The industry knew that, while double features were popular, they did not bring in as much money as single bills. The
Hollywood Reporter noted in June 1940 that 65 percent of industry revenues
came from 18 percent of the theaters in the United States, all of which ran
single bills. Double features accounted for only about 25 percent of total
revenue though they screened in most U.S. theaters. This was largely because first-run theaters, whose higher ticket prices brought in more revenue,
mainly screened single features.[74] And first-run theatres attracted a more affluent clientele than the second-run and neighborhood houses that showed
doubles. Thus class differences were implicit in discussions about exhibition
practices: during the Depression, only the upper-income groups could afford
to patronize more expensive first-run theaters. The question became which
group it would be more profitable to pursue.

Though Hollywood knew that class differences influenced audiences' decisions about what theaters to attend, AIPO's survey provided the first statistical evidence of these differences. The chart that accompanied AIPO's press
release demonstrated a clear split along class lines (table 6.1). A preference
for single features directly correlated to the respondent's income group.

For Samuel Goldwyn, this data led to only one conclusion: the industry
should focus on people who brought in the most money at the box office. He
noted that the bulk of the industry's revenues came from the upper-income
groups who favored single features and patronized large, first-run theaters.
In his *Post* article Goldwyn quoted a Paramount executive who said that box
office revenues come from people who go to Radio City, but the industry
acts as if it should make films for the Meadowville Orpheum.[75] AIPO's press
release offered a similar analysis, perhaps inspired by Goldwyn's. Gallup argued that, "Only by making a greater appeal to those people who have sufficient money to attend theaters more often can the revenues of the industry
be materially increased; and it is precisely these people in the higher income
levels and in the age groups over 24 who register the greatest opposition to

TABLE 6.1 Demographic Groups and Double Features

	FOR SINGLE FEATURES	FOR DOUBLE FEATURES
Upper-income group	75%	25%
Middle-income group	63%	37%
Lower-income group	47%	53%
On relief	42%	58%

Source: George Gallup, "Public Votes Against Double Feature Movie Programs," August 9, 1940 (Public Opinion News Service press release, New York Public Library, microfilm)

double features."[76] *Variety* quoted a highly regarded United Artists executive who also supported Gallup, and who pointed out that even if kids and people on relief liked double bills, they did not contribute enough money at the box office to justify making more "B" pictures. A high quality "A" picture, supported by carefully selected short subjects, seemed to be the best way to reach these groups, he felt.[77]

While the survey results, and Gallup's analysis of them, pleased Goldwyn and other producers, many exhibitors felt that Gallup had ignored the needs of audiences in their communities. As Gregory Waller and Kathryn Fuller have demonstrated in their studies of exhibition practices in small American towns, theater owners in these areas were acutely aware of the backgrounds and interests and economic class of their patrons.[78] To many exhibitors, Gallup's focus on elite, affluent viewers felt like a dismissal of their clientele. The head of one theater circuit argued that people who favored single features were not the steady patrons theater owners wanted. "It is the people who plunk down their 20 cents, 30 cents or 40 cents regularly each week or twice weekly who support theatre operations. And these people want all they can get for that money."[79] Their position won support from the *New York Times'* new critic, Bosley Crowther, who began writing about the cinema for the paper in 1940. In contrast to his predecessor Andre Sennwald, who had vehemently opposed double bills, Crowther appreciated their popular appeal. Even if Gallup's survey found that 57 percent of the public preferred single features, he noted, that was not an overwhelming majority, and it meant that 43 percent of the audience liked what they were getting. "It would seem commercially risky to shoot for a potential audience and let that 43 per cent go hang."[80] Responses to Gallup's work by exhibitors and some journalists highlighted the class biases in his analysis and injected a more populist note into the discussions.

In addition to these debates about class, exhibitors argued about the importance of geographical differences as well. Theater owners who lived outside of large metropolitan areas felt that Hollywood already focused too much attention on key cities and neglected significant markets in the rest of the country. Sam Gill, the former research director for Crossley's radio services, argued that although city dwellers had larger incomes, more of their financial resources were spent on housing and food, whereas "the ruralite puts more of his income into having a good time."[81] The 1940 census revealed that Americans were moving out of cities to suburbs and small towns, and Gill argued presciently that the future of film exhibition would be in these areas.[82] This idea won further support when the Curtis Publishing Company issued a study suggesting that since the population in rural areas was 54 million, and the urban population was only 37 million, Hollywood should do more to increase business in those parts of the country.[83] *Variety* reported that the results of Gallup's survey did indeed launch some efforts to get to know "the great open spaces beyond the Sierras." "The idea is that Hollywood is so wrapped up in the technique of picture-making that it has lost touch with the farmers, clerks, mechanics, and storekeepers who pay for it all." Inspired by this idea, independent producer Walter Wanger toured the country to speak to civic and business clubs, citing Gallup's polls in his speeches.[84]

The range of reactions to Gallup's double-feature survey illustrates how seemingly objective information can be interpreted according to the interests of the analyst. Goldwyn believed that the survey bolstered his case against doubles, and Gallup seems to have agreed; exhibitors and some critics thought the evidence was not sufficient to dismiss double features altogether. One interesting element of AIPO's findings that was ignored in the double-feature debates was the age differences Gallup noted, the fact that people under 30 bought 60 percent of all movie tickets. The double-feature survey provided the first empirical evidence of the importance of teenagers at the box office, but hardly anyone noticed, until a year or two later when Gallup was conducting studies for RKO, which was interested in developing young stars. Instead, various groups within the industry interpreted the results in ways that reflect the larger struggle for control and autonomy at this time. In taking issue with Gallup, theater owners in particular raised the question of who was entitled to speak for the audience.

Speaking for the Audience

Gallup believed wholeheartedly that opinion polls provided a means for people to express their views, to "talk back" to power. One of his primary motivations for establishing his survey organization was his belief that the centers of power in America needed to hear the views of "the common man." Yet by setting up his polls as the means through which Americans could be heard, he displaced other, more established mechanisms through which people expressed their beliefs. In the film industry, one voice that was displaced was that of the local exhibitor. Though Goldwyn was pleased that Gallup supported his opinions, local exhibitors came to feel that their views had been distorted or ignored in the double-feature poll. In the wake of AIPO's survey, they asserted their authority to speak for local audiences, through arguments that were clearly inscribed within the ongoing antitrust disputes.

In its original press release about the double-feature poll, AIPO acknowledged that local theaters reached different demographic groups, some of whom preferred single bills and some of whom preferred doubles. Switching to single-features programs was not a prescription for every theater. "Theaters which draw a large part of their patronage from children and the poorer classes, and theaters located in a part of the country which favors double features, would obviously suffer by changing to single features, particularly if the single features are not of sufficient quality to attract patrons in the higher age and income levels."[85] However, when the trade papers discussed the survey, they focused mainly on the total percentages that liked or disliked duals, and did not delve into regional differences. Trade papers presented the national audience as a monolithic entity, almost ensuring that local exhibitors would react by insisting that their patrons were different from the group that Gallup discussed.

As Margaret Thorp argued in *America at the Movies*, theaters connect Hollywood to the people who pay to see its films.[86] Theaters and their owners created the links between studios and local communities. So it's not surprising that exhibitors prided themselves on knowing their patrons, and on their ability to promote films in their communities. By the 1930s, exhibitors had developed a range of practices to learn about their customers' interests that reflected their deep knowledge of their specific areas. Theater owners saw themselves as a reliable and knowledgeable voice for their patrons when speaking to the studios.

When Gallup portrayed his polls as the voice through which "America Speaks," he challenged the authority of local exhibitors to represent their communities. Many theater owners reacted immediately and angrily to his assertion of authority. *Film Daily* highlighted one theater circuit in Des Moines that said it planned to conduct its own survey of their patrons, and would feature single or double bills according to the percentage of patrons who wanted them. As the general manager of the Tri-States theaters asserted: "We do not believe that Samuel Goldwyn speaks either for all the industry or all the patrons. . . . We have a definite field which the Gallup poll does not consider—the paying patrons at the box office. If Gallup is right, we'll find out for ourselves."[87] The Tri-States survey found that even within the same geographical area, responses varied from theater to theater. One theater found results similar to AIPO's, while another found the opposite.[88]

For months after the conclusion of the AIPO survey, *Variety* carried announcements about local polls. *Film Daily* discussed these countersurveys in nearly every issue during July and August 1940. In St. Louis, for example, the Ambassador Theater conducted a six-week test during which it ran "A" films with reserved seating for five weeks and a double bill of musicals and comedies, at lower prices, for one week. Not surprisingly, patrons preferred the more varied, and cheaper, double bills. The exhibitor announced that despite what Gallup said, he was sticking to duals.[89] One radio station staged a debate that pitted Goldwyn, Texas theater owner Karl Hoblitzelle, and the chair of the California PTA film committee against two independent producers and a California housewife. Goldwyn cited Gallup to support his views, but a panelist who supported double bills argued that "the picture house is community property," and that the industry was taking theaters away from local control.[90]

Exhibitors also banded together to bring patrons back to theaters with strategies that drew on their own experience with their communities. The Interstate chain of theaters in Texas argued that double bills were not a problem in their state because most theaters there showed single features. People must be staying away from the cinema for other reasons, they said, and the best way to find out why was for local theater owners to conduct a house-to-house canvass and ask them. With this information, theater owners could then write personal letters to these residents, inviting them back to the theater and even enclosing free passes as an inducement. The Interstate plan recommended the use of questionnaires and a close attention to demographic characteristics of each town—qualities that Gallup had already publicized in his surveys.[91]

AIPO's survey and the countersurveys it provoked took place in late summer 1940, after the antitrust trial had adjourned and before the majors signed the consent decree. It is not surprising, then, that exhibitors would perceive Gallup's poll, which was requested by a producer, as advancing the interests of producers over those of independent theater owners. The Allied Independent Theater Owners of Eastern Pennsylvania made this belief explicit when it announced that it planned to carry out its own series of surveys, of exhibitors only, to "place sellers and buyers on an equal footing by affording the latter the same market information enjoyed by the former."[92] The group announced its plan in July 1940, when the trade papers were publicizing Gallup's poll, in a move clearly designed to counter his work. The group asked theater owners not only about their policies regarding double features but also about their experiences of buying and renting features, whether distributors forced them to accept short films, the cancellation policies they were given, and how rental fees were calculated. Their work highlighted the fact that in asking about preferences and the kinds of films audiences enjoyed, Gallup was obtaining information that would be more useful to studios who produced the films than to exhibitors who bought them when they were finished. Allied continued to poll its members throughout 1941 about these issues and about their reactions to the consent decree.[93]

For the Allied Independent Theater Owners, challenging Gallup was a way of challenging the studios that supported him. Ironically, Gallup himself felt sympathetic to the exhibitors' plight. In later interviews he spoke of the "brutal methods" distributors used to maintain control. "They always sneered at this man and paid so little to him . . . to run the theaters."[94] Gallup believed that local exhibitors, who were in touch with local audiences, knew better than Hollywood producers what people liked, yet many of those same exhibitors felt that he undermined their authority.

Gallup assumed when he carried out his poll that Hollywood wanted one clear answer about Americans' reactions to double bills. In presenting himself as impartial and scientific, he argued that his polls would be the authoritative voice on this subject. Hollywood, however, had a long tradition of informal surveys of its own. In 1940–41 alone, trade papers ran reports of surveys by 1,100 newspaper editors; by Camp Fire Girls who studied the preferences of junior and senior high school students; and by the Society of Motion Picture Engineers, wanting to find out public preferences for seating.[95] Nearly every component of the industry was ready to swing into action at a moment's notice to poll the public on any issues that concerned it.

Through its political polls, AIPO had convinced the country that a scientifically selected sample of Americans could represent the views of the rest of the population. The reactions to its double-feature polls indicated that many in Hollywood disagreed. Instead, many people in the industry saw through AIPO's assertion that its methods and assumptions were neutral and objective. From the beginning, many in the industry perceived Gallup as being allied with one group—producers. Gallup's desire to be an impartial arbiter was called into question from almost the moment he began working in Hollywood.

"Until the Cows Leave Home"

The double-feature survey was certainly not the last word on the subject, and the battle between distributors and exhibitors continued into the late 1940s. In the year after Gallup's survey, several major studios united with several independent producers to create a plan to eliminate double bills from both independent and affiliated theaters.[96] Yet exhibitors continued to insist that audiences in their communities liked getting two for the price of one, and audiences proved their point. In October 1940 the Better Films Council of Greater St. Louis demanded that local theaters join a movement to support single features. Some did, but when audiences failed to materialize they switched back to duals.[97] Even the entry of the United States into World War II didn't dim the popularity of these films. When in 1942 the government ordered that raw film stock should be conserved, to preserve the chemicals it used for military purposes, some argued that double features were downright unpatriotic; but even this plea for conservation didn't change the public's behavior.[98] Journalist Frank Nugent summed up the contradictions that made this practice so enduring:

> If this proves anything, it is that there is far more to the double-feature situation than meets the weary eye of the filmgoer or the professionally sharpened eye of the Hollywood analyst. It proves . . . that producers are not actually as eager as they have said they were to change from a quantity to a quality basis of production. It demonstrates . . . that exhibitors by [and] large are not—as they have contended—forced into twin-bill bondage and kept there against all their better instincts by the wicked producers. And what it proves of the public is what every double-feature experiment has proved: that public indifference, apathy, and self-contradiction make it unlikely that any change in the existing situation will come "by public demand."

Nugent concluded: "You can cite Dr. Gallup's poll until the cows leave home, but you won't change industry opinion—opinion based, one would have to admit, on experiments rather than straw votes."[99]

While some in Hollywood and elsewhere came to see the double-feature survey as just another viewpoint on an enduring practice, Gallup's survey retains a historical significance. It took place during a crucial time period in the antitrust hearings, when tensions between producer-distributors and exhibitors were at a peak, and became one more vehicle through which those groups could assert power. Though Gallup strove to compose an objective survey that would accurately measure the opinions of U.S. filmgoers, the topics he chose and the way he analyzed the results illustrate the extent to which seemingly neutral material can encode unconscious assumptions. Debates about the survey and its interpretation also brought to light the class biases that infused these discussions during the Depression.

From Goldwyn's desire to use evidence as a club, to the moguls' sense that their experience was being displaced, Hollywood showed that it understood what was at stake in empirical research. As the industry knew, perhaps even better than Gallup did, audience research was one kind of discourse, one imbued with the aura of science but a discourse nonetheless. Contemporary debates about how to interpret this data recognized that it reflected the economic crisis of the time, and film historians who look at this material today, within the broader history of the classical Hollywood system, can see how the double-feature survey marks an important moment in the struggle for power that characterized the studio system in the 1940s.

7

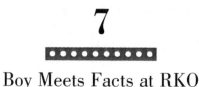

Boy Meets Facts at RKO

The double-feature poll that Gallup conducted during the summer of 1940 launched his career in Hollywood. His analysis of the survey appeared in the *Los Angeles Times* and other newspapers at the same time as Gallup's forecasts for the November presidential election. Gallup's film work, and his new Audience Research Institute (ARI), gained fame and credibility from being associated with his political firm, the American Institute of Public Opinion (AIPO). By tackling double features at the same time that the federal government was examining exhibition practices in general, Gallup ensured that his findings would receive wide press coverage and become part of ongoing industry discussions. But Gallup did not intend to limit his work to a few sporadic, if well-publicized, surveys. Instead, he wanted to establish the kind of ongoing relationships that Young & Rubicam enjoyed with its clients, and to offer a range of services to companies that would underwrite his research.

Shortly before he began the Goldwyn survey in July 1940, Gallup met with executives from several Hollywood studios and eventually signed a contract with RKO Radio Pictures to study public opinion about projects it was developing. RKO had spent most of the 1930s in bankruptcy, and its president, George Schaefer, who had followed Gallup's film research in its early stages, believed that systematic audience studies would be useful in selecting projects when the studio emerged from bankruptcy reorganization. Schaefer had become president of the reorganized company with the support of Nelson

Rockefeller, and the changing positions of these two men within the studio shaped attitudes toward Gallup's work as well.

Gallup's research for RKO marks the first time that a Hollywood studio commissioned nationwide, scientific studies of public opinion on current projects. Gallup drew on both his political polls and advertising background to formulate his methods for studying film. Like AIPO, ARI examined people's reactions to films in relation to their age, gender, class, and place of residence, using carefully constructed samples that mirrored the filmgoing population. As he did at Young & Rubicam, Gallup tried to define the key components of a text that attracted audiences, which he decided were a film's cast and story. Though Gallup developed ARI's basic research methods and made the initial presentation to RKO, it was his assistant director David Ogilvy who handled the day-to-day dealings with the studio. It was Ogilvy who wrote most of ARI's reports, summarizing the survey data and offering his own interpretations of the results. Though he claimed that he was only "reporting the facts," Ogilvy relished the opportunity to make sweeping generalizations about American filmgoers, though he himself was a recent immigrant to the United States from England.[1] His "analysis" of the data encases this material in an interpretive shell that highlights selected aspects of ARI's work and ignores others.

What began as a one-year agreement led to a decade-long working relationship, in which ARI prepared hundreds of reports involving nearly every film RKO produced, and many that did not make it into production. The large number of reports and the extensive correspondence about them make it possible to trace the impact of ARI's work on the studio and the diverse reactions of executives to Gallup's findings. At various times RKO's executives treated Gallup and Ogilvy's reports as top-secret information; criticized their ignorance of Hollywood's inner workings; or used their analyses to justify crucial decisions about actors, producers, and projects.

This chapter focuses on ARI's surveys for RKO from September 1939 until the end of 1942, during Schaefer's administration, and analyzes why the studio decided to commission audience research and how its executives responded to Gallup's findings. Though Gallup conducted studies for RKO throughout much of the 1940s, these years saw the most intensive research. ARI's surveys not only influenced decisions within the studio, but shaped perceptions about films and filmgoing within the rest of U.S. culture during this era.

Tangled Networks

Gallup's research produced conflicting reactions within RKO that were due in part to the studio's complex organizational history and the shifts in power among its executives. The Radio Corporation of American (RCA) and its chair David Sarnoff had founded RKO in October 1928 as a way to extend RCA's patents in sound technology to the entertainment innovation—talking motion pictures. RCA purchased two other companies controlled by Joseph Kennedy, the Film Booking Office (FBO), a producer-distributor of low-budget films, and the Keith-Albee-Orpheum chain of vaudeville theaters. RCA contributed its Photophone division to form a new holding company, the Radio-Keith-Orpheum Corporation (RKO). The corporation encompassed several subsidiaries, including Radio Pictures, which became the fifth largest film studio in Hollywood. The corporation's chain of theaters and its capacity to produce and distribute films created a vertically integrated organization resembling more established Hollywood studios. RKO continued to expand during the early 1930s, borrowing money to buy more theaters and convert them to sound. As the Depression deepened, however, the company found itself unable to repay these debts and, in January 1933, it defaulted on $3.5 million in loans and declared bankruptcy.[2] RKO spent the next seven years in receivership, suffering what Richard Jewell has described as a "perpetual state of transition," with four changes of administration in eight years, changes that brought executives with conflicting loyalties and different approaches to film production.[3]

During this period of reorganization two other business interests became involved in RKO's activities—the Rockefeller family and Floyd Odlum's Atlas Corporation. When RKO declared bankruptcy, it stopped making rental payments on Radio City Music Hall, which it had leased from the Rockefellers to use as its flagship theater in New York. The Rockefellers sued and eventually accepted as compensation 663,500 shares of stock in the reorganized company and a seat on its board of directors. The family appointed Nelson Rockefeller, who had just graduated from Dartmouth, to represent its interests on the new board of directors that emerged from RKO's bankruptcy.[4]

At the same time that the Rockefellers were strengthening their role in RKO, Floyd Odlum's Atlas Corporation also began purchasing shares in the company. Atlas was an investment trust that bought up distressed companies whose assets were more valuable than their stock prices indicated—what is today called value investing. During the 1930s, Odlum purchased a controlling interest in twenty-two companies that he believed were undervalued, including the New Yorker Hotel, the department store Bonwit Teller, and Greyhound bus lines.[5] Bankrupt RKO, with its valuable patents in sound technology and extensive theater holdings, attracted his interest. In October 1935, Atlas and Lehman Brothers, a Wall Street investment bank, paid $5 million for half of RCA's holdings in RKO and also bought stock in RKO's theaters, giving Odlum some control over different parts of the company.[6] Odlum had helped reorganize Paramount in 1933 and prided himself on taking control of a company before its directors realized what was happening. Over the next few years he bought more and more RKO stock before taking control of the company in the summer of 1942.

The executive board that took shape when RKO emerged from bankruptcy in January 1940 reflected the struggle for power among these groups. Odlum selected N. Peter Rathvon, a Wall Street banker, to represent his interests and chair the board, while the Rockefellers chose George Schaefer, who had worked in marketing and promotion at Paramount and United Artists, to be president of the newly reorganized company. J. R. McDonough, a long-term ally of David Sarnoff and an RKO veteran since the mid-1930s, became executive producer in charge of "A" films.[7] Schaefer and McDonough got along well, but relations between Schaefer and Rathvon were difficult from the beginning. Schaefer, the Hollywood insider, believed that RKO's salvation lay in making prestige films based on quality literary and theatrical properties, which meant spending money, while Rathvon, the banker, thought the studio should economize to put the company on a sound financial footing. RKO's emergence from bankruptcy protection signaled a new beginning, but the disparate backgrounds and attitudes of the studio's leaders created the basis for future discord.

Within this tangled network of alliances, Gallup was linked to Rockefeller and Schaefer. Gallup had met Rockefeller through mutual friends, probably in 1938 or 1939, though who brought them together is unclear. They may have been introduced by Jock Whitney or David O. Selznick, who knew Rockefeller socially, or by Gallup's Republican colleagues at Young & Rubicam. However they came to know each other, Gallup and Rockefeller were very close.[8] Gallup appreciated Rockefeller's enthusiasm for his work, in contrast to the resistance he met from industry moguls, and praised Rockefeller for being "dynamic" and "open-minded," "ready to do things in a new way." "Not being a movie man and being young, he was intrigued by the whole idea that research might find a better way to improve on the product . . . it was his insistence that really got us into RKO."[9] In addition to their business activities, the Rockefellers had supported many research projects in the social sciences, and this family history may have taught Nelson the value of empirical studies. Gallup said later, "he knew nothing about the motion picture business, but he did believe in research. So it took little persuasion on my part to get him to finance a research project in Hollywood for RKO."[10] Rockefeller staunchly defended Gallup's work to Rathvon and other members of the board, praising it as "an entirely new and highly sensitized approach" to studying the public's interests in films.[11] Within the studio Schaefer, Rockefeller's appointee, provided the strongest and most consistent support for his work. Gallup's connection to Rockefeller and Schaefer, then, meant that his work was already tainted in the minds of Rathvon and others, and their criticisms of him intensified as Odlum and Atlas gained more control within the company.

To Scientifically Assist and Guide

Gallup first approached RKO with the idea of conducting scientific research in mid-September 1939, at a time when the studio was beset by external and internal troubles. Hitler's invasion of Poland on September 1, 1939, closed many foreign markets, then as now the key source of film industry profits. Half of these foreign profits came from England; when its government decided to limit currency exports, studios were not able to send back much of the money they earned overseas. These restrictions forced producers to cut costs and put more pressure on the domestic box office to earn a profit. Studios found it difficult to pay the high salaries earned by top stars and to meet audience expectations for elaborate productions and multiple stars per film.[12] RKO's net earnings had been dropping steadily, from $2.5 million in 1936, to $1.8 million in 1937, to a mere $19,000 in 1938, Schaefer's first year as president. At the end of 1939, RKO's filmmaking division reported a loss of $545,126, in contrast to its theater operations, which netted $1,234,523 in profit. What profit the studio had earned came from European sales, and the war eliminated them.[13] The other companies with whom Gallup met at this time—Loew's, Twentieth Century-Fox, and Paramount—were keeping afloat, but RKO, after seven years of bankruptcy reorganization, was still hemorrhaging money. These international developments, on top of the studio's already precarious financial state, led Schaefer to become more actively involved in production decisions than his predecessors.[14]

Gallup made his first presentation to RKO executives on September 28, 1939, four weeks after Hitler's invasion of Poland and ten months before he conducted the double-feature poll. The presentation took place in New York, and Gallup prepared a 27-page report that outlined his ideas. He proposed to concentrate on two key factors that he believed defined a film's success—its stars and its story. Gallup had on several AIPO surveys in 1937 and 1938 begun questioning the public about what led them to go to a film, and from these responses he theorized that these two elements were crucial. This effort to isolate the precise elements of a text that influenced viewers and to measure their effects reflected the factor analysis that Gallup used in his advertising research. In the report Gallup outlined various ways that research could aid RKO—by helping to determine the relative interest of the public in various story ideas; uncover new subjects; and chart changing reactions to story genres. Surveys could also provide an early indication of which properties lacked appeal before RKO committed to production. In looking at stars, Gallup argued that research could measure what impact a particular cast had on the public's desire to see a film and enable the studio to compare two stars being considered for the same role. He claimed that he could also track the emergence of new stars and chart changes in the popularity of existing ones.

In each case, Gallup argued for the value of systematic and continuous research, the approach he took in his political polls, rather than single, short-term studies. By studying reactions on a national scale, he argued, he could provide more impartial and scientific information than was currently available to any studio and offer RKO an early glimpse of emerging trends. The idea was particularly appealing to a studio that trade papers portrayed as desperate to become profitable again. In this first report to RKO's executives, Gallup acknowledged that there were some aspects of film that could not easily be measured by scientific research, and mentioned in particular the quality of acting, the impact of direction and dialogue, and the merits of various distribution practices.[15] After he began working for RKO, some studio executives questioned the approach Gallup outlined here, feeling that he did not know as much about film production as they did. Nevertheless, these assumptions guided his first year of work for the studio.

Schaefer circulated Gallup's proposal within the studio over the next few months. McDonough and Lee Marcus, the head of "B" film production, talked about their views over lunch with Gallup and Schaefer in early February 1940. During these discussions RKO selected the kinds of studies it wanted ARI to conduct from the menu of options Gallup provided. The studio was less concerned about general trends and more interested in obtaining reactions to specific story properties and casts it was considering. RKO wanted ARI to test story properties that it was pursuing, but agreed that ARI could propose up to ten ideas a year based on its own studies of reader interest in newspapers, magazines, and books. RKO liked ARI's proposal to study stars' changing popularity, but wanted to choose the players from ones it had under contract. The studio also asked ARI to measure reactions to casting choices RKO had in mind for specific projects. Where Gallup offered to provide continuing surveys of general trends, RKO wanted to use ARI as its own in-house research provider.

The terms of their first contract indicate that both Schaefer and Gallup felt committed to working together. To gain a foothold in Hollywood, Gallup was willing to reduce his fees dramatically and accept terms that were much more advantageous for his client. Schaefer argued that since Gallup did not have a lot of experience in motion picture research, he should give the studio a discount on his fees. Initially Gallup proposed a fee of $10,000 per month, but the final one-year contract signed on March 8, 1940, cut the cost to $5,000 a month for the first six months and $10,000 a month for the remaining six.[16] To illustrate the relative value of this service, a few weeks earlier Schaefer had spent $390,000 on story rights for a collection of Broadway plays and stories published in national magazines, the kind of quality material he believed the studio should produce.[17] So RKO's first contract for film research equaled almost one-quarter of the amount the studio had just spent for story rights—a large sum for a company that was emerging from bankruptcy. At the time he was negotiating with RKO, Gallup was also talking with Darryl Zanuck, but Zanuck broke off those talks when RKO asked for an exclusive contract.[18] Having one client who would underwrite his first foray into motion picture research was more attractive to Gallup than working on smaller projects for a number of producers.

Schaefer formally announced Gallup's hiring at the studio's annual sales convention in May 1940, shortly after Gallup launched the double-feature poll. He told the assemblage of sales managers and theater owners that ARI would "scientifically assist and guide the studio in its selection of stories, casts and titles."[19] The reference to ARI's "scientific" approach implied that RKO had discovered a sure-fire way to develop popular films, and Schaefer presented Gallup's credentials, including the fact that he held a Ph.D., as if they guaranteed success. The May 1940 convention was particularly important because it occurred while the five major studios were negotiating with the Justice Department over its antitrust suit, and RKO and others involved in the case anticipated that they would soon have to change their procedures for renting films. These changes, combined with the drop in foreign sales, would further increase pressures on the domestic box office. By hiring Gallup, RKO implied that it would have a privileged source of information about what the public wanted. Reporters covering the convention portrayed Schaefer's choice as a coup on par with his decision to hire Orson Welles after the 1938 "War of the Worlds" broadcast.[20] At the convention Gallup formally announced the launch of the Audience Research Institute as a separate enterprise working only for RKO. Since he had begun the double-feature survey only two weeks earlier, and Schaefer wanted to make it clear that RKO had an exclusive contract, creating a separate firm allowed Gallup to work for more than one client at a time.[21]

The "Nether Segments"

In order to find out what audiences liked, RKO first needed to know who went to see its films. In his September 1939 presentation Gallup stated that his most important task was to establish an accurate cross-section of the filmgoing public before he began studying their preferences.[22] Under his contract with RKO, Gallup agreed to provide the studio with two kinds of data: demographic information about the U.S. motion picture audience as a whole, and more detailed analyses of viewers in cities where RKO owned theaters. To develop a profile of the national filmgoing population, ARI used information collected from AIPO's surveys, which regularly asked people how often they went to the cinema and how much they paid for their tickets. Gallup then collated this data with information about the respondent's age, gender, income, occupation, and place of residence to construct samples of the filmgoing population as a subsection of the larger national group. Most ARI surveys involved 1,000 to 5,000 people, a number Gallup justified by referring to the principle of sampling used in his political research.

ARI hired interviewers from among the people who contacted its office directly and from those who applied for jobs at AIPO and Young & Rubicam. Substitute schoolteachers were among Gallup's favorite sources for film interviewers. He found them to be friendly, articulate, and used to dealing with people. ARI's interviewer manager, Paul Sheatsley, met with each new recruit on his regular trips around the country and took pains to find interviewers who could talk comfortably with people from different social and economic groups. ARI gave its staff detailed instructions about how to select respondents and expected each to complete about ten questionnaires a week.[23] As with his political polls, Gallup asked interviewers to write down people's responses verbatim, "dialect, blasphemy and all."[24] These comments provide a rich source of material that Gallup and Ogilvy mined in their reports and give today's reader a vivid sense of the language and attitudes of this period.

ARI's thorough research meant that, for the first time, a Hollywood studio had detailed empirical evidence linking people's interests in film to specific demographic characteristics. Gallup pointed out that other methods studios had used, such as fan letters or preview cards, might indicate the writer's gender, place of residence, or general age group, but his studies used scientific samples that included people based on their percentages in the filmgoing population. Gallup's surveys measured everyone who went to the cinema, not just the people who wrote the studios. This method enabled Gallup to provide precise demographic information about which segments of the audience liked or disliked a project. For example, ARI proved that the audiences for *Rebecca* were 71 percent female, while those for *The Fighting 69th* were 62 percent male, and that *My Favorite Wife* attracted many more viewers from prosperous income groups, while *Road to Singapore* was popular among less affluent filmgoers.[25] Hollywood probably knew this already, but ARI offered precise statistics to support its intuition.

As with many kinds of data, however, some findings are ignored while others receive extra emphasis. It is fascinating to see which groups become marginalized and which gain greater visibility in ARI's research. In terms of class, for example, ARI provided conclusive proof of the importance of middle- and lower-income viewers to the U.S. box office. Nearly half of all box office sales came from people who earned less than $30 a week. People from the lower middle class, which ARI defined as anyone with a weekly income of $20–$30, accounted for 22 percent of box office sales, while those who earned less than $20 a week were responsible for 21 percent of the box office. People on relief accounted for another 4 percent. These three groups—people on relief, the poor, and the lower middle class—accounted for 47 percent of Hollywood's total box office income, with the remainder coming from the middle class (38 percent) and upper-middle- and high-income groups (15 percent).[26] Early in its work for RKO, ARI provided solid proof of the large numbers of working- and lower-middle-class Americans who attended films, just as it had brought to light the preference of these groups in the double-feature poll.

David Ogilvy, in charge of interpreting and disseminating these findings, took pride in the panoptic quality of ARI's research. "If Hollywood producers could be persuaded to spend one week every year in the company of our interviewers, exposing their production plans to coal miners and steel workers, shopgirls and school children, plumbers and builders, WPA workers and policemen, colored and white, they would never be surprised or incredulous" at the institute's findings, he wrote.[27] ARI's ability to reach a broad base of film-goers seems to have empowered him to speak boldly on their behalf to studio executives. In many reports, Ogilvy portrays himself as a champion of viewers that he felt Hollywood overlooked. For example, although Schaefer looked to Broadway for story ideas, Ogilvy argued that Americans who lived in the rest of the country didn't keep up with productions in New York and weren't interested in seeing films based on them.[28] "The motion picture audience is *broader-based* than the legitimate theater audience. A play can succeed on Broadway or Shaftsbury Avenue provided it appeals to the upper income levels, but the present organization of motion picture distribution demands that any story which is to succeed on the screen must appeal to *all* income levels."[29] Ogilvy also reminded executives that most Americans couldn't afford to indulge in Hollywood's favorite pastimes. When RKO proposed setting a film at a racetrack, Ogilvy chided executives that while going to the races might be one of their favorite activities, most Americans preferred football or baseball games.[30] Americans were also not interested in films set in countries they had never visited. Summarizing reactions to a film set in Mexico, Ogilvy wrote: "If you, the reader, have been fortunate enough to visit Mexico, you are almost bound to harbor a special interest in stories about that country; the vast majority of theatergoers do not share this special interest because they have never enjoyed an opportunity to visit Mexico."[31] In these reports,

Ogilvy presents himself as the spokesperson for viewers whose interests were ignored by the cultural elites who populated Hollywood.

At other times, though, Ogilvy went out of his way to distance himself from the majority of filmgoers, as if to assure his clients that he too belonged to the same elevated class as they did. In one report about the film *The Corn Is Green*, he sniffed: "We can only report the comments recorded by our interviewers, without attempting to justify the level of taste they reveal."[32] Dismissive remarks about the "nether segments" that love the films of Abbott and Costello, or the "proletarian admirers" of George Raft, indicate that he did not feel much affinity with fans of these actors.[33] On one occasion he urged RKO to try to raise the level of public taste. In the summer of 1940, the studio released the first feature-length film from the *March of Time* series, *The Ramparts We Watch*, based on a book by the same title.[34] Though the film was set during World War I, it had obvious parallels to the contemporary situation in Europe. Ogilvy admired it as "a new kind of picture, the first great American documentary." When the picture failed to do well at the box office, he urged RKO to "whip up" some publicity to support it. "The advertising and publicity should sell the idea that every well-informed person must see this new phenomenon and be able to discuss it intelligently, just as he must be able to discuss the fashionable best-sellers."[35] In this report, Ogilvy portrays the filmgoer more as a habitué of the cocktail party circuit who wants to keep up to date on current events—a far cry from the social circles frequented by many of ARI's respondents. Though Ogilvy waxed eloquent when describing ARI's ability to reach the "mass" of film viewers, at other times he was eager to distinguish himself from many of the groups within that mass.

Ogilvy took pride in speaking for ordinary Americans when he analyzed ARI's research, just as Gallup took pride in speaking for Americans when he discussed his political polls. Gallup's populist commitment reflected his Midwestern roots and feeling that cultural elites should pay more attention to the rest of the country. With Ogilvy, however, this desire to represent the people seems to have been motivated by an economic analysis of the Hollywood box office. The masses mattered because Hollywood's system of production depended on them. As he wrote:

> When films cost fortunes and distribution has only a few main channels, it is imperative that every feature should appeal to the largest possible number of theatergoers. At present there is no room for pictures which appeal to minorities. For better or for worse, the industry is geared to the majority. If the majority does not want the picture, the investment is jeopardized. It therefore becomes of paramount importance for the producer to have a clear picture of the major-

ity. The more he knows about ordinary, average theatergoers, the less likely he is to make costly mistakes in estimating their reactions.[36]

If a project lacked interest for young and low-income audiences, the two groups who dominated the box office, Ogilvy discouraged RKO from producing it. When the studio asked for reactions to a proposed film of *The Devil and Daniel Webster* with Paul Muni, Ogilvy warned that, "Mr. Muni has a problem on his hands. His concentration on highbrow and foreign properties has deprived him of marquee value among two important segments of the population—the young and the poor. All indications are that if he persists in this policy he will progressively alienate more and more ordinary theatre-goers, to a point where his pictures will become the esoteric taste of a few connoisseurs."[37] Muni did not star in the final film, which featured Edward Arnold instead. In discussing a possible screen version of "The History of Mr. Polly," Ogilvy argued against the production because, "With the great mass of ticket-buyers—poor and young—it is definitely weak. As we have shown in so many other instances, this pattern seldom makes for box-office strength."[38] RKO did not produce the film. If lower-income viewers disliked a project, Ogilvy asserted, that was reason enough to end it.

His pragmatic analysis of what mattered at the box office explains why Ogilvy was equally concerned about attracting upper-income viewers, the "infrequent" filmgoers who opposed double features and who Goldwyn believed were crucial to his success. Upper-income viewers contributed only 15 percent of the box office, but they tended to patronize first-run theaters where ticket prices were higher, so if they could be persuaded to go to the cinema more often, profits would increase. In several reports Ogilvy refers to them as "the group whose increased support is so important if national attendances are to be boosted."[39] For this reason he seized on any project that research found appealed to upper-income groups and urged RKO to produce it. Ogilvy never argued that a film should be produced because it appealed to low-income viewers; he just noted that they would enjoy it. The elusive upper classes who might be persuaded to come to the cinema deserved to be courted, but millions of lower-income patrons could be relied on to attend. In his reports Ogilvy pursues a two-pronged strategy, directing attention to films that please the mass audience and also highly praising any project that has a chance of bringing in infrequent filmgoers.

The Importance of Men and Teenagers

The double-feature survey provided the first statistical evidence that teenagers were the dominant force at the U.S. box office. Ogilvy continually stressed their importance in his reports to RKO. People under 30 bought 65 percent of all film tickets, he noted, and people under 20 accounted for half these purchases. Nineteen-year-olds bought more tickets than any other group, nearly two million a week, and ticket buying dropped precipitously after that; people in their early thirties bought only half as many tickets as teens.[40] Ogilvy thought this finding was one of ARI's most important discoveries. "Until Audience Research Institute revealed the fact that 34 per cent of all tickets are purchased by persons under twenty years old, there had been a tendency to dismiss the adolescent market as chicken feed."[41] Historians of adolescence have confirmed that the late 1930s marked the first time that a majority of teenagers were attending high school rather than working. As Grace Palladino has noted in *Teenagers*, "Advertisers and merchandisers were beginning to recognize an attractive new market in the making."[42] ARI brought this market to the attention of Hollywood.

Having proved their importance, Ogilvy urged RKO to develop and publicize films that would appeal to this dynamic teenage market. The institute combed library lists for young adult literature that could be adapted for the screen, and recommended that RKO film the popular novels featuring nurse Sue Barton. Ogilvy even suggested that RKO could alter children's stories to feature teenagers instead.[43] ARI also recommended that RKO build films around popular musicians teenagers liked, such as swing bandleader Kay Kyser. Kyser already had starred in RKO's *That's Right—You're Wrong* (1939) and *You'll Find Out* (1940), and his strong showing on ARI's surveys would have reinforced the decision to feature him again in *My Favorite Spy* (1942) and *Around the World* (1943). Ogilvy offered detailed advice about how RKO could adapt the plot of Kyser's *The Band Played On* so that it would appeal more strongly to teens. "The treatment should minimize the historical aspect and the grim struggles . . . the cast should include a band leader and a colored trombonist (or trumpeter) who are popular with youngsters." [44] According to Palladino, the swing craze was one of the hallmarks of emerging teen culture in the early 1940s, and Ogilvy astutely zoomed in on it as a key space in which RKO could reach this market.[45]

ARI also pushed RKO to develop more teenage stars, arguing that there were not enough actors and actresses with whom young filmgoers could identify. "While 52 per cent of all attendance is by persons under twenty-five years of age, only 2.1 per cent of 'A' actors and 21.3 per cent of 'A' actresses are under twenty-five. . . . Perhaps it would be good business for RKO to concentrate on building up one or more personalities in this age group," Ogilvy wrote.[46] Several months after he made this recommendation, *Film Daily* reported that RKO was grooming many of the young stars ARI had recommended.[47] Since RKO did not have many stars under contract, ARI's research offered a way to identify up-and-coming actors and actresses early, before other studios in Hollywood knew about them, which would give the studio a competitive edge over its rivals.

Though ARI's research may have advanced the careers of younger performers, it hurt older ones. Ogilvy's reports often demeaned older actresses by noting that young people did not like them and could not identify with them. In discussing reactions to Irene Dunne, Ogilvy noted that she was older than 76 percent of all female moviegoers. "Result: to watch Miss Dunne in a drama of emotional development is approximately equivalent to watching the emotional development of one's aunt. The aunt can be very funny and amusing in a comedy situation, but it is embarrassing to observe her in a serious clinch."[48] When RKO planned Gloria Swanson's return to the screen in *Father Takes a Wife*, Ogilvy advised against it, noting that 97 percent of viewers under the age of 17 had never seen her. The comments he reports are nasty and vicious, even the ones from adults. "She's an old woman, ain't she?" "She has had her day." "She reminds me of a vampire." "I have forgotten her. Think we all should." RKO released the film anyway in its 1941–42 season, perhaps thinking that Swanson might appeal to those elusive older viewers, but the film lost $104,000.[49] At times Ogilvy even questioned the ability of RKO's own executives to understand this youthful market, since most of them were over 30 as well. They should rely on ARI's research, he argued, since through it they could gain access to this mysterious element of the filmgoing population.[50]

The emphasis on younger audiences became an inherent part of ARI's research. Once Gallup found that 65 percent of all filmgoers were under 30, ARI constructed its regular samples to reflect this demographic, thus ensuring that its surveys would continue to measure young audiences more than older ones. A decade before teenagers emerged as a target audience for filmmakers in the 1950s, ARI provided Hollywood with regular and detailed reports of their preferences.

In contrast to his interest in teens, Ogilvy minimized the importance of another group at the box office: women. In 1941 several articles appeared stating that women made up the majority of those who attended films. Ogilvy seems to have taken it as his personal mission to debunk this view. "Like the mythical 85,000,000 weekly attendance, the theory of female predominance has too long been taken for granted." Men and women each accounted for about half of box office sales, he noted; women bought 50.5 percent of tickets, while men purchased 49.5 percent.[51] Ogilvy argued that this was because the large number of men in the younger and low-income groups who dominated the box office counterbalanced the high percentage of women among older, wealthier viewers.[52] Ogilvy even provided highly detailed charts which, he said, proved that films could succeed by appealing mainly to men. Even after Pearl Harbor, when more American men left to go overseas, Ogilvy continued to assert that "in spite of the absence of a large segment of the male population in military service, there are now as many males as females in the national film audience."[53]

Though Ogilvy's conclusions seem to defy the reality of World War II America, they circulated in trade papers, as in a *Variety* column entitled "'Men Top Pic Fans'—Gallup."[54] That "Gallup" said men dominated the box office gave the assertion credence. *Time* magazine also published an article in summer 1942 that summarized many of ARI's findings.[55] In April 1944, William Lydgate, who wrote many of the questions used on AIPO's surveys, published article about Gallup's film research for the business magazine *Sales Management* that was later condensed and reprinted in *Reader's Digest*. Lydate expanded on Ogilvy's ideas to develop a broader argument about gender and the imagination. "The closer the situation is to the average woman's experience, the better women like it. Men, on the other hand, are interested in stories portraying not only familiar situations, but lives they would *like* to lead. Their preference is for swift-moving dramas that show them new experiences and fire the imagination. They are less interested than women in emotion on the screen. They want to know what happened, not how people feel about it."[56] In this distillation of ARI's research, empirical data becomes a jumping off point to justify traditional views of women's interests and roles.

Scholars such as Michael Renov, Mary Ann Doane, and M. Joyce Baker have argued that films of the 1940s challenged prevailing gender conventions in their plots, characters, and visual style, creating a space for more flexible representations and enabling new modes of spectator identification.[57] Ogilvy's reports, and the discussions they inspired in and beyond Hollywood, show that many people did not want to let go of ingrained gender biases. While changing social conditions and films themselves were producing new ways of looking at gender, Ogilvy used ARI's research to minimize the importance of women. He and others buttressed their opinions with seemingly authoritative data.

Since ARI provided empirical evidence of the interests of different groups of filmgoers, RKO could have produced pictures aimed at particular segments of the audience, as Hollywood does now, rather than at the mass market. In fact, Gallup pointed this out in a speech that was discussed in *Time* magazine. The article, "Boy Meets Facts," summarized Gallup's presentation at RKO's July 1941 sales convention and noted that it was becoming harder and harder to make a box office success that drew customers from all age groups and social classes. "There is no sure-fire formula for producing that kind of picture." Hollywood, according to Gallup, was faced with the alternative of making pictures aimed solely at 19-year-olds, or "making less costly pictures for distribution to population segments." [58] Both Ogilvy and Schaefer thought in terms of the mass, but as Gallup himself pointed out, ARI's research would have enabled RKO to target specific demographic groups if it chose to do so. While the studio preferred to concentrate on more highbrow properties in the hope of reaching those elusive, affluent audiences, Gallup articulated the value of targeting particular groups a decade before this trend emerged in the 1950s.

"Them Rough and Ready Fellers"

In his proposal to RKO executives in September 1939, Gallup described film narratives as one area where he believed research could be useful. Testing stories in advance would tell RKO about the merits of its projects before they went into production, he argued, and allow the studio to eliminate any from its schedule that proved to be unpopular. Story tests would also provide clues to the elements audiences enjoyed so that these could be accentuated, if RKO wanted to do so.[59] The most difficult aspect of story research proved to be finding the appropriate object to test. ARI experimented with summaries that ranged from one or two sentences to 5,000 words, before deciding on a 60-word synopsis as a practical and efficient way to measure reactions during a personal interview. Some executives at RKO doubted that such a short summary could convey the nuances of a film, but ARI responded that this was about as much information as people received from a newspaper review or a conversation with someone who had seen the film. In some cases RKO wrote the synopses; at other times ARI devised its own. When RKO worded them, ARI sometimes revised the text "so as to insure that the uneducated theatergoer will experience no difficulty in understanding them."[60] ARI then sent the summaries to its interviewers around the country, who presented them to the public and recorded their reactions in relation to the same demographic variables used in other reports. The synopses were usually presented in groups, and ARI used some that it had tested repeatedly as "controls." Sometimes the institute also tested multiple versions of a synopsis that emphasized different themes.[61]

After completing the surveys, interviewers mailed them to ARI's headquarters in Princeton, where staff members coded the results and punched the data on IBM cards so the material could be analyzed by age, gender, region, size of community, and income level.[62] Ogilvy's analysis of the data circulated among the people who had the responsibility to approve or cancel productions: after McDonough read them, he forwarded the reports, or his summaries, to Schaefer and also sent copies to Harry Edington, who succeeded him as production head for "A" films when McDonough was put in charge of overall studio production. Schaefer and McDonough did not share these reports with individual producers on the RKO lot. The synopses ARI used and the comments people made about them went through the same kind of filtration and interpretation that its data on film audiences received.

In addition to testing projects that RKO was developing, ARI was also expected to supply the studio with original story ideas, "certified" ideas "that have been tested for their interest value with the motion picture public."[63] Of the three hundred story tests ARI conducted during the first two years of its contract, one-third came from RKO and rest were the institute's own suggestions.[64] ARI obtained some of its ideas from the studies of magazine readership that Gallup conducted at Young & Rubicam. ARI also recommended that RKO adapt best-selling novels and popular library books because they had a built-in audience.[65] That ARI continually suggested best-sellers for RKO's consideration reinforced the popularity of these already established works and perpetuated narrative models that had proven successful in the past.

In Ogilvy's summaries of their responses, American filmgoers emerge as a blunt, outspoken group who knew what they liked and disliked. The quotes that pepper his reports convey the down-to-earth quality of people's attitudes. Viewers come across as unabashed seekers of relaxation and entertainment, enjoying films that "take your mind off everyday worries."[66] One man spoke for a multitude when he enthused: "*action* is what I like."[67] He and others readily admitted that they liked "fellers like James Cagney and Clark Gable, them rough and ready fellers," more than intellectual actors such as Paul Muni, who was "too deep."[68] Americans wanted stories of today, they said, not films based on the past. "I don't like duels. They are kinda stupid. They don't have them in America," one complained.[69]

To Ogilvy, these remarks indicated the public's desire to escape from present circumstances through films that "picture a happier world than that in which the unfortunate theatergoer happens to be situated."[70] Most Americans did not want to see economic differences dramatized on screen, he argued. Responding to a proposed project about the life of labor leader Samuel Gompers, they said: "You read so much of this stuff in the papers all the time that I wouldn't care for it in the movies." "If you understand labor problems it would be all right, but I don't."[71] ARI instead recommended projects that revolved around overcoming class differences. The institute urged RKO to produce a film about Hetty Green, "The Witch of Wall Street," the first woman to become a successful financier. "For the poor and for the hinterlanders there seems to be something admirable about anyone who can get the better of Wall Street," Ogilvy told the studio.[72] Other projects they proposed featured young women who bewitched wealthy bachelors into falling in love with them.

ARI's story tests revealed many gaps between RKO executives and the public. ARI recommended that the studio make films about Lou Gehrig and Houdini, while RKO asked for studies on the humanitarian Urbain Ledoux. ARI tested stories that had been serialized in the *Saturday Evening Post, Redbook, Collier's*, and the *Ladies' Home Journal*, and urged RKO to make films based on comic strips and popular radio programs, while the studio sought reactions for projects based on the works of Charles Dickens and George Bernard Shaw. The institute championed Broadway hits that were enjoying successful national tours, such as *Life with Father*, while RKO wanted to test plays from the 1920s. RKO repeatedly asked ARI to test films about prizefighters and race horses, no matter how often the institute said people didn't like those subjects.[73] Of the ninety-five stories that ARI tested in its first year with RKO, 80 percent of the ones ranked in the top class were ARI's own proposals, not the studio's.

ARI's research also documented the failure of many of the independent producers upon whom Schaefer had pinned his hopes for success. When he became president of the studio, Schaefer revived the unit production system that David O. Selznick had introduced to RKO in the early 1930s.[74] Though his predecessors had fired many independent producers, Schaefer reversed course by signing contracts with Broadway producers Harry Goetz and Max Gordon and the screenwriting team of Gene Towne and Graham Baker. As a result, fifteen of the fifty-three films the studio released in the 1940–41 season were independent productions or coproductions.[75] ARI conducted multiple story and cast tests for the independent productions RKO had on its schedule. Unfortunately, the public expressed only moderate interest in most of them.

Gordon and Goetz's recent Broadway hits included *Abe Lincoln in Illinois* and *The American Way*, and to do their screen versions justice, Schaefer budgeted $2 million for each film, making them two of RKO's most expensive productions for 1939 and 1940.[76] Neither fared well at the box office. Their adaptation of Carl Sandburg's biography of Lincoln, produced before RKO hired Gallup, debuted at the same time as John Ford's magisterial *Young Mr. Lincoln*, released by Fox, and RKO's film lost nearly three-quarters of a million dollars.[77] After Schaefer hired ARI, he asked Gallup to test reactions to their second project, *The American Way*. ARI found little enthusiasm for a film depicting events in America over the last fifty years as told "through the story of a poor German immigrant couple," at a time of Nazi aggression.[78] Towne and Baker's proposed adaptation of *Little Men* fared much better.

Many respondents said they had read and loved the book and looked forward to seeing one of their favorite novels brought to the screen. However, a follow-up survey that described the proposed treatment in more detail elicited many negative reactions, with people saying that it left out many of the elements they had enjoyed in the book. ARI forecast that the film would lose money, and indeed it received hostile reviews and lost $215,000. ARI also predicted that Towne and Baker's adaptation of *Tom Brown's School Days* would fail, and it lost money as well ($110,000).[79]

In December 1940, at the end of ARI's first year of research for RKO and Schaefer's second year as president, RKO showed a deficit of $988,191.[80] In the face of this decline, Schaefer reversed course again and announced that RKO would reduce the number of independent films on its roster. He canceled the studio's contracts with Gordon and Goetz, and Towne and Baker.[81] That their productions lost money was reason enough, but ARI's forecasts of failure gave Schaefer additional ammunition. After United Artists, which relied solely on outside producers, RKO had the most independent producers under contract at this time. What began as a way to assure product for distribution without entering into long-term contracts became another financial drain for Schaefer's regime.

Unadulterated Escapism

The frank opinions expressed in these reports often contradict the assumptions of groups that criticized Hollywood during this period, such as the Hays Office and the Legion of Decency. In a nationwide survey he conducted in January 1941, Gallup found that 46 percent of Americans had not even heard of the Hays Office. Those who had were not impressed. "Considering some shows that came out early last year, I think it must have been on vacation." A few complained that its enforcers let too much slip by. "Some of the studios must pay 'hush money' what they get away with." Others felt the industry censors were "blue-noses" who "ruined good motion pictures" and sympathized with the studios that had to abide by the censors' restrictions: "must be a pain in the neck to producers."

According to Gallup, many Americans didn't care about the things the Hays Office was protecting them from. The Production Code prohibited scenes of people drinking and smoking, but ARI found that only 25 percent of Americans objected to scenes in which women drank, and a mere 13 percent objected to scenes of them smoking, mainly because they felt these images set a bad example for children.[82] Films about divorce didn't bother people either, nor did the divorces of Hollywood stars. "It doesn't mean anything, especially out there," one respondent said. The public had no trouble separating on-screen images from off-screen reality. "They're *fine actors*," one noted, "even though they may be marital failures."[83] And viewers didn't pay much attention to allegations about Communist influence in Hollywood being raised by the Red-hunting Dies Committee in Congress. In one study, 52 percent of those polled could identify at least one star that had been labeled a Communist, but 68 percent said they would still buy a ticket to see that person on screen.[84]

Schaefer did not share these findings with the Hays Office; in fact, he later hired Joseph Breen, its director, to run the studio. But ARI's research on other pertinent social issues did make their way into broader social discourse. Gallup's work for RKO encompassed the period before and after Pearl Harbor. At RKO's request, the institute began tracking attitudes toward war-related films in June 1940 and continued to ask about this topic through the end of 1942, providing a longitudinal survey of changing attitudes during this crucial time. In its first survey on the subject, ARI found clear gender differences in reactions to war films: men relished them, in keeping with their love of action and adventure, but women did not. Men wanted to see films that explained "modern warfare methods, how they move troops quickly," how ammunition worked. "We may have to fight soon ourselves. I guess we'll have to know about it." "They would give us an idea what to expect." Women, by contrast, said they went to the cinema to escape news of the war, not see more of it.[85]

After Pearl Harbor, however, 30 percent more people said they wanted to see additional war coverage in newsreels. Stories that had ranked among the lowest in ARI's ratings zoomed to the top during the weeks after the attack. ARI found that war films appealed to filmgoers who were most likely to be drafted— men, young people, and low-income groups—but that even young women found pleasure in imagining their husbands and boyfriends taking part in some of the more adventurous scenarios. Many men in the audience expressed a blunt desire for revenge. "Anything we see where the Nazis are blown up appeals to us," one said. Older women, however, seemed more aware of the dangers soldiers were facing and did not want to see any more depictions of war on screen. ARI kept RKO apprised of these sentiments on a regular basis and provided the studio with analyses of the reactions of specific demographic groups, but the data could not shake Schaefer's conviction that war films would be unpopular.[86]

As with ARI's studies of audiences' age and gender, these findings about people's interest in different types of narratives gave rise to broad generalizations that circulated beyond RKO to the rest of Hollywood and into the media. For example, Gallup drew on the early studies before Pearl Harbor to argue against those who said that Hollywood should educate viewers about current issues. In a radio broadcast in February 1941, writer Leo Rosten and independent producer Walter Wanger stated that Hollywood could make pictures that were enlightening as well as entertaining. Gallup wrote Schaefer to say that he strongly disagreed. "I cannot see how any individual studio which is publicly owned can afford to feed the public what they *ought* to see instead of what they *want* to see."[87] Several months later Gallup wrote Schaefer again after another similar program to say that, "The reformers in Hollywood will wake up to the fact some day that entertainment, unadulterated escapist entertainment, really does perform a pretty useful function in the world after all."[88]

In February 1941, Schaefer asked Gallup to study public opinion about propaganda in motion pictures. Gallup talked about how difficult it would be to carry out such a study but gave Schaefer useful information nonetheless. A survey on that subject would be hard to construct, he said, because "no two people agree on the meaning of the word 'propaganda.'" Some identify it "with an objective with which they don't sympathize," but may think something is not propaganda if they agree with its message. For illustration he cited an AIPO survey from November 1940 that asked people if they thought there was too much propaganda in films at that time. Seventy percent said no. Those who answered yes were asked what kinds of propaganda they had seen, and most identified films that were blatantly anti-Nazi. Gallup noted that most people did not complain about propaganda that supported England, and theorized that people disliked it only when the political message weakened the entertainment value of a film. "What they objected to was the inclusion of such doleful material in an entertainment which they had paid to see, in the hope that they would derive enjoyment and relaxation."[89]

Schaefer combined this statement from Gallup with other reports from Ogilvy about reactions to war films, and packaged this information in a statement that he sent to the *Motion Picture Herald*, whose editor Martin Quigley was leading a campaign in favor of "pure" entertainment. Schaefer quoted verbatim Gallup's remark about feeding the public what it wanted to see, and cited Gallup as his source of information. Schaefer argued that, "In Hollywood there are men with an instinct for politics, social reform, moral uplift, education. Apparently they cannot accept the fact that motion pictures are an entertainment medium, *the* entertainment medium. These men would like to flood the screen with pictures of the 'message' type. They have no mandate from the public to do any such thing."[90] A few months later Schaefer's campaign against socially oriented films and the *Herald*'s support of it were discussed in the congressional hearings led by Sen. Gerald Nye to investigate propaganda in motion pictures. Armed with Gallup's scientific data,

Schaefer felt emboldened to charge into a battle over the social implications of cinema.[91] Though the pre- and post–Pearl Harbor studies indicated that men at least were very interested in war-related films, Schaefer and Gallup clung to an ideology of entertainment that overrode the evidence.

Another Argument for Typecasting

The other area Gallup proposed to treat in his first presentation to RKO involved public opinion about individual Hollywood stars. This area was of particular interest to the studio, because during the 1940s RKO had failed to develop long-term strategies for creating stars out of contract players. Many well-known performers were reluctant to cast their lot with a company that had spent so much time in bankruptcy and whose leadership changed so often. As a result, RKO ended up borrowing actors and actresses from other studios for one or two picture deals, but did not have many major stars under contract.[92] Besides these conditions within RKO, it was becoming increasingly difficult for the industry as a whole to find new stars from its usual sources on Broadway and in radio and regional theaters. Of the fifteen tests ARI carried out during the first three months of its contract with RKO, seven asked the public about stars. The first test RKO asked ARI to conduct involved Ginger Rogers, the studio's biggest star and, as *Variety* put it, "the essence of the RKO meal ticket."[93]

In mid-1940 Rogers' contract with RKO was about to expire. Her films with Fred Astaire had been the foundation of much of RKO's success during the 1930s. Their screen debut, *Flying Down to Rio* (1933), had earned a profit of $500,000, and their next film together, *the Gay Divorcee* (1934), netted RKO $583,000. *Top Hat* (1935), possibly their most famous film, earned $1,295,000, making it RKO's most profitable release of the decade. Rogers' last film with Astaire, *The Story of Vernon and Irene Castle* (1939), a nostalgic look back at the turn-of-the-century dance team, did not do as well at the box office, and she had begun to branch out beyond musicals to dramatic roles in films such as *Vivacious Lady* (1938) and *Having Wonderful Time* (1938), which were not as successful financially. For his part, Astaire wanted to work with other leading ladies and had filmed *Broadway Melody* (1940) with Eleanor Powell.[94] The Astaire-Rogers team was at a turning point, and RKO asked ARI for advice.

ARI showed a list of Rogers' recent films to a cross-section of filmgoers and asked which they had seen and enjoyed the most. *Bachelor Mother* (1939), which had earned $827,000 in profits, proved to be the public's favorite, but nearly all the other films chosen were musicals with Astaire. The institute also conducted a survey designed to learn whether the box office failure of

Broadway Melody was due to a decline in Astaire's popularity. In fact, he was the main reason people said they went to see the film, and 89 percent said they planned to see his next one. When given a choice between seeing a picture with Astaire and Rogers, or one with Astaire and Powell, 68 percent voted for the first pair.[95] Though the favorable response to *Bachelor Mother* could be seen as supporting Rogers' desire to take on more dramatic roles, ARI concluded that the public wanted to see her in another dancing picture with Astaire more than in another comedy.[96] During the course of ARI's research, however, Rogers had already begun filming *Kitty Foyle*. ARI's research failed to override her strong desire to perform more dramatic roles, and she did not make another film with Astaire until *The Barkleys of Broadway* (1949), their last film together. Rogers' box office clout resulted in a new contract in May 1941 in which she agreed to make one picture a year for three years for RKO. *Variety* considered this arrangement to be an act of generosity on her part toward the studio that had made her famous.[97]

ARI also conducted surveys about RKO's newest sensation, Orson Welles. In May 1940, as New Yorkers were watching *Citizen Kane*, ARI asked audiences in the rest of the country for their reactions to three other projects he was considering: the suspense film *Smiler with a Knife*; an adaptation of Joseph Conrad's *Heart of Darkness*; or a film adaptation of his 1938 radio broadcast "War of the Worlds." Welles's Mercury Theatre production of the H. G. Wells story was broadcast on CBS on October 30, 1938, and had scared some viewers, who really believed that an invasion from Mars was in progress (fig. 7.1). As one might expect, ARI found that the public wanted to see Welles in a screen version of "War of the Worlds," either because they had enjoyed the radio version or regretted missing it. RKO producer Harry Edington liked ARI's suggestion and felt that it would capitalize on his famous broadcast; but when Welles said that he did not want to be catalogued as "the horror man," Schaefer supported his decision. At the same time, ARI also tested public interest in another project that RKO was developing, "Parachute Invasion," which featured an Army division that parachuted into cities and tied up their communication systems. When one of the survey participants suggested that it would suit Welles, ARI ran additional tests with him in the cast and found that this new project scored higher than any of the others.[98] However, Welles's star power, and Schaefer's desire to showcase him in a unique way, outweighed Gallup's evidence and these projects were not produced.

As the studies of Rogers and Welles indicate, ARI's casting tests presented evidence that the public wanted to see actors in the same roles they had starred in before. The tests reinforced a performer's established screen persona and did not encourage the studio or the stars to experiment with new

FIGURE 7.1 Orson Welles with reporters on the day after the "War of the Worlds" broadcast in October 1938. Gallup found that the public had a hard time imagining Welles in
anything other than a science fiction film, but Welles's own ideas about his image outweighed the polls. *(Courtesy Corbis)*

roles. As Ogilvy put it, "We do not imply that a player should never be cast in
a part different from those he has been playing in the recent past. But we believe that a radical departure in casting *may* . . . handicap the immediate audience acceptance of the picture."[99] And he added, "We are well aware that
this finding seems to be another argument for type casting."[100] This result
can be explained in part by ARI's methods: since the institute gave people
a list of projects from which to choose, with only a short synopsis for each,
filmgoers would be inclined to select stories that resembled a star's previous roles. In addition, many people do not cast films in their minds, and it
might have been difficult for them to think up alternate roles on the spot. For
example, ARI advised against casting Ronald Colman in a romantic comedy
because audiences had begun to think of him more recently as the adven-
turer of *Lost Horizon*. Though the public liked Colman, they told ARI they
could not imagine him starring in a light romantic comedy with Ginger Rogers. RKO went ahead with *Lucky Partners* anyway, and audiences responded

well to the pairing of these two performers. The film earned a respectable profit of $195,000.[101] Again, RKO ignored ARI's advice to please the few top stars it had under contract.

As the experience of Ginger Rogers shows, ARI's research did not always indicate if a star would succeed in breaking out of his or her established screen identity. Nor could the institute predict if an actor or actress might break out of "B" films to emerge as a full-fledged star. In March 1941, RKO asked ARI to test three possible westerns for John Wayne. Ogilvy was very gloomy, as Wayne's recent films, including the somber Eugene O'Neill adaptation The Long Voyage Home, had not been blockbusters. "John Wayne's marquee value is small. An actor with such low marquee value in a story with such low audience appeal, can only have one result."[102] Ogilvy also could not see the potential for stars that had not been on the screen for a while. When RKO planned a return for silent film comedian Harold Lloyd in late 1940, Ogilvy said that anything but a low-budget picture would be "highly speculative" and suggested the studio be prepared to spend a lot of money for publicity and advertising. Since Lloyd was taking longer than Schaefer liked to finish his film, it was easy to decide not to renew his contract.[103]

Though ARI's research did not indicate whether actors could break out of an established screen persona or revive a dormant career, the institute did a good job of suggesting new stars of the future. ARI developed what it called a "Dark Horse" survey to gauge which actors and actresses were likely to gain popularity in the next few years. This was determined by measuring the intensity of a star's following, on the theory that fans who felt strongly about the actor or actress would make them a star. ARI gave people a list of performers who did not rank in the top 200 of the Motion Picture Herald's poll and asked whether they remembered seeing any of them, and if they did, which performer they especially enjoyed. The "Dark Horse" survey was meant to have predictive value, unlike trade paper polls, which measured a star's popularity in the recent past.

For example, in Gallup's earliest study of this type, a pilot study in March 1937, he found evidence that Tyrone Power and Jimmy Stewart showed great promise, even though the Herald had not placed them in its top 200. ARI's predictions in these "Dark Horse" surveys proved remarkably accurate. In surveys from 1940 through 1942, the institute picked as emerging stars Ingrid Bergman, Van Heflin, Roddy McDowall, Alan Ladd, Teresa Wright, Linda Darnell, and Lana Turner.[104] The institute also noted that Lucille Ball was very popular with theatergoers under 18, the same people who would be young parents during the heyday of her television show of the 1950s. Ogilvy singled out teens as good indicators of emerging stars, explaining that "very frequent filmgoers . . . normally become aware of a new star long before the bulk of the theatergoing public gets around to noticing her. These frequent theatergoers are concentrated in the 12–17 age group."[105]

RKO valued these "Dark Horse" surveys because they provided advance information about who would become successful, before the actor or actress became too expensive to hire. As ARI explained, their "dollars and cents value to RKO Radio will depend on the extent to which you are now able to invest in the personalities at the top of the poll, and the extent to which you are able to remain free from long-term commitments to the personalities at the bottom of the poll."[106] McDonough used the surveys to evaluate every performer RKO had under contract. And in June 1941, when the studio announced the names of performers it was grooming for the future, the list included many who ranked high in ARI's survey.[107] That RKO relied so heavily on these reports is symptomatic of its uncertainty about how to use the performers it had under contract, and how much of its meager resources to spend on actors from other studios.

In addition to special studies of less well-known performers, ARI conducted a quarterly study that it called the "continuing audit of marquee values." The audit asked the public whether seeing a particular person's name on a theater marquee would in itself induce them to buy a ticket to the film. ARI compared these studies to the ratings that Archibald Crossley had carried out for the Cooperative Analysis of Broadcasting, so these audits represented a direct transference of personality ratings from radio to film. ARI presented the results of these surveys in graphs that charted fluctuations in audience interest in the form of lines or bars. ARI also assigned each performer a numerical rating so that executives could compare them more easily.[108] The reports were bound in red leather with gilt-edged pages and embossed with the names of executives who received them. *Variety* compared these studies to Gallup's surveys of presidential popularity. "Method of plotting the ebb and flow of a performer's reception by Joe and Jane America is precisely the same as the familiar barometer of President Roosevelt done by Gallup's American Institute of Public Opinion."[109]

Before ARI began a survey it sent RKO a list of names and asked for additions or deletions. McDonough circulated the lists to Ben Piazza, RKO's talent chief, and reviewed it with Edington and J. J. Nolan, the production heads for "A" and "B" films.[110] McDonough urged Schaefer to limit the circulation of the final reports to the two of them and to Schaefer's assistant, arguing that the material "is of such value that it should be treated with the utmost confidence and used as one of the main bases for passing on the casting suggestions of producers and associate producers."[111] No evidence survives to document how the information was used in these decisions, but McDonough's remarks indicate that the studio valued these reports highly.

Schaefer found another use for these audits: to argue that stars should make more films. The high tax rates of 1940 and 1941 meant that highly paid performers had no incentive to make more than one or two films a year. Schaefer complained to the trades on June 4, 1941, that RKO had nearly two dozen scripts ready for production but could not get enough big-name performers to act in them. Three weeks later, ARI issued a report proving that a star's marquee value declined unless he or she made at least three films a year. The institute drew this conclusion by comparing the marquee value of stars with the number of films they had made in the past year. Stars who had not made a film suffered an average decline of 43 percent in marquee value.[112] The obvious pro-management implications of this report were not lost on the *New York Times*, which pointed out that it was convenient for Hollywood to have information supporting the studio's position "carefully set forth by attractive statistics."[113] RKO's publicity department worked the information into press releases that appeared in several newspapers, and Schaefer sent copies of the report to Myron Selznick and seventeen other agents. Many replied that they were also trying to persuade their clients to make more films—for different reasons.[114]

Changes in the tax code and opportunities for independent production began to alter the position of stars relative to the studios in the early 1940s, giving actors and actresses more opportunities and more reasons to move outside studio hierarchies. The information ARI provided through its quarterly audits, "Dark Horse" studies, and surveys of individual casting choices gave RKO ammunition to manage and keep in check the slippery power of stardom—or at least gave it the illusion of control. The studio's need for what star power it could muster meant that actors or actresses with outsize followings or reputations, like Rogers and Welles, could still exercise their own control over projects.

A Theory of Self-Identification

Though his personal opinions pervade these reports, Ogilvy continued to insist that his analyses were objective. "It is the constant endeavor of those of us who are charged with the responsibility of drawing conclusions from the polls to avoid intruding our private opinions. Any mere opinions are always plainly labelled as such, and are always offered with the greatest diffidence."[115] In less diffident moments, however, Ogilvy speculated freely from the results of these surveys. Just as Gallup generalized about Americans' political opinions from the information he gathered through AIPO, Ogilvy's immersion in ARI's research led him to theorize about why people enjoyed certain actors and actresses. ARI's methods may have been scientific, but what Ogilvy did with the results was another matter.

In Ogilvy's opinion, people liked "to imagine themselves in the position of the star," and it was easier to do that if the star resembled you in some way.[116] What he called his "theory of self-identification" explained why "boys wanted to see boy stars, old women wanted to see old women stars, sophisticated people wanted to see Katharine Hepburn and Laurence Olivier."[117] This vital part of film viewing could be hindered, however, if audiences did not feel enough similarity between themselves and the characters onscreen. George Raft's "proletarian admirers" could easily "project themselves into the adventures of the truck drivers of *They Drive By Night*," but characters from the upper class "who cross the continent in Pullman drawing-rooms are foreign to them."[118] Female viewers also needed to feel some sort of resemblance between themselves and the women onscreen to immerse themselves fully in the drama. In discussing how romance affected women in the audience, Ogilvy explained:

> We have reason to believe that romances succeed only when large numbers of the audience can project themselves into the clinches—when Miss and Mrs. John Citizen can identify themselves with the heroine. This is psychologically difficult unless the heroine bears some reasonable resemblance to the ladies in the audience. If she speaks with a strong foreign accent, or wears a crinoline, the illusion is impossible, and the ladies in the audience remain detached and unmoved.[119]

Ogilvy's statement that a foreign accent would deter audience identification illustrates one of his most firmly held beliefs: that U.S. audiences wanted to see U.S. culture on screen. In his critique of *Cyrano de Bergerac* as a film subject, Ogilvy wrote that, "A foreign background is a powerful obstacle to that process of self-identification upon which most motion pictures depend for their success."[120] After RKO bought the rights to a story called "Water Gypsies," Ogilvy complained that "a Chicago stenographer simply cannot project herself into the life of a bargee's daughter on the Thames." When the studio asked ARI to test public reaction to Maureen O'Hara for the role of the daughter, Ogilvy told them that "she needs an American role before the American public will take her to their hearts."[121] Paul Muni brought trouble on himself by playing the roles of Pasteur and Zola, according to Ogilvy, because viewers no longer thought of him as an American actor.[122] Ogilvy urged RKO to make a film based on Dr. Victor Heiser's bestseller, *An American Doctor's Odyssey*, because he is "an *American* doctor, and is therefore more interesting to theatre-goers."[123] Many of the survey participants he cites do in fact express these opinions, but Ogilvy's summaries give them greater weight.

Ogilvy's conviction that U.S. filmgoers wanted to see native-born stars in familiar U.S. settings led him to seriously underestimate the appeal of actors who did not fit into these categories. Gallup hardly ever reported results in terms of race or ethnicity in the 1930s and early 1940s, though both AIPO's and ARI's surveys included a space for interviewers to note if a respondent was "colored" or white. Ogilvy himself almost never discussed race or ethnicity in his reports to RKO, and he discounted even the strongest evidence that U.S. citizens might have an interest in actors and actresses from other countries. As he wrote: "So much of an actor's marquee value depends on the theatregoer's ability to identify himself with the actor that any obstacle which interferes with this process is bound to militate against that actor ever becoming a first-class marquee name. American theatregoers cannot easily identify themselves with foreign actors."[124]

A remarkable example of Ogilvy's misrepresentation of this data can be found in a poll that asked the public about fourteen stock players whom RKO had under contract. Since the actors were not widely known, interviewers showed people their photographs and asked whom they would most want to see in a film. The winner by far was Desi Arnaz, with 23 percent of the vote, followed closely by Alberto Vila, with 18 percent. Forty-two percent of teenagers expressed a desire to see Arnaz in films, and 22 percent of those surveyed voted him the "most handsome." In his report to RKO, however, Ogilvy recommended that the studio focus on developing actors Edmund O'Brien and Jack Briggs, who had each received only 12 percent of the "most want to see" vote. Ogilvy explained his recommendation this way:

> On the basis of these results, Desi Arnaz and Alberto Vila look the most promising, but our respondents had no means of knowing that these two actors are Latins with Latin accents. If we are not very much mistaken, their votes should be considerably discounted on this account. All we have discovered about marquee values would indicate that a foreign accent is a grievous handicap to any actor—it obstructs the normal processes of self-identification. . . . Unfortunately a substantial number of persons recognized the pictures of Desi Arnaz. . . . It is probable that the vote . . . was thus somewhat inflated.[125]

This survey indicated that people's interests were much less ethnocentric than Ogilvy thought, but he ignored the evidence it revealed in favor of his own preconceptions.

Though Ogilvy did not think the public wanted to see Desi Arnaz on screen, Schaefer knew better. In 1939, Arnaz appeared on Broadway in the musical *Too Many Girls* as a Cuban who performed the conga and loved Notre Dame football. On the strength of its success, RKO invited Arnaz to Hollywood to appear in the film adaptation of the play (fig. 7.2), and RKO shot additional footage after production to build up his role.[126] In October 1940, he married Lucille Ball, whom RKO had under contract. A few hours after their wedding, Arnaz appeared onstage in New York, where a packed theater of screaming fans threw rice from the balconies. Schaefer was there, and within a few months RKO signed him to a three-year contract.[127] His Broadway success and obvious appeal to young audiences, and Schaefer's personal friendship with him and Ball, seem to have outweighed the argument Ogilvy advanced only a few months later. The success of the studio's *Mexican Spitfire* (1940) with Lupe Velez and its six sequels (1940–1943), and the movement within Hollywood to promote its films in Latin America, may also have reinforced Schaefer's decision to ignore Ogilvy.

"How Accurate Are Our Results?"

Though Gallup and Ogilvy presented ARI as a source of objective and impartial information, it is obvious that ARI's reports contain a great many speculations, suppositions, and massaging of the data. While Ogilvy seemed to enjoy teasing out every last ounce of meaning from these studies—and adding some of his own—Gallup recognized that he and his polling staff had much to learn about the ways of Hollywood. In his first presentation to RKO's executives in fall 1939, he argued that his previous experiences in advertising and political polling were readily transferable to film, that in fact "the methods of the Audience Research Institute are similar to those of the Institute of Public Opinion."[128] Although Gallup found a logical link between his political polls and his work in film, not everyone at RKO shared this view. The assumption that these two enterprises could be compared prompted attacks on his work even before he signed his first contract with the studio.

Some of the earliest criticism came from Odlum's representative Rathvon, who doubted the basic value of market research. One might expect Odlum's ally to raise objections, but even if Rathvon's motivations were partly political, his remarks go right to the heart of audience surveys. His three-and-a-half-page memo in January 1940 directly challenged Gallup's assertion that film research was comparable to political surveys.

FIGURE 7.2 Lucille Ball, Desi Arnaz, and Ann Miller in *Too Many Girls* (1940). David Ogilvy rejected research that found Arnaz was one of Hollywood's most popular stars because he believed that U.S. audiences could not identify with anyone who had a foreign accent.

(Courtesy Corbis)

There is a great difference between asking a simple question such as the choice of candidates for office and presenting a story or story idea in a way which will give the full flavor of its proposed treatment. Is the quizzer to become a raconteur or will he hand out printed matter? . . . *Love Affair* was a great picture. A summary of the story of *Love Affair* would probably elicit the response, "Why do they want to re-hash that old plot?" And how about the answers? They will surely be qualified in all sorts of ways. How can these be conveyed intelligibly and codified in a useful manner?[129]

Though Rathvon agreed that it would be useful to eliminate haphazard ways of selecting stories and casts, he pointed out that Gallup had not developed his procedures in consultation with RKO, but had relied on his own sense of what mattered in films. Gallup's lack of firsthand experience with film production also bothered McDonough, ARI's chief contact at the studio. Though he supported Schaefer in many other areas, he had doubts about Gallup. Like Rathvon, McDonough found problems with Gallup's methods for analyzing stories. ARI's story tests were problematic, he felt, because they ignored "a number of highly variable factors intimately concerned with production, such as acting, directing, etc., which can not be predicted or controlled." [130] ARI didn't tell experienced executives much more than they already knew, he felt. Ogilvy usually sent his reports to McDonough first, and McDonough in turn forwarded them to Schaefer, after adding his own comments.[131] For example, his cover letter for the Ginger Rogers' study compared ARI's findings with the actual box office grosses for her films. Although the public chose *Bachelor Mother* as their favorite, he noted, two of her films with Astaire had in fact earned more money. McDonough speculated that people picked the more recent release because it was fresh in their minds, and argued that this was not a reliable way to gauge the true popularity of her musicals.[132]

While he criticized ARI, McDonough did not help the institute resolve the problems he noted. For one story test, RKO sent ARI a 15-page synopsis and suggested Ogilvy could find several story ideas in it. When ARI asked for more information about what RKO wanted, the studio instructed Ogilvy to use the entire 15-page summary for the survey—not a practical solution in an interview situation.[133] With *Kitty Foyle* McDonough sent ARI the entire script and said, "you can draw your own synopsis."[134] When ARI prepared summaries for story ideas it found on its own, McDonough insisted they be sent to RKO for review before they were tested on the public, and criticized them relentlessly.[135] By late 1941, ARI was conducting two nationwide surveys for every story test, using different synopses that were prepared independently of each other, which increased the time it took to respond to

RKO's requests.[136] McDonough also did not want to provide ARI with the information it needed to estimate box office returns. One of the institute's aims was to predict a film's general box office gross before its release—a major accomplishment for any studio if it could be done. McDonough repeatedly refused to supply ARI with the information it requested about previous grosses and the rental agreements it had with theatres—a sensitive subject during a time of antitrust investigations, but crucial information for predicting box office returns.[137]

While Rathvon and McDonough criticized ARI for failing to appreciate the complexities of filmmaking and the sensitivity of some kinds of information, others attacked ARI's fundamental method of cross-section sampling. In August 1941, McDonough turned over his responsibilities for ARI to staff member George Cecala, who had had some experience in statistical research.[138] Between August and December 1941, Cecala fired off criticisms of ARI's work to Schaefer every three or four days, and sometimes for several days in a row. Some of his memos question the basic premise of asking the public for their opinions. "Polling necessarily assumes that an audience is articulate on its likes and dislikes—that it has a critical spirit. But this is an extremely doubtful assumption. Yet, even granting this, how can any serious and stable organization expect to adapt its production to the whimsies of public opinion."[139] Gallup and Ogilvy were concerned enough about Cecala's attacks to prepare a 170-page summary of ARI's work for RKO's board.[140] Ogilvy displayed masterful skill in flattering Cecala's rudimentary knowledge, telling him that, "Criticisms and suggestions must have formulated themselves in your mind and I urge you not to pull your punches in bringing them to Gallup's attention. A constant barrage of criticism and questioning is the life's blood without which we cannot hope to make progress."[141]

Even George Schaefer, who hired Gallup, does not seem to have applied ARI's services consistently. RKO made many decisions about story purchases and casting without consulting the institute. ARI tested *The Hunchback of Notre Dame*, *Vigil in the Night*, *Swiss Family Robinson*, and *Nurse Edith Cavell* after RKO announced the films as part of its 1939–40 slate of releases, when it was too late to change production plans. Schaefer's record-breaking purchase of story rights in February 1940 was made while he was in the process of hiring Gallup, but ARI did not do any research before the decision. ARI did not conduct any preproduction tests on many of the studio's major films of this time, including *Citizen Kane* (1941) and Goldwyn's *Little Foxes* (1941). In late 1941, Ogilvy complained that ARI did not learn about RKO's production plans until it read about them in the papers. In one case, the studio did not ask ARI to conduct a story test for a project until four days before shooting began.[142] Many of Ogilvy's reports in early 1942 begin by complaining that RKO had already purchased a property before it got around to asking whether audiences wanted to see it on screen. When the studio announced its slate of productions for the 1941–42 season, the list contained many that ARI had already predicted would be unpopular, such as *Father Takes a Wife* and *The Devil and Daniel Webster*.[143]

Given RKO's poor financial results, one might ask how well the studio could have done if it had paid more attention to ARI's advice. Of the twenty-one stories ranked "first class" in ARI's studies, seventeen originated with ARI and not with RKO. The institute tested many of RKO's projects several times with different synopses and casts, but one property after another met with little enthusiasm.[144] Ogilvy spoke bluntly about the general weakness of RKO's product, "those medium budget star-less pictures in which RKO has come to specialize."[145] He pointed out that the studio was consistently below average in appealing to younger ticket buyers and those from low-income groups and that the projects it proposed usually appealed more to high-income patrons and older viewers.[146] If ARI was right in arguing that the young and the poor were the key demographic groups, then RKO did not pay enough attention to them, and the films it made for older, more affluent patrons did not bring in enough money to compensate for this failure. Though Ogilvy sometimes displayed an elitist attitude in speaking about "the people," he at least brought them to RKO's attention, and the studio might have been more profitable if it had listened.

For its part, ARI undermined its own position through its lack of familiarity with the norms of Hollywood production. That Gallup was brought into RKO by its president and a member of its board of directors meant that his work was linked more closely with New York than with Hollywood. Historically, New York has been the site for finance, sales, and distribution, where executives focused on the bottom line and strove to reduce costs and boost efficiency, while their counterparts in Hollywood dealt with the day-to-day demands of stars, scripts, and shooting.[147] Gallup held most of his meetings with RKO in the company's New York office, which would have reinforced the sense among some in RKO's Hollywood studio that his work reflected the concerns of corporate management rather than production executives.[148] Ogilvy also recognized that an East Coast research institute might inadvertently trample on the legendary egos of Hollywood executives. In the introduction to one report he shamelessly flattered McDonough and Schaefer by telling them that audience research "is for the producer whose genius derives its impetus from divine discontent. It is for the man who is still learning—for the mind which is still open."[149]

Though both men acknowledged that they did not have firsthand experience in the field, Ogilvy did not seem as concerned as Gallup about the problem. In one report he noted that although "the variables which intervene between our pre-production polls and the release of the picture" prevented ARI from predicting the success of a picture with "mathematical accuracy," the institute was usually pretty close. Among the "variables" which "intervened" between a poll and a finished film were such elements as acting and direction. "We cannot contribute much to an appraisal of acting ability," he wrote, "since all major stars must possess a certain minimum level of acting competence before they become stars; and since acting ability is so largely a matter of personal judgment." As for direction, "we have found that direction is *very seldom* either good enough or bad enough to upset our predictions."[150] McDonough took issue with this view and pointed out to Schaefer that studio executives had a better grasp of films than ARI did. "The attractiveness of the cast and the appeal of the story I assume can be measured by the Gallup polls. In estimating before production . . . the quality of the completed picture . . . we have to rely upon the reputation of the producer and the director and the script writer"—qualities that studio executives such as himself were in the best position to judge.[151]

ARI's lack of awareness regarding the norms of Hollywood production was also apparent in some of its research on stars. In one report, "Believe-It-Or-Not Equations," ARI asserted that certain stars were equivalent in terms of their marquee value. Some of its pairings seemed reasonable, like James Cagney and Pat O'Brien, or Ginger Rogers and Loretta Young. But it was hard to believe that others matched in any way, such as the linkage of Greta Garbo and Joan Blondell, Shirley Temple and Jane Withers, or Marlene Dietrich and Anna Neagle. ARI argued that each star in the pair was equal in his or her ability to sell tickets; RKO disagreed.[152] ARI drew other conclusions that flew in the face of Hollywood practice. The institute argued that a film did not need two or three marquee stars because "two big marquee names can sell more tickets appearing separately in two films than appearing together in one."[153] Ogilvy based his argument on a disingenuous arithmetic formula that doesn't hold water. He presented a chart indicating that Myrna Loy's appearance in a film would attract 29 percent of the audience, while William Powell's appearance would attract 22 percent. When audiences were told that both of them would appear together in a film, 45 percent said they would buy a ticket to see it. While to most people this would look like a potent combination, Ogilvy claimed these numbers showed that their total as a duo (45 percent) was less than their combined individual totals (51 percent and, therefore, the studio would do better to feature them separately. Another way to look at this data, of course, is to say that the team of Loy and Powell created synergy, that together they were greater than the sum of their individual scores.[154] Ogilvy's reasoning ignored the tradition of Hollywood casting and would have eliminated films such as *The Thin Man* series that made the two famous in the 1930s.

When it came to story tests, ARI was right in forecasting the failure of many of RKO's program pictures. However, ARI's success at predicting failures was outweighed by its failure to predict the success of RKO's biggest moneymaker, *Kitty Foyle*, Christopher Morley's story of a girl who married up but found that life among the wealthy did not guarantee happiness. The film fit ARI's criteria for success, since it was based on a novel that ranked as the second all-time favorite on library lending lists, but tests showed that it was not popular with men and teens under 18, groups whom Ogilvy believed were vital to the box office. Besides diminishing the significance of female filmgoers, Ogilvy discouraged RKO from making films aimed primarily at them. ARI had demonstrated that there were distinct gender differences in the audiences for various films. Instead of acknowledging these differences and urging RKO to make films for each gender, Ogilvy insisted that the interests of both groups had to be represented in each film. When research indicated that *Kitty Foyle* appealed more strongly to women than to men, Ogilvy argued that its popularity with women would not be enough to compensate for its lack of interest for men. He urged RKO to add some action-oriented elements to increase the film's appeal for men. *Kitty Foyle* was a love story, and men did not like love stories, he noted, quoting one who grumped: "It's all about love. I don't like love." This led him to conclude that the film would not break even, but as it turned out, it was so popular that women of all ages and incomes turned out to see it, thus negating the lack of interest among men. *Kitty Foyle* earned $865,000, was the most successful production under Schaefer's regime, and won Rogers an Oscar (fig. 7.3).[155] ARI admitted its error, but the misstep damaged its reputation within RKO.

Ogilvy also seems to have succumbed to the lure of "going Hollywood." Don Cahalan, Gallup's colleague at AIPO, remembers that Ogilvy was fascinated by the industry and, despite his assurances that audience research was but a "supplement" to the creative and business functions of the studio, had his own ideas about what RKO should be doing.[156] When ARI found that the public was interested in the Mayo Brothers as a film subject, Ogilvy convinced Gallup to contact the American Medical Association for approval. Its board met and responded that they would support the film if they had script approval and a special prerelease preview. Ogilvy then wrote the Mayo Clinic to ask them to sponsor the project, and promised that RKO would make a "substantial contribution" to its work. McDonough was livid, saying that Ogilvy had "gone too far," and that RKO would not make a film with so much "interference" from others.[157] When RKO did agree to film another one of ARI's story ideas, "Army Surgeon," Ogilvy fussed that the studio's treatment

FIGURE 7.3 Jan Wiley and Ginger Rogers in a scene from RKO's *Kitty Foyle* (1940). Though Gallup predicted it would be a box office flop, the film proved to be one of RKO's biggest hits and won Rogers an Oscar.   *(Courtesy Corbis)*

did not match his view of what the film should be. As he imagined it, the title character should be "an over-worked, over-strained, entirely normal young man in whom war has submerged normal impulses of light-hearted-ness." RKO eliminated the romantic subplot that Ogilvy found essential, and didn't stress enough about the adventurous side of medicine, which is what the public wanted. In the studio's script, the surgeon became "rather a dull stick." Ogilvy may have been right, however, since *Army Surgeon* lost $46,000 when it was released in 1942.[158]

Even Gallup himself seems to have become infected with the desire to join the ranks of Hollywood producers. In June 1941 he announced that Edmund Dorfman's Film Institute would produce a series of 10-minute shorts based on the findings of the Gallup Poll. At first Schaefer supported the idea, and even arranged for Dorfman to meet with the head of Pathé News, whose newsreels RKO also distributed, before Ned Depinet, the studio's head of sales, complained that the project would undermine RKO's existing commitment to the *March of Time*. Gallup reluctantly agreed that the topicality of his political polls would lose their value in the time it took to produce a newsreel.[159]

Gallup also infuriated RKO's executives by his efforts to position himself as an alternative voice to the film industry. On the eve of the 1941 Academy Awards, ARI released a "people's choice" opinion poll that indicated what awards the general public would make if it were voting. The survey "was not confined to a special group, but shows how the moviegoing public generally—Mr. and Mrs. John Citizen whose nickels and dimes keep the motion picture industry going—would vote." The press release came from AIPO and received extensive coverage in the trades, including a front-page story in *Film Daily*. Gallup emphasized the poll's nationwide coverage and the fact that AIPO's staff of interviewers had questioned 10,000 Americans. As he noted, America's moviegoers chose only one film that appeared on the Academy's list—*Rebecca*. In the year that Oscars were awarded to *How Green Was My Valley* (Best Picture), *Sergeant York* (Best Actor for Gary Cooper), and *Suspicion* (Best Actress for Joan Fontaine), audiences selected as their favorites *Boom Town*, *Knute Rockne—All-American*, and *Northwest Passage*. "Apparently," Gallup said, "there is considerable difference of opinion between Hollywood and its customers." A film historian today might also note the gap between the overwhelmingly popular films of 1941 and the academic canon, which includes all of the Academy winners but none of Gallup's. But what riled RKO was Gallup's statement in the press release that the public's top six choices included three films made by MGM, two by Warners, and one by Selznick. The Academy, by contrast, included five RKO films among its nominees.[160] Schaefer complained to McDonough that the studio was paying for Gallup's research, and there weren't even any RKO films on the list, though the Academy sought fit to nominate five for its awards.[161] Gallup's desire to serve as the voice of the people offended the client who funded his research.

An Open Fight for Control

Gallup's unfamiliarity with Hollywood, as well as his desire to assert his public voice, augmented by Ogilvy's tendency to speculate freely and offer his own suggestions about what RKO should do, meant that they communicated much more to the studio than facts and statistics. RKO's decisions to adopt or discard ARI's recommendations reflected the beliefs and experiences of its executives and internal financial pressures at the studio. In any case, the overriding determinants on Schaefer's decisions were the impact of the consent decree, World War II, and the shifting power structures within RKO.

The consent decree that RKO and four other major studios signed in the fall of 1940 mandated that studios had to preview their films before signing rental agreements with exhibitors, and that these agreements could cover no more than blocks of five films. Journalist Douglas Churchill argued that these restrictions hit middle-range studios such as RKO the hardest. "Hollywood feels that under the new order resulting from the consent decree that studios which have existed half way between the top and bottom either must be rejuvenated and assume an importance equal to that of the dominating companies or must resign themselves to an inconspicuous position with the small independents."[162]

To Schaefer, the consent decree meant that studios would have to cut back on the number of films they produced, since some films would have to sit on the shelf until a block of five could be completed. In January 1941 he announced that RKO would not release the fifty-three films it had promised at the May 1940 convention, where he had also optimistically announced Gallup's hire. The final number would be more like thirty-five or forty. Given the requirements of the consent decree, he felt that RKO was producing "too many little pictures," and that it would be more profitable to concentrate on a smaller number of big-budget films.[163] Schaefer also announced that he was reorganizing the studio and would take over day-to-day production responsibilities himself. Lee Marcus and J. J. Nolan left RKO in April 1941, and in June Schaefer appointed Joseph Breen, the former head of the Production Code Administration, as general manager of the RKO studios and vice president in charge of production, though he had never produced a film. By mid-1941 nearly all of ARI's established contacts at RKO had left.[164]

When Schaefer announced in June that the studio had lost $988,191 during the previous calendar year, industry insiders began to ask openly how long he would last. RKO's stockholders meeting, which was always held in June, was postponed, and rumor had it that Odlum was accumulating more stock. Nearly every day trade papers carried reports of conflicts between Schaefer, Rathvon, and Odlum. *Variety* reported that even the Rockefellers, who had chosen him as president, had withdrawn their support. As Catherine Benamou and Richard Jewell have documented, Schaefer was also in trouble because of the growing expenses on Orson Welles's Latin American production *It's All True*.[165]

As Schaefer's position became more and more tenuous within the studio, so did ARI's. Ogilvy's reports from this period reflect an increasing sense of marginalization and confusion. When Rathvon began to assert more authority, Gallup and Ogilvy had to meet with him to explain ARI's work and prepare lengthy reports justifying their methods. In December, Rathvon became a vice president of the RKO Corporation and put a close ally in place as the studio's controller. RKO did renew Schaefer's contract in December 1941 for a short period, but it was mainly because both Odlum and Rockefeller were engaged in war work in Washington and wanted a familiar face in place for the time being.[166]

Despite his own troubled position, Schaefer still went to bat for Gallup. At the end of February 1942, when his own contract was once again up for discussion, Schaefer negotiated a renewal of ARI's contract for an even lower monthly fee than its original price.[167] Later that month, McDonough re-signed as executive producer, ending one of ARI's most consistent contacts at the studio. In April and May, RCA sold Odlum its remaining shares in the studio, as rumors flew that RCA head David Sarnoff had lost patience with Schaefer. The *Hollywood Reporter* announced that there was an "Open Fight for RKO Control." After announcing yet again that the studio had lost money, Schaefer resigned in June, and Odlum gained the control he had long sought. To replace Schaefer's men Odlum elevated executives from RKO's distribution and exhibition arms, the key source of what profits the studio had earned. Rathvon became head of the RKO Corporation, while Ned De-pinet, the director of sales during Schaefer's regime, took over as head of the film studio. Charles Koerner, who had been in charge of RKO's theater chain, became vice president in charge of studio operations.[168]

Since Koerner and Depinet had worked in sales and exhibition, they felt comfortable relying on their own knowledge of the public and did not see a need for ARI's research. On June 30, 1942, the studio notified Gallup that his contract would be canceled. Gallup persuaded Koerner to reconsider by offering three months of free service, in addition to the discount that Schae-fer had already negotiated, in exchange for a one-year extension. Gallup was willing to work for free to retain his most vital and prestigious client. Rathvon renewed the contract, but demanded a two-month cancellation clause, and then threatened to cancel it again in November, before renewing it one more time. RKO also scaled back the number and kinds of services it required from ARI, paying only for the audits of marquee values, a few story tests, and some publicity reports.[169] For the remainder of the war, ARI provided mini-mal research for the studio, but maintained its connection.

Though Koerner and Depinet felt they didn't need Gallup, their ideas of what the public wanted, and the changes they made in RKO's production schedule, matched ARI's earlier recommendations very closely. Koerner an-nounced that RKO would abandon Schaefer's focus on "prestige films and artistic features" and that instead "the company's entire production setup will be aimed to supply commercial and saleable pictures."[170] Under his regime RKO produced several war films as well as films based on popular novels, magazine stories, and radio characters. Baseball pictures were in and racetrack pictures were out, as Koerner strove to "give exhibitors the kind of pictures I always wanted the companies to give me."[171]

Reporting the Facts

Despite Gallup and Ogilvy's insistence that they were merely "reporting the facts," it is obvious that the hundreds of reports ARI presented to RKO include many creative interpretations of empirical data. ARI's research and RKO's responses to it can be seen as a competition to assert the power of interpretation over seemingly objective material. Rockefeller and Schaefer hired Gallup to harness the power of his political polls for the studio's use, and Gallup himself used AIPO as a foundation for building ARI. Gallup and Ogilvy referred often to Gallup's political surveys and sent RKO's executives advance copies of some of their findings. Even Koerner, who was so confident that he could rely on his own ideas about what the public wanted, didn't hesitate to refer to the Gallup polls when it would enhance his stature in the industry. In September 1942, Koerner wrote to Ed Mannix of MGM's publicity department about a question he had raised during a breakfast for Vice President Henry Wallace. Mannix wondered whether the pro-British propaganda of *Mrs. Miniver* was effective or not. "As you undoubtedly know," Koerner wrote, "we use the Gallup Poll for many purposes and I am submitting the following that I know will be of great interest to you." He then went on to quote a recent ARI report about the film and others depicting the war in Britain, which found that the attitude of filmgoers who had seen several of these pictures was measurably more favorable toward England.[172] Koerner's eagerness to advertise that RKO "used" the Gallup Poll underscores the sense of power executives accrued from their connection with Gallup.

The Audience Research Institute was more than George Gallup, however, and one of the most memorable voices in this period is that of David Ogilvy, exhorting the studio to "whip up" publicity to support a film he liked, or sniffing at the strange tastes of the "nether elements." Ogilvy is at once the most distinctive voice in these reports, and the most problematic, because his freely embroidered interpretations of the data often exceeded the bounds of what most would call science. It was precisely because he was engaged in so many other endeavors—the political polls and his work at Young & Rubicam—that Gallup hired Ogilvy to be the chief contact and analyst for ARI; yet this choice added another layer of commentary that drew criticism from RKO. When Koerner and Rathvon decided to renew some of ARI's services, they asked only for barebones data, not the interpretive reports that distinguished Ogilvy's tenure with the institute.

ARI had mixed results during Schaefer's regime. Though it succeeded in identifying stars of the future, and helped RKO to negotiate better terms with some it already had under contract, its data did not override the choices of the few powerful stars that were willing to work with the studio. Box office returns from the period indicate that McDonough and Schaefer would have done well to listen to Ogilvy's urgings that films based on popular narratives would be more profitable than the highbrow properties Schaefer bought. Schaefer's decision to hire Gallup heightened his stature within the corporation and affirmed to the rest of the company his determination to make profitable films. But the executive didn't seem to be willing to take the chances that Gallup's research mandated. The instability in RKO's management and ownership meant that there was no long-term support for ARI's research.

From Gallup's perspective, the opportunity to work in depth with a major Hollywood studio broadened his horizons. His time in Hollywood marked one of the most exciting periods of his research, and it is clear that he was willing to make huge sacrifices to carry out work in film.[173] Though he expressed confidence that the skills and methods used in advertising and politics could transfer to film, he needed to work out his ideas in more detail, and RKO gave him the chance to do that. For Gallup, RKO provided on-the-job training in film audience research.

Beyond the effect of this work on Gallup's professional development and the effect on RKO's corporate history, perhaps the most enduring aspect of this period is that film research became a significant part of the fabric of popular culture. Gallup and Ogilvy's statements about teenagers, gender differences, and the value of escapism made their way into mass magazines and even congressional hearings as "facts" about the way people thought. Through the Gallup polls, popular opinion became reified, fluctuations in beliefs and feelings were encoded into percentages and graphs that were then taken up and used in other contexts. Through Gallup, public opinion became a tool that could be used for many purposes, often far beyond the contexts in which "the people" had first expressed themselves.

8

David O. Selznick Presents

Audience Research and the Independent Producer

The responses to Gallup's work within RKO illustrate how a vertically integrated Hollywood studio reacted to empirical audience research. From Schaefer's decision to commission research in order to improve the studio's profitability, to other executives' reluctance to cede the power of interpreting audiences that they had so carefully amassed, RKO's experience with survey research reveals how this data could become caught up in the internal power struggles of a corporation. For the most part, however, major Hollywood studios were not interested in commissioning Gallup's studies at this time because their chief executives felt confident they understood what the public wanted. Instead, further interest in Gallup's work came from another quarter, from independent producers such as Samuel Goldwyn and David O. Selznick. As Goldwyn's battle against double features demonstrates, independent producers, though they were some of the most esteemed people in Hollywood, occupied an uncertain space within the studio system.

RKO relied on many independent producers to meet its distribution schedules, and they were among the first to be cut during budget crises. Most of the independents that worked for the studio used its facilities to produce their films, but there were some independents in Hollywood who owned their own production facilities. Even then, they needed majors such as RKO to distribute their films, and often to supply actors and actresses for them. The economic structure of the studio system placed these independent producers at a distinct disadvantage. Before the consent decree of 1940, studios rented the films they distributed in large blocks, and the work of an independent producer might be lumped together with films of lesser quality that the studio itself had produced. Even if a producer tried to release one or two films close together, there was no guarantee that a distributor would package them that way. Selznick's work was so highly regarded that his distributor in the mid-1930s, United Artists, packaged his films with others they had produced themselves, in order to sell their own product.[1] The consent decree required studios to rent films in groups of five or less, a provision that stood to benefit independents because it would make individual films more visible. Even in this more favorable environment, however, the time it took to produce a quality film and recoup its costs meant that independent producers were often in precarious financial circumstances.

Research by Janet Staiger and Matthew Bernstein has demonstrated that independent production was the site of continual battles over control and creativity, as producers with a more individualistic or even visionary bent competed for financing and distribution from the major studios that controlled exhibition. As Staiger argues, the industry supported an ideology of creativity, believing that special films from a few gifted directors could reap as much profit as the mass-produced films of the studio system, but this commitment to individualism was tempered by the need to supply their theaters with regular programs. Independent producers who were under contract to the majors suffered competing demands: they were expected to produce innovative films that also returned high profits and fit easily into existing systems of promotion and distribution. According to Bernstein, this unceasing demand for profitability, and the expectation that independents would cooperate with the majors' distribution schedules, mitigated the freedom they appeared to enjoy in experimenting with innovative narrative and visual forms.[2]

In an article for the *Washington Post* in June 1941, journalist Hubbard Keavy articulated what motivated people to become independent producers. "The man who feels restricted, artistically or commercially, under studio supervision becomes an independent producer. He is his own boss, he makes the kind of pictures he likes."[3] For Selznick, film, and the desire to "be his own boss," were in the blood. His father Lewis had immigrated to the United States from Russia and launched several production companies in New York and Hollywood before declaring bankruptcy in 1925. An incessant gambler, Lewis Selznick took his wife and four sons from wealth to destitution, living at the height of his career in a 17-room Park Avenue apartment, before dying in 1933 in a three-room flat.[4] Undeterred by these changes in fortune, he is reported to have told his sons: "Always remember to live beyond your means. It gives a man confidence."[5] David and Myron Selznick accompanied their father to business conferences before beginning their own careers in film.

Myron became one of the legendary Hollywood agents, one that *Life* magazine described in 1939 as "more important in Hollywood than all other agents combined."[6] David became one of the most highly sought-after and highly paid Hollywood producers of the 1930s.

Selznick worked in various roles in most of the major studios and rose swiftly through their corporate hierarchies. He began as script reader at MGM in 1923 and within a few months became an associate producer at triple his starting salary. In 1927, Selznick left to go to Paramount where he moved rapidly from head of the writers' department to assistant to Paramount's production chief, to become head of production himself. In October 1931 he moved over to RKO to become executive vice president of RKO Radio Pictures.[7] The industry regarded Selznick so highly that the *Wall Street Journal* cited his involvement in RKO as one of the few reasons to be optimistic about its future.[8] Selznick returned to MGM in 1933 as an associate producer. In the midst of these moves he had also married Irene Mayer, the daughter of one of MGM's founders, so his return to the company was seen as that of a favored son and heir apparent who would some day take over.[9]

Despite his solid position within a leading film studio and personal link to its founder, Selznick felt driven to establish his own production firm. As he explained in one of his legendary memos: "I simply had to fulfill my ambitions of starting my own company. It had always been an obsession of mine, unquestionably inherited from my father . . . that there be no interference with our work; that we must have authority."[10] In the summer of 1935 he formed David O. Selznick Productions, which a few months later became Selznick International Pictures, after he obtained financing from John Hay Whitney. Whitney in turn brought in other investors from among his relatives and business associates, including his cousin Cornelius Vanderbilt Whitney and sister Joan Payson, and Robert Lehman of the Wall Street investment bank Lehman Brothers. Whitney and his family invested $2.4 million in Selznick's company, providing three-quarters of its starting capital, with the rest coming from Selznick's own associates in the film industry: his brother Myron, Norma Shearer, and Irving Thalberg. Selznick himself did not invest any money, but owned half the company.[11] A second merger in June 1936 combined Selznick International with Pioneer Pictures, the company Whitney had formed to produce Technicolor films, and Selznick assumed Pioneer's contracts to produce color features.

Selznick was among the most fervent proponents of color film and showcased its possibilities in productions such as *The Garden of Allah* (1936), *A Star Is Born* (1937), *Nothing Sacred* (1937), and most notably, *Gone with the Wind* (1939), the film that defined his career. Regarded as one of the most skilled adapters of literary works, and a producer with a knack for discovering new stars, Selznick exemplified the independent producer with the studio system. Yet even such a powerful figure was in the end, in Matthew Bernstein's phrase, a semi-independent producer.[12]

The independent producers whom Keavy described often used their own capital to finance films, and were limited in the amount of funds they could raise. And the interest rates independents paid were twice that of other businesses.[13] Unlike other independent producers, however, Selznick had a wide network of professional contacts and substantial financial support from one of America's wealthiest men. Yet even though he had his own production company, he still had to rely on other studios that owned networks of theaters in order to distribute his films. For Selznick, a ferociously independent person working within a highly structured studio system, the conflict and tensions were ongoing. In the early 1940s he turned to audience research to gather ammunition he could use to support his ideas to more powerful figures with whom he worked. Selznick realized literally the day that Gallup's election polls began that the techniques could be applied to motion pictures. Though Gallup began to study Selznick's films at first without his authorization, Selznick soon began to use survey research for his own purposes. Gallup's surveys helped him negotiate the distribution, promotion, and re-release of *Gone with the Wind* with its distributor MGM, and when Whitney chose to dissolve their company in 1940, Gallup continued to provide information that gave Selznick at least an illusion of control over a situation in which he had in fact very little power. Selznick's use of audience research illustrates how this information could help one articulate figure gain leverage and clout in the complex system that was Hollywood in the early 1940s.

"A Really Intelligent Survey"

On Wednesday, July 8, 1936, during the same week that the *Washington Post* announced the launch of the American Institute of Public Opinion, the *Los Angeles Times* reported that it too would carry Gallup's syndicated columns about the surveys. Gallup's new polling service, according to the paper, "is believed to be the first in history to show authoritatively the relative standing of the leading candidates so soon after the nominations."[14] Later that same day, Selznick wrote to the chief executive officer of his company, Daniel O'Shea, about the article and asked him to look into the possibility of hiring AIPO to carry out research in film. "It occurs to me that it might be worthwhile, if the cost were not prohibitive, getting a really intelligent survey of the tastes and desires of the public in motion picture entertainment."

O'Shea in turn wrote to Gallup, who replied on July 20 that he was in fact already experimenting with ways of studying the public's tastes and interests in motion pictures, and thought he would have some results to show in the next few months. Gallup spoke confidently of the parallels between political surveys and film research. "The task of determining the taste of the public in respect to motion picture entertainment is not unlike that of determining public opinion in respect to issues or candidates. The same basic procedure can be followed in both cases, allowing of course for the difference in the makeup of the two publics."[15]

Though Gallup felt these projects were complementary, the intense effort required to develop his presidential polls hampered his work in film, and he wrote O'Shea in mid-October that he would have to delay his motion picture studies until after the election. "Our efforts at the moment are confined chiefly to predicting as accurately as we can the [outcome] of the November election. As soon as this is over we plan to concentrate our efforts on our motion picture research." Despite the delay, Gallup's success in predicting the outcome of the election reinforced O'Shea and Selznick's determination to work with him. A few days after Roosevelt's victory, O'Shea sent Selznick another *Times* article describing Gallup's methods and wrote that in his mind AIPO was "far and away the best poll."[16] Thus, from literally the first day Gallup launched his election polls, they were inextricably intertwined with his research on film. And even though Gallup was not able to take on other work immediately, his syndicated column in the *Times*, like his regular features in the *Washington Post*, kept his name before potential clients and reminded them of the benefits of working with him.

Shortly after the election, in January 1937, Whitney commissioned the studies of public attitudes toward Technicolor which Gallup had included as part of his political polls. At the same time, Gallup also began to formulate ways to study the public's responses toward film actors and actresses. These studies were not part of the AIPO surveys, and the only evidence of them appears in Gallup's correspondence with Whitney, Selznick, and Whitney's lawyer, John Wharton, in this period. The letters indicate that Selznick sought Gallup's advice on casting and that he realized immediately how research could give added weight to his own ideas. In early February 1937, for example, Selznick wrote Wharton to say that, "Jock has told me of the Gallup preliminary information concerning Edward Arnold and Myrna Loy, respectively. This more or less coincides with my own impressions concerning these two players and makes me doubly anxious to secure such information as you can from Gallup concerning players who are or might be available to us, including especially [Janet] Gaynor, [Charles] Boyer, Irene Dunne, [Frederic] March, Madeleine [Carroll], and [Freddie] Bartholomew."[17] Gaynor and

March had just appeared in *A Star Is Born*, and Selznick wanted to sign them for his next color film. It appears that Whitney paid for these studies, as Selznick sent his request for more information to Wharton. Two days after Selznick asked for these star studies, Wharton told Whitney:

> I am somewhat worried about the Gallup situation. He is devoting most of his time at the moment to the Star Service, which you told me you felt was an absolute waste of time. On the other hand, I got a teletype from David asking me to get information from Gallup on about six different people. As a result, I don't know whether to tell Gallup that you are definitely not interested in that phase of the work, or whether to let him go ahead with it.

Wharton did in fact provide Selznick with some answers to his questions: that Frederic March ranked high in public opinion, and that Janet Gaynor was popular among low-income customers. Like the executives at RKO, Wharton also offered his own analysis of Gallup's data, noting his own favorites and repeating what he had heard at dinner parties.[18]

These studies from late 1936 and early 1937, as well as the ones discussed earlier that involved reactions to color films, suggest that Gallup was working on several fronts simultaneously: testing the kinds of questions that he could study through survey research; composing population samples that mirrored the filmgoing audience; isolating elements of films that could be studied; and developing sources of funding for this new venture. The focus of his research reflected both his own interest in methodology and the concerns of his industry clients. None of this material appeared in the Hollywood trade papers in 1937 or 1938, nor did Gallup publicize them, suggesting that he regarded these studies as experimental. Instead, Gallup's first public foray into film research began because of a request, not by Hollywood, but by the newspapers that underwrote his political polls. Their interest in the national bestseller *Gone with the Wind* spurred Gallup to undertake a survey that in turn led David Selznick to become his client.

One of the Greatest Audiences

Gone with the Wind became a national obsession as soon as it was published in June 1936. Margaret Mitchell's novel had the largest advance sale of any book in history, and went through eight printings within the first month of its publication. By Christmas it had become the fastest-selling book in history. It took two printing plants working 24-hour shifts to meet the insatiable demand for the novel about the plantation era in the South. So it was not surprising that bidding for film rights to the book was fierce before David Selznick won them for $50,000 one month after the book's publication.[19]

Americans almost immediately began to debate which actress should play the role of Scarlett O'Hara. Selznick turned this public fascination into a major promotional gambit. For more than two years, beginning in November 1936, his talent scouts scoured the country in a national search to find a leading lady. They visited community theaters, university drama societies, and Federal Theater performances to interview candidates for the role. Selznick's agents met with actresses from the MGM stock company, dozens of New York models, and women whose claim to fame was that they had appeared in magazine ads or on the cover of *Life* magazine. Selznick also solicited nominations from readers of fan magazines and from radio listeners. Most major actresses of the time were considered or rumored to have signed at some point, including Tallulah Bankhead, Jean Arthur, Miriam Hopkins, Norma Shearer, Paulette Goddard, and Carole Lombard. One radio commentator received 70,000 letters indicating that the public wanted either Bette Davis or Katharine Hepburn for the part.[20] Still, a great many people shared Selznick's belief that an actress who was not well known would be best for the part. On January 13, 1939, after more than a two-year search, Selznick announced that he had signed the British actress Vivien Leigh to fill the role. The news broke during the same week that Gallup published his *New York Times* piece about Hollywood's influence on America's reading habits, the essay in which he reported that *Gone with the Wind* was second only to the Bible in popularity.[21]

Southerners roundly attacked Selznick for choosing a British actress to play a quintessential American character. A letter to the *New York Times* from the "grandson of a Confederate soldier" revealed some of the passion that surrounded the decision. John Alexander condemned the choice of "an alien English woman" to play Scarlett as "a direct affront to the men who wore the Gray and an outrage to the memory of the heroes of 1776 who fought to free this land of British domination." Alexander applauded a Florida chapter of the Daughters of the Confederacy that planned to boycott the film because, he said, "it is high time those Hollywood producers find out that there are still those to whom the honor of Southern womanhood is no empty phrase."[22] Sentiments such as Alexander's may have been the reason that the *Atlanta Constitution* and several other newspapers commissioned a survey from Gallup about public reactions to Leigh.[23] Though Selznick didn't hear about the survey until it was nearly completed, Gallup's findings gave him ammunition that he used to support his ideas about the film.

AIPO's *Gone with the Wind* survey took place nine months before Gallup's first presentation to RKO and marked the first time that he conducted in-depth research on one specific production. Seven questions relating to the film appeared on the Gallup poll for the period January 27–February 1, 1939, amounting to one-quarter of the survey. By including questions about the film in a poll that also measured public opinion on government spending, Roosevelt's presidency, and organized labor, AIPO treated the production as if it were a topic of national interest. Interviewers asked Americans whether they intended to read the book, which character they thought was the most interesting, and whether they planned to see the film when it was released. The survey also inquired whether audiences wanted to see the film in color or in two parts, which actress they wanted to play Scarlett O'Hara, and whether they approved of the selection of Vivien Leigh.[24]

Before carrying out the national survey, Gallup conducted small-scale pilot studies with residents of New Jersey in which he tested various ways to word several questions.[25] Tracing how the questions changed between these pilot studies and the final AIPO survey reveals the issues Gallup confronted in developing his film research and illustrates how data can be interpreted in dramatically different ways. One question that changed from the pilot studies to the final poll asked whether people had read the novel. In the pilot studies, researchers asked people directly: "Have you read *Gone with the Wind*?" One quarter of the respondents answered yes. However, Gallup and his staff believed that this number might not be accurate because, if they asked respondents directly whether they had read a popular book, people might say they had when they hadn't, to avoid embarrassment. By contrast, Gallup and his staff believed that if they asked whether someone "intended" to read the book, people who had already done so would volunteer that information.[26] The final AIPO survey asked people whether they intended to read the book, but the press release only reported the percentage that said they actually had read it.

Gallup also experimented with the question asking whether people planned to see the film. One pilot study asked people whether they thought they would go to the movie "when it comes to your local theatre," while another asked whether they thought they would go to the movie "after it comes out." The final AIPO survey asked more broadly: "When *Gone with the Wind* comes out as a movie, what are your chances of seeing it?"—which left open the possibility that respondents might travel beyond their local theater to see it at a first-run venue instead of waiting for the film to appear in neighborhood theaters on its second or third run. This way of wording the question captured the public's general desire to see the film independently of its venue. Gallup also tried different ways to gauge the public's level of commitment to seeing the film. When the pilot studies asked people whether they intended to see it, the options for response included yes, probably, can't say, probably not, and no. In this format, three out of five options indicated doubt ("can't say") or lack of desire ("probably not," "no"). The final nation-wide survey, by contrast, included six options, four of which were positive: "almost certain," "probably," "better than even," "50–50," "less than even," and "probably not." The most negative response on the final survey was "probably not," in contrast to the absolute "no" option which had appeared in the pilot studies. AIPO's press release stressed the percentage of respondents who reported at least a "better than even" chance of seeing the film and did not mention how many said they would probably not go (about one quarter). By structuring the question in this way, and by reporting answers indicating a "better than even" chance that the respondent would see the film, the press release revealed a potential audience for *Gone with the Wind* that exceeded any previously known. The possible size of the audience became one of the most important facts to emerge from the national survey.

The nationwide survey also showed the special care that Gallup took to assess reactions to Vivien Leigh. As he did with the double-feature poll, Gallup used a split ballot on this survey, with two questionnaires that varied in wording. The first six questions were the same on both forms, but the last question about reactions to Vivien Leigh differed in wording and emphasis. One form asked the public if they were satisfied with Leigh's selection for the part of Scarlett, while the other asked whether the respondent was more or less interested in seeing the film, now that Leigh had been chosen. Only 12 percent said they were more interested since she had been cast, while 37 percent said they were still undecided, and 34 percent said they hadn't heard of her selection. Gallup staffers felt that this second version of the question was confusing and chose to report only the responses to the first form, which indicated that 35 percent were satisfied with the choice.[27] This number presented a public that was eager to see Selznick's choice on screen.

Selznick heard about the survey when it was nearly completed and sent a frantic telegram to Whitney on February 11. "I knew nothing of this poll. Did you? Aren't you pretty close to the Gallup people? Do you think you could telephone them and get an advance slant on how it is going and, if it looks as though it's going to be damaging perhaps do something to stop its publication?"[28] Whitney in turn telegraphed his lawyer Wharton and asked him to intercede.

We understand Gallup has recently conducted a poll regarding nation wide reaction to casting of Leigh as Scarlett. If this were unfavorable it could of course do great deal of harm and lend encouragement to further attacks from other sources. Could you tactfully, on the basis of our past friendship with him, discover what approximate result of the poll has been? I cannot believe he would publish something which would have a seriously damaging effect on an enormous investment if he were aware that such might be the case.[29]

Gallup offered to show Wharton the figures in person, and Wharton promised to phone Whitney from Gallup's office. Gallup himself later sent Wharton a personal note with the information he released to the newspapers.[30]

Though the survey took Selznick by surprise, he found much in it that pleased him. According to Gallup's research, fourteen million people had read all or part of the book, and 65 percent of those surveyed said there was an "above even" chance that they would see the film. This meant that *Gone with the Wind* had a potential audience of 56,500,000, what AIPO's press release called "one of the greatest potential film audiences in picture history." Respondents said they would still see the film if it were in two parts, and almost 60 percent wanted to see it in color. When asked who they thought was the most interesting character, about half said Scarlett, with Rhett Butler a close second. Besides the 35 percent of respondents who said they were satisfied with Selznick's decision to cast Vivien Leigh, 20 percent were undecided, and only 16 percent said they were dissatisfied. Despite the publicity surrounding Leigh's hiring, 29 percent of AIPO's respondents didn't know she had been chosen.[31] For them, the survey functioned as a news release that simultaneously announced and validated this information as important. Overall, then, the national survey offered empirical proof that U.S. filmgoers were eager to see the film and felt satisfied with Selznick's plans for the production so far.

"A Gross So Staggering"

Though Selznick had not commissioned the survey, Gallup's decision to conduct it was a major publicity coup for the producer. He wasted little time in putting these findings to work for him. Don Cahalan, Gallup's associate at AIPO, believed that some of Gallup's clients commissioned surveys "not just to fit the ostensible purpose, to find the facts, but to clobber somebody or to win some argument."[32] This appears to have been the case with Selznick. Over the next several years, while *Gone with the Wind* was in production and while he was negotiating the terms of its distribution with MGM, Selznick evoked Gallup's polls again and again as evidence that the public supported his work. AIPO's research influenced the ticket prices and screening times for the film's initial release, its advertising campaign in the trades, and decisions about marketing and pricing for later re-releases of the film. AIPO's survey provided scientific proof of what Selznick already believed, that *Gone with the Wind* would be a major cultural phenomenon. In contrast to his own subjective opinion, however, AIPO's numbers and percentages appeared impartial and objective and could therefore be used as "proof" of the value of his film and himself.

Gone with the Wind meshed well with the kinds of films for which Selznick had become famous. Critics and industry insiders alike admired his adaptations of great works of English literature such as *David Copperfield* (1935) and *A Tale of Two Cities* (1935) and American classics such as Mark Twain's *The Adventures of Tom Sawyer* (1938). The Museum of Modern Art presented *Tom Sawyer* as a model of filmmaking in an exhibit entitled "The Making of a Contemporary Film" in January and February of 1938. The exhibit cited the research that went into the film's sets and costumes and its process of script development as an exemplary instance of contemporary film production.[33] Thus *Gone with the Wind*, as the most recent contender for the title of "great American novel," fit well within the canon of his previous films.

The work ethic that produced these films had also become the stuff of legend. A 1939 article in *Life* magazine that appeared shortly before the premiere of *Gone with the Wind* described Selznick as "the most dictatorial and irregular executive in an industry where irregularity is commonplace." Selznick often acted as both producer and director of his films—along with writing the scripts, casting the actors, and advising on costumes and hairstyles. A classic perfectionist, he spoke bitterly of working until midnight without dinner, but didn't feel he could trust anyone else to do as well.[34] When colleagues urged him to delegate some of his responsibilities, he complained that he couldn't find people who were good enough.[35] The thousands of boxes of documents about the film that fill the Selznick archive in Austin, Texas, include hundreds of 10- and 20-page memos on every aspect of *Gone with the Wind*. At least ten writers are said to have worked on the script, and Selznick approved every line—besides writing a great deal of it himself. He also reviewed the film's lighting and use of color.[36] His heroic work was so legendary that it became the subject of a play in 2004, Ron Hutchinson's "Moonlight and Magnolias."[37]

Given his ferocious commitment to the project, it is not surprising that for Selznick the most notable fact to emerge from AIPO's survey was the size of the audience waiting to see it. As the *New York Times* noted, "For the first time, scientific calculation has been employed to justify Hollywood's customary optimism over success . . . a Gallup poll was conducted which indicated that 56,500,000 customers were practically standing in line with money in their hands."[38] Selznick saw immediately the economic value of these eager millions. "The figures of the Gallup poll will indicate a gross so staggering as to be beyond even our hopes . . . even if the Gallup poll is only 50% correct, an average admission scale of 60 cents would give a domestic theatre gross of about $17,000,000, of which 70% to 75% would come to the distributors. If the Gallup poll is correct, the figure is Thirty-four million dollars!!!!!!"[39]

Selznick found many ways to make use of this information. He suggested that Wharton print two or three hundred copies of a press release highlighting these figures and distribute them to MGM's exchange managers and others connected with the film's production.[40] Selznick also cited Gallup's figures when he discussed the production with the stockholders in his company.[41] Besides using Gallup to prove the film's box office potential, Selznick referred to his research to demonstrate that the public approved of his choice of Vivien Leigh. He considered asking Margaret Mitchell herself for an endorsement, but when she declined to let her name be used in any advertising, Selznick turned to Gallup instead.[42] When he wrote to Ruth Waterbury, the editor of *Photoplay*, to respond to criticisms of his choice, Selznick devoted nearly half the letter to discussing Gallup's finding that only 16 percent of the public was dissatisfied.[43] At one point he even composed a trade paper ad that highlighted Gallup findings, but it was apparently never published.[44] Just as AIPO's double-feature survey gave Goldwyn ammunition to support his opposton toward that practice, Gallup's *Gone with the Wind* survey gave Selznick concrete evidence of public support. Gallup himself understood the extent to which his research supported Selznick. Many years later he recalled: "The experts in Hollywood were saying . . . that it was a great pity that David Selznick had wasted so much time selecting the stars for the show that he had lost most of the ticket buyers. Our findings showed the exact opposite."[45] For both the pollster and the producer, these surveys validated new ideas that others in Hollywood had criticized.

The Dollar Plan and the Roadshow Plan

In order to reach this enormous potential audience, however, Selznick had to arrange distribution for the film, and this necessity brought him up against the hard reality of being an independent producer within the studio system. An effective distribution plan was vital to the film's economic success, he knew. "We are not going to . . . make the profits that we hope out of the picture unless it is handled as no picture that has ever been made with the possible exception of *Birth of a Nation*."[46] And there was one other aspect of the production he couldn't ignore: the public's firmly held belief that Clark Gable was the only person who could play Rhett Butler. Gallup did not even ask the public who they thought should play that role because America had already decided. To secure Gable, Selznick had to negotiate with the studio that held his contract—MGM, his former employer and father-in-law's company. Selznick's other pictures were being distributed by United Artists, so obtaining Gable required skilled negotiations, some of which Jock Whitney conducted. As Whitney explained when he announced the agreement in September 1938, "Mr. Selznick has felt all along that Clark Gable was the one and only 'people's choice' to play the part of Rhett Butler, and only through an arrangement with Metro-Goldwyn-Mayer, to whom Mr. Gable is exclusively under contract, would we have been able to make *Gone with the Wind* as the world wants to see it."[47] In addition to lending Gable, MGM's parent company Loew's advanced half the film's estimated negative cost, for a total of $1.25 million. Under the terms of their contract, if the film cost more than $2.5 million (which it did), Selznick was to assume all the overage but would not be paid back until after Loew's had recouped its investment. Loew's demanded 70 percent of the box office take from exhibitors, but guaranteed them 10 percent of the box office. Loew's was also to receive 15 percent of the gross receipts as a distribution fee.[48]

Though it seemed that Loew's held the upper hand, its agreement to distribute *Gone with the Wind* stood to help its filmmaking subsidiary MGM as well. MGM was the only one of the five integrated majors to weather the Depression without going into bankruptcy or reorganization, but by the time of the film's release it too was feeling the same pressures that were affecting the rest of Hollywood. In 1938, when RKO was still in bankruptcy, MGM had earned profits of $10 million on gross revenues of $122,700,000. Of that ten million, $7 million came from film rentals to theaters, so the potential profits on *Gone with the Wind* were hugely important. Though the company did well in 1938, its films in the first half of 1939, such as *Marie Antoinette*, *The Great Waltz*, and *Ice Follies of 1939*, did not perform well; in fact, *Fortune* magazine labeled them a "crop of turkeys." As the most profitable company in Hollywood, Loew's also received special scrutiny in the antitrust suit the Justice Department had filed in July 1938. William Rodgers, the studio's head of distribution, and Howard Dietz, its publicity manager, were especially sensitive to the demands of exhibitors who rented its films.[49] By providing theaters with the most sought-after release in Hollywood, Loew's hoped to reduce tensions with exhibitors. Loew's wish to avoid further antitrust complaints, along with Selznick's desire to burnish his reputation and squeeze the most profits from the production, played out in a drama over distribution.

To Selznick, *Gone with the Wind* promised to be one of the greatest films ever made, one that would make anything else MGM had produced pale in comparison. He expressed these feelings in a series of letters to MGM executives. *Gone with the Wind*, he wrote, "is not simply another picture, it is an enterprise that has no precedent in the theater. . . . I don't think that anyone has any conception . . . of the drawing power of this picture, and of the public anxiety to see it, and of how much the public will pay to see it."[50] "All precedent will have to go by the boards. It cannot be measured in terms of ordinary admission prices . . . it will have to be approached as an institution, as an industry in itself. . . . *The Wizard of Oz* and *Northwest Passage* will be fine films, but forgive me if I say that these are mere pygmies alongside of *Gone with the Wind*."[51]

How this unprecedented production should be exhibited to the public became the subject of debates that lasted nearly all of 1939. To Selznick, the film's special quality meant that it deserved to be exhibited in a roadshow format. "There is no film on the horizon that deserves it as much," he wrote.[52] To "roadshow" a film meant that it was screened at fixed times no more than twice a day, with reserved seats and at prices comparable to those of stage productions, at $1.65 or more. The practice began around 1913 with films such as *Birth of a Nation* and *Quo Vadis* and served to elevate the cultural status of films by putting them on par with theatrical productions. To roadshow a film came to be seen as an indicator of its importance and of the belief that it would earn top dollar from exhibitors. The format had almost disappeared by 1939 due to the need for economy during the Depression, but MGM had continued to distribute more films in this way than any other studio.[53]

On the other hand, MGM wanted to recoup its investment as quickly as possible and proposed to open the film nationally at ticket prices of fifty cents to one dollar and run continuous screenings with no reserved seats.[54] By opening the film simultaneously around the country at these prices, the studio would please both exhibitors and the public who were clamoring to see the film. Selznick's roadshow plan would bring in more money per ticket, but fewer theaters would be able to provide the luxurious accommodations that audiences would expect. And if the film played for a long time at these first-run theaters, people who could not afford such high ticket prices might become resentful. Better to open it widely and rake in the profits that would follow, MGM believed. MGM may also have favored this arrangement because, under the terms of its agreement with Selznick, it would not receive its distribution fee if it was decided to roadshow the film.[55] To Selznick, MGM's "dollar plan" was an insult to his film, himself, and the waiting public. *Gone with the Wind* and its eager audiences deserved the special treatment roadshows afforded, he felt. "With the countless millions of people that are going to see this picture, a plan *must* be devised that will insure people who pay their good money that they will at least see the picture sitting down, and under decent conditions." Reserved seats and an intermission were a must to ensure the audience's comfort, he argued, because "it would be a defiance of the laws of nature" to assume that people wouldn't have to go to the bathroom, and if seats weren't reserved, there would be a "mad scramble" for the seats of anyone who went to the lavatory. The film's quality and the intense public interest in it mandated a distribution plan that provided reserved seats and fixed running times, and audiences would pay more for the privilege of seeing it that way, he felt.[56]

What emerges again and again in the correspondence about *Gone with the Wind* is the sense that there was no precedent for the film, and that neither Selznick nor Loew's could predict how much business it would do at the box office, or how best to exhibit this one-of-a-kind film. And no one wanted to miss a dollar of profit. This uncertainty about how to distribute the film spurred Loew's and Selznick to study public opinion in their own ways. Loew's, according to *Fortune* magazine, was more attentive than other studios to exhibitors' needs. The company owned 125 theaters in the United States, 76 of which were in New York City. These theaters contributed only 15 percent to the company's theatrical gross, so it was critical to negotiate favorable agreements with independent exhibitors and theaters owned by the other majors.[57] Loew's conducted its own studies of public opinion, using channels of information that were readily available to it. Rodgers and Joe Vogel, who oversaw Loew's theaters outside of New York, conferred with individual exhibitors and heads of theater chains and asked what they thought the public would be willing to pay, what time the film should start, whether it needed an intermission, and whether they preferred reserved seats. While it was not unusual for a vertically integrated studio such as Loew's to talk often with its theater subsidiaries, the internal disagreements and simple lack of precedents for a film such as *Gone with the Wind*, combined with the antitrust investigations and national interest in polling, seems to have inspired the company to look more systematically at public opinion.[58]

Selznick, the film's very independent producer, did not have direct access to this channel of information, and so sought evidence from America's pollster. While MGM asked its sales force what to do, Selznick conducted his own previews in theaters in Santa Barbara and other cities, where he asked people for their views on these questions. And he continued to refer to Gallup's research. "Nobody on earth knows how *Gone with the Wind* should be handled; and nobody on earth can find out without experimentation. Even the hours at which the picture should be exhibited should . . . be determined by a nation-wide Gallup poll, so that in each city it could be learned what hours were most convenient for the public to see this extraordinarily long film."[59] Public opinion became a kind of evidence, and the way Loew's and Selznick evoked this evidence reflected each side's positions within the studio system.

Opinions on both sides vacillated. Some Loew's executives, such as Joe Vogel, the head of theater operations, and Rodgers, the head of distribution, began to agree with Selznick that they should charge $2.00 or $2.20 in major cities, with reserved seats.[60] Then for a time Selznick adopted Loew's view and argued that maybe it would be better to open the film quickly in many theaters and at a lower ticket price. "The whole thing comes down to a matter of reaching the greatest number of people in the fastest possible time," he said. If the top price were $1.50 instead of $2.20 or $2.50, maybe people would pay the extra fifty cents.[61] Hitler's invasion of Poland on September 1, 1939, triggered another round of reevaluations, and Selznick swung back to the roadshow idea, feeling that with markets in Europe so uncertain, he wanted to glean as much as possible from domestic ticket sales.[62] We can always lower prices, he pointed out, but we couldn't raise them later if they weren't high enough at the beginning.[63] He also felt that the price should reflect the quality of the theater and not be the same everywhere.[64]

The plan that Selznick and Loew's finally agreed upon represented a victory for both sides. After the film's premiere in Atlanta, it opened in a few key cities in a modified roadshow format. In New York, Los Angeles, and Boston the film screened in two theaters simultaneously. At one theater in each city, *Gone with the Wind* showed twice a day, at set times, with reserved seats and ticket prices ranging from 75 cents to $2.20—the format that Selznick desired. At the other theater, the film screened three times a day, continuously, with ticket prices from 75 cents to $1.10—the format Loew's preferred. Loew's referred to this policy as a "streamlined" roadshow because it combined fixed screening times and continuous showings. Lichtman took pains to note that wherever *Gone with the Wind* screened, tickets would cost no less than 75 cents during the day and $1.00 in the evening, and that prices would not go lower during its first run.[65]

MGM maintained this pattern of mixing two and three shows a day and unreserved and reserved seats for the duration of the film's first run. *Gone with the Wind* even played simultaneously in first-, second-, and third-run theaters in New York (fig. 8.1). Even when audiences could see the film in less expensive theaters, many chose to attend those offering reserved seats at higher prices—just as Selznick had predicted. In New York, while the film attracted over 900,000 viewers at the Capital, which ran three shows a day, half a million people paid higher prices to see the film at the Astor Theater, where it screened at fixed times twice a day. Even after the film began appearing in smaller neighborhood theaters around the city, *Gone with the Wind* could still command top prices at the Astor. By mixing formats, MGM met the needs of its theaters during the antitrust investigations in Washington and satisfied Selznick's demands at the same time, all while raking in 70 percent of each box office's take.[66]

Under terms of their agreement, MGM also handled all the advertising for the film. Selznick had definite ideas about how to publicize *Gone with the*

FIGURE 8.1 Gallup's research influenced the exhibition and promotion of David O. Selznick's *Gone with the Wind*. In New York the film played at two theaters simultaneously—at the Astor (shown here), with higher ticket prices and fixed screening times, and at the Capitol, with lower prices and continuous screenings.   *(Courtesy Corbis)*

Wind, but he did not have final authority in the matter. To gain leverage, he cited Gallup. Selznick favored a restrained approach, one that built on the public's knowledge of the book. Ads for the film should mirror the cover of the book that millions had read, he felt. This meant that "we should establish as a sort of trade mark color and type face for all the advertising and posters, what was used on the jacket of the book, using the same combination of colors and the same lettering. This has after all appeared on almost two million copies of the book and has been seen by perhaps fourteen million people (Gallup figures) or more and we might as well capitalize on it by using it throughout our campaign, practically without deviation." Trade paper ads for both the film's initial run and later releases share the same style of bold, Gothic lettering as the book jacket (fig. 8.2). Ads also explained the two exhibition formats for the film and made sure that audiences understood the times *Gone with the Wind* would screen at different theaters. "All that is

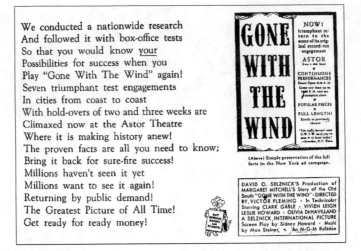

We conducted a nationwide research
And followed it with box-office tests
So that you would know your
Possibilities for success when you
Play "Gone With The Wind" again!
Seven triumphant test engagements
In cities from coast to coast
With hold-overs of two and three weeks are
Climaxed now at the Astor Theatre
Where it is making history anew!
The proven facts are all you need to know;
Bring it back for sure-fire success!
Millions haven't seen it yet
Millions want to see it again!
Returning by public demand!
The Greatest Picture of All Time!
Get ready for ready money!

FIGURE 8.2 Gallup found that the film version of *Gone with the Wind* had a potential audience of 56 million people, many of whom had read the book. On the basis of his research, Selznick decided to mimic the visual style of the book's jacket cover in ads for the film's initial and later releases. *(Courtesy Variety, April 15, 1942, 4)*

necessary is dignified announcement copy, and to be sure that everybody in town knows that it is playing," Selznick argued. "The picture, God knows, is already sold and it would be simply a matter of letting people know that it is playing."[67] Since he and Loew's hoped to run the picture for many months at advanced prices, Selznick also felt that it was essential to maintain curiosity about the film. Ads for its initial release did not include any pictures, to avoid spoiling the public's first look at its characters and scenes. As *Film Daily* put it, "It is Metro's assumption that *Gone with the Wind* has been pre-sold to the public. (The Gallup poll indicated an audience expectancy of 56,000,000.) Accordingly, the Dietz campaign is essentially factual, frank, and definite. Claims are carefully avoided; rather there is what Dietz terms 'a tremendous attempt to be truthful.'"[68] Gallup's figures served as a rationale for the advertising campaign as well as the exhibition plans for the film.

Gone with the Wind set many records on its first run. It was one of the longest films ever made and double the usual length of a film, though only a little longer than the double bills Goldwyn had railed against. Its minimum ticket price of 75 cents was twice the usual price of admission, and the evening price of $1.10 set a new standard for second- and third-run theaters. The film took in an average of $1 million a week in the first three months of screenings and earned back its cost in eight weeks. Its domestic gross in first run topped $17 million, the highest in U.S. history to that time. The figure met Selznick's estimate of what the gross would be if Gallup were half right but, as we shall see, this was only the film's first run. *Gone with the Wind* saw similar business when it opened in London on April 18, 1940. The film enjoyed the first triple opening in English film history, at the Empire, Ritz, and Palace Theatres simultaneously, and nearly doubled the previous record for one week's gross at any theater in England. (Interestingly, British audiences gave more praise to Hattie McDaniel's performance as Mammy than they did to British-born Vivien Leigh.) In mid-1940 the British government relaxed restrictions on currency imports for U.S. film studios, allowing Loew's and Selznick to export half the film's profits. For Loew's, the success of *Gone with the Wind* offset nearly all the company's losses in foreign markets for 1940.[69]

"While the Getting Was Good"

MGM withdrew *Gone with the Wind* from theaters in July 1940 with the intention of re-releasing it again in January 1941. In March 1940, three months after the film first opened, Selznick and MGM asked Gallup to assess how many people had yet to see it. An AIPO survey during the last week of March 1940 found that 39 percent of those surveyed said they intended to see the film, indicating that it still had a large potential audience.[70] Gallup estimated the number of people who had seen the film, how many had seen it more than once, and how many planned to see it again or for the first time. To gather this information, Gallup used AIPO's regular weekly surveys, since ARI was under an exclusive contract with RKO. MGM combined the information from this report with its own discussions with exhibitors and determined that the film did more repeat business at lower-price theaters.[71] This suggested that a key selling point for the film in the future would be a lower ticket price.

For the rest of the year, Loew's and Selznick discussed again what release strategy to follow.[72] Just as the industry had marveled at the potential audience for the film's first release, and cited Gallup's numbers as evidence, trade papers highlighted his numbers when speculating at the number of people who would come to see the film again, or see it first for the first time because prices were reduced.[73] Selznick wanted his distributor to carry out another Gallup poll, but MGM felt confident in its own long-standing sources within the industry and chose instead to converse informally with theater owners and hold test engagements to help set admission prices. MGM felt that the information it gathered in this way was very useful, "even though the poll method may be defective according to Gallup's standards."[74]

MGM launched the film for a second time with another Atlanta premiere. Ads appearing in trade papers announcing the film's reissue referred to Gallup's original findings to remind theater owners that millions of Americans planned to see the film. An announcement in *Film Daily* told theater owners that this was their chance to book "the picture that Gallup Poll figures reveal 55 million Americans want to see. That includes *your* patrons."[75] Exhibition arrangements for the film largely followed the plan MGM had sketched before the film's initial opening: screenings that began as early as 9:15 a.m. and ran continuously until after midnight; some reserved seats but mainly general admission; and reduced prices. During the film's first run MGM had announced widely that ticket prices would not be cut until at least 1941. By reissuing the film nationwide in January 1941, the studio lived up to its promise but was able to take advantage of the demand for reduced prices. MGM's plan succeeded, as the film took in more than $7 million on its re-release, or about 40 percent of its original box office take. Gallup's estimate that 39 percent of Americans intended to see it was not far off, as about 30 percent of the people who saw it the first time came back again.[76]

In the summer of 1940, as *Gone with the Wind* neared the end of its initial run, Jock Whitney decided to liquidate his investment in Selznick International. Faced with the unstable economic and political situation caused by the war in Europe, Whitney did not want to tie up his capital, and he and Selznick's other investors also wanted to cash in the large profits they had reaped from *Gone with the Wind*. As *Variety* put it more bluntly, Whitney wanted "to get out while the getting was good."[77] The early Technicolor films that Whitney had financed had not always earned back their costs, but the success of *Gone with the Wind* more than made up for any losses. Whitney and the film's other investors received their entire investment, plus interest of 24 percent, and shared an additional dividend of $1 million in cash and Technicolor stock. Selznick worked to put a positive light on what became in effect the end of his company by announcing that the liquidation would enable him to launch his own production firm independently of outside investors. Though he formed a new company, David O. Selznick Productions, in August 1940, for the next two years he was preoccupied with dissolving his business and dividing its assets. Thus the profits to be brought in with the reissue of *Gone with the Wind* became crucial to his investors and to his own future.[78]

In his biography of the producer, David Thomson characterizes the period from mid-1940 to the end of 1942 as one of anxiety and uncertainty. Selznick, exhausted after the relentless pace of production on *Gone with the Wind*, had to reorganize his staff and locate new sources of funding in an increasingly uncertain market. Like other studio heads, he hoped to go to Washington to help with the war effort, and wanted to keep his plans flexible.[79] For much of 1941, trade papers buzzed with news of possible projects: Selznick hired Somerset Maugham to develop a script; he was about to produce *Life with Father*. In October 1941, Selznick paid $1.2 million for a quarter share in United Artists and announced that he would produce films based on the popular play *Claudia*, Charlotte Bronte's *Jane Eyre*, and A.J. Cronin's current bestseller *Keys of the Kingdom*. Two months later he secured $6 million in financing from UA and several banks.[80] Though he hired a production designer for *Jane Eyre* and *Keys* in January 1942, and announced in February that *Keys* would mark his return to the screen, he in fact sold all three properties to Twentieth Century-Fox in November 1942 and did not produce another film until *Since You Went Away* in 1944.[81]

These changes in Selznick's business position affected his attitude toward the third playoff of *Gone with the Wind* that began in February 1942. Since his company was being dissolved, and all expenditures had to be approved by the liquidators, Selznick had to persuade MGM to pay the cost of any surveys. And MGM was reluctant to do so because the studio placed more confidence in its own tried-and-true methods of talking with exhibitors and holding test engagements. Selznick wrote William Rodgers that "whether we have a potential audience of five million or ten million or twenty million is a matter of the merest guesswork without any accurate scientific research." Selznick wanted a national release for the third playoff, with simultaneous openings in 150–300 cities supported by an advertising campaign in national magazines such as the *Saturday Evening Post* and *Life*. "It is my personal opinion," he wrote, "that both Metro and Selznick International must be prepared to spend money to put the picture over again this year in a very big way. Whatever difference advertising and publicity makes to the usual picture, and regardless of whether *Wind* needed publicity and advertising on its initial releases, there can be little question that we have got to take important and carefully thought out steps to revivify the film for the third playoff." Rodgers, however, resisted the idea, arguing that it was better to gather information through Loew's tried-and-true methods, but he eventually agreed to fund a survey if the cost didn't exceed $5,000. "Frankly I am not too enthused about the Gallup poll as it affects the third playoff on *GWTW*. It is my belief that a better line on the possibilities will be had by the actual engagement of the production, and we plan to have several tests sometime during February."[82]

One can sense Selznick's frustration at the seeming lack of commitment within MGM to promote the third playoff as strongly as he wanted. In subsequent memos he argued that the studio should consult with him before choosing these test cities, and visit each one to examine the ad campaigns that exhibitors prepared. Even after Loew's agreed to pay for a survey, Selznick wasn't sure he trusted Gallup either. His statements about the survey demonstrated how much Selznick had learned from Gallup. "I particularly request that I be consulted on the exact questions after they have been drafted, and before they have been propounded to the public. I should also appreciate being consulted on just how the poll is to be conducted, in order to insure our having a true cross-section from a potential audience, rather than from a public which could not be expected to be an audience."[83] Selznick wanted to manage the film, the advertising, and the poll itself in order to collect evidence to prove its continuing value. "We have no way of knowing whether 'WIND' will pick up just a few dollars on its third playoff, or a few millions—but certainly the result is going to be entirely dependent upon the approach of the Metro sales and publicity departments. . . . I feel confident that we have a sympathetic audience in the Metro executives, but we can't expect them to have the same interest in the matter that we have unless we keep goosing them."[84]

Loew's and Selznick discussed how to use these different sources of information, polls, and test engagements for several weeks in January 1942. Gallup could not conduct the survey Selznick wanted without getting permission from RKO, with whom ARI had an exclusive contract, and RKO was suffering from the internal struggles that led to Schaefer's ouster later that year.[85] In the meantime, Loew's was eager to get started with its test engagements. Eventually, Selznick and his distributor developed a neat solution that met several goals: they would hold test engagements in six to eight cities and conduct polls in two of them to gather more detailed information from specific demographic groups.[86] They would chose one city (eventually Buffalo) to reflect those where the defense economy was strong and one (Milwaukee) where it had less impact, to study a range of economic conditions. In addition, Gallup proposed that this close-up study be supplemented with a national survey that looked at which groups in the population as a whole had yet to see the film. By conducting polls in cities where Loew's was holding its test engagements, Gallup could also determine whether the company's advertising campaigns for the film's re-release were effective in attracting audiences.

The idea of using Gallup to test the effectiveness of Loew's advertising campaign originated with Selznick, and the producer's sense of urgency increased when he saw the ads his distributor had compiled. They featured well-known scenes from the film, such as the one in which Mammy laced up Scarlett's corset, and the scene of Rhett and Scarlett standing by the fence after they fled Atlanta, accompanied by captions with fictitious taglines. The scene with the corset, for example, showed Scarlett telling Mammy that she had to look beautiful for the barbecue because Rhett Butler would be there. In fact, she meets Rhett for the first time at the picnic and does not know he will be there when she's getting dressed. In the ad showing Scarlett and Rhett embracing near the fence, Scarlett tells Rhett, "Now we have only each other!"—a sentiment she did not express in the film (fig. 8.3). Selznick strongly objected to the approach taken in these ads and drew on the philosophy that had served him well in adapting classic works of literature to the screen.[87] "I have discovered that the public will forgive you for any number of omissions—particularly of subordinate material which is not directly connected with the main plot—but it won't forgive you for deliberate changes." It is acceptable to move dialogue from one part of the book to another, or to condense character, if "the audience is given the illusion of seeing and hearing that with which they are already familiar," but MGM's additions, he felt, would offend a public who knew the film and novel well.[88] Selznick hoped that Gallup's survey would prove these ads didn't work.

ARI carried out the *Gone with the Wind* survey during the last week of January 1942. As in earlier studies, Gallup used a split ballot in which the wording of some questions varied. One form of the survey included a three-part question that asked: "The movie *Gone with the Wind* may soon be shown here again. Do you intend to see it? Have you already seen it? If so, how many times?" In response, 46 percent said they had not yet seen it; of those who had, 44 percent had seen it once, 6 percent twice, and 1 percent three times. When asked if they intended to see the film on its third release, 25 percent said they did, while 74 percent did not. Thus this form of the survey yielded the fact that 25 percent of the people questioned planned to see the film again, a not insubstantial number.

However, the other form of the survey yielded more useful information. This format presented people with a card containing a choice of statements and asked which one best represented their point of view. Options included: "I have not seen *Gone with the Wind* and I do not want to see it. I have not yet seen *Gone with the Wind* but I would like to see it. I have already seen *Gone with the Wind* and I do not want to see it again. I have already seen *Gone with the Wind* and I would like to see it again." This form of the question revealed the same 25 percent who had not seen the film but wanted to, but also brought to light the existence of another 20 percent who had seen the film once and wanted to see it again. The wording of the first format might have given people the idea that they should only say they were going to see the film if they hadn't seen it already, and would not necessarily pick up anyone who intended to see it again. The second format, however, uncovered this hidden group of repeat viewers, an audience that would greatly increase the film's box office potential.[89]

After evaluating the data from both the local and national surveys, Gallup told Selznick and Loew's that 40,254,000 people had seen the film once,

FIGURE 8.3 Selznick objected to the ads MGM developed for the second anniversary release of *Gone with the Wind* because they contained dialogue that didn't occur in the film. The producer drew on his own experiences adapting works of literature for the screen and on Gallup's studies of the film's audience to support his case.

(Courtesy David O. Selznick Collection, Harry Ransom Humanities Research Center, The University of Texas at Austin)

5,032,000 twice, and 457,000 three times or more. AIPO estimated the potential audience for the film's third release to be about 12.5 million, but cautioned that the final number depended on the number of theaters, playing times, price structure, and exploitation campaigns—all issues that Selznick had raised repeatedly in his correspondence with Loew's, and that Gallup probably included at his behest. Most importantly, Gallup noted that only 34 percent of the potential audience for the third release had seen the film before, which meant that most had not, and the ones who had not were young and from lower-income groups. Those who had already seen *Gone with the Wind*, Gallup said, were for the most part over 30 and were infrequent filmgoers, in contrast to the audience for most Hollywood films, which consisted of frequent filmgoers who were under 30. This meant that the groups whom Gallup had identified as crucial in its correspondence with RKO, the young and the poor, were waiting for the right opportunity to see the picture.[90]

To reach this eager and untapped audience, Gallup offered several specific advertising strategies. Most people who had not seen the film were waiting for ticket prices to go lower and did not realize that they would on this release, so to reach them Gallup recommended using a bargain appeal, either by stressing that prices had been lowered or emphasizing how much film they got for their money. For those who had already seen the film and planned to see it again, Gallup urged Loew's to use a "repeat rationale," with ads that stressed how many other people had seen the film more than once, or that featured celebrities talking about their enjoyment of it. This audience might also respond to quizzes that tested their knowledge of plot points and characters, he noted. Seventy-one percent of the people who said they planned to see the film on this release rarely went to the cinema, so Gallup argued that they would require special kinds of advertising. More than half of the 12,655 people AIPO interviewed thought the film would be cut, and most did not want it to be shortened. Ads should stress that it would screen uncut, he urged. No one needed to be convinced of the film's quality, but Gallup also argued that the historical nature of its subject might deter younger viewers. Ads should stress the more human aspects of the story. The report concluded with a list of best remembered scenes, beginning with the burning of Atlanta, followed by the overhead shot of the wounded soldiers at the depot and Scarlett falling down the staircase. Rhett's famous "I don't give a damn" remark came in fourth.[91]

Ads publicizing the film's third release reflected Gallup's suggestions. Most announced that the film would screen "Full Length! Uncut! Exactly as previously shown." Some ads directly appealed to the two groups Gallup found would most be interested in the film—repeat viewers and first-time patrons. "If you haven't seen it—now's your chance! If you have seen it—you'll want to see it again!" Others, particularly ads that ran in New York, used the testimonial strategy Gallup had advocated and featured pictures of stars on one side of the ad with quotes from them down the center praising the film. In one, Spencer Tracy enthused, "You have to see it at least three times to appreciate all of its greatness," while Hedy Lamarr gushed, "I have seen it four times and enjoyed it more each time." Other ads used the basic design from the film's first release, the one mimicking the cover of the book, but played up the fact that this time the film was showing continuously, from morning until night, at reduced prices.[92]

Both Selznick and Loew's explicitly credited Gallup's research for inspiring these testimonial ads and for prompting a change away from the "circus type" ads that Selznick had opposed, the ones featuring deceptive taglines from the film. Gallup's research had indeed supported Selznick's opposition to these ads, and Selznick used the data successfully to persuade Loew's to change its approach.[93] Loew's also acknowledged that, as a result of Gallup's work, they enlarged the part of the ad that mentioned the lowered ticket price. "We are paying attention to Gallup," Lowell Calvert wrote to Selznick.[94] Thanks to the empirical evidence Gallup provided, Selznick felt vindicated. "We advertised in accordance with what I have been screaming about all along, ever since the Gallup report, and the ads were strictly in accordance with Gallup's suggestions—no billing, no sales copy, nothing but the prices featured as large as the title and the only other strong selling line dealing with the fact that the picture was full length and unchanged."[95]

"Like Something Out of Ripley"

In March 1942, shortly before the film's third release, MGM prepared an oversize ad for the Hollywood trade papers that embodies the power that Gallup had come to represent for Selznick. Under a headline in all capital letters that read, "GONE WITH THE WIND TO REOPEN AT ASTOR, N.Y.; MILLIONS HAVE SEEN EPIC FILM TWICE OR MORE," the text read:

> It sounds fantastic . . . like something out of Ripley . . . but the fact is— 5,489,999 persons have seen David O. Selznick's production of Margaret Mitchell's GWTW—twice or more . . . That figure comes from the Audience Research Institute . . . And it's a figure that's growing and will continue to grow as this greatest movie money-maker of all time makes its third appearance on the nation's screens . . . In all, more than fifty-one million patrons have seen the production since its memorable world premiere in Atlanta . . . 5,032,000 have seen it twice or more and 457,000 have seen it three times or more.[96]

Trade papers including the *Hollywood Reporter* and *Motion Picture Herald* used these numbers as a starting point for many discussions of the film after its release.[97]

In April 1942 these same papers announced that ARI no longer worked under exclusive contract to RKO and that the organization had signed a contract with Selznick.[98] In May, Selznick wrote to support ARI when it was being considered for a survey to be conducted by the Motion Picture Producers Association (MPPA) as part of a long-range program of public relations research. A telegram composed by "100 men and women of the Audience Research Institute" (but more likely written by David Ogilvy) appealed to Selznick for assistance. "It is probably important that the research organization which undertakes this program should command the respect and credence not only of industry leaders but also of government and press. As our most distinguished salesman can you advise us [h]ow best to proceed?"[99] Selznick obliged: "You may be sure I will swing into action." "On the face of it it seems ridiculous to me that any organization but your own would even be considered."[100]

His passionate, and lengthy, defense of ARI serves as a testament to the extent to which Gallup influenced the promotion and exhibition of his most famous film, and his sense of himself as an independent producer within the studio system. Selznick begins by questioning Hollywood's engrained assumption that it doesn't need any outside experts to find out what audiences like.

> I have just learned that [the] Producers Association is planning a long range program of public relations research, and that toward this end it is contemplating establishing its own research and polling department. I should like to urge just as forcibly as I can my opinion that an attempt by the motion picture business to enter the research field is the equivalent of an attempt by an established research organization to enter motion picture production and distribution; and I cannot understand why the picture business should be egotistical enough to think that it overnight can acquire an expertness in this field that it has taken existing organizations years of study and a very large investment . . . to acquire. . . .

Selznick draws on his own experiences with research to attest to the value of outside experts, and to argue that only an independent company can provide trustworthy information.

> I have experimented with amateurs, with individuals who had had some sort of experience either on their own or as members of the staff of the larger research groups, and with the research groups themselves, and I can tell you from personal knowledge that there is simply no comparison in the result to be obtained by individuals or newcomers as against that which can be secured by an established organization. And out of this experience I can tell you that I would discount 90 percent of any result obtained by any research department started by the industry itself, whereas I should regard as pretty close to being completely accurate the determinations arrived at by one of the few larger groups in this field, and more particularly by Gallup, who is so clearly head and shoulders over anyone else in his equipment to undertake this work that I cannot understand how an intelligent group of men could even consider anyone else. . . .

Speaking directly about Gallup's role in the distribution and marketing of *Gone with the Wind,* he tells the association that

The results of Gallup's work on "GWTW" at the time of its first release were so accurate as to be almost uncanny. Furthermore, his work in connection with the third release was equally thorough, went way beyond what we were trying to find out, showed us exactly what was wrong with our advertising, and estimated results with a remarkable degree of accuracy, going as far as to tell us individual cities in which the results would be different from those in the country as a whole, predictions which were thoroughly borne out by the final results.

Selznick also attests to Gallup's personal integrity and the fact that he does not rely on Hollywood for his living. It is this independence, Selznick argues, that confirms the integrity of his research.

Gallup has a huge organization, with years of experience in the field of public relations. . . . He is personally a man of complete integrity, and of intellectual stature, and can be depended upon to give the industry thoroughly honest reporting, without fear or favor, without prejudice, without catering to any individuals. He does not need the industry, and his livelihood is not dependent upon doing a job that might please the industry, or any individuals in it, without giving the industry what it wants to know. He has on his staff men whom the industry could not possibl[y] duplicate, in any organization of its own. His audience research institute already has an experience of years in studying motion picture problems; and it is characteristic of his thoroughness that he spent years in studying the motion picture field before he would even accept a commission to do a job for any of its component parts. It is significant that the industry is willing to rush in where Gallup, for all his experience, feared to tread, until he had completely analyzed and decided upon proper approaches.

Finally, Selznick reminds the association of Gallup's reputation in American life outside of Hollywood, and argues that his political polls gave him unparalleled access to public opinion. By retaining his services, the industry could gain the respect Gallup already enjoys.

Gallup is in daily touch with the country's thinking on every problem of importance; and it is quite obviously superficial thinking, to say the least, to assume that the industry's public relations problems can be studied without relation to the country's thinking on more major problems. . . .

I should think the industry would want an organization whose results would be accepted by the press, by people in the industry, and by such people outside the industry as we might wish to approach as a result of the findings. I ask you to consider, for instance, the difference in presenting to government officials findings of our own research department, as against the findings of Dr. Gallup. Which findings do you think would be more likely to be regarded seriously, to be treated importantly? Which findings do you think would be regarded as being more accurate, more honest, more unprejudiced?

We are entering crucial times. If the industry is to survive, it must consider its problems in adult fashion, and not with the top-of-the-head thinking that has unfortunately characterized so many of its activities in the past, and which has led to so many of its mistakes. Perhaps the industry is still in its infancy, but I like to believe that at least its leaders are adult, and are approaching the stage where they will treat with problems in the same manner as important individuals and groups in other fields.[101]

Selznick's long and heartfelt testimonial to Gallup's strengths and importance illustrate how, in his view, empirical research had completely supplanted the industry's long-cherished idea that it could rely on itself to understand the public. The MPPA did indeed hire ARI, and Ogilvy wrote Selznick to request that he send the staff a big photo of himself, "so that we can remember the source of this generosity."[102] And the final results from Gone with the Wind's releases at this time bore Gallup out. By July 1943, in its fourth year of release, the film had grossed $31 million and had attracted 59,979,000 people to see it—numbers very close to Gallup's original prediction that 55 million people would come to see it, and that the film might gross as much as $34 million.

Selznick's uses of Gallup's surveys in his negotiations with MGM illustrate how audience research became embroiled within the power structure of Hollywood during the studio era. Compared with many other independent producers, Selznick had stronger personal and professional connections and financial support from one of the wealthiest men in America, yet even he struggled to maintain his vision of what a film should be in the face of the studio system. For Selznick, Gallup's research provided scientific evidence that he could use in his struggle to maintain his autonomy. Selznick put Gallup's cultural capital to work for him, and the strength of Gallup's poll enhanced his own power. Having proven to himself the value of these studies, Selznick urged other independent producers to employ his services as well, most notably, Walt Disney. Gallup's work at the Disney studio challenged him to find ways to apply empirical research to the ineffable pleasures of cartoons.

9

Gallup Meets Goofy

Audience Research at the Walt Disney Studio

Using scientific techniques to study animation might seem to be taking audience research to an extreme. After all, what could be more natural than the pleasure we take in cartoons? Whether we're enjoying the inventive play of abstract shapes in Robert Breer's films, or the never-ending struggle between Road Runner and Wile E. Coyote, cartoons seem to exist in a world beyond reason and logic. Yet in the 1940s one cartoon producer saw the value of audience research. Walt Disney became aware of Gallup's work, first through his distributor RKO, and then through his association with David Selznick in the Society of Independent Motion Picture Producers (SIMPP). ARI's initial studies in 1940 and 1941 served RKO's interests more than Disney's, but it wasn't long before the animation producer began to use ARI for his own purposes. After World War II, when Disney began to expand beyond animation into other forms of entertainment, he turned to Gallup for assistance. ARI's techniques played a role in *every* film Disney produced in the late 1940s and early 1950s. At first Gallup followed the same procedures that he had used with other studios, but later Disney adapted ARI's methods to suit its own particular needs. Even after Gallup left Hollywood in the late 1940s, ARI's research had become such an integral part of Disney's work that Bob Thomas included it along with other production departments in his 1958 book about the studio.[1]

Disney's changing relationship to ARI reflects the dramatic shifts in its position in Hollywood during this period. At the beginning of the decade, the

Disney studio struggled to meet RKO's expectations while trying to fulfill its own ambitious goals. Disney wanted to explore new artistic ideas, but RKO expected it to produce a steady stream of shorts and features that could easily be sold to theaters. Disney's first experience with ARI came when RKO asked Gallup to find out how the public felt about Disney's experiments in film form. During World War II and in the postwar period, Disney wanted to diversify beyond animation. The studio adopted a more corporate form of organization that emphasized quick and efficient production and began to branch out into live-action films and eventually theme parks. Walt Disney began to rethink the place and even the value of animation in this new world. During this period Disney hired ARI of its own volition to assist in evaluating films it had in production. ARI developed procedures that Disney used to track reactions to its projects among animators and representatives of the general public. Among all of Gallup's clients, Disney found the most creative uses for audience research, adapting ARI's methods to meet its own goals.

Shifting Power: Disney and RKO

Like other animation producers, Disney financed and distributed its films through a major studio. ARI conducted its first research on Disney films in 1941 at RKO's request, when its client questioned the new directions Disney was taking with *Fantasia*. RKO needed Disney financially, and Disney was not producing as many profits as its distributor expected. The subject and purpose of these initial surveys reflect RKO's concerns much more than Disney's.

During the 1930s and '40s, most major studios included cartoons, along with newsreels and features, as part of the packages they sold to exhibitors. Each major served as exclusive distributor for one cartoon producer's output, and these films both enhanced the distributor's prestige with exhibitors and gained attention for its live-action releases.[2] As animation's most visible practitioner, Disney possessed enormous cachet within the film industry and within American culture as a whole. The studio won every Academy Award given for cartoon shorts from 1932 to 1939; in fact, the category seems to have been invented to honor its films.[3] Disney's characters became an integral part of American popular culture: images of Mickey Mouse, Donald Duck, and the Three Little Pigs saturated the country in comic strips, storybooks, watches, and toys. The company that distributed Disney's cartoons gained immediate respect. When RKO signed its distribution agreement with Disney in March 1936, *Variety* heralded the news by saying, "Radio Captures Disney."[4]

In addition to enhancing its status among its peers, RKO hoped to capital-ize on Disney's success to resolve its own financial difficulties. During the period when it was in bankruptcy, RKO made one or two picture deals with independent producers in order to minimize its fixed costs yet still guaran-tee a supply of films to theaters. Its spring 1936 contract with Disney rep-resented one of these agreements. At the time of its first negotiations with America's leading cartoon producer, RKO had suffered a series of flops and two of its major stars, Fred Astaire and Katharine Hepburn, were arguing over contracts and script approval. An alliance with Disney promised to en-hance RKO's prestige within the industry and give it access to popular and profitable films.[5] Disney, for its part, looked to RKO for financial assistance and opportunities for expansion it had not found with its previous distribu-tor, United Artists. RKO offered Disney an advance against negative costs, which would reduce the amount of operating capital it needed, and access to the major's chain of first-run theaters, which Douglas Gomery believes was crucial in strengthening Disney's position in the industry.[6]

Though the initial agreement between the companies promised to benefit both of them, the release of Snow White and the Seven Dwarfs in December 1937 shifted the balance of power toward Disney. Snow White became the highest-grossing film in American history; only Gone with the Wind, released two years later, would supplant it. More than 800,000 people saw the film at Radio City Music Hall, RKO's flagship theater, where it grossed half its production costs in five weeks.[7] According to Variety, Snow White "gobbled up everything in sight," and RKO's share of the profits brought the company twice as much net return as it had earned on any previous picture.[8] Internal memos state bluntly that Snow White's revenues "saved" RKO.[9]

Disney's stature within the cartoon industry, and the studio's economic importance to RKO, gave the cartoon producer extraordinary clout with its distributor. RKO received only 25 percent of the gross revenues from Snow White, compared with the 35 percent it demanded from other independents, and accepted the same profit split for foreign revenues as for domestic in-come, rather than varying the fee from country to country, as was customary. For Snow White, RKO prevailed upon theater owners to show the film as a single bill, the first for a cartoon, and to charge higher admission prices, in some cases even for children's tickets. What is most astonishing from today's perspective is that Disney kept all the merchandising revenue from the film; RKO never received a dime.[10]

Disney's distribution contract with RKO did not expire until spring 1939, but the two companies began discussing terms for renewal a year in advance, at the height of Snow White's success. Trade papers linked the two events, marveling over Snow White's grosses while speculating about the progress of the negotiations.[11] RKO, for its part, had no major box office hits in 1938 and was losing money. In October, George Schaeffer became president of the studio and inaugurated a drive for "quality" films.[12] Disney's box office success and cultural status placed its projects in this category. Disney and Schaeffer signed their renewal agreement at RKO's annual sales meeting in June 1939, where it was a highlight of the conference and earned headlines in the trades.[13] The contract represents the zenith of Disney's power in relation to its distributor. Beginning in 1940, control in the relationship began to shift toward RKO.

During these contract negotiations, Disney announced an ambitious expansion program. Inspired by Snow White's success, the studio decided to put four more features into production and to increase its release schedule from one feature every two years to between two and four features each year. Disney had tripled its staff to finish Snow White and estimated that it would need several hundred more employees to produce these additional films. To provide enough space for all this activity, Disney also announced that it planned to build a new studio in Burbank, at a cost of nearly $2 million.[14] Snow White's profits and Disney's merchandising revenues paid many of these expenses, but Disney still needed the financing and distribution RKO provided to ensure its cash flow. Disney's plans for expansion represented an assertion of its newfound power, but the company needed RKO to achieve its goals.

Though it relied on RKO, Disney did not always meet the terms set out in their distribution contract. In an interview from this period Walt Disney admitted that, "We never work on a schedule. In that way if we don't like something we can keep working on it until we do like it."[15] The perfectionism that had brought him so much critical and popular acclaim conflicted with the demands of a fixed release schedule. By May 1940 the studio had completed only half the number of shorts specified in its contract for that season.[16] When RKO's income from short films that year fell $300,000, executives blamed the drop on Disney.[17] Disney's feature films also fell behind schedule. The studio had four features in production but couldn't guarantee when one of them would be finished.

Disney's inability to meet its distributor's deadlines became apparent during production on Pinocchio. During their negotiations in 1938, Walt Disney had predicted the film would be finished within a year, but it was not completed until early 1940.[18] RKO, in the meantime, was counting on Pinocchio to provide the same hefty profits as Snow White.[19] RKO and Disney marketed the feature as the equal of Snow White: sixty-three national magazines carried articles about the film; Lux Radio Theater dramatized its story on Christmas Day; seventy-two department stores featured Pinocchio displays;

and Disney licensed nearly eighty manufacturers to produce merchandise. RKO also demanded the same percentage split and higher ticket prices it had commanded with Disney's first feature.[20]

Although many reviewers felt that Pinocchio surpassed Snow White in terms of artistic achievement, Disney's second feature failed to match the box office gross of its first.[21] Disney lost money on the film in the first year of its release, mainly because its European markets had closed after Hitler's invasion of Poland. Disney had earned $2 million in Europe from Snow White, but took out only one-tenth that amount for Pinocchio. These troubled conditions overseas were partly responsible for the studio's posting a loss of $1.2 million in 1940.[22] The film was a major disappointment for RKO as well, though Pinocchio still accounted for half the increase in its billings for features that year.[23]

The 1940 antitrust decree also changed Disney's relationship with RKO. A little-discussed aspect of the decree is that it ended the "forced" selling of short films. Distributors could no longer package cartoons, newsreels, and live action comedies with feature films but had to sell them separately.[24] This meant that a reliable distribution network was even more vital to Disney, and thus its commitment to RKO became more attractive. RKO heavily promoted Disney's films among its short subject bookers and staged special events to publicize them. RKO announced that it would continue to sell Disney films individually, and not package them in the blocks of five that the consent decree allowed.[25] Thus, changing financial circumstances inside each studio, and legal and economic conditions outside, combined to shift power away from Disney to RKO in 1940–41.

Pinocchio's box office failure and Disney's own push to enlarge its operations exacerbated financial difficulties within the cartoon company. When its contract with RKO came up for renewal in September 1940, Disney abandoned the idea of negotiating the release of one feature at a time and gave RKO the rights to both of the features it was planning to produce after Fantasia—Bambi and The Reluctant Dragon. RKO still only received a 25 percent distribution fee, however.[26] Despite these plans, Fantasia brought matters to a head. The most unusual film the studio had yet produced, Fantasia's very originality made it difficult to market within the industry. The challenge of promoting and distributing this unique work led RKO to call in ARI.

At the Disposal of Mr. Disney

Fantasia is still considered one of the most innovative films Disney has ever produced. Unlike Snow White or Pinocchio, it was not based on children's literature and employed the most well-known Disney character, Mickey Mouse, in only one sequence. *Fantasia* also broke with the established Disney tradition of strongly plotted, character-centered narratives to present a series of imagistic sequences designed to associate visuals with music. Though there are narratives within several sequences, there is no overarching structure to link them; rather, the film is driven more by musical contrasts and changes of tone and design. As Moya Luckett has noted, the film's unique combination of image and sound created a generic instability that caused critics to wonder whether it was a film or the visual accompaniment to a concert.[27] *Film Daily* referred to *Fantasia* as "the picture, if that is what it will be" and noted that "the enterprise can not be described as a feature cartoon, nor can it be termed as a picture with live talent."[28] Newspapers didn't know whether to have their film, music, or theater critics review it. One Boston paper sent all three to cover *Fantasia*'s debut.[29]

From RKO's perspective, this originality was cause for concern because it meant that the film would be difficult to sell to theaters. Disney was already behind in its distribution commitment, and now it wanted to release a film that many found hard even to describe. In addition to its unusual visual qualities, *Fantasia* also marked an innovation in sound design. "Fantasound" was one of the first multichannel systems in which the music track was recorded with multiple microphones from within the orchestra and channeled into four tracks. Each track was then sent through multiple speakers in a theater so that sound appeared to be coming from different directions within the auditorium. The system required special projectors designed to accommodate a wider filmstrip, and a theater that screened *Fantasia* had to be shut for one week before opening and one week after to assemble and take apart the equipment, which weighed eight and a half tons and required the services of a supervising engineer. Each of these units cost $30,000 and RCA was not able to manufacture more than eleven of them because of the military demands on its production capabilities.[30] Because of the unusual nature of the film, Disney decided to distribute *Fantasia* itself and make its own arrangements with theaters. The studio felt that it would build interest in the film with an extended playing period of two years, which would greatly increase the time required to recoup its investment.[31] From RKO's point of view, Disney was lavishing attention on a dubious experiment when it should have focused on producing films starring its already popular characters (fig. 9.1).

RKO asked ARI to study reactions to *Fantasia* two weeks after it opened. The idea originated within ARI, when Gallup wrote to J. R. McDonough to ask, "There has been considerable discussion in this office [ARI's Princeton office] about Walt Disney's recent choice of subjects. I am wondering whether RKO would like to place the facilities of this Institute at the disposal of

FIGURE 9.1 Walt Disney, Deems Taylor, and conductor Leopold Stokowski discuss plans for *Fantasia* (1940). RKO opposed Disney's innovative use of music and imagery in the film, and Gallup provided evidence to support the studio's objections.   *(Courtesy Corbis)*

Mr. Disney, to help him measure audience reactions to his ideas?"[32] The letter was dated December 11, 1940, the same day that Disney discussed his ideas about the film in *Variety*.[33] ARI often cited trade paper articles in its correspondence with RKO, so the column probably spurred this suggestion. Since ARI worked exclusively for RKO at this point, it could not approach Disney directly, though Gallup may have felt that he could lay the groundwork for future dealings with the animator. RKO discussed the proposal with Walt and Roy Disney, Walt's brother and the company's chief financial officer, and decided that RKO would pay for the studies as part of its own contract with Gallup.[34] RKO was generally wary about sharing ARI's research with anyone outside the studio, so its willingness to include Disney is striking. By contrast, when ARI suggested that Samuel Goldwyn might also want to use its services, RKO refused to authorize any.[35]

ARI did not begin its work on *Fantasia* immediately, but waited until July 1941. This delay may have been because RKO took over distribution of the film from Disney in May 1941. *Fantasia* did not earn enough in its first engagements to cover its budget, and trade papers estimated that it would take seven years to pay off its costs. When RKO took over, it jettisoned the special sound equipment Disney was using and compressed the multiple channels of sound onto standard 35mm film. RKO also increased its distribution fee from 25 percent to 30 percent.[36] Since RKO had assumed responsibility for the film, it was even more concerned to know what people thought about it.

After discussions with Disney, McDonough asked ARI to include *Fantasia* as part of its regular Index of Publicity Penetration in July 1941. "Publicity penetration" measured the percentage of the filmgoing public that had been "penetrated" or reached by the advertising and publicity for a picture. Penetration measures indicated the effectiveness of a distributor's campaign which, according to ARI, included the amount of money spent, the fame of a film's cast, the film's release date, and the length of time a promotional campaign was conducted before a film's release. Penetration studies, ARI asserted, allowed a studio to judge the success of marketing campaigns. In addition, knowing how many people had heard about a picture and wanted to see it made it possible to predict box office performance. Through a complicated formula, ARI believed it could use these figures to predict revenue before a film opened.[37]

ARI included *Fantasia* on its indexes for the weeks of July 26 and August 12, 1941. Before adding the film to ARI's list, Ogilvy wrote McDonough to ask how to pronounce its title. He felt that many people would not understand the word, and thus it would be difficult to test with ARI's usual procedures.[38] Despite this drawback, both ARI surveys found very high penetration or public awareness of the film. The poll showed that *Fantasia*'s national penetration was higher than average at 61 percent, and in areas where it had not yet opened it was 45 percent. By comparison, the percentages for *Sergeant York*, for which Gary Cooper later won an Academy Award, were 54 percent and 46 percent, respectively. These findings indicated that Disney's campaign to market the film and the press coverage of its technological innovations had succeeded in reaching audiences. Unfortunately, ARI also found that only 63 percent of the people who knew about *Fantasia* wanted to see it, which was 5 percent less than average. Of those who had seen the film, 48 percent enjoyed it less than they had expected. The public knew about *Fantasia*, all right, but they weren't motivated to see it, and many of those who did were not happy.[39]

Fantasia's lack of success further weakened Disney's position in relation to RKO.[40] Disney's vulnerability became apparent in its next distribution agreement. After signing over both *Bambi* and *The Reluctant Dragon* in September 1940, six months later Disney gave RKO distribution rights to *Dumbo* and a new Mickey Mouse feature. RKO, once eager to take even one film from Disney, now held distribution rights to four features, marking a major shift of power in their relationship.[41]

RKO's concern about the new direction Disney had chosen was reinforced by ARI's surveys regarding *The Reluctant Dragon*. The film was the first Disney feature to combine live action and animated sequences and, like *Fantasia*, departed from the fully animated, character-driven Disney classics such as *Snow White*. The plot features comedian Robert Benchley, who visits the new Burbank facility to try to persuade Walt Disney to make a film about a book he is reading, "The Reluctant Dragon." On his way to meet Disney, Benchley wanders through different rooms in the studio and encounters animators involved in various stages of the production process. As Benchley learns about the steps needed to create cartoons, we see several Disney shorts and get previews of upcoming releases, including *Bambi* and *Dumbo*. Disney marketed this film as "a new Disney FEATURE!" but the infomercial quality of a behind-the-scenes look was not lost on the press. Today the film stands as one of the earliest glimpses of life inside the Disney studio, but many critics at the time derided it as Disney's trailer for itself and a "super de luxe commercial."[42]

In April 1941, Ned Depinet, the head of RKO's sales department, asked Schaefer to have ARI include *The Reluctant Dragon* in its next penetration report. He also asked if ARI could determine what percentage of the public knew the film was a feature and not a short. Schaefer wrote McDonough, who in turn wrote Gallup with the request.[43] At this time, the studio was telling its sales force that RKO would distribute four new Disney features that would contain all the studio's well-known characters.[44] Depinet wanted to be able to advertise the Disney who was already familiar to audiences, while Disney wanted to experiment with new forms of animation. ARI's research offered a means to test public awareness of the film and reactions to the changes Disney was making.

The Reluctant Dragon appeared on ARI's penetration studies beginning the week of June 14, 1941, a week after the film opened, and continued for seven reports, through July 26, when it appeared in the same study as *Fantasia*. The surveys confirmed Depinet's fears, as ARI found that even as the film was making its debut, its publicity penetration was nine points below average. Only 34 percent of those surveyed knew that *The Reluctant Dragon* was a feature.[45] Among those who knew something about it, *The Reluctant Dragon*'s want-to-see was 4 to 5 percent below average, and declined even further after the film opened. As with *Fantasia*, even when people did go to see the film, they were not enthusiastic.[46] Critics, too, complained that it was "sub-par" Disney and not up to the standards of the studio's earlier features. *Time* described it as "two and a half shorts" with a tour thrown in for good measure, and *Motion Picture Herald* felt that it had been "welded together" from several shorts.[47]

These low numbers triggered a war of blame between Disney and RKO. Under its distribution agreement with RKO, Disney was responsible for the cost of advertising its films in trade papers and magazines.[48] Ogilvy argued that Disney should have started its promotional campaign for the film sooner, and Depinet accused the studio of deliberately holding back so as not to conflict with *Fantasia*.[49] Disney changed the date of *The Reluctant Dragon*'s premiere several times and did not settle on a final location until ten days before the opening, which did not allow much time for promotion.[50] The most obvious reason that Disney did not heavily advertise the film is that it presented a happy-go-lucky view of the studio at a time when most of its staff was on strike. The walkout resulted partly from jurisdictional disputes between the American Federation of Labor (AFL), the Screen Cartoonists Guild, and the International Alliance of Theatrical Stage Employees (IATSE), who were competing to organize the Hollywood animation studios, and from workers' complaints about conditions within the new studio. The strike began in late May 1941 and lasted until the end of July. The trade papers carried reports of the dispute in nearly every issue that summer.[51]

During this period RKO was also using ARI's surveys to track interest in projects proposed by other independent producers that it had under contract. Often the institute's research found little enthusiasm for these productions. Public opinion toward Disney films of the early 1940s followed a similar path. According to ARI, audiences were not excited about the innovations in form and subject that Disney presented. As was the case with many of RKO's other films, the public wanted to see the kinds of characters and stories with which it was already familiar. The theory that audiences would respond better to more traditional Disney films was borne out by the success of *Dumbo*, released in October 1941. The film cost less than any of Disney's previous features and was produced quickly, in one year, while *Bambi* was experiencing production delays.[52] Both critics and the public praised the film as "a return to Disney first principles."[53] *Newsweek* noted that while *Fantasia* was "arty," and *The Reluctant Dragon* "experimental," with *Dumbo*, "Disney was back again." Reviewers also praised the film's visual style, comparing its drawing and coloring with *Snow White* and *Pinocchio*, even though, as Mark Langer has pointed out, the film combines disparate styles of animation that were operating simultaneously within the studio at that time: a "West Coast" style that mimicked the narrative and stylistic conventions of classical Hollywood cinema, and an "East Coast" style that celebrated the flexibility and unpredictability that animation afforded.[54] ARI tracked *Dumbo*'s publicity penetration from the film's opening week through November 8, 1941, and found that the film enjoyed a steady increase in public awareness matched by a strong desire to see it. By returning to its roots, Disney had found the approach audiences wanted.[55]

One might argue, then, that ARI provided solid evidence that the public didn't like these innovations, and that Disney should have stayed with its tried-and-true approach to cartoon production. This was RKO's conclusion and seems to have been Ogilvy's as well, though he may have been telling his client what it wanted to hear. On the other hand, one might also argue that these studies revealed a weakness in ARI's methodology, a fundamental inability to measure the effects of new ideas. Low want-to-see numbers might have meant that people needed time to absorb these new changes, time that admittedly wasn't available in the tight exhibition schedules of the 1940s. ARI's methods privileged film styles that were familiar; as Gallup himself admitted, penetration studies were designed for well-publicized "A" films that featured major stars. It was not clear whether they would work for "B" films, or films that did not have marquee names, let alone cartoons.[56] ARI provided a read-out of public sentiment at the time, which is what mattered to RKO, but it could not adequately gauge the more enduring value of these films.

RKO subjected all of Disney's features of the early 1940s to the scrutiny of publicity penetration studies. The extra attention they received underscores Disney's importance to RKO at a time when its president was counting on quality films to return the company to profitability. By allowing ARI to study public reactions to its films, RKO was giving Disney special treatment, but the fact that it was singled out also meant the studio expected something in return. In Depinet's opinion, ARI offered proof that the public did not like the innovations in sound and design that Disney introduced at this time. Clearly, the cartoon producer should return to his roots and create the trademark films for which he was known. Yet even Gallup admitted that his research might not be able to convey the full complexity of the public's responses to animated films. And Disney cannot be blamed for losses caused by the war in Europe. In RKO's hands, this research hampered the artistic innovations Disney was struggling to achieve. When Disney met Gallup on other projects, however, he saw another side to this work and realized that it could help him achieve his goals.

Looking Ahead

Though Walt Disney depended on RKO for financing and distribution, he continued to maintain his own filmmaking studio and to retain his identity as an independent producer. Along with David Selznick, he belonged to the Society of Independent Motion Picture Producers, an organization that also included Samuel Goldwyn. The society organized itself in 1941 in order to campaign for legal and economic conditions that would foster creative and innovative filmmaking.[57] SIMPP formed at the same time that Selznick was dissolving his own production company and when he was beginning to work with Gallup, and he spoke often to his colleagues about ARI.[58] Disney also met Gallup himself through his war work in Washington. These experiences gave Disney a different perspective on the value of audience research.

Gallup and Walt Disney first met in person in Washington, D.C., in January 1942, when Gallup was conducting studies for the government. The Treasury Department asked Disney to make a film explaining the new laws that would require many Americans to pay taxes for the first time. Their meeting in Washington illustrates the kinds of connections forged during World War II between executives in different fields, an interplay of influence resulting from the crisis conditions of the time. As Eric Smoodin documents in *Animating Culture*, this film—*The New Spirit*—was intended to inspire particular economic groups, lower- and lower-middle-income citizens, to pay the new taxes willingly.[59] Gallup offered to help Disney determine whether the film had succeeded by providing a demographic analysis of its viewers.[60] David Ogilvy also attended the meeting in Washington and, as he wrote to Selznick later, took the opportunity to suggest "casually" that ARI might be able to help Disney choose among possible subjects for his next feature film. Disney was putting all his resources into *Bambi*, however, and felt it might be a while before he made another feature.[61]

Still, the contact was made, and Gallup and Ogilvy built on it. In June 1942, the same month that Schaefer left RKO and when ARI's future with the studio looked uncertain, ARI went ahead with this proposal on its own. Gallup conducted a nationwide poll in which interviewers showed respondents five titles and asked which they would most like to see as a Disney cartoon. The choices were "Alice in Wonderland," "Peter Pan," "Peter Rabbit," "Uncle Remus," and "Bambi," which was then in production. Disney had already announced plans to film some of these works in the trade papers, but asking about "Peter Rabbit" may have been ARI's idea. The survey found "Alice" the favorite by far, with 48 percent of the vote, but "Bambi" was next to last, at only 11 percent. Only 24 percent even knew it was in production. Ogilvy wrote to Selznick about the results and said that he was afraid to tell Disney for fear that he "might become depressed." He asked Selznick to tell him instead. Selznick demurred, but agreed to talk to his friend about the general value of ARI.[62]

Selznick's endorsement, and perhaps the Disney studio's own precarious state, spurred Walt Disney to commission his own Gallup survey in September 1942. As Richard Shales documents in his extensive study of Disney during World War II, Disney had just begun production on a film adaptation of Alexander Seversky's *Victory Through Air Power*, and paid ARI $5,000 to provide a detailed analysis of its potential audience. Seversky, a Russian naval lieutenant, had emigrated to the United States after World War I and eventually became a major in the U.S. Air Corps Reserve. Recognized as a leading expert on air warfare, Seversky published the book to promote his idea that the United States needed to upgrade its aviation program. The book became an immediate bestseller when it was published in spring 1942.[63] Gallup conducted the same kind of study he made for *Gone with the Wind* and estimated that twenty million people had heard of Seversky, and that five million had either read his book or the *Reader's Digest* condensation of it. ARI noted that the film was strong among men and boys but drew a great deal of interest generally. Gallup encouraged Disney to make the film, but warned that the public's appetite for war films was diminishing.[64] The film grossed only a little more than it cost to make.[65]

The Disney studio committed nearly all its resources during the early 1940s to government work, producing training films and films designed to promote good relations with Latin America. In late 1943, though, Walt Disney seems to have stepped back from the day-to-day demands of production to begin to assess what directions the studio might take after the war. In this period he asked ARI to conduct several studies that looked at general reactions to the studio's films and characters. In a survey carried out on August 11, 1943, ARI asked a representative sample of Americans which Walt Disney character they like best. Donald Duck won by a landslide, followed by Thumper with 51 percent, and Bambi with 47 percent. Mickey Mouse ranked lower than Bambi in the public's estimation, at 45 percent.[66] A few months later, on November 9, 1943, ARI queried another cross-section of Americans about which of six subjects it would like to see as a Disney film: "Cinderella," "Peter Pan," "Alice in Wonderland," "Lady and the Tramp," "Uncle Remus," or "Hiawatha." The survey aimed to uncover both positive and negative reactions, how different demographic groups responded, and whether people preferred to see each subject as a live-action or animated film. Though no subject reached 100 on the acceptance scale (the number ARI set as "average"), "Cinderella" ranked highest at 95. Younger audiences liked it, and even men were positive, while the subject was off the charts with women. Viewers at all income levels said they would enjoy seeing the tale on film, and as a Disney cartoon, rather than in live action. These responses offered a resounding affirmation of both Disney's animation and the value of fantasy in a world emerging from war. By contrast, reactions to "Peter Pan" and "Alice" revealed a general dislike of cartoons and classic literature among younger and less educated audiences.[67]

Many factors entered into Disney's choice of subjects for his features, but it is interesting to note that the first full-length cartoon he released after the war was indeed *Cinderella* in 1950. Disney's growing interest in audience research during the war presaged a full commitment to studying public response in the postwar period. As the studio returned to commercial production after 1945, Walt Disney continued to rethink the studio's direction and focus. ARI's methods helped him manage an increasingly complex enterprise even as he ventured out beyond animation to live-action and industrial films. ARI became an integral part of the filmmaking process at Disney after the war, helping the studio both to maintain its traditions in a changing culture and to integrate new ideas.

The Entertainment Factory

Though Disney films dominated American studio animation during the 1930s, after World War II economic, industrial, and sociological factors combined to weaken its position. Animation production as a whole became less profitable, and the Disney studio in particular suffered financially. Critical and popular reaction began to turn against Disney in this period, and within the company, attention shifted from animation to live-action production. To maintain its output, Disney adopted an industrial mode of organization that emphasized efficiency and productivity. ARI helped the company manage this shifting internal and external environment.

Animation production declined rapidly after World War II. Studios that had taken pride in their cartoon series dropped them completely in 1946–47. The primary reason was cost: in 1945 the average cartoon short cost $17,000 to produce, but two years later this had risen to an average of $25,000 per picture, an increase of nearly 50 percent. Labor costs increased by 41 percent in this period, and Technicolor raised the cost of processing color film. Exhibitor fees, the main source of revenue for shorts, did not keep pace with these increases.[68] The financial situation at Disney was especially difficult. In its annual report for 1947 the company announced that profits were 40 percent less than the year before.[69] Revenues were tied up in new features that would not return a profit for several years. Full-length cartoons were even less cost-effective than shorts: they took three or four years to produce, and two or three more to return their investment. In 1948 and 1949, Disney posted losses for the first time since the beginning of World War II, of $39,038 and $93,899.[70]

In addition to these economic difficulties, Disney lost its preeminence among animation producers. The mid- to late 1940s marked the ascendancy of Warner Bros. and MGM cartoons. Disney had won every Oscar for cartoon shorts awarded between 1932, when the category was first announced, and 1939, but between 1943 and 1952 it failed to win any. MGM's Tom and Jerry dominated the awards from 1943 to 1946 and again in 1948, interrupted only by the debut of Warner's Sylvester and Tweetie in 1947, which earned that studio an Oscar as well.[71] Critics matched these snubs from the Motion Picture Academy. Arthur Knight, writing in *Theatre Arts* in August 1951, asserted that Disney's celebrated naturalism had reached a dead end, that his imagination had "worn thin." Knight praised instead the modernist flatness of the cartoons produced by UPA, whose *Gerald McBoing-Boing* had won an Oscar in 1950.[72]

Within the studio, live-action films began to displace animated ones in the company's production schedule. Disney's interest in live action developed during the war, when the studio produced documentaries for government agencies and private industry. When the war ended, the studio continued producing live-action films to maintain cash flow, since profits returned more quickly for live action than for animation. Between 1950 and 1955, Disney produced more live-action features than animated ones. For a time in the late 1940s, it even seemed possible that Disney would no longer produce fully animated features. Where animation did appear in full-length films, it was often combined with live action, as in *Song of the South* (1946) and *So Dear to My Heart* (1949). In June 1946 all the projects announced in the company's upcoming schedule were described as combinations, including *Cinderella*.[73] Even Roy Disney pressed his brother to give up producing animated films.[74]

To meet the demands of this changing environment, Walt Disney introduced a new managerial style that stressed efficiency and cost-effectiveness. In an article published when the new Burbank facility had opened, he described the studio as an "entertainment factory" and "a machine for the manufacture of entertainment."[75] The design itself served as a synecdoche for the rationalization and efficiency governing the company. According to its engineers, the new Burbank headquarters aimed to "provide a smooth and efficient . . . flow line" for "optimum per capita production."[76] A postwar memo from Walt and Roy Disney to the studio staff demonstrated that this stress on efficiency extended to the use of money as well as time and energy. The memo called for "a constructive attitude toward every dollar which goes into developing, producing and selling the pictures." Film production should be planned in advance to avoid uncertainty and save money. "The production schedule should be buttoned up and not changed," the memo said. Animators should also stay within their budgets and bring films "across the finish line" under their projected cost.[77]

During the 1930s Walt Disney had introduced several changes designed to streamline animation production: he instituted storyboard conferences and pencil tests to check films at an early stage of development, and organized workers into specialized groups similar to the production units employed at live-action studios.[78] In the postwar era, he turned to audience research. According to the studio's annual report for 1946–47, Disney's primary motivation for hiring Gallup was to hold down production costs, which had increased 75 percent since 1941. By taking audience reactions into account in the early stages of production, before a film was completed, the studio felt it could head off potential failures.[79] Undertaking a program of "scientific" research would also enhance its status as a serious business enterprise and allay the concerns of its creditors and stockholders. The earlier research ARI had carried out served RKO's needs, but in the postwar era Disney realized that it could use research for its own purposes. Disney's reworking of ARI's methods illustrates how techniques that appear to be cast in stone can be reshaped to suit the needs of the people who use them.

Calculating Pleasure

The worldwide popularity of Mickey Mouse, Donald Duck, and other Disney characters promoted the belief that Walt Disney possessed an instinctive understanding of his audiences' likes and dislikes. Though his affinity with the audience had acquired almost mythic proportions, Disney had from the beginning studied people's reactions firsthand. Disney and his animators often went to theaters to listen to audiences' reactions and note what sequences or types of characters appealed to them. He and his colleagues would then gather outside for a postmortem analysis of the film's structure, music, animation, and backgrounds.[80] According to Shamus Culhane, who worked at other animation studios before joining Disney, Walt Disney was one of the few cartoon producers who was willing to change a film based on audience response. Other studios used everything their animators produced because they didn't want to take extra time or pay for footage that didn't appear in the film.[81] For Disney, though, understanding what audiences liked was as important to cartooning as good draftsmanship and the ability to develop gags.[82]

Disney's first large-scale effort to study audiences more systematically began in 1945, when the studio initiated a series of previews for carefully selected groups of people. The year before, ARI had begun conducting preview screenings with audiences who were carefully selected according to their representation in the general filmgoing population. Studios had long held sneak previews for anyone who came to the theater, but ARI argued that viewers at these screenings did not represent the American public as a whole.[83] While the idea of holding advance screenings for scientifically chosen audiences originated with ARI, Disney modified the technique to fit his production schedule and budget. Instead of going outside the studio, Disney commissioned ARI to survey its own employees to determine how well they corresponded to the national filmgoing population. ARI found that, except for viewers over 30, Disney's employees mirrored the majority of American filmgoers pretty well.[84] After learning this, the studio began to hold in-house previews for audiences of forty employees at a time, employees who had been selected to represent the rest of the country in terms of age, gender, and level of education. Participants came from the general office staff and groundsworkers, and from the ranks of junior production personnel, such as the women in ink and paint, and the men who worked as assistant animators and in-betweeners. Card Walker, the executive in charge of advertising at the studio, arranged these screenings. For the next ten years, until the mid-1950s, Disney submitted all its productions, whether shorts or full-length features, to this employee scrutiny.

Disney first used these "studio ARI's," as they were called, to gather reactions to its short films. The audience chosen for a screening would watch a rough cut of a film then in production, a reel that combined footage produced by various animators assigned to the project. After looking at the reel, viewers completed a form that asked these questions: Do you like this type of cartoon? Which gags or situations did you enjoy most? Least? Are there any parts that are dull or uninteresting, so shortening would help? Were there any gags or situations you did not understand? Any dialogue? Some of these queries are closed-ended, that is, answers were expressed in a "yes or no," binary form. Walker or his secretary typed the responses about which gags were enjoyed most or least on a separate sheet, indicating that this issue received particular attention. Most questions focused on a film's intelligibility and tried to uncover problems that could be solved through reediting. Walker sent transcripts of these responses to the director of animation for each film, who reviewed them and recommended appropriate changes to the animators whom he supervised. Usually the alterations were cuts designed to clarify the action or shorten the pace of a scene.[85] He also sent reports of each screening and summaries of the audiences' reactions to Walt Disney.

From the standpoint of efficiency, this procedure seemed to ensure that the most unpredictable variable in a film's success—audience reaction—could be studied in advance and incorporated into the production process itself. The animators' firsthand experiences of audiences in the 1930s were replaced by carefully designed questionnaires that raised issues that could be addressed through existing production procedures. Though the questions are logical ones to ask about a cartoon, they nonetheless narrow the potential range of audience responses to these films. The discursive form of these responses made them difficult to manage; however, Walker soon found a way to convert them into numerical form. The extent to which audience response could be codified is vividly illustrated by the way he handled the first question, the one asking viewers to rate their enjoyment of each film on a scale of one to seven.

After several months of reporting individual scores, Card Walker developed a decimal rating for each film by multiplying the number of "most enjoyed" votes by seven, the next highest level by six, and so on. His memos to Walt Disney and to the animation supervisors began to contain statements such as, "This film received a 5.67 enjoyment rating." Since the studio subjected every short cartoon to this process, Walker also began to tabulate a running average; each project was compared with the overall enjoyment ratings from other screenings. He then compiled long lists that positioned each film in relation to previous ones according to their rating.[86] George Heinemann, a Peabody award-winning television producer who knew Walker, has said that Walker felt more secure with numbers and graphs because they were tangible and concrete, unlike the creative process.[87] Walker's background in advertising had accustomed him to the same kinds of rating measurements that Gallup knew at Young & Rubicam, and his efforts to create a similar system at Disney marks a point of intersection between animation production and advertising research.

This effort to quantify pleasure, to develop a precise numerical measurement for happiness, set off reverberations within the studio. As the Canadian media theorist Dallas Smythe has pointed out, during the 1940s corporate executives viewed the control of information as a crucial part of efficient management.[88] At Disney, the decimal rating system that Walker developed offered a convenient method for evaluating the productivity of animation units, their success at producing humorous cartoons. The memos that routinely circulated from Walker to Walt allowed the studio's founder to keep tabs on employees' work when he was no longer involved in day-to-day production. Among the animation staff, however, this rating system fostered a sense of competition. In one memo, a secretary informs Walt Disney that an animator altered the statistics on one film to lower the enjoyment score for another group.[89] By adapting ARI's idea of sampling audiences for its own purposes, Disney found another tool to rationalize production and maintain control over an increasingly complex environment. This effort at control, however, set off counter-efforts by his employees to maintain their own power over their productions.

The Critical and the Non-Critical

While the carefully chosen studio audience was screening rough cuts, the animation staff continued the studio's tradition of holding storyboard conferences. Disney pioneered the use of storyboard meetings in the 1930s as a way to evaluate a film's narrative structure and character development before it went into production. Animators drew key scenes, gags, and actions on storyboards that the rest of the staff reviewed with Walt Disney. This process enabled them to plan scenes in detail before committing to the expense of drawing and painting cels. Two years after the studio began working with in-house audiences, Disney began posing some of the same questions that it asked of other employees to its animation staff during storyboard meetings. In contrast to the general studio audience, which was called the "non-critical" group, the animation staff that filled out these forms was called the "critical" group. This group consisted of senior animators, story men, and background and layout artists, many of whom had been with the studio since the early 1930s and had imbibed Disney's beliefs about animation. Their responses rarely questioned the studio's approach to filmmaking but, rather, talked about how a film could be made to look more like a Disney production.[90]

Before long, differences began to emerge between the critical group's view of the storyboards and the studio audience's reactions to the rough reels that resulted from those storyboards. In April 1950 the studio began to invite the non-critical audiences to view the storyboards as well, often in back-to-back sessions with the critical group.[91] As with the rough cuts, having the non-critical group look at storyboards was intended to detect problems earlier in production, even before the rough reels. Usually the non-critical group reacted more positively to the storyboards than the critical group, and even came to serve as a court of appeals for animators who felt that their peers had not evaluated their projects fairly.[92] If the non-critical group gave a storyboard a strong positive response, it often moved into production even if the critical group had reservations about it.

At other times, however, the responses from the non-critical audience were more negative than those of the senior staff. Since the studio audience was partly composed of junior production personnel, many seized this opportunity to express their own views of how animated films should be handled. These questionnaires then became an arena where tensions within the studio played out, and where different groups articulated competing ideologies of animation. Respondents often critiqued the classic Disney style and extolled the merits of the cartoons coming out of Warner Bros. or the UPA style of animation that produced the Mr. Magoo series.[93] As Walt Disney turned to other projects at the studio, his dominance in cartoon production waned, and the studio's in-house audience research allowed opposing views to emerge. The responses on these questionnaires may have supported the shift toward a more modernist drawing style that some animators, such as Ward Kimball, adopted during this period.

Though this double-preview system was supposed to simplify cartoon production, it had the opposite effect. By 1952 the Disney studio was engaged in a veritable frenzy of audience research: not only did the studio audience attend storyboard conferences, but the critical group began to fill out questionnaires at the rough screenings as well. With opinions circulating constantly, films often required two or three storyboard conferences, and as many rough screenings, before they were approved for release.[94] In addition, the time lag between these stages increased in the early 1950s, as the studio pulled more animators into feature production for *Cinderella* and *Peter Pan*. Often the audiences' responses at one screening didn't match their views at all a few months later. Viewers who loved a rough cut in January sometimes hated it when they saw it again in September.[95] Disney began to shelve many short films because the studio could not reach a consensus on their value, and in 1954 stopped producing them altogether. The decision to discontinue cartoon shorts is usually explained in purely economic terms, but the breakdown of the studio's system for measuring audience response undoubtedly contributed to it.

"I Want to Know"

Walt Disney was very proud of his use of audience research. He told Pete Martin in an interview in 1956:

> I've never tested a picture with children. I test with adults. . . . And I test them in my own studio and never go beyond my own studio. . . . I have enough people working in my studio that actually have nothing to do with the creating of the pictures. They don't know the first thing about production. They're bookkeepers, they're stenographers, janitors. There's people from all walks of life within my studio. I pull an audience from there. And I throw my picture at them. And I let them write on a piece of paper. They can say it stinks. Yes sir, I want to know.[96]

Disney's attitude toward this research underscores its utility as a management tool at a time of rapid change within the company. Walker recalls that Walt Disney was firmly committed to audience studies, believing they could provide important advance information about public reaction.[97] The quantitative form of this research, its numbers and ratings, may have satisfied both a desire for knowledge and a need for control, at a time when the studio and animation as a whole were changing rapidly. By contrast, Maurice Rapf, who worked on *Song of the South* later in the 1940s, took a different view of this work. In his mind, Walt Disney's decision to use research was symptomatic of the fear and uncertainty that pervaded the studio after the war. Challenged by Warner and UPA, Walt Disney began to lose faith in his own judgment and hired Gallup for reassurance as well as evidence. Rapf recalls that Walt Disney "brought in Gallup every time he could. Conferences would be going along well and he'd say, 'Let's put it to a test.'"[98] Rapf felt that Walt Disney knew his audiences well enough not to need this outside intervention, but that the economic pressures of the postwar era, combined with financial strains within the studio, led him to rely on audience research. From the animators' perspectives, these conferences were a nightmare, as their work became an object of intense scrutiny not only by their peers but also by employees throughout the company.[99]

The late 1940s marks a critical juncture at the Disney studio, a time when the company began to transform itself from a small cartoon producer to a diversified major with a full slate of short and feature cartoons, live-action films, and documentaries. It was during this period that Disney started to become the entertainment conglomerate that it is today. Many factors contributed to this change: the ambitions of its executives, changes within the film industry as a whole, and the aftereffects of World War II. But along with these forces, ARI played a crucial role in Disney's alteration. The decision to hire Gallup signaled a fundamental shift within the company, a desire to adopt the business practices and organizational strategies of a major studio. As this shift took place, the studio's approach to animation changed as well. The opportunities for innovative narrative forms and image and sound design that so inspired Disney before the war came to be seen as elements that required management and measurement. Animation, the cinematic medium with perhaps the greatest potential for fluidity and transformation, was expected to meet carefully defined corporate goals, and ARI assisted in that process. While Disney's audience research was a far cry from the national polls that ARI conducted for RKO, the studio's use of questionnaires and translation of emotions into decimal ratings illustrates how scientific techniques can be modified and absorbed into media companies.

10

Like, Dislike, Like Very Much

World War II brought many changes to the Audience Research Institute. Most of its key staff members had left by the end of 1942. Don Cahalan, who joined ARI in November 1938, fresh out of graduate school at Iowa, moved to Washington in June 1941 to conduct survey research for the government. He went on to earn a doctorate in psychology and carried out studies on alcoholism before retiring from the faculty at Berkeley. Paul Sheatsley, the head of ARI's interviewing staff, left the institute in January 1942 to join the recently established National Opinion Research Center at the University of Chicago, where he worked for forty-five years. He later served as president of the American Association for Public Opinion Research in 1967–68. After David Ogilvy left in September 1942 to participate in the English war effort, Gallup's sister-in-law Barbara Miller Benson took over his duties as head of the research staff, analyzing data and writing reports for ARI's clients. In January 1943 Gallup hired Albert Sindlinger, a sales executive from the *March of Time*, to set up a New York office for ARI, and asked Jack Sayers to be the institute's representative in Hollywood. In 1946, ARI expanded further, bringing in James Wolcott and Bob Jones from the *March of Time* when Sindlinger left to form his own company.[1] With Ogilvy's departure, a distinctive voice disappeared from ARI's reports. Instead of the creative interpretations and freely offered conjectures that characterized his correspondence with RKO, ARI's reports in the postwar era are written in a more neutral, less poetic style and rarely take wing in flights of speculation.

Even its named changed: at some point in 1943, for reasons that are not clear, the Audience Research "Institute" became Audience Research, Inc.

The turmoil of World War II created additional strains for Gallup and ARI. Gallup found it more and more difficult to hire the personable and articulate people he needed to conduct interviews. In Cleveland, for example, where RKO owned four theaters, ARI could find only one interviewer, who decided to move to California. Back home in Gallup's Princeton headquarters, the demands for up-to-date opinion polling in a rapidly changing political climate created a logjam, as ARI's tabulators and ballot processors competed for space and computer time with AIPO's staff members.[2] The staff and equipment that his political polls required cut into the time and resources he could devote to film research. On a broader level, however, World War II created conditions in which Gallup was able to expand his network of professional connections. In the pressure conditions caused by the United States' all-out commitment to the war effort, executives from different kinds of industries began to collaborate on government work. Gallup conducted surveys for four government departments, including the Treasury Department, where he met Walt Disney. Nelson Rockefeller's work as Coordinator for Inter-American Affairs created opportunities for RKO, Gallup, Walt Disney, Orson Welles, and Jock Whitney. Just as in the First World War, World War II spurred massive survey research projects that opened new avenues of research, such as Samuel Stouffer's work on *The American Soldier.* As survey historian Jean Converse has noted, the war brought about a tremendous surge of interest in polls and spurred business and government officials to explore new ways of using them.[3]

The increased interactions between business executives and government officials during this period promoted awareness of opinion polling among many Hollywood leaders as well. In addition, economic changes within the industry led many studios that had rejected research before the war to reconsider its value. Between 1941 and 1946 the cost of producing a feature film rose 75 percent.[4] This increase forced studios to manage costs more carefully and prove the value of each expenditure. Like Disney and RKO, other companies saw audience research as a way to prove their commitment to sound financial management. In addition to increased production costs, changes in exhibition and competition from other forms of entertainment motivated producers to use audience research after the war. The postwar import quotas that many European governments imposed on Hollywood films severely reduced the income studios derived from their overseas markets. As box office profits in the United States became more important, executives devoted more resources to studying the interests of American audiences. Competition from other forms of leisure entertainment, such as radio and television, also spurred studios to examine the interests of film audiences more carefully.[5]

During the 1940s, the system of vertical integration that had defined relationships between producers and exhibitors loosened under the impact of antitrust decrees that prohibited blind bidding and block booking. Since films were no longer marketed as part of a package, producers had to demonstrate the merits of each production. In negotiating with exhibitors, studios used ARI's research to prove the popularity of their films and to establish a rental price.[6] Some even took out ads in the trade papers to draw attention to ARI's ratings. In a 1946 *Variety* ad, MGM highlighted an ARI survey that found its films ranked highly with the public. "Said Doctor Gallup to the Nation—What's Your Favorite Recreation? It's Leo's pictures, Dr. Gallup. They give us folks the biggest wallup." The scientific research conducted by "Doctor" Gallup proved the value of MGM's productions.

In the early 1940s, as we have seen, the clients who used Gallup's services were studios that were suffering financial difficulties, like RKO, or chief executives who thought that survey research would lend additional credence to their views, like Samuel Goldwyn and David Selznick. In the postwar period, everybody liked surveys. From 1946 through 1951, ARI carried out surveys for nearly every major studio, including MGM, whose executives were reluctant to use Gallup's work when Selznick wanted them to. By 1946, William Rodgers, the studio's vice president for sales and marketing, admitted that, "We have commenced to acknowledge the wisdom of research."[7] ARI's clients included Paramount and Columbia, and many independent producers such as Edward Small and Benedict Bogeaus. In many cases ARI conducted only one or two studies for these producers, and many of them no longer survive, but trade paper reports indicate that interest in the institute's work was widespread.

During the postwar period ARI added new techniques to the repertoire of strategies it used to analyze films. In addition to the preproduction studies of casts and stories, the institute continued its penetration studies and developed carefully structured previews designed to pinpoint the exact moments in a film where audiences lost interest. ARI also focused more heavily on marketing and began to offer specific ideas for advertising campaigns. Before the war, ARI offered its clients mainly preproduction research; after the war, it provided comprehensive strategies for managing postproduction as well. In the late 1940s ARI's function became similar to that of an advertising agency rather than a research institute, as it sought to provide total management services for a film. ARI's efforts to totalize control of film spectatorship triggered a backlash against its work from writers, actors, and many journalists. In the end, Gallup's stinging defeat in the 1948 election brought his work in Hollywood nearly to a close.

Total Film Management

Gallup's advertising research at Young & Rubicam worked to pinpoint the exact features of a text that affected viewers. In addition to its studies of story and cast, ARI also identified film titles as a key element that shaped audiences' expectations for a film. ARI carried out some title tests for RKO in the early 1940s, but the bulk of this research was done in the postwar era.

ARI determined that one quarter of the public bought tickets on the basis of a film's title.[8] As Gallup explained, this meant that it was "of paramount importance to insure that every picture carries the strongest possible title." A picture's name bore a direct relationship to its box office success: "the fact remains that a weak title always impairs box office performance, and a strong title always helps it." In addition to enhancing the value of a film, title tests could also uncover information that would assist in developing promotional campaigns. Just as Gallup had argued in his early advertising research, studying titles through empirical research could eliminate "guesswork and argument" and save "costly hours of executive time."[9]

To determine the most successful title for a project, ARI tested as many as forty choices, usually in groups of four. Interviewers read the selections or presented them on a written list to respondents chosen to correspond with the general filmgoing population. Their reactions were reported using a scale of 1 to 100, with 50 considered the median. The simple numerical measurement these tests provided seemed to guarantee their accuracy, and executives often made decisions based purely on this number. During preproduction for *Mr. Lucky* (1943), for example, RKO changed the title six times, as each new survey discovered a more popular name.[10]

In addition to providing a quantitative measure of a title's popularity, these tests were designed to uncover the connotations names evoked. ARI determined whether a title was intelligible to the ordinary viewer and whether it created positive or negative associations. The surveys also revealed the kind of audience a film might attract, so that studios could tailor their advertising campaigns accordingly. ARI argued that clarity was a major factor in a title's popularity. If audiences couldn't pronounce a name, or didn't understand what the title meant, they felt less desire to see the picture. For this reason, ARI cautioned studios against using large words, or references that would not be understood by the majority of the population. Rather, titles should serve as an accurate reflection of a film's content, guiding audiences into the narrative in the same way that newspaper headlines led readers into a feature story.[11] Through testing, studios discovered what associations a title produced and could judge whether they matched the actual subject of the film. One of the most amusing studies of this type concerned J. Arthur Rank's pro-

duction of *The Rake's Progress*. In its study of American filmgoers, ARI found
that most people expected the film to be a documentary about the evolution
of the garden tool. Rank later changed the title to *Notorious Gentleman*.[12]

Once aware of the implications a title possessed, studios could adjust a
film's name to target particular segments of the audience. This approach is
reflected in title studies that ARI carried out at the Disney studio during the
late 1940s. As part of its quest to move beyond animation, Disney wanted to
expand its audience beyond the traditional juvenile one to include adults.
The studio used ARI's research to determine whether a title evoked too many
reminders of childhood, and what changes could be made to enhance a films'
attraction for adults. For example, Disney chose *Song of the South* over *Uncle
Remus* as the title for its 1946 live-action/animated feature because older
viewers liked it more.[13]

Though Gallup's letters to producers stressed the benefits of early research,
the main function of title tests and other preproduction studies was to provide evidence of viewer preferences that could be used to construct marketing campaigns. By learning at an early stage what associations a title evoked,
a studio's advertising and sales departments could develop promotional strategies around them. ARI's extensive work on Columbia's 1946 production of
Carmen illustrates this practice. ARI determined that most audiences had
no desire to see a film about Bizet's opera and categorically rejected oper-
atic performances in general; as one respondent put it, "I can't stand them
squawkers."[14] Since Columbia intended to develop its production from the
novel by Prosper Mérimée, and use music composed especially for the film,
ARI advised the studio to emphasize these facts in its advertising. The film's
title was changed to *The Loves of Carmen*, and posters stressed that it was
"NOT THE OPERA . . . but a dramatic version of the story of Carmen."[15]

Title tests illustrate some of the key features of ARI's research: its attempt
to define the basic factors affecting audience response and to manage the
associations they evoked. Implicit in this research is the assumption that
films should attract as many viewers as possible, and that clarity and simplicity were to be prized over ambiguity or complexity. These features are also
evident in the story tests ARI conducted after the war. While its tests for
RKO sought to measure the public's general perceptions and expectations of
a project, story tests in the postwar period aimed to uncover information that
studios could use to plan marketing campaigns.

Though its title was the first thing audiences heard about a film, the story
was the most important influence on whether they chose to see it. As we
have seen, story tests presented variations on a film's plot, setting, and characters to determine which combination aroused the most interest. ARI recommended that whatever formula earned the best response become the basis

for a film's advertising.[16] For example, when Columbia was planning a film about the life of Frederic Chopin (*A Song to Remember*, 1945), initial studies found that audiences were lukewarm about a biography of a composer. When ARI created new summaries that stressed the love interest between Chopin and George Sand, interest quickened.[17] As we will see, writers believed these tests infringed on their creative autonomy, but many producers felt they provided a useful basis on which to construct marketing campaigns.

The preferences that emerged in story tests helped determine which aspects of a film were stressed in promotional campaigns. Since these surveys provided a general indication of an audience's likes and dislikes, the advertising developed from them often used broad emotional appeals rather than specific references to unique features in the film. Tests for RKO's *Notorious*, for example, found little interest in its plot but great curiosity about the director, Alfred Hitchcock, and the film's stars. Accordingly, posters for the film featured oversize images of Cary Grant and Ingrid Bergman locked in an embrace.[18]

As in its other surveys, ARI presented its conclusions using the demographic variables of age, gender, geographical location, and frequency of attendance.[19] Reports to studio executives indicated where interest was highest and lowest among these categories. Since ARI had found that 19-year-olds purchased most film tickets, it often recommended changes that would boost interest among this group. Story tests for Columbia's *The Jolson Story* (1946) provide an instructive example. ARI's first synopsis asked whether viewers would like to see a film based on the life of Al Jolson. Few 19-year-olds expressed interest. New story synopses inquired whether audiences would enjoy "a story about the 1920s, with songs such as 'Mammy' and 'Swanee River.'" At this, teenage attention rose. To maintain the interest of this key group, posters and ads featured a banner down one side that listed twenty-six songs performed during the film.[20]

Though title, story, and cast tests provided early indications of a film's potential, they did not measure its overall effect. As Gallup himself admitted, preproduction tests could not evaluate the impact of an inventive script, witty dialogue, or imaginative direction.[21] In response to the limitations of its early research, ARI began conducting preview screenings with carefully selected audiences in late 1943 and early 1944. Though studios had conducted advance screenings for many years, ARI presented its screenings as a more scientific assessment of viewer interest.

Before 1940, executives made little effort to select the audience for a preview screening. Most previews took place in theaters around Los Angeles and attracted large numbers of industry insiders.[22] As ARI pointed out, previews conducted this way did not reflect the interests and preferences of the average American filmgoer, and may have biased responses in favor of particular films or directors.[23] In assembling the audience for its screenings, ARI used the same method of cross-section sampling employed in its other work, and selected participants according to their representation in the general film-going population. Each demographic group was included, and the company also chose viewers to reflect the same percentage of positive and negative responses that were found in earlier studies for the film. The sampling methods ARI used to assemble a preview audience were designed to guarantee that it was "a replica in miniature of the movie masses."[24]

This view of the audience as a mass was also reinforced by the mechanism ARI used to collect spectators' responses—the Hopkins "Televoting" Machine. The device was modeled after the Program Analyzer developed in the late 1930s to monitor listener reactions to radio programs. Audiences working with the Analyzer held one button in each hand, one red and one green. If they enjoyed a segment of a program, they were instructed to press the green button and to hold it down for as long as they felt a positive reaction. If they disliked a section of the program, they pushed the red button. If they did not press either button, the lack of response registered as indifference. Each listener's responses were recorded on a moving paper strip, with the "likes" encoded as a solid line, and the "dislikes" encoded as a separate dotted line. The pens recording these responses were synchronized with the program second by second, and at the end of the test, researchers combined the individual graphs to develop an overall audience profile.[25]

The machine ARI used differed from the Program Analyzer in the range of responses it offered to viewers and the profile it developed of their reactions. Instead of two buttons, the Televoting Machine featured a luminous dial offering respondents five choices; the switch could be turned to positions marked "dull, dislike, like, like very much." However, unlike the Program Analyzer, the Televoting machine did not record individual reactions; rather, it combined the responses of different audience members to provide a cumulative reaction for each moment. The flow of current from each electrical meter registered on a central machine that printed the combined reactions in the form of a bar graph. The recording device for the Televoting machine was attached directly to the projector and thus synchronized the graph with the film. The chart that resulted from this process provided a second-by-second account of audience reaction and could extend as much as four feet. Analysts noted the beginnings and ends of scenes so that dips and crests in the graph could be correlated with specific parts of the film.[26]

Studios used these "preview profiles" as a guide in editing rough cuts, and deleted or shortened sequences that failed to reach a particular level of response. In *The Jolson Story*, for example, one song and the dialogue between two minor characters were cut based on ARI's previews.[27] Charts also brought to light areas of confusion in a film. At a preview for *Gilda*, for example, audiences became confused when the character's husband returned after having been apparently lost at sea. Based on ARI's profile, Columbia filmed an additional sequence showing that he had been rescued after his accident.[28]

In addition to machine read-outs, ARI used postscreening interviews and questionnaires to gather information about viewers' reactions.[29] These methods provided a check on the data provided by the charts and allowed ARI to follow up on audiences' responses. They were intended to discover if people had forgotten to turn the dial during a particularly absorbing scene, or reveal precisely which features of a sequence stimulated their reactions. These follow-up questions functioned in much the same way as Gallup's earlier studies of newspaper and magazine reading—as an effort to pinpoint the factors motivating viewer response. Preview profiles were one of ARI's most popular features and were widely used between 1944 and 1947. The institute tested and retested films until audiences displayed a level of enthusiasm that satisfied studio executives. The information obtained from previews was also used to determine a film's release pattern and the nature and extent of its publicity.

As ARI concluded early in its research, the success of a film depended on both its intrinsic qualities and whether it received adequate publicity. ARI's research also aided executives in planning exploitation campaigns that built on the desires audiences had expressed. When a film earned a poor response in previews, and its title and story tests were low, studios spent less money on advertising and opened it quickly to avoid negative word of mouth.[30] If early responses were strong, a film might open slowly, with a big promotional campaign to build public interest. In the case of Goldwyn's *The Best Years of Our Lives* (1946), early reactions were so positive that ARI recommended the film be screened in roadshow engagements at special prices.[31]

In planning publicity campaigns, ARI urged studios to start at least six months in advance of release, and use gossip, background articles, and other pieces of news to build audience awareness. As the company argued, early publicity for a film established a "mental rallying point that can be built up and reinforced repeatedly by the release date."[32] To reach the largest possible audience, the company urged studios to employ many different campaigns that could be tailored to particular markets, rather than use one type of promotion. On ARI's advice, Goldwyn promoted *The Kid from Brooklyn* (1946) in sixty newspaper and magazine stories, radio plugs, and product tie-ins with cereals, soaps, cigars, and mattresses.[33]

As Goldwyn's promotional strategy illustrates, ARI's research increased producers' awareness of particular segments within the audience and stimulated the development of marketing campaigns targeted to them.[34] ARI brought to film promotion techniques that were widely used in advertising campaigns for different kinds of business. Its audience research served to link film reception more firmly with the purchase of other goods and reinforced the status of Hollywood films as items to be consumed.

The impact of studio promotion on the public was measured through tests of "publicity penetration." Although these began in the early 1940s, their use increased dramatically after the war, when they became part of the overall coordination that ARI offered. Interviewers asked respondents whether they had heard of a film, and whether they knew something about it. If they were able to correctly identify its cast or some element of the story, they were said to have been "penetrated" by the publicity. ARI further divided its studies into "shown area" and "not shown area" penetration, to measure the effect of local versus national publicity.[35]

Penetration tests allowed studios to gauge the effectiveness of different forms of advertising and to determine the level of audience interest in a film before its release. At the Disney studio, advertising executive Card Walker constructed elaborate charts to track changes in audience penetration after ads appeared in national magazines and local newspapers This enabled the studio to compare the relative effectiveness of different media in reaching viewers, and to coordinate promotional campaigns with releases in different cities. This synchronization between promotion and release recalls similar practices in advertising and radio during this period.

After several years of research, ARI announced that it could use penetration studies and preproduction research to estimate the box office return of a film. Through a complicated formula computing "want-to-see," the marquee value of a cast, and penetration research, the company developed charts that allowed producers to determine the level of awareness a film had to achieve in order to earn a given amount of money. With this information, David Selznick held off on releasing *Duel in the Sun* for six months after it was ready in order to build its penetration to a level where he could recuperate the film's expenses. Aware of the flaws in his production, Selznick played the film off quickly, before negative word of mouth could hurt its financial return.[36]

A Totalizing View?

ARI's efforts to analyze audience response at all levels of production illustrate its goal of managing spectatorship to achieve a greater profit for the studios. As more and more executives began to commission this work, other groups within the industry attacked its methods and assumptions. The debates that ARI's research generated highlight the historical and ideological forces that were reshaping Hollywood during the 1940s.

The scientific aura surrounding Gallup's research was due in part to its effort to provide a totalizing view of film spectatorship. ARI's battery of techniques worked to isolate and define every element influencing viewer response, from narrative and cast to advertising and exhibition. Using empirical methods that had been tested in national polls, ARI promised executives advance information about the most unpredictable element of film economics—audience reaction. Its surveys seemed to provide an element of control over the risks and uncertainty of film manufacture. By minimizing risk and increasing cost efficiency, executives believed they gained a competitive edge.

That producers relied so heavily on audience research is symptomatic of the pressures operating in Hollywood during the late 1940s. In this period studios lost the near-total control they had exercised over production and exhibition, due to the increasing efforts to unionize on the part of actors and writers, and government antitrust decrees that gave more power to theater owners. The widespread use of audience research after the war can be seen as an effort to maintain dominance even as the industry's monopolistic structure was disintegrating.

Ernest Bornemann forcefully articulated the terms of battle against audience research during the postwar period in a July 1947 article for *Harper's* magazine. In a scathing attack on viewer surveys and the executives who relied on them, Bornemann charged that Hollywood's "utter dependence" on Gallup's polls had turned film production into "a sterile, glutted and intractable thing." The slavish devotion to empirical research made producers less willing to take risks, he asserted, since it was easier to create films that satisfied a preestablished demand than to experiment with new approaches. Surveys allowed no room for variations among viewers and failed to recognize that films are complex works of art, not industrial products.[37]

Bornemann's diatribe illustrated how studies of spectatorship became intertwined with debates about the nature of film and the place of individual creativity within an industrial system. His attack defined the two issues that came to govern disputes about ARI's research—creativity and control. Objections to ARI advanced by writers, stars, and theater owners all focused on these concerns. In speaking of spectators, they were at the same time referring to broader issues at stake in film production.

When ARI conducted its double-feature poll in 1940, exhibitors were the most vocal critics of its work. In the postwar era, further attacks came from members of the Screen Writer's Guild. The group invited Gallup to address a special meeting in March 1947, and his speech, along with members' reactions to it, was discussed in the organization's professional journal. In critiquing ARI's methods, writers focused in particular on the use of story tests as a guide to developing screenplays, preview machines, and the implications of the demographic samples ARI used.

In attacking story tests, Robert Shaw argued that "the evanescent beauty and tenderness of a great film cannot be captured in 60 words."[38] Dudley Nichols deplored the inhibitions that such tests placed on screenwriters, who had to develop characters and narratives to match predetermined patterns. "This new scientific era in movie-making [is] sometimes tough on writers and filmmakers, who can work with enthusiasm on something they personally happen to like, and can grow strangely apathetic when told to work on 'public demand.'"[39]

The English producer Alexander Korda shared their sentiments. "To sell pictures on the basis of poll-indicated popularity as to title and story elements is a very sound practice and one I might use myself. But to try to determine public interest in a story on the basis of a few questions is absurd. How would you react if someone stopped you on the street, or rang your doorbell, and asked, 'Would you like to see a picture about a sixteenth century English king and his several wives?'"[40] Korda's reference to his own *The Private Life of Henry VIII* (1933) underscores how the form of Gallup's surveys limited the kinds of responses people could make.

Particular scorn was reserved for the Televoting machine that ARI used to monitor preview audiences. Ranald MacDougall, screenwriter for *Objective Burma* and *Mildred Pierce*, recounted his experiences with a similar machine when he worked at CBS radio. As he described, many people forgot to move the dial when they became absorbed in a film, thus registering their reaction as indifference. Audiences also showed a slight delay in reaction time, so that "a moving scene will register nothing and slightly afterwards a dissolve from a door opening to a door closing will appear on the graph as one of the finest pieces of acting yet this year." Most important, MacDougall noticed that film audiences tend to view characters and situations as real, rather than as representational constructs. In one experience at CBS, audiences reacted so negatively to a Nazi documentary that the machine broke down and had to be overhauled.[41]

In both its story tests and preview screenings, writers argued, the cross-section ARI used meant that films had to appeal to teenage audiences. Previews were often filled with "vivacious, gum-chewing bobby soxers," and narratives seemed designed to fit their level of experience. By defining the audience as a mass, ARI ignored the interests of other segments of the population. As MacDougall demanded, "We *know* what junior wants, and he gets it. Why not find out *what senior wants*?"[42] In the opinion of these writers, audience research perpetuated mediocrity in films by gearing characters and narratives to satisfy the lowest common denominator among audiences.

Actors and actresses also complained that executives used audience research to control production and limit creativity. During the emergence of the star system in the 1910s, evidence of audience affection increased actors' bargaining power with producers. Gallup's studies of box office power, on the other hand, supported the studio's hegemony over players. In the late 1940s, as many actors began to set up their own production companies and tried to wrest control from the studios, stars came to view Gallup's empirical methods as another tool for producer control. In an article entitled "Audience Research Blues," *Variety* noted that "columns of statistical surveys" were beginning to play a "deadly decisive" role in actors' careers. Stars felt ARI's quarterly index was often the determining factor in casting a film. Some described walking into a producer's office and watching him "open that secret drawer, look down on a column of figures, and say, 'Sorry, you're not the type.'"[43]

In the postwar period, the studies of actors and actresses that Gallup first carried out for RKO became an ongoing, industry-wide phenomenon. Gallup also continued to conduct the "people's poll" he had begun at RKO in 1943, in which he announced the public's favorite films and film stars right before the Academy Awards.[44] In February 1945, Gallup took over *Photoplay*'s annual awards to the most popular stars and made it a continuing survey. Trade paper ads presented the polls as the film equivalent to Gallup's election surveys. "The same scientific methods will be used which have enabled Dr. Gallup to predict the winner in five presidential elections."[45] Gallup also made quarterly "check-ups" of stars' popularity and these were reported regularly in the trades.[46]

Though studio publicity often depicted a star's life as the epitome of freedom and autonomy, many experienced audience research as a threat to their identity. Appearing on a radio talk show, Paulette Goddard and Burgess Meredith expressed fear that somewhere there was "a machine-made estimate of us all."[47] In his study of the procedures ARI used to measure actors' popularity, Gorham Kindem discovered that it grossly underestimated the earning power of Hollywood stars, and concluded that actors and actresses were not paid according to their actual value to the company.[48] ARI's numerical estimates of popularity constrained both the emotional and financial freedom of actors and actresses.

In describing his film research near the end of his life, Gallup complained that Hollywood producers during the 1930s and 1940s were too distant from the small towns where most Americans lived.[49] Part of the impetus for his work was the desire to bring to Hollywood's attention the interests of local audiences. As they had with the double-feature poll, exhibitors felt that he was undercutting their autonomy and continued to commission polls of their own. Many ARI surveys drew contrasts between the interests of viewers in rural and urban areas. In 1949 the Allied Association of Motion Picture Exhibitors commissioned a study that concluded viewers in large cities did not differ significantly from their small-town counterparts.[50] As ARI continued to issue its quarterly audits of box office power, some theater owners declared that the star system was dead. In a 1951 study, Detroit exhibitors surveyed over 22,000 audience members and found that, contrary to ARI's assertion that stars influenced attendance, only a handful of viewers went to the theater to see their favorite actors.[51]

The failure of Gallup's political poll in the 1948 election dealt the final blow to the Audience Research Institute. AIPO's prediction that Thomas Dewey would defeat Harry Truman nearly ruined its image in the public's mind. Both RKO and Disney, which had been negotiating contract renewals with the company, decided instead to commission its services on a case-by-case basis. Though Gallup insisted that his film and political research were entirely separate, the associations he had fostered between them made producers skeptical of this claim. In 1947, Gallup had left Young & Rubicam to form his own advertising research firm, Gallup and Robinson. Though he tried for several years to drum up interest in advertising research, after 1948 studios began to turn away from his techniques.

Reporting the Facts

The 1940s mark an important juncture in media research because it was during this period that the discourses of the 1930s, which were organized around a view of the audience as a mass, evolved into the 1950s' conception of audiences as fragmented and selective.[52] The 1930s witnessed the development of public opinion and communication research that assessed the effects of propaganda and other messages on large groups of people. By the 1950s, this view of audiences as impressionable and easily influenced was changing to a conception of them as more selective viewers whose motivations and choices could be examined in detail.

During the 1940s, studios became aware of differences among viewers, but still wanted to bring in the largest possible audience. Though Gallup's research revealed contrasts among demographic groups, ARI urged executives to attract as many viewers as possible from each category. In the 1950s, as divestiture increased competition between studios and made a wider range of exhibition spaces available, film companies began to market their products to increasingly specialized audiences.[53] Films such as *Sunset Boulevard* (1950), which earned a strong profit in urban markets despite poor regional showings, fueled arguments about whether films had to appeal to the masses or could earn enough income by attracting only a segment of the audience.[54]

Changes in exhibition patterns, and the desire to reach more specialized audiences, promoted the development of new research techniques that eventually replaced many of ARI's methods. During the 1950s, machines such as Bernard Cirlin's Reactograph helped producers determine how a film affected particular groups of viewers. Used at previews, it recorded audiences' reactions as separate profiles before combining them into a composite picture. With the Reactograph, producers could study the reactions of the portions of the audience they wanted to reach, such as women, teenagers, and people with high incomes, and reedit or reshoot sequences to strengthen their intended effect.[55]

These changes also made audience research attractive to the growing numbers of industrial filmmakers. During the 1950s, AT&T, among others, used preview machines to assess the effectiveness of public relations messages. The replacement of ARI's Televoting machine by devices like the Reactograph illustrates the trend toward increasingly precise demographics in market research and heralds the movement of opinion research into other areas of American business.

Though ARI's formal contacts with Hollywood studios ended in the 1950s, many of its techniques were assimilated into industry practice and continue to affect film production today. At Disney, for example, the practice of gathering responses to a film became known as "doing an ARI."[56] Today, film companies that use audience research measure responses to titles and proposed casts, screen rough cuts for preview audiences, and test the effectiveness of advertising strategies.[57] In 1994 the Gallup organization launched a comeback into film research by establishing a Motion Picture Research Division based in Irvine, California. Unlike its Hollywood predecessor of the 1940s, this new service offered an 800 number that people could call after a screening to give their opinions of a film, indicate whether they would recommend it to a friend, and if they planned to buy the movie soundtrack or video. Though the company no longer employs such techniques as continuing audits of marquee values, its new approach offered studios a quick indication of a film's word-of-mouth.[58]

This account of Gallup's audience research has analyzed a critical historical period in the development of theories of film spectatorship. As this study demonstrates, empirical research encodes values and assumptions that reflect the impact of cultural, economic, social, and ideological forces. Used to maintain power, audience research can also be seen as a symptom of its limitations. Though they strive to pinpoint the factors that influence our responses, ARI's battery of techniques illustrates the ultimate impossibility of predicting and managing the audience. Rather than providing definitive answers, Gallup's research illustrates the continuing challenges involved in translating the complexity of our desires into quantitative forms.

Abbreviations Used and Collections Consulted

The following abbreviations are used in the notes.

Newspapers and Magazines

FD   *Film Daily*
HR   *Hollywood Reporter*
MPH   *Motion Picture Herald*
NYT   *New York Times*
WSJ   *Wall Street Journal*

Collections Consulted

AFI—The American Film Institute, Louis B. Mayer Library, Hollywood, California: "RKO Radio Flash"

American Institute of Public Opinion Surveys, The Roper Center for Public Opinion Research (RCPOR), University of Connecticut at Storrs

AMPAS—The Academy of Motion Picture Arts and Sciences, The Margaret Herrick Library, Beverly Hills, California: George Stevens Collection

Audience Research Institute Reports: The Walt Disney Studio Archive (WDSA), Burbank, California

Daily Iowan: Special Collections Department, University of Iowa, Iowa City, Iowa. *See also* Iowa Authors Collection

David Ogilvy Papers: Manuscript Division, The Library of Congress, Washington, D.C. *See also* George Gallup Papers

DOS Papers: The David O. Selznick Papers, Harry Ransom Humanities Research Center (HRHRC), University of Texas at Austin. *See also* JHW Papers

Gallup, George: Interview with Paul Sheatsley, March 22, 1978 (NORC, University of Chicago, Chicago, Illinois)

Gallup, George, "The Reminiscences of George Horace Gallup": Oral History Collection, Butler Library, Columbia University, New York, New York. *See also* Meyer, Eugene

George Gallup Papers: Manuscript Division, The Library of Congress, Washington, D.C. *See also* David Ogilvy Papers

George Stevens Collection: *See* AMPAS

HRHRC: Harry Ransom Humanities Research Center, University of Texas at Austin. *See also* DOS Papers; JHW Papers

Iowa Authors Collection: Special Collections Department, University of Iowa, Iowa City, Iowa. *See also Daily Iowan*

JHW Papers: The John Hay Whitney Papers, Harry Ransom Humanities Research Center (HRHRC), University of Texas at Austin. *See also* DOS Papers

J. Walter Thompson Collection: *See* JWT Papers

JWT Papers: J. Walter Thompson Collection, Perkins Library Special Collections, John W. Hartman Center for Sales, Advertising, and Marketing History, Duke University, Durham, North Carolina

Meyer, Eugene, "Reminiscences": Oral History Collection, Butler Library, Columbia University, New York, New York. *See also* Gallup, George, "Reminiscences"

Nelson Rockefeller Papers: The Rockefeller Family Archives (RFA), Tarrytown, New York

NORC: The National Opinion Research Center, University of Chicago. *See* Gallup, George: Interview with Paul Sheatsley

Ogilvy, David. *See* David Ogilvy Papers

The Orson Welles Papers: Lilly Library, Indiana University, Bloomington, Indiana

RCPOR: The Roper Center for Public Opinion Research, University of Connecticut at Storrs. *See* American Institute of Public Opinion Surveys

RAC: The Rockefeller Family Archives, Rockefeller Archives Center, Tarrytown, New York. *See also* Nelson Rockefeller Papers

RKO Papers: RKO Radio Pictures Archive, Turner Entertainment, Culver City, California

"RKO Radio Flash": *See* AFI

Rockefeller, Nelson: *See* Nelson Rockefeller Papers

Walter Wanger Papers: Wisconsin Center for Film and Theater Research (WCFTR), Madison, Wisconsin

WCFTR: Wisconsin Center for Film and Theater Research. *See* Walter Wanger Papers

WDSA: The Walt Disney Studio Archive, Burbank California. *See* Audience Research Institute Reports

Welles, Orson. *See* The Orson Welles Papers

Y&R: Young & Rubicam Archive, New York, New York

Notes

1. What Do Audiences Want?

1. Adolph Zukor, with Dale Kramer, *The Public Is Never Wrong* (New York: Putnam's, 1953), 42.

2. Annette Kuhn, "Women's Genres," *Screen* 25.1 (Jan.–Feb. 1984): 23.

3. Mary Ann Doane, *The Desire to Desire: The Woman's Film of the 1940s* (Bloomington: Indiana University Press, 1987), 8. For recent examples of this approach, see Warren Buckland, *The Film Spectator: From Sign to Mind* (Amsterdam: Amsterdam University Press, 1995).

4. See, for example, Judith Mayne, *Cinema and Spectatorship* (New York and London: Routledge, 1993), 54.

5. Virginia Nightingale, *Studying Audiences: The Shock of the Real* (London and New York: Routledge, 1996), and see also essays by Ann Gray and Kim Christian Schroder in Pertti Alasuutari, ed., *Rethinking the Media Audience* (London and Thousand Oaks, Calif.: Sage, 1999), 22–68.

6. Keith Michael Baker, *Inventing the French Revolution* (Cambridge: Cambridge University Press, 1990), 167–99; John Durham Peters, "Historical Tensions in the Concept of Public Opinion," in Theodore L. Glasser and Charles T. Salmon, eds., *Public Opinion and the Communication of Consent* (New York and London: Guilford Press, 1995), 3–32.

7. Mona Ozouf, "'Public Opinion' at the End of the Old Regime," *Journal of Modern History* 60 (Sept. 1988): S3–S9; and Elisabeth Noelle-Neumann, "Public Opinion and Rationality," in Glasser and Salmon, eds., *Public Opinion and the Communication of Consent*, 33–54.

8. Ang, quoted in Peters, "Historical Tensions," 18.

9. Ien Ang, *Desperately Seeking the Audience* (New York and London: Routledge, 1991), 7–8.

10. Susan Herbst, *Numbered Voices* (Chicago: University of Chicago Press, 1993), 43–68.

11. James R. Beniger, *The Control Revolution* (Cambridge: Harvard University Press, 1986).

12. Mary Poovey, *A History of the Modern Fact* (Chicago and London: University of Chicago Press, 1998), xii.

13. Patricia Cline Cohen, *A Calculating People: The Spread of Numeracy in Early America* (Chicago and London: University of Chicago Press, 1982), 40.

14. Ibid., 44.

15. Warren I. Susman, *Culture as History* (New York: Pantheon, 1984), 158.

16. Ang, *Desperately Seeking the Audience*, 8.

17. Pierre Bourdieu, "Public Opinion Does Not Exist" (1972), trans. Mary C. Axtmann, in Armand Mattelart and Seth Siegelaub, eds., *Communication and Class Struggle*, vol. 1, *Capitalism, Imperialism* (New York: International General, 1979), 127.

18. Ang, *Desperately Seeking the Audience*, 41.

19. Ibid., 8.

20. For examples of recent studies that focus on the particularities and complexities of film reception, see Annette Kuhn, *Dreaming of Fred and Ginger: Cinema and Cultural Memory* (New York: New York University Press, 2002); Melvyn Stokes and Richard Maltby, eds., *Identifying Hollywood's Audiences: Cultural Identity and the Movies* (London: British Film Institute, 1999); Will Brooker and Deborah Jermyn, *The Audience Studies Reader* (London and New York: Routledge, 2003).

21. Leo Handel, *Hollywood Looks at Its Audience* (Urbana: University of Illinois Press, 1950; rpt., New York: Arno Press, 1976).

2. Guesswork Eliminated

1. Marty S. Knepper and John S. Lawrence, "Visions of Iowa in Hollywood Film," *Iowa Heritage Illustrated* 79.4 (Winter 1998): 157–69. The well-known 1962 version of *State Fair* took place at the Texas State Fair.

2. Thomas J. Morain, *Prairie Grass Roots: An Iowa Small Town in the Early Twentieth Century* (Ames: Iowa State University Press, 1988), 26–32; Eric Pace, "George H. Gallup Is Dead at 82," *New York Times* (hereafter, *NYT*), July 28, 1984, 9; George Gallup, "The Reminiscences of George Horace Gallup" (1962), Columbia University Oral History Collection, New York, New York, transcript, 4–5.

3. George Gallup, interview with Paul Sheatsley, Mar. 22, 1978, National Opinion Research Center, University of Chicago (Chicago, Ill.), transcript, 1; Gallup, "Reminiscences," 2–3 and 14; Morain, *Prairie Grass Roots*, 11–12.

4. Gallup, interview with Sheatsley, 2.

5. Gallup, "Reminiscences," 11.

6. Ibid., 12–13.

7. Morain, *Prairie Grass Roots*, 30.

8. Gallup, interview with Sheatsley, 3, and "Reminiscences," 13.

9. As Jean Converse notes in *Survey Research in the United States: Roots and Emergence, 1890–1960* (Berkeley: University of California Press, 1987), 115.

10. W. A. Jessup, "How Education Grows in Iowa," *Des Moines Register & Tribune*, Mar. 18, 1929, 4; and "Memorial Union," *Daily Iowan*, Apr. 28, 1921, 4.

11. Gallup, "Reminiscences," 18; "Iowan Grows 40 Per Cent," *Daily Iowan*, Sept. 22, 1921, 9; "Elect Gallup and Upton," *Daily Iowan*, May 3, 1922, 1; "Iowan Editors Outline Plans," *Daily Iowan*, May 4, 1922, 1.

12. Dorothy Schwieder, *Iowa: The Middle Land* (Ames: Iowa State University Press, 1996), 148–51; Joseph Frazier Wald, *Iowa: A Bicentennial History* (New York: Norton, 1978), 176.

13. "Hard Times," *Daily Iowan*, Dec. 14, 1921, 1.

14. Advertisements, *Daily Iowan*, Mar. 4, 1921, 3, and Mar 31, 1922, 6.

15. For examples of ads that announce rapid changes in programs, see the ad for D. W. Griffith's *Way Down East*, *Daily Iowan*, Jan. 16, 1921, 4; Charlie Chaplin's *The Kid*, *Daily Iowan*, Mar. 8, 1921, 4. This policy was typical of the time, according to Richard Koszarski, *An Evening's Entertainment: The Age of the Silent Feature Picture, 1915–1928* (New York: Scribner's, 1990), 34–51.

16. Richard DeCordova, *Picture Personalities: The Emergence of the Star System in America* (Urbana: University of Illinois Press, 1990), Gaylyn Studlar, *This Mad Masquerade: Stardom and Masculinity in the Jazz Age* (New York: Columbia University Press, 1996).

17. Richard Dyer, *Stars* (London: BFI, 1979), 45.

18. Ad for *What Women Will Do*, *Daily Iowan*, Apr. 24, 1921, 5.

19. Ad, *Daily Iowan*, Nov. 9, 1922, 4.

20. Morain, *Prairie Grass Roots*, 169.

21. Studlar, *This Mad Masquerade*, 81.

22. Ibid., 147.

23. Donald S. Napoli, *Architects of Adjustment: The History of the Psychological Profession in the United States* (Port Washington, N.Y.: Kennikat Press, 1981), 47.

24. Otto Klemm, *A History of Psychology* (New York: Scribner's, 1914), 1.

25. Arthur L. Blumenthal, "Wilhelm Wundt and Early American Psychology," in R. W. Rieber, ed., *Wilhelm Wundt and the Making of a Scientific Psychology* (New York and London: Plenum Press, 1980), 129–32; James F. Brennan, *History and Systems of Psychology* (Englewood Cliffs, N.J.: Prentice-Hall, 1982), 201–202; K. B. Madsen, *A History of Psychology in Metascientific Perspective* (Amsterdam and New York: Elsevier, 1988), 116–25; and David J. Murray, *A History of Western Psychology*, 2d ed. (Englewood Cliffs, N.J.: Prentice-Hall, 1988), 199–222.

26. Michael M. Sokal, "James McKeen Cattell and American Psychology in the 1920s," in Josef Brozek, ed., *Explorations in the History of Psychology in the*

United States (Lewisburg, Penn.: Bucknell University Press, 1984), 284; Loren Baritz, *Servants of Power* (Middletown, Conn.: Wesleyan University Press, 1960), 45–47; Edmund C. Lynch, "Walter Dill Scott: Pioneer Industrial Psychologist," *Business History Review* 42.2 (Summer 1968): 150–52, 162–67. For further discussion of psychologists' contribution to World War I, see Kerry W. Buckley, *Mechanical Man* (New York: Guilford Press, 1989), 99–111.

27. For histories of scientific management, see Reinhard Bendix, *Work and Authority in Industry* (New York: John Wiley, 1956), 254–340; Judith Merkle, *Management and Ideology* (Berkeley: University of California Press, 1980); and Daniel Nelson, *Managers and Workers: Origins of the New Factory System in the United States, 1880–1920* (Madison: University of Wisconsin Press, 1975), 48–78. An excellent history of Taylorism is Robert Kanigel, *The One Best Way: Frederick Winslow Taylor and the Enigma of Efficiency* (New York: Penguin, 1997); pages 486–503 analyze the diffusion of his theories into other areas of business beyond the factory.

28. Bendix, *Work and Authority*, 278; Baritz, *Servants of Power*, 60–71; Sokal, "James McKeen Cattell," 284.

29. Napoli, *Architects of Adjustment*, 5.

30. Carl E. Seashore, *Pioneering in Psychology*, University of Iowa Studies No. 398 (Iowa City: University of Iowa Press, 1942), 6–7.

31. Gallup, interview with Sheatsley, 4.

32. "Carl Emil Seashore," in Carl Murchison, ed., *A History of Psychology in Autobiography*, vol. 1 (Worcester, Mass.: Clark University Press, 1930), 225–37; Carl Seashore, *Introduction to Psychology* (New York: Macmillan, 1923). See also "Seashore's Text Book Ready Soon," *Daily Iowan*, Mar. 21, 1923, 2.

33. "Carl Emil Seashore," in *A History of Psychology*, 260–64, 280–82; Seashore, *Pioneering in Psychology*, 160–162.

34. Susan Porter Benson, *Counter Cultures: Saleswomen, Managers, and Customers in American Department Stores, 1890–1940* (Urbana: University of Illinois Press, 1988). See also Ralph M. Hower, *History of Macy's of New York, 1858–1919* (Cambridge: Harvard University Press, 1943), 141–56.

35. Charles W. Hoyt, *Scientific Sales Management Today* (New York: Ronald Press, 1929), 24–25; Lynch, "Walter Dill Scott," 152–60; Mary Carsky, "One Hundred Years of Retail Education: Will the Wheel Continue to Turn?," paper presented at the Conference on the History of Advertising Research and Marketing, Duke University, May 17–20, 2001.

36. George Gallup, "A Study in the Selection of Salespeople for Killian's Department Store, Cedar Rapids, Iowa," unpublished M.A. thesis, University of Iowa, June 1925, 6–25. See also the article he published from his thesis: George H. Gallup, "Traits of Successful Retail Salespeople," *Journal of Personnel Research* 4 (Apr. 1926): 474–82. For a discussion of the role and work of the sales manager in this period, see Beulah Elfreth Kennard, *The Educational Director* (New York: Ronald Press, 1918).

37. Gallup, "A Study in the Selection of Salespeople," 24–30, 46–60.

38. Ibid., 69.
39. John G. Jenkins, *Psychology in Business and Industry* (New York: John Wiley, 1935), 82–84.
40. Dorothy Ross, *The Origins of American Social Science* (New York: Cambridge University Press, 1990), 433
41. Baritz, *Servants of Power*.
42. Napoli, *Architects of Adjustment*, 34.
43. David H. Weaver and Maxwell E. McCombs, "Journalism and Social Science: A New Relationship?" *Public Opinion Quarterly* 44 (1980): 480–81; and David T. Z. Mindich, *Just the Facts: How "Objectivity" Came to Define American Journalism* (New York: NYU Press, 1998).
44. Gallup's work in journalism at Iowa is discussed in Becky Wilson Hawbaker, "Taking 'the Pulse of Democracy': George Gallup, Iowa, and the Origin of the Gallup Poll," *The Palimpsest* 74.3 (Fall 1993): 105, and in "Iowans Honored in Journalism," *Des Moines Sunday Register*, May 19, 1929, 6. The winning student entries were published in George Horace Gallup, ed., *The Best Creative Work in American High Schools, 1927–1928* (Iowa City, Iowa: National Honorary Society for High School Journalists, 1928), and in H.A. Berens, ed., *The Best Creative Work in American High Schools, 1929–1930* (Iowa City, Iowa: National Honorary Society for High School Journalists, 1930). Harry S. Bunker, George H. Gallup, W. Harry Harper, and Charles H. Stout, *The Business Department of School Publications* (Iowa City, Iowa: Lombard Press, 1927) recounts the more business-oriented methods he advocated for student journalists.
45. Gallup, interview with Sheatsley, 5.
46. George Gallup, "An Objective Method for Determining Reader Interest in the Content of a Newspaper," unpublished Ph.D. diss., University of Iowa, Aug. 1928.
47. Ibid., 1–11.
48. Gallup, "An Objective Method," 27–37; "The Cowles Boys," *Newsweek*, July 4, 1949, 52, 54; William B. Friedricks, *Covering Iowa* (Ames: Iowa State University Press, 2000), 45–82. Gallup describes how he met Mike Cowles in Gallup, "Reminiscences," 43–44.
49. Gallup, "An Objective Method," 17–19, 128–36. The study was published as George Gallup, "A Scientific Method for Determining Reader-Interest," *Journalism Quarterly* 7.1 (Mar. 1930): 1–13.
50. George Gallup, "Guesswork Eliminated in New Method for Determining Reader Interest," *Editor & Publisher* (Feb. 8, 1930): 5.
51. Roland Marchand, *Advertising the American Dream* (Berkeley: University of California Press, 1985), 110.
52. Gallup, "Reminiscences," 31.
53. Ibid., 28–29, 42–51; George Mills, *Harvey Ingham and Gardner Cowles, Sr.: Things Don't Just Happen* (Ames: Iowa State University Press, 1977), 107–108; "Cowles Brothers Build a $50,000,000 'Empire,'" *Advertising Age*, Aug. 1, 1949, 38, Friedricks, *Covering Iowa*, 86–88.

54. "Comic Pages," *Tide* 5 (May 1931): 10–11; also see "Competitive Comics" *Tide* 6 (June 1932): 14.

55. "Comic Pages," 11.

56. "Ads in Funnies," *Time*, June 13, 1932, 49; "Competitive Comics," 14; and Otis Pease, *The Responsibilities of American Advertising* (New Haven: Yale University Press, 1958), 185–86.

57. See, for example, George Burton Hotchkiss, *An Outline of Advertising: Its Philosophy, Science, Art, and Strategy* (1933) (rpt., New York: Macmillan, 1940), 170–71; and Harold J. Rudolph, *Attention and Interest Factors in Advertising* (New York: Funk and Wagnalls, 1947), 100. *Printer's Ink* cited the campaign in a special issue highlighting advertising milestones of the 1930s: "1932," *Printer's Ink* (July 28, 1938,): 420.

58. Merle Curti, "The Changing Concept of 'Human Nature' in the Literature of American Advertising," *Business History Review* 41 (Winter 1967): 335–47. Also see David Kuna, "The Concept of Suggestion in the Early History of Advertising Psychology," *Journal of the History of the Behavioral Sciences* 12 (1976): 347–53; and Kerry W. Buckley, "The Selling of a Psychologist: John Broadus Watson and the Application of Behavioral Techniques to Advertising," *Journal of the History of the Behavioral Sciences* 18 (July 1982): 210.

59. Pease, *Responsibilities of American Advertising*, 183.

60. Ibid., 187.

61. A staff member of the J. Walter Thompson agency, quoted in Marchand, *Advertising the American Dream*, 112.

62. J. J. O'Malley, "Black Beans and White Beans," *New Yorker*, Mar. 2, 1940, 20.

3. The Laws That Determine Interest

1. Stephen Fox, *The Mirror Makers: A History of American Advertising and Its Creators* (New York: Morrow, 1984), 101.

2. Stuart Chase and F. J. Schlink, *Your Money's Worth* (New York: Macmillan, 1927), 26.

3. Ralph Hower, *The History of an Advertising Agency* (Cambridge: Harvard University Press, 1939; rev. ed., 1949), 151.

4. Helen Woodward, *Through Many Windows* (New York: Harper, 1926), 282.

5. James Rorty, *Our Master's Voice* (New York: John Day, 1934), 5.

6. James Playsted Wood, *The Story of Advertising* (New York: Ronald Press, 1958), 417–31.

7. Estimates of the Consumers' Counsel Division of the Department of Agriculture, cited in Hower, *History of an Advertising Agency*, 151.

8. Theodore Peterson, *Magazines in the Twentieth Century* (Urbana: University of Illinois Press, 1956), 25.

9. George Burton Hotchkiss, *An Outline of Advertising: Its Philosophy, Science, Art, and Strategy* (1933) (rpt., New York: Macmillan, 1940), 66–67; Frank Luther Mott, *American Journalism, A History: 1690–1960*, 3d ed. (New York: Macmillan, 1967), 674–76.

10. Hower, *History of an Advertising Agency*, 148.
11. *Adversiting & Selling* 22 (Dec. 7, 1933): 9.
12. Hower, *History of an Advertising Agency*, 149.
13. "Macfadden Buys 'Liberty,' Sells 'Detroit Daily,'" *Advertising Age*, Apr. 4, 1931, 1, 14; "*Liberty* Is Sold," *Advertising & Selling* 16 (Apr. 15, 1931): 27; William H. Taft, "Bernarr Macfadden: One of a Kind," *Journalism Quarterly* 45 (1968): 632.
14. George Gallup, "Survey of Reader Interest in *Saturday Evening Post, Liberty, Collier's, Literary Digest*" (The *Liberty* Research Department, 1931); "Dr. Gallup's Next Job," n.d. (1932), 4 (George Gallup file, Young & Rubicam Archive, New York, New York; hereafter Y&R).
15. "Field Survey," *Tide* 5 (Nov. 1931): 41; Henry C. Link, *The New Psychology of Selling and Advertising* (New York: Macmillan, 1938), 51–52.
16. Walter Mann, "Survey of Surveys," *Sales Management* (Oct. 17, 1931): 78; "The Gallup Method of Advertising Research," *Advertising & Selling* 18 (Mar. 16, 1932): 30.
17. Hotchkiss, *An Outline of Advertising*, 214–15, 234–35, 545; and L. E. Firth, *Testing Advertisements* (New York: McGraw-Hill, 1934), 227–29.
18. "Staff Meeting Minutes for November 17, 1931" (box 4, folder 6, J. Walter Thompson Archives, Perkins Library, Duke University, Durham, N.C.; hereafter JWT).
19. "Research: Gallup," *Tide* 6 (Mar. 1932): 47–48.
20. George Gallup, "Factors of Reader Interest in 261 Advertisements" (Liberty Publishing, 1932), 2–8.
21. Hower, *History of an Advertising Agency*, 343.
22. "Gallup Survey Paves Way for Stronger Copy," *Advertising Age*, Jan. 30, 1932, 5; and Raoul Blumberg and Carroll Rheinstrom, "How Advertising Techniques Are Rated by Gallup Survey," *Printer's Ink* (Mar. 24, 1932): 17–20.
23. Gallup, "Factors of Reader Interest," 20–21.
24. Another article published during the same time period found a similar pattern of interests, but attributed them to the different educational and life experiences of men and women. See Key Lee Barkley, "A Consideration of the Differences in Readiness of Recall of the Same Advertisements by Men and Women," *Journal of Applied Psychology* 16 (June 1932): 312–13.
25. "Research: Gallup," *Tide*, 47–48.
26. For examples of how *Liberty* cited Gallup's research in *Advertising Age*, see "Which Is America's Best Read Weekly?" (Oct. 17, 1931, 11); "Three Little Ads Went to Market" (Oct. 31, 1931, 7); and "In Your Space Buyer's Hands" (Nov. 28, 1931, 7).
27. Blumberg and Rheinstrom, "How Advertising Techniques Are Rated," 17–20; "Research: Gallup," *Tide*, 47–48; "The Gallup Method of Advertising and Research," 30, 46–49; "Gallup Surveys for *Liberty*," *Advertising Age*, July 16, 1932, 7. Gallup discusses the importance of the address to the journalists' association in Gallup, "The Reminiscences of George Horace Gallup" (1962), Columbia University Oral History Collection, New York City, transcript, 39–41.
    The articles based on his talk appeared in *Editor & Publisher* as "Store Ad-

vertising as Important as News, Gallup Surveys Show" (Jan. 9, 1932): 25; George A. Brandenburg, "Research Shows Reader Preference" (Jan. 16, 1932): 9, 30; and "Stores Should Study Customers to Make Copy More Effective" (Jan. 23, 1932): 16.

28. Gallup, "Reminiscences," 40.

29. James D. Scott, *Advertising: Principles and Problems* (1950) (rpt., New York: Prentice-Hall, 1953), 278–79.

30. "Special Production and Representatives Meeting," Apr. 9, 1928 (Stanley Resor, 1916–1950 file, Henderson Papers, box 1, JWT). Jane Gaines notes that this was one of the earliest attempts to tie a brand-name product with motion pictures on a national scale in "From Elephants to Lux Soap: The Programming and 'Flow' of Early Motion Picture Exploitation," *Velvet Light Trap* 25 (Spring 1990): 40.

31. "Lux Soap Mail Investigation in Worchester, Massachusetts," July 1926; "Lux Mail Investigation," Aug. 1927; "Lux Toilet Soap Test Campaign," Mar. 1931 (all on microfilm reel 47, JWT).

32. Gallup, "Reminiscences," 40, and "Lux Toilet Soap—Gallup Test," Feb. 1933 (microfilm reel 250, JWT); "Memo to Mr. Palmer," Sept. 20, 1932 (microfilm reel 251, JWT).

33. Consultant and textbook author Percival White took over the study for *Liberty* in May 1932, and Daniel Starch succeeded him from November 1932 until May 1933. For an example of how ads continued to refer to Gallup, see "Were These America's Best Read Advertisements?" *Advertising Age*, June 11, 1932, 8–9.

34. Gallup, "Reminiscences," 40; and George Gallup, letter to the editor, *The Link* 4 (Fall 1982): 1 (Y&R).

35. Sigurd Larmon, "The Book of Young & Rubicam," 112 (Y&R).

36. Gallup, "Reminiscences," 39.

37. "A Story in the Stars," *Fortune* 2 (Sept. 1930): 95; "Young & Rubicam Prepares Advertising for These Companies and Products," *Fortune* 13 (Mar. 1936): 113; "These Shows Are Good Box-Office," *Fortune* 13 (Feb. 1936): 93; Fox, *The Mirror Makers*, 139–40, 157.

38. "Raymond Rubicam," *Current Biography* (New York: H. W. Wilson, 1943), 639.

39. "Creative Staff Meeting," May 4, 1932, 12, and "Staff Meeting Minutes" (box 5, folder 3, JWT).

40. Fox, *The Mirror Makers*, 127.

41. "Raymond Rubicam," *Current Biography*, 639.

42. Nathaniel A. Benson, "Raymond Rubicam: A Close-up," *Forbes* (Feb. 1, 1944): 15.

43. "Creative Staff Meeting," 12–13 (JWT).

44. "Dr. Gallup's Next Job," 1–7, and "Young & Rubicam Establish Separate Copy-Testing Bureau," Apr. 28, 1932 (Gallup file, Y&R).

45. "Dr. Gallup's Next Job," 3.

46. Ibid., 8.

47. "Young & Rubicam Establish," 2.
48. "The Story of Young & Rubicam," *Advertising Agency and Advertising & Selling* 42 (Dec. 1949): 52.
49. "What Newspaper Readers Read," Oct. 1, 1931, 1 (Gallup file, Y&R).
50. Walter Dill Scott, *The Psychology of Advertising* (1903) (rpt., New York: Dodd, Mead, 1931), 8.
51. David P. Kuna, "The Concept of Suggestion in the Early History of Advertising Psychology," *Journal of the History of the Behavioral Sciences* 12 (1976): 347–53; Edmund C. Lynch, "Walter Dill Scott: Pioneer Industrial Psychologist," *Business History Review* 42.2 (Summer 1968): 151–52; A. Michal McMahon, "An American Courtship: Psychologists and Advertising Theory in the Progressive Era," *American Studies* 13 (Fall 1972): 5–18.
52. George Gallup, "Outstanding Advertisements" Apr. 21, 1938 (Raymond Rubicam binder, Y&R); "Says Position on Right-Hand," *Advertising Age*, Feb. 17, 1936, 22; Gallup, letter to the editor, 1.
53. "Position on Right-Hand," 22; George Gallup, "Memo on *Life* Magazine," Nov. 19, 1937, 4 6 (Raymond Rubicam binder, Y&R).
54. Gallup, "Reminiscences," 59–60.
55. Scott, *Psychology of Advertising*, 136.
56. Gallup, "Reminiscences," 80–81.
57 Joseph H. Jackson, "Should Radio Be Used for Advertising?" *Radio Broadcast* 2 (Nov. 1922): 76, quoted in Susan Smulyan, *Selling Radio: The Commercialization of American Broadcasting, 1920–1934* (Washington, D.C.: Smithsonian Press, 1994), 68.
58. Michele Hilmes discusses the characteristics of integrated commercials in *Hollywood and Broadcasting: From Radio to Cable* (Urbana: University of Illinois Press, 1990), 86 96.
59. Gallup, "Memo on *Life* Magazine," 1
60. "How a Good Radio Show Is Built," *Fortune* (Feb. 1937): 121.
61. "Young & Rubicam Hails 25th Milestone," *Advertising Age*, May 24, 1948, 44; "Notes on Young & Rubicam in 1934," Memo, Mar. 4, 1970 (George Gallup file, Y&R); "Radio Audience Much Like Vaude," *Variety*, Jan. 24, 1940, 25.
62. Gallup, "Reminiscences," 85–86; Gallup, "Outstanding Advertisements," 1–6.
63. Copy Research Department, "Magazine Checking Methods," Dec. 18, 1935, 11 (Raymond Rubicam binder, Y&R).
64. George Gallup, "New Magazine Report Form," Memo, Oct. 24, 1935, 1–3 (Raymond Rubicam Binder, Y&R).
65. Copy Research Department, "Magazine Checking Methods."
66. George Gallup, "General Magazine Memorandum," Aug. 9, 1937, 1 (Raymond Rubicam Binder, Y&R).
67. For good histories, see E. P. H. James, "The Development of Research in Broadcast Advertising," *Journal of Marketing* 2 (July 1937–Apr. 1938): 141–43; Daniel Starch, *Measuring Advertising Readership and Results* (New York: McGraw-Hill,

1966), 260; James G. Webster and Lawrence W. Lichty, *Ratings Analysis: Theory and Practice* (Hillsdale, N.J.: Erlbaum, 1991), 68–69.

68. Herman Hettinger, *A Decade of Radio Advertising* (Chicago, Ill.: University of Chicago Press, 1933; rpt., New York: Arno Press, 1971), 41–48; and Karen Buzzard, *Chains of Gold: Marketing the Ratings and Rating the Markets* (Metuchen, N.J.: Scarecrow Press, 1990), 3–14.

69. Hugh Malcolm Beville, Jr., *Audience Ratings: Radio, Television, and Cable* (Hillsdale, N.J.: Erlbaum, 1988), 3–7; and G. T. Sewell, "Young & Rubicam & Crossley Radio Ratings," Sept. 23, 1937, 1–11 (Raymond Rubicam binder, Y&R).

70. For a discussion of the coincidental method, see George Gallup, interview with Paul Sheatsley, Mar. 22, 1978, NORC, University of Chicago, transcript, 7; Gallup, "Reminiscences," 37–38; Gallup, letter to the editor, 2; Gallup, "Survey Shows Radio Advertisers Reach But Small Portion of Public," *Editor & Publisher* (Jan. 3, 1931): 28; George A. Brandenburg, "Telephone Surveys Puncture Radio Claims to Intensive Coverage," *Editor & Publisher* (Jan. 30, 1932): 6; Frederick H. Lumley, *Measurement in Radio* (Columbus: Ohio State University Press, 1934), 28–30.

71. Charles Hull Wolfe, "Radio Audience Measurement," *Advertising & Selling* (July 1948): 37–38, 53; Webster and Lichty, *Ratings Analysis*, 71–73; Larmon, "The Book of Young & Rubicam," 117–18; Gallup, letter to the editor, 2.

72. Gallup, "Survey Shows Radio Advertisers Reach," 28; and Brandenburg, "Telephone Surveys Puncture Radio Claims," 6; Sewell, "Young & Rubicam & Crossley Radio Ratings," 1–6, and "Revised Charts of Radio Listening Habits," June 22, 1937, 1–3 (Raymond Rubicam binder, Y&R); Archibald M. Crossley, "Why We Should Bring Radio Research Up to Date," *Advertising & Selling* (Nov. 1946): 41–42, 106–114.

73. Smulyan, *Selling Radio*, 85.

74. Larmon, "The Book of Young & Rubicam," 104–106. Also see Cyrilla Ecker, untitled memo, June 10, 1937, 1–2 (Raymond Rubicam binder, Y&R).

75. Matthew N. Chappell and C. E. Hooper, *Radio Audience Measurement* (New York: Stephen Daye, 1944), 209; and Fred H. Fidler, "Agencies Demand New Facts about Radio," *Broadcasting* (July 1, 1933): 7, 30.

76. Larmon, "The Book of Young & Rubicam," 118.

77. Gallup, letter to the editor, 2.

78. Gallup, "Outstanding Advertisements."

79. Fox, *The Mirror Makers*, 139.

80. "William H. Johns Is Awarded Medal," *NYT*, Feb. 27, 1936, 28; and "Citations," advertisement, *Fortune* (Apr. 1936): 133.

81. Benson, "Raymond Rubicam: A Close-Up," 14–15; "Raymond Rubicam," *Current Biography*, 639.

82. "How Long Is Interesting?" advertisement in *Fortune* (Mar. 11, 1935): 101.

83. Larmon, "The Book of Young & Rubicam," 114–15.

84. Donald Hurwitz, "Market Research and the Study of the U.S. Radio Audience," *Communication* 10 (1988): 237–39.

4. America Speaks

1. Henry C. Link, "Some Milestones in Public Opinion Research," *International Journal of Opinion and Attitude Research* 1 (Mar. 1947): 36–38.

2. The confluence of market research and social science studies during this period is discussed in Jean Converse, *Survey Research in the United States: Roots and Emergence, 1890–1960.* (Berkeley: University of California Press, 1987), 87–114; Archibald M. Crossley, "Early Days of Public Opinion Research," *Public Opinion Quarterly* 21 (Spring 1957): 159–64; and David Wallace, "A Tribute to the Second Sigma," *Public Opinion Quarterly* 23 (1959–1960): 313–14.

3. "Polling America," *Business Week*, Nov. 30, 1935, 27.

4. Lowell Calvert to Selznick, Feb. 25, 1942, "The Gallup Poll 1939–41–42" (box 3562, DOS Papers, HRHRC).

5. George Gallup, interview with Paul Sheatsley, Mar. 22, 1978, NORC, University of Chicago, transcript, 6.

6. American Institute of Public Opinion, "The Story Behind the Gallup Poll" (Princeton, N.J.: AIPO, 1957), 5; American Institute of Public Opinion, "The New Science of Public Opinion Measurement" (New York, N.Y.:, n.d. [c. 1938]), 9–12; George Gallup, "Reminiscences" (1962), Columbia University Oral History Collection, New York City, transcript, 105–115.

7. Gallup, interview with Sheatsley, 9.

8. AIPO's origins are described in various sources, most notably in "Gallup Says Measuring Public Opinion," *Editor & Publisher* (Nov. 14, 1936): 14; "Dr. Gallup Closes a Gap," *Newsweek*, Nov. 14, 1936, 14–16; Richard G. Hubler, "George Horace Gallup: Oracle in Tweeds," *Forum* 103 (Feb. 1940): 94; "How Gallup Poll Samples," *Business Week*, June 19, 1948, 42–44. The number of papers that subscribed to his column varied, but the *Washington Post* listed forty-five subscribers by November 1935; see "Editors Assist," Nov. 10, 1935, sec. 3, p. 1.

9. "Papers of Wide Political Views Publish Polls," *Washington Post*, Oct. 20, 1935, sec. 3, p. 1.

10. George Gallup, "Measuring Public Opinion," *Vital Speeches of the Day* 2 (Mar. 9, 1936): 372 (emphasis in the original).

11. Hadley Cantril, *The Human Dimension: Experiences in Policy Research* (New Brunswick, N.J.: Rutgers University Press, 1967), 25.

12. George Gallup, "Gallup Explains 'Opinion Sampling,'" *NYT*, May 17, 1938, 18; George Gallup, James Pollock, and Louis Wirth, "A Radio Discussion of Testing Public Opinion," *The University of Chicago Roundtable No. 86* (Chicago: University of Chicago, 1939), 5–10; Archibald Crossley, "Straw Polls in 1936," *Public Opinion Quarterly* 1 (Jan. 1937): 24–35.

13. Harwood Childs, *An Introduction to Public Opinion* (New York: John Wiley, 1940), 53–54; Jerome H. Spingarn, "These Public-Opinion Polls," *Harper's*, Dec. 1938, 98.

14. "Dr. Gallup to Take the National Pulse," *Newsweek*, Oct. 26, 1936, 23–24; *The Gallup Poll: Public Opinion, 1935–1971*, vol. 1, *1935–1938* (New York: Random

House, 1972), vii–viii ; George Gallup, "Putting Public Opinion to Work," *Scribner's*, Nov. 1936, 38; Hadley Cantril, "Straw Votes This Year," *NYT*, Oct. 25, 1936, D3. Researchers could not always agree on which characteristics influenced voting and whether or not they could be separated from one another. Partly for these reasons, quota sampling was replaced by area probability sampling in the early 1940s, where people were chosen by random. For a discussion of the limitations of quota sampling, see Harwood Childs, *Public Opinion: Nature, Formation, and Role* (Princeton.: Van Nostrand, 1965), 79; and Hadley Cantril, *Gauging Public Opinion* (Princeton: Princeton University Press,1944), 146–49.

15. "54 Polls Taken," *Washington Post*, Nov. 3, 1935, sec. 3, p. 1.

16. David W. Moore, *The Superpollsters* (New York: Four Walls Eight Windows, 1992), 64–65.

17. "Polling America," 26–27; Cantril, *Gauging Public Opinion*, 146–49.

18. Daniel Katz and Hadley Cantril, "Public Opinion Polls," *Sociometry* 1 (July 1937–Apr. 1938): 160–61. For an indication of the kinds of questions the *Fortune* survey asked, see "The *Fortune* Survey: II," *Fortune* (Oct. 1935): 57.

19. "54 Polls Taken," sec. 3, p. 1.

20. George Gallup and Saul Forbes Rae, *The Pulse of Democracy* (New York: Simon and Schuster, 1940; rpt., New York: Greenwood Press, 1968), 65. Daniel J. Robinson analyzes AIPO's approach to race in the 1940s in *The Measure of Democracy: Polling, Market Research, and Public Life, 1930–1945* (Toronto: University of Toronto Press, 1999), 54–56.

21. Daniel Katz, "Psychological Tasks in the Measurement of Public Opinion," *Journal of Consulting Psychology* 6 (1942): 59–65.

22. "Poll Is a National Election on a Small Scale," *Washington Post*, Oct. 20, 1935, sec. 3, p. 1.

23. "Democrats Leading," *Washington Post*, Nov. 24, 1935, sec. 3, p. 1.

24. "Does the Forgotten Man Still Feel Forgotten?" *Washington Post*, Oct. 20, 1935, sec. 3, p. 1.

25. Williston Rich, "The Human Yardstick," *Saturday Evening Post*, Jan. 21, 1939, 9; "News and Notes," *American Journal of Sociology* 42 (Sept. 1936): 256.

26. Meyer's Wall Street career and acquisition of the *Washington Post* are detailed in Tom Kelly, *The Imperial Post* (New York: Morrow, 1983), 11–83.

27. Merlo J. Pusey, *Eugene Meyer* (New York: Knopf, 1974), 266–69; Eugene Meyer, "Reminiscences," Part II, no. 132, pp. 715–22 (Columbia University Oral History Collection, New York, New York).

28. See Eugene Meyer, "A Newspaper Publisher Looks at the Polls," *Public Opinion Quarterly* 4 (June 1940): 238–39. Gallup discusses Meyer's use of mining analogies in Barry Sussman, *What Americans Really Think* (New York: Pantheon, 1988), 82.

29. Moore, *The Superpollsters*, 31–32.

30. For a history of these early polls, see Tom W. Smith, "The First Straw? A Study of the Origins of Election Polls," *Public Opinion Quarterly* 54 (1990): 21–36.

Robinson discusses them in Claude Robinson, *Straw Votes* (New York: Columbia University Press, 1932), 48–52 and 79–83.

31. "Institute Findings," *Los Angeles Times,* Aug. 9, 1936, 14; and "Poll Methods Used Daily," *Los Angeles Times,* Aug. 23, 1936, 8.

32. Gallup and Rae, *Pulse of Democracy,* 38–41; Robinson, *Straw Votes,* 57.

33. "The *Digest* Presidential Poll Is On!" *Literary Digest* (Aug. 22, 1936): 3.

34. "*Digest* Poll Machinery Speeding Up" (Aug. 29, 1936): 5; "*Digest's* First Hundred Thousand" (Sept. 12, 1936): 5–6; "Half-Million Votes in *Digest* Poll" (Sept. 26, 1936): 7; "*Digest* Poll Passes Million Mark" (Oct. 10, 1936): 7.

35. Robinson, *Straw Votes,* 58–65.

36. Ibid., 90–93.

37. "Final Poll Report," *Literary Digest* (Jan. 11, 1936): 10–11.

38. Robinson, *Straw Votes,* 116–17.

39. "Results Today Point to Close November Race," *Washington Post,* July 12, 1936, sec. 3, pp. 1, 3.

40. Gallup and Rae, *Pulse of Democracy,* 46–50.

41. Gallup, interview with Sheatsley, 10.

42. "George Gallup," *Current Biography* (New York: H. W. Wilson, 1940), 320, and Rich, "Human Yardstick," 9.

43. "Results Today," and "New York, 11 Other States," *Washington Post,* July 12, 1936, sec. 3, pp. 1, 3.

44. Funk, quoted in "Dr. Gallup Chided by *Digest* Editor," *NYT,* July 19, 1936, 21.

45. By November 1936, a total of 78 papers subscribed to "America Speaks." "*Post* Shares in Experiment," *Washington Post,* Nov. 1, 1936, sec. 3, p. 1.

46. Cantril, "Straw Votes," 3.

47. Mildred Parten, *Surveys, Polls, and Samples* (New York: Harper, 1950), 30–31.

48. Robinson, *Straw Votes,* 107–112.

49. "1936 Election Scorecard," *Washington Post,* July 11, 1936, 4.

50. "Election Will Show," *Washington Post,* Oct. 4, 1936, sec. 3, p. 1, "Voting Tuesday to Test," *Washington Post,* Nov. 1, 1936, sec. 3, p. 1.

51. Katz and Cantril, "Public Opinion Polls," 156; Moore, *The Superpollsters,* 33.

52. *The New York Times Index for 1936,* 2315–16.

53. "The *Fortune* Quarterly Survey: VI," *Fortune* (Oct. 1936): 130–31. The election results are discussed in "The *Fortune* Quarterly Survey: VII," *Fortune* (Jan. 1937): 86–87.

54. J. J. O'Malley, "Black Beans and White Beans," *New Yorker,* Mar. 2, 1940, 22.

55. Converse, *Survey Research in the United States,* 119.

56. Crossley, "Straw Polls in 1936," 27.

57. AIPO ballot, May 28, 1937 (Roper Center for Public Opinion Research; hereafter, RCPOR).

58. Peverill Squire, "Why the 1936 *Literary Digest* Poll Failed," *Public Opinion Quarterly* 52 (1988): 125–33. The impact of non-response bias is also analyzed in Maurice Bryson, "The *Literary Digest* Poll: Making of a Statistical Myth,"

American Statistician 30 (Nov. 1976): 184–85; and Katz and Cantril, "Public Opinion Polls," 158–59.

59. "What Went Wrong with the Polls?" *Literary Digest* (Nov. 14, 1936): 7–8.

60. "*Digest* to Seek Reason," *NYT*, Nov. 4, 1936, 4.

61. Gallup and Rae, *Pulse of Democracy*, 77–78; Parten, *Surveys, Polls, and Samples*, 30.

62. William J. Enright, "Market Guide Seen," *NYT*, Nov. 29, 1936, sec. 3, p. 1.

63. Mrs. Don Cahalan, statement to the author, Feb. 20, 1992, tape recording, Berkeley, California.

64. "How Scientific Poll Forecast Unprecedented Roosevelt Landslide," *Washington Post*, Nov. 8, 1936, sec. 3, p. 1.

65. "Advertising News and Notes," *NYT*, Nov. 5, 1936, 50; and "Sales Are Votes," *Scholastic* 35 (Oct. 2, 1939): 34–36.

66. "Straw Polls Help Market Research," *NYT*, Nov. 8, 1936, sec. 3, p. 9.

67. "Faith in Power of Editors Shaken," *Literary Digest* (Dec. 19, 1936): 42.

68. Robert P. Post, "Polls in Disfavor," *NYT*, Nov. 8, 1936, sec. 4, p. 5; Carl W. Ackerman, "Public Opinion and the Press," *Vital Speeches* 3 (June 15, 1937): 521–24.

69. "Gallup Says," *Editor & Publisher* (Nov. 14, 1936): 14.

70. Meyer, "A Newspaper Publisher Looks at the Polls," 240.

71. Francis Sill Wickware, "What We Think About Foreign Affairs," *Harper's*, Sept. 1939, 397.

72. "Reforms in Relief Favored," and "Health Insurance Favored by Millions," both in *NYT*, Jan. 22, 1939, 9; "Social Workers Urged to Politics," *NYT*, June 24, 1939, 18; "Use of U.S. Forces," *NYT*, June 19, 1940, 11.

73. "What Maine's September Election Means," *Congressional Digest* 15 (Aug. 1936): 217; "Institute of Public Opinion Poll, 1938," *Congressional Digest* 17 (May 1938): 147–48. Also see "Dr. Gallup Closes a Gap," *Newsweek*, Nov. 14, 1936, 15; and Robert D. Updegraff, "Democracy's New Mirror," *Forum* 103 (Jan. 1940): 11–12.

74. Richard W. Steele, "The Pulse of the People: Franklin D. Roosevelt and the Gauging of American Public Opinion," *Journal of Contemporary History* 9 (Oct. 1974): 195–207.

75. Melvin G. Holli, *The Wizard of Washington: Emil Hurja, Franklin Roosevelt, and the Birth of Public Opinion Polling* (New York: Palgrave, 2002), 39–80.

76. Cantril, *Human Dimension*, 38–41. See also Gerald Lambert, *All Out of Step* (Garden City, N.Y.: Doubleday, 1956), 251–79.

77. Steele, "Pulse of the People," 215–16; and Betty Houchin Winfield, *FDR and the News Media* (Urbana: University of Illinois Press, 1990): 215–29.

78. For example, Gallup, "Putting Public Opinion to Work," 36–39, 73–74; and George Gallup, "Public Opinion in a Democracy," Stafford Little Lectures (Princeton University: Herbert L. Baker Foundation, Spring 1939).

79. Gallup and Rae, *Pulse of Democracy*.

80. Irving Crespi, *Public Opinion, Polls, and Democracy* (Boulder, Colo.: Westview, 1989), 3.

81. George Gallup, "The Way People Are Thinking," *Reader's Digest* 32 (June 1938): 1–2.

82. Useful surveys of the history of public opinion are Vincent Price, *Public Opinion* (Newbury Park, Calif.: Sage, 1992); and Carroll J. Glynn, Susan Herbst et. al., *Public Opinion* (Boulder, Colo.: Westview, 1999), 31–64.

83. Paul A. Palmer, "The Concept of Public Opinion in Political Theory," in Carl Wittke, ed., *Essays in History and Political Theory in Honor of Charles H. McIlwain* (Cambridge: Harvard University Press, 1936), 230–33; Susan Herbst, *Numbered Voices* (Chicago: University of Chicago Press, 1993), 49.

84. Rousseau, quoted in Palmer, "The Concept of Public Opinion," 237.

85. Bentham, quoted in Jürgen Habermas, *The Structural Transformation of the Public Sphere*, trans. Thomas Burger (Cambridge: MIT Press, 1962; rpt., 1989), 100.

86. "Auslander Warns," *NYT*, Nov. 26, 1939, 28.

87. In Gallup's time, doubts about the intelligence of the masses were expressed by Robert Lynd in "Democracy in Reverse," *Public Opinion Quarterly* (June 1940): 218–20, who felt that the great mass of Americans lived in "operational poverty" and that to let them decide their fate was "naive." Walter Lippmann also detailed the factors limiting the public's ability to form accurate ideas in *Public Opinion* (1922; rpt., New York: Macmillan/Free Press, 1965). For a discussion of this distopian strain in public opinion theory, see Habermas, *Structural Transformation*, 132–34.

88. Gallup and Rae, *Pulse of Democracy*, 12; Crespi, *Public Opinion, Polls, and Democracy*, 3–4.

89. Gallup and Rae, *Pulse of Democracy*, 14.

90. George Gallup, "Government and the Sampling Referendum," *Journal of the American Statistical Association* 33 (1938): 133.

91. "Gallup Says," 14.

92. Gallup and Rae, *Pulse of Democracy*, 32.

93. George Gallup, "We, the People, Are Like This," *NYT Magazine*, June 8, 1941, 3, 24; George Gallup, "Can We Trust the Common People," *Good Housekeeping* 111 (Oct. 1940): 21; George Gallup, "Making Democracy Work Every Day," *Scholastic* 35 (Oct. 2, 1939): 29–30.

94. American Institute of Public Opinion, "The New Science," 15.

95. Updegraff, "Democracy's New Mirror," 11–14; and James Wechsler, "Polling America," *Nation*, Jan. 20, 1940, 64–67.

96. Gallup and Rae, *Pulse of Democracy*, 7.

97. Ibid., 4.

98. See Converse, *Survey Research in the United States*, 91–106. See also Edward G. Benson, "Problems and Techniques: Wording Questions for the Polls," *Public Opinion Quarterly* 4 (Mar. 1940): 129–34; Hadley Cantril, "Problems and Techniques: Experiments in the Wording of Questions," *Public Opinion Quarterly* 4 (June 1940): 330–32; and Albert B. Blankenship, "Does the Question Form Influence Public Opinion Poll Results?" *Journal of Applied Psychology* 24 (1940):

27–30. The American Association for Public Opinion Research and *Public Opinion Quarterly* provided regular, ongoing forums for these debates.

99. Wechsler, "Polling America," 65.

100. Arthur Kornhauser, "Are Public Opinion Polls Fair to Organized Labor?" *Public Opinion Quarterly* 10 (1946–47): 485–86.

101. Ibid., 486.

102. Daniel Katz, "Do Interviewers Bias Poll Results?" *Public Opinion Quarterly* 6 (1942): 248–68.

103. "F.D.R. Gains Again in Poll But . . . ," *Washington Post*, June 7, 1936, sec. 3, p. 1.

104. "Roosevelt's Popular Lead Is Reduced," *Washington Post*, July 12, 1936, sec 3, p. 1.

105. "Country-Wide Ballot Gives Roosevelt Lead," *Washington Post*, Oct. 27, 1935, sec. 3, p. 1; and "FDR More Popular Than New Deal Tenets," *Washington Post* Nov. 24, 1935, sec. 3, p. 1.

106. "33 States Are Now in Roosevelt Camp," *Washington Post*, Dec. 22, 1935, sec. 3, p. 1.

107. AIPO Ballot 59, conducted the week of November 30, 1936 (RCPOR).

108. Spingarn, "These Public-Opinion Polls," 102.

109. Pusey, *Eugene Meyer*, 272–73.

110. Spingarn, "These Public-Opinion Polls," 98–99.

111. Herbst, *Numbered Voices*, 43–68.

112. Ibid., 153.

113. James Bryce, *The American Commonwealth*, vol. 2 (London and New York: Macmillan, 1889), 241.

114. Leo Bogart, *Silent Politics: Polls and the Awareness of Public Opinion* (New York: John Wiley, 1972), 17–18.

115. Susan Herbst, "On the Disappearance of Groups: Nineteenth and Early Twentieth Century Conceptions of Public Opinion," in Theodore L. Glasser and Charles T. Salmon, eds., *Public Opinion and the Communication of Consent* (New York and London: Guilford Press, 1995), 93.

116. Hadley Cantril, *The Invasion from Mars* (Princeton: Princeton University Press, 1940; rpt., 1982).

117. Paul F. Lazarsfeld, Bernard Berelson, and Hazel Gaudet, *The People's Choice: How the Voter Makes Up His Mind in a Presidential Election* (New York: Columbia University Press, 1948). Though it was published in 1948, the book describes research conducted during the 1940 campaign.

118. A good overview of the factors that researchers believed could influence public opinion is given in Emory S. Bogardus, *The Making of Public Opinion* (New York: Association Press, 1951).

119. Crespi, *Public Opinion, Polls and Democracy*, 6.

120. John Durham Peters, "Historical Tensions in the Concept of Public Opinion," in Glasser and Salmon, eds., *Public Opinion and the Communication of Consent*, 18–20.

121. Pierre Bourdieu, "Public Opinion Does Not Exist" (1972), trans. Mary C. Axtmann, in Armand Mattelart and Seth Siegelaub, eds., *Communication and Class Struggle*, vol. 1: *Capitalism, Imperialism* (New York: International General, 1979), 125.

122. Herbst, *Numbered Voices*, 39–41 and 153–75.

123. For specific examples of this, see Michael B. Salwen, "The Reporting of Public Opinion Polls During Presidential Years, 1968–1984," *Journalism Quarterly* 62 (1985): 272–77; James Glen Stovall and Jacqueline H. Solomon, "The Poll as a News Event in the 1980 Presidential Campaign," *Public Opinion Quarterly* 48 (1984): 615–23; and Albert E. Gollin, "Polling and the News Media," *Public Opinion Quarterly* 51 (Winter 1987): S86–94. The film *The War Room* (Chris Hegedus/D. A. Pennebaker, 1993) also illustrates how campaigns are planned around polls.

124. Herbst, *Numbered Voices*, 168.

125. Peters, "Historical Tensions," 20.

126. Bogart, *Silent Politics*, 15.

127. Herbst, *Numbered Voices*, p. 166.

5. Piggybacking on the Past

1. Don Cahalan, interview by author, Feb. 20, 1992, tape recording, Berkeley, California.

2. Herbert I. Schiller, *The Mind Managers* (Boston: Beacon Press, 1973), 117.

3. George Gallup, "Reminiscences" (1962), Columbia University Oral History Collection, New York City, transcript, 126.

4. George Gallup, interview with Paul Sheatsley, Mar. 22, 1978, NORC, University of Chicago, transcript, 14.

5. Gallup, "Reminiscences," 127.

6. Gallup, interview with Sheatsley, 14.

7. Michele Hilmes, *Hollywood and Broadcasting: From Radio to Cable* (Urbana: University of Illinois Press, 1990), 53–60.

8. Erik Barnouw, *The Golden Web: A History of Broadcasting in the United States*, vol. 2, *1933–1953* (New York: Oxford University Press, 1968), 103–104.

9. "Agency, P. A. Winners," *Billboard*, Apr. 26, 1941, 6.

10. "Young & Rubicam Marks 10th Anniversary," *HR*, Aug. 12, 1946, 10. In "The Book of Young & Rubicam," Sigurd Larmon gives the address as 6252 Hollywood Boulevard, but memos from David Selznick to Young & Rubicam executives indicate the location was 6253. See David Selznick, memo to Tom Lewis, May 7, 1942 ("Gallup Poll, 1939–1941–1942" file, box 3562, DOS Papers, HRHRC).

11. Richard Alleman, *The Movie Lover's Guide to Hollywood* (New York: Harper and Row, 1985), 43.

12. "Raymond Rubicam," *Current Biography* (New York: H. W. Wilson, 1943), 640; "You Ought to Know . . . Sigurd Larmon," *Advertising Age*, May 20, 1946, 83. See also George Gallup, letter to the editor, *The Link* 4 (Fall 1982): 2 (Y&R).

13. Gallup, interview by Thomas Simonet, Princeton, New Jersey, Sept. 21, 1977, transcript, part 2, p. 8. Transcript courtesy of Thomas Simonet.

14. David Ogilvy, memo to Francis Ogilvy, Sept. 26, 1947 ("September-December 1947 Correspondence" file, David Ogilvy papers, container 32, Library of Congress Manuscript Division, Washington, D.C.; hereafter, Ogilvy Papers).

15. "Sindlinger Wanted," *Variety*, Oct. 2, 1946, 4. Rubicam's obituary in the *Washington Post* also says that he and Gallup owned ARI jointly between 1944 and 1948 ("Raymond Rubicam," *Washington Post*, May 9, 1978, C7).

16. Cahalan, interview by author, Feb. 20, 1992.

17. Sigurd Larmon, letter to David Selznick, Dec. 16, 1940 ("Gallup Poll, 1939–1941–1942" file, box 3562, DOS Papers, HRHRC).

18. "Wanger Strong Advocate," *Variety*, Sept. 11, 1940, 8.

19. David Ogilvy, *Confessions of an Advertising Man* (New York: Atheneum, 1971), 96.

20. "David Mackenzie Ogilvy," *Current Biography* (New York: H. W. Wilson, 1961), 348–49; and David Ogilvy, *The Unpublished David Ogilvy*, ed. Joel Raphaelson (New York: Crown, 1986), 3–16.

21. Spencer Klaw, "Is Ogilvy a Genius?" *Fortune* (Apr. 1965): 171.

22. Ogilvy, quoted in Thomas Whiteside, "Ogilvy the Ineffable Ad Man," *Harper's* (May 1955): 54.

23. Gallup, letter to the editor, *The Link*, 2.

24. David Ogilvy to Francis Ogilvy, Sept. 26, 1947 ("September-December 1947 Correspondence" file, container 32, Ogilvy Papers).

25. Bart Cummings, *The Benevolent Dictators* (Chicago: Crain Books, 1984), 102 (emphasis in the original).

26. David Ogilvy, "Ogilvy Comes to New York, Ogilvy Goes to Hollywood," *New York* (Feb. 6, 1978), 57. For further discussion of how Gallup influenced Ogilvy's own approach to advertising, see *Confessions of an Advertising Man*, 116–32.

27. David Ogilvy, *Blood, Brains, and Beer* (New York: Atheneum, 1978), 82.

28. Cahalan, interview by author, Feb. 20, 1992.

29. Ibid. Cahalan was not sure of the exact date when ARI acquired its own office space, but Gallup signed his first contract to do motion picture research in March 1940, so the move may have occurred around that time.

30. "Conversation with Don Cahalan," *British Journal of Addiction* (1989): 125.

31. Cahalan, interview by author, Feb. 20, 1992.

32. Ibid.; and *NORC Report [National Opinion Research Center], 1985–86* (Chicago: University of Chicago, 1987): 73; "In Memoriam: Paul B. Sheatsley, 1917–1989," *Public Opinion Quarterly* 53 (1989): 395–96.

33. As an example of Gallup's frequent insistence that AIPO and ARI were separate, see Gallup to Selznick, Aug. 20, 1943 ("Gallup Poll, 1943" file, box 3562, DOS Papers, HRHRC).

34. "An Analysis of American Public Opinion Regarding the War," Sept. 10, 1942 ("George Gallup confidential" file, box 4504, DOS Papers, HRHRC).

35. Ogilvy to Selznick, June 4, 1942 ("Gallup Poll, 1939–1941–1942" file, box 3562, DOS Papers, HRHRC).

36. Selznick to Gallup, Aug. 9, 1943, and Gallup to Selznick, Aug. 20, 1943 (both in the "Gallup Poll, 1943" file, box 3562, DOS Papers, HRHRC).

37. AIPO Ballot 59, Nov. 30–Dec. 10, 1936 (RCPOR). The date for the first appearance of a film question on an AIPO survey was determined by a hand search of the AIPO materials at the Roper Center.

38. "Fortune Survey: Motion Pictures," Fortune (Apr. 1936): 222; Hadley Cantril and Mildred Strunk, Public Opinion, 1935–1946 (Princeton: Princeton University Press, 1951): 485.

39. AIPO Ballot 61, Dec. 16–21, 1936 (RCPOR).

40. AIPO Ballot 65, Jan. 20–25, 1937 (RCPOR).

41. Paul Perry, interview by Thomas Simonet, Princeton, New Jersey, Feb. 15, 1978.

42. Elmo Roper's April 1936 poll for Fortune found similar results. When the magazine asked people how often they went to the movies, 63.2 percent said at least once a month.

43. Cahalan, interview by author, Feb. 20, 1992.

44. AIPO Ballot 80, Apr. 28–May 1, 1937 (RCPOR).

45. Fred Basten, Glorious Technicolor (Cranbury, N.J.: A. S. Barnes, 1980), 47–61; Ronald Haver, David O. Selznick's Hollywood (New York: Knopf, 1980), 176–91.

46. "Selznick Pictures," NYT, Oct. 10, 1935, 30; "News of the Screen," NYT, June 22, 1936, 22; Douglas W. Churchill, "Hollywood Tumult and Shouting," NYT, June 28, 1936, sec. 10, p. 3; "News of the Screen," NYT, Nov. 24, 1936, 35.

47. Basten, Glorious Technicolor, 59–65.

48. Cahalan, interview by the author, Feb. 20, 1992.

49. Haver, David O. Selznick's Hollywood, 183.

50. Ibid., 202–206.

51. Roland Flamini, Scarlett, Rhett, and a Cast of Thousands (New York: Collier/Macmillan, 1975), 103–104; Irene Mayer Selznick, A Private View (New York: Knopf, 1983), 204–229.

52. Gallup to Whitney, Jan. 30, 1937 ("Dr. Gallup" file, box 142, John Hay Whitney Papers, HRHRC; hereafter, JHW Papers).

53. Whitney to Wharton, Jan. 20, 1937 ("Gallup" file, box 2974, DOS Papers, HRHRC).

54. AIPO Ballot 65, Jan. 20–25, 1937 (RCPOR).

55. AIPO Ballot 67, Feb. 3–8, 1937 (RCPOR).

56. AIPO Ballot 72, Mar. 3–8, 1937 (RCPOR).

57. G. Cleveland Wilhoit and David H. Weaver, Newsroom Guide to Polls and Surveys (Bloomington: Indiana University Press, 1980), 11–12. Also see Earl Babbie, Survey Research Methods (Belmont, Calif.: Wadsworth, 1973), 146–47.

58. Paul Snell to Ned Depinet, Apr.–May 1935 (file "S," box 67, JHW Papers, HRHRC).

59. AIPO Ballot 92, July 21–26, 1937 (RCPOR).

60. Wharton to Selznick, Aug. 11, 1937 ("Gallup" file, box 2974, DOS Papers, HRHRC).

61. AIPO Ballot 95, Aug. 11–16, 1937 (RCPOR).
62. AIPO Ballot 135, Oct. 10–15, 1938 (RCPOR).
63. In a memo to Al Lichtman, the MGM executive in charge of distribution, on October 20, 1939, Selznick mentioned that MGM had repeatedly opposed the use of Technicolor ("Gallup Poll, 1939–1941–1942" file, box 3562, DOS Papers, HRHRC).
64. Selznick to Whitney, Feb. 6, 1937 ("Gallup" file, box 2974, DOS Papers, HRHRC).
65. Schiller, *The Mind Managers*, 117.
66. See Gerald Lambert, *All Out of Step* (Garden City, N.Y.: Doubleday, 1956).

6. Singles and Doubles

1. "Survey Institute Marks Third Year," *NYT*, Oct. 20, 1938, 16.
2. "Appendix," George Gallup and Saul Forbes Rae, *The Pulse of Democracy* (New York: Simon and Schuster, 1940).
3. "Sales Are Customers' Votes," *Scholastic* 35.3 (Oct. 2, 1939): 34.
4. "Movie Anti-Trust Suit," *Business Week*, July 30, 1938, 17–18; "Trust Drive Enters Crucial Phase," *Business Week*, Apr. 27, 1940, 15–16; "Movie Trade Bemoans Unhappy Lot," *Business Week*, June 29, 1940, 22–23; "Plan Worked Out," *NYT*, Aug. 24, 1940, 15; "Film Trust Truce Nears," *Business Week*, Aug. 31, 1940, 39; "Movies Arbitrate," *Business Week*, Nov. 2, 1940, 15. See also Simon Whitney, "Antitrust Policies and the Motion Picture Industry," in Gorham Kindem, ed., *The American Movie Industry* (Carbondale: Southern Illinois University Press, 1982), 165–71; and Thomas Schatz, *Boom and Bust: Hollywood in the 1940s*, vol. 6: *History of the American Cinema*, ed. Charles Harpole (New York: Scribner's, 1997), 11–21.
5. "Selznick Not To Sell," *Variety*, May 15, 1940, 5.
6. Leo H. Rosten, *Hollywood: The Movie Colony, the Movie Makers* (New York: Harcourt, Brace, 1941), 346n2.
7. "Hays May Survey Public," *Variety*, Jan. 10, 1940, 3.
8. Sydney Self, "Movies Face 'The Axe,'" *Barron's*, July 29, 1940, 20.
9. "The *Fortune* Survey VI: Industries That Satisfy," *Fortune* (Aug. 1938): 75.
10. Self, "Movies Face 'The Axe,'" 20.
11. "Movie Promotion Up," *Business Week*, June 8, 1940, 47; "War Hits Hollywood," *Business Week*, Feb. 3, 1940, 49–50; Thomas M. Pryor, "Film News of the Week," *NYT*, May 19, 1940, sec. 9, p. 4. For a more extended analysis of these factors, see Ian Jarvie, *Hollywood's Overseas Campaign: The North Atlantic Movie Trade, 1920–1950* (Cambridge: Cambridge University Press, 1992), 135–212, and 336–97.
12. "National Survey," *Variety*, May 1, 1940, 5, 22.
13. AIPO Ballot 136, Oct. 19–24, 1938 (RCPOR).
14. George Gallup, "The Favorite Books of Americans," *NYT Book Review*, Jan. 15, 1939, 2.

15. For criticism of Gallup's emphasis on film, see "Mr. Gallup Searches Literature," *Commonweal* 29 (Jan. 27, 1939): 366–67; and Frederic G. Melcher, "Gallup Among the Books," *Publishers Weekly* 135 (Jan. 21, 1939): 181.

16. "Deuces Wild," *MPH*, Jan. 21, 1939, 7.

17. "Early ARI Poll Results" in "Gallup Looks at the Movies: Audience Research Reports 1940–1950" (Princeton: American Institute of Public Opinion; Wilmington, Del.: Scholarly Resources, 1979), microfilm, reel 1, hereafter GLM.

18. "Increasing Profits Through Continuous Audience Research," p. 2 (GLM).

19. George Gallup, "Reminiscences" (1962), Columbia University Oral History Collection, New York City, transcript, 137–38; Rosten, *Hollywood: The Movie Colony*, 153, 160; "Gallup to Do Poll," *HR*, Feb. 16, 1940, 1.

20. Don Cahalan, interview by author, Feb. 20, 1992, tape recording, Berkeley, California.

21. "Not So Different," *MPH*, Jan. 7, 1939, 1; "Survey Shows Films," *FD*, Sept. 21, 1939, 1, 8; Ralph Wilk, "Launches Pix Survey," *FD*, Jan. 25, 1940, 3.

22. "Hays May Survey Public," *Variety*, Jan. 10, 1940, 55.

23. W. R. Wilkerson, "Trade Views," *HR*, May 2, 1940, 1.

24. W. R. Wilkerson, "Trade Views," *HR*, Apr. 30, 1940, 1.

25. Silverman, quoted in "Industry Pacts Can't Halt Duals," *MPH*, May 11, 1940, 16.

26. "Radio's Coast Nightmare," *Variety*, Mar. 22, 1939, 1, 19.

27. "Hollywood Office History," n.d. (1963–64) (box 8, Sidney Ralph Bernstein Papers, JWT Papers).

28. "Admen Minimize Hollywood's New Anti-Radio Stance," *Variety*, Feb. 15, 1939, 1, 2.

29. "Films, Radio Differ . . . ," *Variety*, Jan. 17, 1940, 4.

30. Ibid., 20.

31. Gallup, "Reminiscences," 138, 144–45

32. Richard Maltby, "The Political Economy of Hollywood: The Studio System," in Philip Davies and Brian Neve, eds., *Cinema, Politics, and Society in America* (New York: St. Martin's, 1981), 54.

33. Ibid., 55.

34. Rosten, *Hollywood: The Movie Colony*, 63, 377. George Custen has suggested that Fox's West Coast theater location and patronage resembled middle America's, and that Zanuck and the studio thereby had access to the kinds of ordinary Americans through their own previews that Gallup sought out via surveys. He may have felt, then, that there were other ways of obtaining the information Gallup provided. See Custen, *Twentieth Century's Fox: Darryl F. Zanuck and the Culture of Hollywood* (New York: Basic Books, 1997), 14–15.

35. Rosten, *Hollywood: The Movie Colony*, 48–49. Rosten discusses the origins of the book in "A 'Middletown' Study of Hollywood," *Public Opinion Quarterly* 3 (Apr. 1941): 317.

36. Gene Lyons, *The Uneasy Partnership: Social Science and the Federal Government in the Twentieth Century* (New York: Russell Sage Foundation, 1969), 11.

37. An excellent analysis of Goldwyn's career can be found in A. Scott Berg, *Goldwyn: A Biography* (New York: Knopf, 1989).

38. "Goldwyn's Solo Deals," *Variety*, May 29, 1940, 6, 20.

39. Edward R. Beach, "Double Features in Motion-Picture Exhibition," *Harvard Business Review* 10 (July 1932): 505; "Pros and Cons on Duals," *Variety*, Oct. 29, 1937, 29; Robert W. Chambers, "The Double Feature as a Sales Problem," *Harvard Business Review* 16 (Winter 1938): 230–31; Andre Sennwald, "Two for One Price," *NYT*, Sept. 15, 1935, sec. 9, p. 3; "H'wood Told Off," *Variety*, Jan. 13, 1937, 5, 21.

40. Thomas Brady, "Hollywood Has 'Double' Trouble," *NYT*, July 7, 1940, sec. 9, p. 3; "Pros and Cons on Duals," 6, 29; Chambers, "The Double Feature as a Sales Problem," 230–231; Bosley Crowther, "Double Feature Trouble," *NYT Magazine*, July 14, 1940, 8, 20.

41. Beach, "Double Features," 514.

42. "H'Wood Told Off," *Variety*, Jan. 13, 1937, 5, 21; "Screen Fans Organize," *Newsweek*, Oct. 4, 1937, 25.

43. Chambers, "The Double Feature as a Sales Problem," 227.

44. "S. Goldwyn Urges Higher Admission Prices," *NYT*, May 8, 1940, sec. 10, p. 3; "Goldwyn Advocates H'wood Cut," *Variety*, May 8, 1940, 5; "Goldwyn Urges Price Scales," *MPH*, May 11, 1940, 17; "Goldwyn Hits Block Booking," *FD*, May 8, 1940, 1, 3; Thomas M. Pryor, "The Screen Grab-Bag," *NYT*, May 12, 1940, sec. 9, p. 3.

45. "Sam Goldwyn Insists . . . ," *Variety*, May 15, 1940, 5.

46. "Film Survey to be Taken," *NYT*, May 16, 1940, 29; "Goldwyn-Gallup Poll," *MPH*, May 18, 1940, 9; Edwin Schallert, "Gallup to Conduct Poll," *Los Angeles Times*, May 16, 1940, pt. 2, p. 11.

47. "Gallup Will Poll Country on Duals," *FD*, May 16, 1940, 3; Pryor, "Film News of the Week," *NYT*, May 19, 1940, sec. 9, p. 4; W. R. Wilkerson, "Trade Views," *HR*, May 16, 1940, 1.

48. "RKO Follows Goldwyn," *Variety*, May 29, 1940, 18.

49. "Fate of Duals Placed in Hands of Eighty Million Theatregoers," *MPH*, May 9, 1936, 70–72; John T. McManus, "Thumbs Down on Doubles," *NYT*, May 31, 1936, sec. 10, p. 4.

50. "Exhibitors in 132 Spots Polled," *Variety*, June 12, 1940, 7, 20; "*Variety* Survey 70% vs. Twin Pix," *Variety*, June 12, 1940, 7, 10; "74% of Public Don't Like Twin Pix," *Variety*, June 19, 1940, 6, 19; "2D Summary of 'Variety' Poll," *Variety*, June 19, 1940, 6, 19; "Summary of 51 Cities," *Variety*, June 26, 1940, 15, 24.

51. AIPO Ballot 106, Dec. 16–20, 1937, and AIPO Ballot 108, Jan. 13–18, 1938 (both RCPOR).

52. AIPO Ballot 201, Form T and Form K, July 13–18, 1940 (RCPOR; emphasis in the original).

53. "Gallup Revamps Double-Feature Poll Question," *Variety*, June 5, 1940, 7.

54. Don Saunders, Instructions for Bulletin AIPO 201, July 11, 1940 (RCPOR). AIPO's press release about the survey said that it included children as young

as six, but this is not indicated in the instruction booklet. Gallup's efforts to construct a sample of filmgoers is discussed in Paul K. Perry, "Marketing and Attitude Research Applied to Motion Pictures," paper presented at the International Gallup Conference, New Delhi, India, Mar. 26, 1968 (given to the author by Thomas Simonet).

55. George Gallup, "Public Votes Against Double Feature Movie Programs," Aug. 9, 1940 (Public Opinion News Service, New York Public Library, microfilm).

56. Letter from Lois Timms-Ferrara, Coordinator for User Services, RCPOR, to the author, July 2, 1990.

57. George Gallup, A Guide to Public Opinion Polls, rev. ed. (Princeton: Princeton University Press, 1948), 82.

58. "Gallup Finds 57 P.C. Off Duals," HR, Aug. 8, 1940, 1; "57% Movie Fans Favor Single Films," NYT, Aug. 9, 1940, 19; "Goldwyn-Gallup Survey," MPH, Aug. 10, 1940, 21; "Gallup Poll Findings," FD, Aug. 12, 1940, 1, 10; George Gallup, "Polls Show Majority Opposed," Los Angeles Times, Aug. 9, 1940, pt. 1, pp. 1, 9; "Poor's Survey Bullish on Pix B.O.," Variety, Aug. 28, 1940, 4.

59. David Ogilvy, Blood, Brains, and Beer (New York: Atheneum, 1978), 81; Samuel Goldwyn, "Hollywood Is Sick," Saturday Evening Post, July 13, 1940, 18–19, 44, 48–49.

60. "Quarterly Survey V: Movies and Movie Stars," Fortune (July 1937): 104; "Cue Poll Shows One Feature Wanted," FD, Mar. 21, 1940, 1, 6; Chambers, "The Double Feature as a Sales Problem," 234–35.

61. "Film Audience of 32 Millions Untapped—Gallup," FD, Aug. 9, 1940, 1, 7.

62. "Kids, Reliefers Favor Duals," HR, Aug. 9, 1940, 4.

63. "'Just Not Interested' in Films Any Longer," Variety, Aug. 28, 1940, 12.

64. Gallup, interview by Thomas Simonet, Princeton, New Jersey, Sept. 21, 1977, transcript, part 2, p. 10. Transcript courtesy of Thomas Simonet.

65. "Five Million More Fans Weekly," HR, Jan. 20, 1942, 4.

66. Rosten, Hollywood: The Movie Colony, 415n1.

67. "Where Are the Lost Film Fans?" Variety, Apr. 15, 1942, 5, 20; "5% More Pix Fans Than '41," Variety, Apr. 22, 1942, 3, 54.

68. "Topics of the Times," NYT, Aug. 20, 1940, 18; "Gallup's Pan on Pix," Variety, Aug. 14, 1940, 5

69. "54,000,000 Tickets . . . ," HR, Aug. 8, 1940, 1.

70. "Film Audience of 32 Millions Untapped, " FD, Aug. 9, 1940, 7

71. John Q. Adams, in collaboration with the Interstate Theatre Managers, "How to Bring 'Em Back," unpublished report, May 10, 1941 ("Gallup Poll 1939–1941–1942" file, box 3562, DOS Papers, HRHRC).

72. "Foreign Markets Lost, Movies to Improve Selling," Advertising Age, Sept. 30, 1940, 27; "Indie UA, S.F., Makes Bid for Gallup's 32,000,000," Variety, Sept. 25, 1940, 8.

73. "Duals 'Solution,'" MPH, Oct. 5, 1940, 8; "Public Wants Duals, Says Arthur," MPH, Nov. 2, 1940, 15; "New Experiment on Duals," Variety, Feb. 5, 1941, 7, 23; "Extend Earlier Screening," MPH, Feb. 8, 1941, 17; "Spotting 'A' Film at 9–9:30,"

Variety, Feb. 12, 1941, 8; "National Interest in '9 O'Clock Plan,'" *Variety*, Feb. 19, 1941, 8.

74. W. R. Wilkerson, "Trade Views," *HR*, June 5, 1940, 1; and "Growing Tendency for Features," *Variety*, Dec. 17, 1941, 22.

75. Goldwyn, "Hollywood Is Sick," 18.

76. Gallup, "Public Votes Against Double Feature Movie Programs," n.p.

77. "Silverman OKs Gallup Poll," *FD*, Aug. 21, 1940, 1, 3.

78. Gregory A. Waller, *Main Street Amusements: Movies and Commercial Entertainment in a Southern City, 1896–1930* (Washington, D.C., and London: Smithsonian Institution Press, 1995); and Kathryn H. Fuller, *At the Picture Show: Small-Town Audiences and the Creation of Movie Fan Culture* (Washington, D.C., and London: Smithsonian Institution Press, 1996).

79. "Jack Shea on Why Duals Do OK Biz," *Variety*, June 5, 1940, 7.

80. Bosley Crowther, "Doubles, Or Maybe Nothing," *NYT*, Aug. 11, 1940, sec. 9, p. 19.

81. "Researcher Finds One Solution," *MPH*, Aug. 31, 1940, 39.

82. "New Suburban Markets," *MPH*, Aug. 31, 1940, 39.

83. "Curtis Publishing Researcher Makes Survey," *Variety*, July 10, 1940, 5.

84. "After 25 Years H'wood Decides to Ask Joe Public," *Variety*, Sept. 25, 1940, 61.

85. Gallup, "Public Votes Against Double Feature Movie Program," n.p.

86. Margaret Farrand Thorp, *America at the Movies* (New Haven: Yale University Press, 1939).

87. "Des Moines Patrons to Vote on Duals," *FD*, Aug. 23, 1940, 3.

88. "Des Moines Patrons Reverse Gallup," *MPH*, Sept. 7, 1940, 18; also see "Des Moines Voting on Duals Question," *FD*, Aug. 27, 1940, 1, 7.

89. "Singles a Flop," *FD*, Oct. 25, 1940, 1, 4.

90. "Noisy Debate on Dueling via CBS," *Variety*, Aug. 28, 1940, 12; also "Hoblitzelle, Goldwyn, Chadwick, Carr, Housewives Debate Doubles," *MPH*, Aug. 31, 1940, 14.

91. "Interstate Refutes Gallup Poll, But Admits More Selling Needed," *MPH*, June 14, 1941, 35.

92. "Allied Asks That Pix Buying Wait on Its Survey," *FD*, July 25, 1940, 8.

93. "Allied to Poll Patrons on Pix Favored," *FD*, May 26, 1941, 1, 12; "AID in 'Scientific Forecasts' on Biz," *FD*, June 5, 1941, 1, 5; "Exhibitor Poll Favors Law," *Variety*, Jan. 21, 1942, 14.

94. Gallup, "Reminiscences," 158.

95. "Rural America Against Dual," *MPH*, Oct. 19, 1940, 27; "Survey Shows Varied Film Tastes," *FD*, July 11, 1941, 8; "Owners Asked to Aid Youth Groups," *MPH*, Feb. 15, 1941, 46; "Seat-Preference Survey," *NYT*, Oct. 22, 1941, 27.

96. "Exhibition Meets with Production to Stop Duals," *MPH*, June 21, 1941, 15.

97. "Showdown on Duals," *MPH*, Oct. 19, 1940, 8; Chester B. Bahn, "Duals Again," *FD*, Oct. 23, 1940, 1, 2.

98. "Speech on Duals," *MPH*, Nov. 21, 1942, 13; and "Exhibs Move to End Duals," *Variety*, Nov. 18, 1942, 7.

99. Frank Nugent, "Double, Double, Toil and Trouble," *NYT Magazine*, Jan. 17, 1943, 11, 21.

7. Boy Meets Facts at RKO

1. ARI's reports for RKO are found on the four-reel microfilm set "Gallup Looks at the Movies: Audience Research Reports, 1940–1950" (Princeton: American Institute of Public Opinion; Wilmington, Del.: Scholarly Resources, 1979), hereafter GLM. ARI changes its numbering system from Roman to Arabic numerals midway through these reports and I have preserved this arrangement. Ogilvy stated that he wrote these reports in a letter to Alec Gallup, George's son, that was shown to the author at Gallup headquarters in Princeton, New Jersey, on Feb. 13, 1992. The tone of the reports is consistent with the rhetorical style of Ogilvy's published books and with his collected papers in the Manuscript Division of the Library of Congress, Washington, D.C.

2. For information about RKO's early history, see Richard Jewell, "A History of RKO Radio Pictures, Incorporated, 1928–1942" (Ph.D. diss., University of Southern California, 1978), 17–33; Douglas Gomery, *The Hollywood Studio System* (New York: St. Martin's, 1986), 124–27; Betty Lasky, *RKO: The Biggest Little Major of Them All* (Santa Monica, Calif.: Roundtable, 1984; 1989), 12–34; Janet Wasko, *Movies and Money: Financing the American Film Industry* (Norwood, N.J.: Ablex, 1982), 77–80. A useful compendium of the studio's films can be found in James L. Neibaur, *The RKO Features* (Jefferson, N.C.: McFarland, 1994).

3. Richard Jewell, with Vernon Harbin, *The RKO Story* (New York: Crown/Arlington House, 1982), 10.

4. Memo, "Re: Reorganization of RKO," Jan. 24, 1936, and John D. Rockefeller III, letter to attorney Thomas M. Debevoise, July 17, 1936 (both in folder 675, box 90, Record Group III, 2C, Rockefeller Family Archives, Rockefeller Archive Center, Tarrytown, New York, hereafter RAC).

5. "Odlum of Atlas," *Fortune* (Sept. 1935): 50–55, 102–110; and "Investment Trusts," *WSJ*, Sept. 23, 1941, 7.

6. "Atlas (Odlum) Buys," *Variety*, Jan. 1, 1941, 5; "Simplification of RKO's Corporate Setup," *Variety*, June 11, 1941, 7; Wasko, *Movies and Money*, pp. 86–90.

7. Odlum (?), memo to David Sarnoff and Nelson Rockefeller, Sept. 30, 1938 (folder 675, box 90, Record Group III, 2C, RAC); "See Geo J. Schaefer to RKO," *Variety*, Oct. 12, 1938, 3; "George Schaefer Takes Over," *MPH*, Oct. 29, 1938, 22.

8. George Gallup, interview with Paul Sheatsley, Mar. 22, 1978, NORC, University of Chicago, transcript, 14–15. Evidence that Whitney, Selznick, and Rockefeller knew each other socially can be found in memos in the "John Hay Whitney" file (box 168, DOS Papers, HRHRC). Don Cahalan confirmed that Gallup and Rockefeller were very close (interview by author, Feb. 20, 1992, tape recording, Berkeley, California).

9.   George Gallup, "Reminiscences" (1962), Columbia University Oral History Collection, New York City, transcript, 138–40.

10. George Gallup, letter to the editor, *The Link* 4 (Fall 1982): 2 (Y&R).

11. Nelson Rockefeller, letter to N. Peter Rathvon, Jan. 22, 1940 (folder 681, box 90, Record Group III, 2C, RAC).

12. "Moving Picture Industry," *WSJ*, Jan. 2, 1940, 32; and Sydney B. Self, "Wartime Boom," *Barrons's*, Aug. 11, 1941, 3.

13. Leo C. Rosten, *Hollywood: The Movie Colony, the Movie Makers* (New York: Harcourt, Brace, 1941), 377; and "Final RKO Report," *Variety*, Mar. 27, 1940, 6; "Expects Bigger Foreign and Domestic Grosses," *FD*, June 21, 1939, 4.

14. Jewell "History of RKO," 466–73.

15. "Scientific Research as Applied to the Motion Picture Public," Sept. 28, 1939 (ARI Agreements file, RKO Papers, Culver City, California; hereafter, RKO Papers).

16. J. R. McDonough to producer Bob Sisk, Sept. 25, 1939; Gallup to RKO Radio Pictures, Dec. 8, 1939; Gallup to Schaefer, Dec. 26, 1939, Jan. 17, 1940, Feb. 26, 1940, and Mar. 8, 1940 (all in ARI Agreements file, RKO Papers).

17. "RKO's Important Script Buys," *Variety*, Feb. 21, 1940, 3.

18. David Ogilvy, *Blood, Brains, and Beer* (New York: Atheneum, 1978), 74–75.

19. Gallup, quoted in "53 Feature Films," *NYT*, May 28, 1940, 29.

20. "RKO Follows Goldwyn," *Variety*, May 29, 1940, 18; "Gallup Will Poll," *FD*, May 28, 1940, 1; "RKO to Have," *MPH*, June 1, 1940, 30; Edwin Schallert, "Welles Will Portray," *Los Angeles Times*, May 28, 1940, 12.

21. Gallup to McDonough, May 15, 1940 (ARI Correspondence File No. 1, RKO Papers).

22. "Scientific Research," 11 (RKO Papers).

23. Paul B. Sheatsley to David Ogilvy, Nov. 18, 1941 (ARI Correspondence File No. 3, RKO Papers); and Paul Perry, interview by Thomas Simonet, Princeton, New Jersey, Feb. 15, 1978.

24. "Increasing Profits Through Continuous Audience Research," 48 (GLM).

25. ARI Report LI, "A Generalization Examined," Feb. 21, 1941 (GLM).

26. Ogilvy to McDonough, Jan. 30, 1941 (ARI Correspondence File No. 1, RKO Papers); "Increasing Profits," 144–45, and "Composition of the Motion Picture Audience, 1940–1941," p. XII (both GLM).

27. "Increasing Profits," 69 (GLM).

28. ARI Report LIX, "The Corn Is Green," Mar. 13, 1941 (GLM).

29. "Increasing Profits," 68 (GLM; emphasis in the original).

30. ARI Report XLIV, "Wrapped in Cellophane," Feb. 12, 1941, and Report XLV, "The Blind Stallion," Feb. 12, 1941 (both GLM).

31. ARI Report 118, "Gilded Pheasant," Nov. 3, 1941 (GLM).

32. ARI Report LIX, "The Corn Is Green," Mar. 13, 1941 (GLM).

3.   "Increasing Profits," 87, and ARI Report XLIV, "Wrapped in Cellophane," Feb. 12, 1941 (both GLM).

34. *"The Ramparts We Watch,"* *MPH*, July 27, 1940, 34.

35. "Increasing Profits," 89–90 (GLM).
36. Ibid., 139 (GLM).
37. ARI Report XXX, "The Devil and Daniel Webster," Oct. 5, 1940 (GLM).
38. ARI Report 145, "The History of Mr. Polly," Mar. 17, 1942 (GLM).
39. ARI Report XXIII, "For the Record," Aug. 27, 1940 (GLM).
40. Ogilvy to J. R. McDonough, Jan. 30, 1941 (ARI Correspondence File No. 1, RKO Papers); "Increasing Profits," 142–43 (GLM).
41. ARI Report XCIII, "Sue Barton II," June 30, 1941 (GLM). Ogilvy excludes children under 12 in this discussion.
42. Grace Palladino, *Teenagers: An American History* (New York: Basic Books, 1996), 52.
43. ARI Report XXI, "Sue Barton," Aug. 19, 1940, and Report 130, "Angel Face," Dec. 16, 1941 (both GLM).
44. ARI Report XLVI, "The Band Played On," Feb. 12, 1941 (GLM).
45. Palladino, *Teenagers*, 49–61.
46. ARI Report LII, "Demand for Stars Under 25, " Feb. 24, 1941 (GLM).
47. "'All Out' Effort to Groom New Stars," *FD*, June 2, 1941, 1, 7.
48. ARI Report LXVI, "Sister Carrie," Apr. 17, 1941 (GLM).
49. ARI Report 101, "More About Gloria Swanson," Aug. 25, 1941 (GLM); Jewell, "History of RKO," 762.
50. ARI Report XCIII, "Sue Barton II," June 30, 1941 (GLM).
51. ARI Report LI, "A Generalization Examined," Feb. 22, 1941 (GLM).
52. ARI Report XIX, "Variations in the Composition of Audiences," July 29, 1940, and Report LXXXII, "Males versus Females," June 2, 1941 (both GLM).
53. ARI Report 165, "The Importance of Men," July 14, 1942 (GLM).
54. "'Men Top Pic Fans'—Gallup," *Variety*, Aug. 5, 1942, 3.
55. "What Sex Are Cinemaddicts?" *Time*, Aug. 10, 1942.
56. William A. Lydgate, "Hollywood Listens to the Audience," *Reader's Digest* (Apr. 1944): 84–85.
57. M. Joyce Baker, *Images of Women in Film: The War Years, 1941–1945* (Ann Arbor, Mich.: UMI Research Press, 1980); Michael Renov, *Hollywood's Wartime Woman: Representation and Ideology* (Ann Arbor: UMI Research Press, 1988); Mary Ann Doane, *The Desire to Desire: The Woman's Film of the 1940s* (Bloomington: Indiana University Press, 1987).
58. "Boy Meets Facts," *Time*, July 21, 1941, 73–74.
59. "Scientific Research," 12–13 (RKO Papers).
60. "Increasing Profits," 47 (GLM).
61. Paul K. Perry, "Marketing and Attitude Research Applied to Motion Pictures," 3–4 (paper presented at the International Gallup Conference, New Delhi, India, Mar. 26, 1968; given to the author by Thomas Simonet).
62. "Increasing Profits," 47–52 (GLM).
63. Gallup to RKO Radio Pictures, Dec. 8, 1939 (ARI Agreements file, RKO Papers).
64. "Increasing Profits," 53 (GLM).

65. ARI Report XXXVIII, "Parachute Invasion," Dec. 12, 1940 (GLM).
66. ARI Report 132, "A Plague on You," Jan. 2, 1942 (GLM).
67. ARI Report LXXVI, "East from Halifax," May 22, 1941 (GLM).
68. "Increasing Profits," 39 (GLM).
69. ARI Report 127, "Arms and the Man," Dec. 10, 1941 (GLM).
70. ARI Report 120, "Brazilian Adventure," Nov. 3, 1941 (GLM).
71. ARI Report 102, "I *Ought* to Like This One—But I Don't," Aug. 27, 1941 (GLM).
72. ARI Report 125, "The Witch of Wall Street," Nov. 24, 1941 (GLM).
73. ARI Report XLIX, "Marquee Value of Radio Stars," Feb. 18, 1941; Report LVI, "Interest in Radio Serials," Mar. 3, 1941; Report LXXXVII, "Three Comic Strips," June 12, 1941; Report 123, "Pickwick Papers," Dec. 9, 1941; Report 127, "Arms and the Man," Dec. 10, 1941; Report LXXXVIII, "Life with Father," June 23, 1941; Report XCVI, "Results of 29 Story Tests," Aug. 14, 1941; Report 103, "49 More Story Tests," Sept. 5, 1941 (all GLM).
74. "RKO-Selznick Deal," *Variety*, Mar. 22, 1939, 2.
75. "Film Unit Trend," *Variety*, Apr. 3, 1940, 3; "RKO May Go," *Variety*, July 17, 1940, 5; "Unit System to Help," *FD*, Sept. 16, 1940, 1.
76. "Gordon's RKO Deal," *Variety*, Mar. 22, 1939, 2.
77. "RKO Budget," *Variety*, June 28, 1939, 6; and Jewell, "History of RKO," 587–89.
78. ARI Report V, "The American Way," Apr. 8, 1940, and Report LXXXVI, "The American Way II," June 5, 1941 (both GLM).
79. ARI Report VIII, "Little Men," Apr. 25, 1940; Report XXIV, "How Accurate Are Our Results?" Aug. 30, 1940; Report XXXVII, "Little Men II," Dec. 11, 1940 (all in GLM); Jewell, "History of RKO," 579–80.
80. "RKO, Columbia Report," *MPH*, June 14, 1941, 45.
81. "RKO Earmarks," *Variety*, Apr. 14, 1940, 4; "RKO Trims," *FD*, Dec. 9, 1940, 1, 7; "Too Many Disappointments," *Variety*, Oct. 30, 1940, 7; "Indies Chief Loser," *Variety*, Dec. 25, 1940, 5, 50.
82. Ogilvy to McDonough, Jan. 29, 1941 (ARI Correspondence File No. 1, RKO Papers).
83. ARI Report XXIX, "Incidental Intelligence," Oct. 4, 1940 (GLM).
84. ARI Report XXV, "Communism and Hollywood," Sept. 10, 1940 (GLM).
85. ARI Report XVI, "The Audience Acceptance Value of War Pictures," June 21, 1940 (GLM).
86. ARI Report 117, "Audience Acceptance of War Subjects," Oct. 30, 1941; Report 134, "72 Hours by Train," Jan. 8, 1942; Report 141, "Ticket-Buyers React to War," Jan. 23, 1942; Report 148, "Battle Stations or Pay to Learn," Mar. 23, 1942 (all GLM).
87. Gallup to Schaefer, Feb. 18, 1941 (ARI Correspondence File No, 1, RKO Papers).
88. Gallup to Schaefer, Apr. 2, 1941 (ARI Correspondence File No, 2, RKO Papers).
89. Gallup to Schaefer, Feb. 18, 1941 (ARI Correspondence File No. 1, RKO Papers).

90. Schaefer to Martin Quigley, Apr. 22, 1941 (ARI General Correspondence File No. 2, RKO Papers).

91. "Propaganda in Motion Pictures," U.S. Senate, *Hearings before a Subcommittee of the Committee on Interstate Commerce*, S.R. 152, 77th Cong., 1st sess., Sept. 9–26, 1941 (Washington, D.C.: GPO, 1942), 112–19.

92. Jewell, "History of RKO," 419, 480, 550.

93. "Ginger Rogers No. 1," *Variety*, Jan. 3, 1940, 23; McDonough to Gallup, Feb. 23, 1940 (ARI Correspondence File No. 1, RKO Papers).

94. Jewell, "History of RKO," 257–58, 318–21, 342–45, 448–51.

95. ARI Report I, "Ginger Rogers," Mar. 21, 1940, and Report XI, "Is Fred Astaire Washed-Up?" May 15, 1940 (both GLM).

96. Ogilvy to Schaefer, Nov. 21, 1940 (ARI Correspondence File No. 1, RKO Papers).

97. "Inside Stuff—Pictures," *Variety*, May 7, 1941, 27.

98. ARI Report XII, "*Smiler with a Knife, Heart of Darkness, or Invasion from Mars?*" May 15, 1940; Report XXXVIII, "Parachute Invasion," Dec. 12, 1940 (both in GLM); Jewell, "History of RKO," 555–56.

99. ARI Report XXVI, "Notes on the Casting of *Lucky Partners*," Sept. 16, 1940 (GLM; emphasis in the original).

100. ARI Report XLIV, "Wrapped in Cellophane," Feb. 12, 1941 (GLM).

101. Ogilvy to George Schaefer, Nov. 21, 1940 (ARI Correspondence File No. 1, RKO Papers). See also ARI Report XXVI, "Notes on the Casting of *Lucky Partners*," Sept. 16, 1940; Report XXVIII, "The Swan for Ronald Colman," Oct. 1, 1940; and Report XLII, "My Life with Caroline," Jan. 10, 1941 (all in GLM); Jewell, "History of RKO," 572–73.

102. ARI Report LXXV, "Warpath, Bitter Creek, Blood on the Moon," May 15, 1941 (GLM).

103. ARI Report XXXIX, "Harold Lloyd," Dec. 16, 1940 (GLM).

104. ARI Report XX, "Dark Horses," Aug. 14, 1940, Report LXXVIII, "Dark Horses II," May 28, 1941; Report 167, "Dark Horses of 1942," Aug. 31, 1942; "Increasing Profits," 28 (all in GLM).

105. ARI Report LXXVII, "Lucille Ball," May 27, 1941; "Increasing Profits," 35–36 (GLM).

106. ARI Report XX, "Dark Horses," Aug. 14, 1940 (GLM).

107. "Increasing Profits," 9–20 (GLM); McDonough to George Gallup, June 4, 1941 (ARI Correspondence File No. 2, RKO Papers); "'All Out' Effort," *FD*, June 2, 1941, 1, 7.

108. "Increasing Profits," 9–20 (GLM).

109. "Gallup Rating Pix Stars," *Variety*, Sept. 18, 1940, 1.

110. Schaefer to McDonough, Mar. 4, 1940, and McDonough to Schaefer, Mar. 6, 1940 (both in ARI Agreements file, RKO Papers).

111. McDonough to Schaefer, Jan. 20, 1941 (ARI Correspondence File No. 1, RKO Papers).

112. "Scarcity of Marquee Stars," *Variety*, June 4, 1941, 1; ARI Report XCII, "How Many Pictures Should a Star Make Every Year?" June 27, 1941 (GLM).

113. "After More Than a Year," *NYT*, Aug. 3, 1941, sec. 9, p. 3.
114. Schaefer to Myron Selznick, July 15, 1941 (ARI Correspondence File No. 2, RKO Papers). For trade paper accounts, see "Stars Told to Make 3 Per Year," *HR*, July 23, 1941, 1, 4, and "High Salaries Prove Boomerang," *Los Angeles Times*, July 24, 1941, 8.
115. "Increasing Profits," 4 (GLM).
116. ARI Report LI, "A Generalization Examined," Feb. 22, 1941 (GLM).
117. Ogilvy, *Blood, Brains, and Beer*, 78.
118. ARI Report XLIV, "Wrapped in Cellophane," Feb. 12, 1941 (GLM).
119. ARI Report LXI, "Silas Marner, Ivanhoe, Lorna Doone," Mar. 25, 1941 (GLM).
120. ARI Report LXXIV, "Cyrano II," May 17, 1941 (GLM).
121. ARI Report LIII, "Water Gypsies," Feb. 26, 1941 (GLM).
122. ARI Report XXX, "The Devil and Daniel Webster," Oct. 5, 1940 (GLM).
123. ARI Report XXII, "An American Doctor's Odyssey," Aug. 19, 1940 (GLM).
124. ARI Report LX, "George Sanders," Mar. 20, 1941 (GLM).
125. ARI Report LXII, "RKO Stock & Contract Players," Mar. 26, 1941 (GLM).
126. "Arnaz Footage Added," *Variety*, Aug. 22, 1940, 12.
127. Desi Arnaz, *A Book* (New York: Morrow, 1976), 92–115.
128. "Scientific Research," 11 (RKO Papers).
129. N. Peter Rathvon to Nelson Rockefeller, Jan. 12, 1940 (folder 681, box 90, Record Group III, 2C, RAC).
130. McDonough to Gallup, Aug. 5, 1941 (ARI Correspondence File No. 2, RKO Papers).
131. McDonough to Schaefer, July 10, 1940, and Schaefer to McDonough, July 15, 1940 (both ARI Correspondence File No. 1, RKO Papers).
132. McDonough to Schaefer, Mar. 25, 1940 (ARI Correspondence File No. 1, RKO Papers).
133. ARI Report 143, "Young Man of Caracas," Feb. 5, 1942 (GLM).
134. McDonough to Ogilvy, Oct. 3, 1940 (ARI Correspondence File No. 1, RKO Papers).
135. Ogilvy to McDonough, Apr. 6, 1940 (ARI Correspondence File No. 1, RKO Papers).
136. ARI Report 136, "Cheyenne," Jan. 10, 1942 (GLM).
137. McDonough to Schaefer, Jan. 6, 1941, and Feb. 1, 1941 (ARI Correspondence File No. 1, RKO Papers).
138. McDonough to Gallup, Aug. 12, 1941, and Gallup to McDonough, Aug. 15, 1941 (both in ARI Agreements file, RKO Papers).
139. George Cecala to RKO sales executive Reg Armour, Aug. 19, 1941 (ARI Correspondence File No. 2, RKO Papers).
140. Gallup to Cecala, Dec. 29, 1941 (ARI Correspondence File No. 2, RKO Papers). The report is "Increasing Profits Through Continuous Audience Research" (GLM).
141. Ogilvy to Cecala, Aug. 26, 1941 (ARI Correspondence File No. 2, RKO Papers).

142. ARI Report 128, "Powder Town," Dec. 17, 1941; Report 129, "The Fighting Littles," Dec. 17, 1941; Report 132, "A Plague on You," Jan. 2, 1942 (all in GLM).

143. "1941–42 Product Listing," *MPH*, June 21, 1941, 29.

144. ARI Report 151, "Father Malachy's Miracle II," Apr. 11, 1942, and "Increasing Profits," 54–55 (both in GLM).

145. "Increasing Profits," 95 (GLM).

146. ARI Report 126, "Attack Alarm," Nov. 24, 1941, and Report 128, "Powder Town," Dec. 17, 1941 (both GLM).

147. Rosten, *Hollywood: The Movie Colony*, 82n1.

148. Cahalan, interview by author, Feb. 20, 1992.

149. "Increasing Profits, " 5 (GLM).

150. ARI Report XXIV, "How Accurate Are Our Results?" Aug. 30, 1940 (GLM).

151. McDonough to Schaefer, Feb. 1 1941 (ARI Correspondence file No. 1, RKO Papers).

152. ARI Report XXXIV, "Believe-It-Or-Not Equations," Nov. 28, 1940 (GLM).

153. "Increasing Profits," 21 (GLM).

154. ARI Report LXXX, "Marquee Value of Teams," May 28, 1941 (GLM).

155. ARI Report XXXII, "Kitty Foyle," Oct. 29, 1940, and Report LXV, "8 Good, 2 Fair and 2 Bad," Apr. 17, 1941 (both GLM); Jewell, "History of RKO," 633.

156. Cahalan, interview by author, Feb. 20, 1992; "Scientific Research," 4 (RKO Papers).

157. McDonough to Ogilvy, Mar. 3, 1941, and to Gallup, Apr. 11, 1941 (both in ARI Correspondence File No. 2, RKO Papers).

158. ARI Report XLVII, *Army Surgeon*, Feb. 13, 1941 (GLM); Jewell, "History of RKO," 764.

159. "Gallup Shorts," *MPH*, June 21, 1941, 9; "Gallup Surveys," *FD*, June 18, 1941, 6. Also, Gallup to McDonough, Mar. 17, 1941; Schaefer to Gallup, Apr. 4, 1941; to Ullman, Apr. 11, 1941; Depinet to Schaefer, Apr. 15, 1941; Ullman to Schaefer Apr. 17, 1941; Depinet to Schaefer, Apr. 18, 1941; Schaefer to Dorfman, Apr. 21, 1941 (all in ARI Correspondence File No. 2, RKO Papers).

160. "*Boom Town* Named Best-Liked," press release from Public Opinion News Service, Feb. 26, 1941, New York Public Library, microfilm; "'Best-Liked Pix Via Gallup," *FD*, Feb. 26, 1941, 1, 4. Information on the 1941 Academy Awards was taken from www.oscars.org.

161. Schaefer to McDonough, Feb. 26, 1941 (ARI Corresponsdence File No. 2, RKO Papers).

162. Douglas W. Churchill, "Hollywood Reports," *NYT*, May 4, 1941, sec. 9, p. 5.

163. "Sees No Film Shortage," *Variety*, Jan. 1, 1941, 5.

164. "RKO Exec Realignments," *Variety*, Apr. 9, 1941, 3; "RKO's Revamp," *Variety*, Apr. 30, 1941, 5; and "Breen Signs Contract," *FD*, June 19, 1941, 1.

165. "Predict Atlas Control," *FD*, Aug. 13, 1941, 1; "Schaefer-RKO Deal," *HR*, Aug. 13, 1941, 1, 5; "Clarify RKO Setup," *Variety*, Nov. 12, 1941, 5 ; "Schaefer and Nelson Rockefeller Reach Accord," *Variety*, Nov. 26, 1941, 5; Richard B. Jewell, "Orson Welles, George Schaefer, and *It's All True*: A 'Cursed' Production," *Film*

History 2 (1988): 330–32; Catherine Benamou, "*It's All True* as Document/Event: Notes Towards an Historiographical and Textual Analysis," *Persistence of Vision* 7 (1989): 121–52.

166. "Increasing Weight of Floyd Odlum's Atlas Corp.," *Variety*, Dec. 24, 1941, 5; "Rathvon V.P. of RKO," *Variety*, Dec. 17, 1941, 5.

167. Schaefer to Rathvon, Feb. 26, 1942 (ARI Agreements file, RKO Papers).

168. "Sarnoff, Angry," *Variety*, Mar. 25, 1942, 5; "RCA Selling," *Variety*, Apr. 7, 1942, 6; "Open Fight," *HR*, May 22, 1942, 1; "Schaefer Resigns," *NYT*, June 12, 1942, 29, 30; "Odlum at RKO Helm," *Variety*, July 1, 1942, 5, 54. "Rathvon Heads RKO; Depinet, RKO Radio," *FD*, June 26, 1942, 1, 3; "Rathvon, Depinet," *MPH*, July 4, 1942, 23.

169. Rathvon to George Gallup, June 30, 1942; lawyer Gordon Youngman to Gallup, Mar. 1, 1942; Youngman to Gallup, Aug. 20, 1942, and Nov. 30, 1942 (all in ARI Agreements file, RKO Papers).

170. "Koerner Rules," *Variety*, Aug. 26, 1942, 5.

171. "RKO Radio Starts Season," *MPH*, Aug. 29, 1942, 53.

172. Koerner to Eddie Mannix, Sept. 21, 1942 (ARI Correspondence File No. 3, RKO Papers).

173. John Rindlaub, Vice President of External and Government Relations, Young & Rubicam, telephone conversation with the author, February 1992.

8. David O. Selznick Presents: Audience Research and the Independent Producer

1. John Wharton to David Selznick and John Hay Whitney, Jan. 27, 1937 ("Gallup" file, box 2974, DOS Papers, HRHRC).

2. Janet Staiger first developed this argument in "Individualism Versus Collectivism," *Screen* 24.4–5 (July–Oct. 1983): 68–79, and elaborated on it in more detail in David Bordwell, Janet Staiger, and Kristin Thompson, *The Classical Hollywood Cinema: Film Style and Mode of Production to 1960* (New York: Columbia University Press, 1985), 317–30. Matthew Bernstein presented his analysis, "Hollywood's Semi-Independent Production," in *Cinema Journal* 32.3 (Spring 1993): 41–54, and more fully in *Walter Wanger, Hollywood Independent* (Berkeley: University of California Press, 1994), 93–113.

3. Hubbard Keavy, "Independent Movie Makers," *Washington Post*, June 1, 1941, L3.

4. "Selznick Suit," *NYT*, Aug. 23, 1925, 11; Henry F. Pringle, "Hollywood's Selznick," *Life*, Dec. 18, 1939, 83.

5. "The Producer Prince," *Time*, July 2, 1965, 62.

6. Pringle, "Hollywood's Selznick," 83.

7. Thomas Schatz, *The Genius of the System* (New York: Pantheon, 1988), 48–57, 69–81, 125–34.

8. "Inquiring Investor," *WSJ*, Nov. 21, 1931, 6.

9. Rudy Behlmer, *Memo from David O. Selznick* (New York: Viking, 1972), 67–72.

10. Behlmer, *Memo*, 97.

11. "North Formosa Novelties," *Time*, Oct. 21, 1935, 46; and Pringle, "Hollywood's Selznick," 76–85.

12. Bernstein, "Hollywood's Semi-Independent Production," 41–54.

13. Keavy, "Independent Movie Makers," L3.

14. "National Poll Will Show Roosevelt-Landon Score," *Los Angeles Times*, July 8, 1936, 1.

15. DOS to Daniel O'Shea, July 8, 1936; O'Shea to Gallup, July 11, 1936; Gallup to O'Shea, July 20, 1936 (all in the "Pi" file, box 633, DOS Papers, HRHRC).

16. Gallup to O'Shea, Oct. 19, 1936; O'Shea to DOS, Nov. 5, 1936, enclosing the article "Final Standings in American Institute Poll," *Los Angeles Times*, Nov. 1, 1936, 2 (ibid., DOS Papers, HRHRC).

17. DOS to Wharton, Feb. 1, 1937 ("Selznick teletype messages 1937" file, box 47, JHW Papers, HRHRC).

18. Wharton to Whitney, Feb. 3, 1937; Wharton to DOS, Feb. 5, 1937 (both in "Gallup" file, box 2974, DOS papers, HRHRC).

19. Malcolm Cowley, "Going with the Wind," *New Republic*, Sept. 16, 1936, 161–62, reprinted in Darden Asbury Pyron, ed., *Recasting "Gone with the Wind" in American Culture* (Miami: University Presses of Florida, 1983), 17–18; Belle Rosenbaum, "Why Do They Read It?" *Scribner's*, Aug. 1937, 23; David O. Selznick, "For the Defense," in Richard Harwell, ed., *GWTW as Book and Film* (New York: Paragon, 1987), 130.

20. Chronology of *GWTW* casting, undated ("GWTW Casting—General" file, box 178), and Max Arnow to DOS, Sept. 6, 1938 ("GWTW—Casting—Talent Search" file, box 179; both in DOS Papers, HRHRC). Selznick's own account of the search can be found in David O. Selznick, "Discovering the New Ones," *Collier's*, Mar. 8, 1941, 13, 56–57. For fan magazine coverage of the search, see Adelheid Kaufmann, "Heartaches in the Search for Scarlett O'Hara," *Photoplay*, Dec. 1937, 20–21, 82. For a list of actresses, see Lucie Neville, "Film Fans Were Ready," *Washington Post*, Sept. 25, 1938, TT1. Information about radio fans appears in Jimmie Fidler to DOS, Oct. 19, 1938, reprinted in Ronald Haver, *David O. Selznick's Gone with the Wind* (New York: Random House, 1986), 6.

21. "Vivien Leigh Gets Role of Scarlett," *NYT*, Jan. 14, 1939, 12.

22. John Alexander, letter to the editor, *NYT*, Jan. 29, 1939, sec. 9, p. 4.

23. Wharton to Whitney, Feb. 13, 1939 ("Gallup Poll 1939–1941–1942" file, box 3562, DOS Papers, HRHRC).

24. AIPO Ballot 146 A & B, Jan. 25–Feb. 1, 1939, RCPOR.

25. The three pilot studies for the *GWTW* national survey took place during December 1938 and are included in the "Early ARI Poll Results" in "Gallup Looks at the Movies: Audience Research Reports 1940–1950" (Princeton: American Institute of Public Opinion; Wilmington, Del.: Scholarly Resources, 1979), microfilm, reel 1, hereafter GLM.

26. Don Cahalan, interview by author, Feb. 20, 1992, tape recording, Berkeley, California.

27. "Film-Goers Give Views on Choice of Vivien Leigh," AIPO press release, Feb. 19, 1939 ("Gallup Poll 1939–1941–1942" file, box 3562, DOS Papers, HRHRC).

28. DOS to Whitney, Feb. 11, 1939 (ibid., HRHRC).

29. Whitney to Wharton, Feb. 11, 1939 (ibid., HRHRC).

30. Wharton to Whitney, Feb. 13, 1939, and Gallup to Wharton, Mar. 3, 1939 (ibid., HRHRC).

31. "Film-Goers Give Views on Choice of Vivien Leigh," AIPO press release, Feb. 19, 1939 (ibid., HRHRC).

32. Cahalan, interview by author, Feb. 20, 1992.

33. Stirling Bowen, "Tom Sawyer on the Screen," WSJ, July 9, 1936, 13, and Bowen, "The Theatre: Tom Sawyer," WSJ, Jan. 22, 1938, 5.

34. DOS to Wharton, Apr. 16, 1937 ("Gallup" file, box 2974, "Selznick Administration 1936," DOS Papers, HRHRC).

35. Pringle, "Hollywood's Selznick," 78.

36. Ibid., 78–80.

37. Ron Hutchinson's "Moonlight and Magnolias" premiered in Chicago at the Goodman Theatre, May 25–June 13, 2004, directed by Steven Robman. See www.goodman-theatre.org/primg_magnolias.asp.

38. Douglas W. Churchill, "The Coming of Gone," NYT, Apr. 23, 1939, sec, 10, p. 5.

39. DOS to Whitney, June 28, 1939 ("Gallup Poll 1939–1941–1942" file, box 3562, DOS Papers, HRHRC).

40. DOS to Wharton, Mar. 10, 1939 (ibid., HRHRC).

41. DOS to Leonard Case, Feb. 27, 1940 ("Gallup Poll 1939–1941–1942" file, box 3562, DOS Papers, HRHRC); and Roland Flamini, Scarlett, Rhett, and a Cast of Thousands (New York: Collier/Macmillan, 1975), 277.

42. For evidence that Mitchell would not allow her comments to be advertised, see her letter to Susan Myrick, June 10, 1939, in Susan Myrick, White Columns in Hollywood: Reports from the GWTW Sets, ed. Richard Harwell (Macon, Ga: Mercer University Press, 1982), 21–22. Selznick to Nicholas Schenck, president of Loew's, Inc., Jan. 16, 1939 (JHW Papers, box 4445, HRHRC).

43. DOS to Ruth Waterbury, Mar. 10, 1939 ("GWTW Casting—Scarlett," box 179, DOS Papers, HRHRC).

44. Ad (in the "Gallup Poll 1939–1941–1942" file, box 3562, DOS Papers, HRHRC).

45. George Gallup, letter to the editor, The Link 4.4 (Fall 1982): 2 (Y&R).

46. DOS to L. V. Calvert, Apr. 5, 1939 ("Gallup Poll 1939–1941–1942" file, box 3562, DOS Papers, HRHRC).

47. Jock Whitney, quoted in "GWTW Finally Goes to M-G-M," MPH, Sept. 3, 1938, 75.

48. "Agreement Regarding GWTW," Aug. 12, 1938 ("MGM-GWTW, including Whitney correspondence" file, box 159, DOS Papers, HRHRC).

49. "Loew's Inc.," Fortune (Aug. 1939): 25–26.

50. DOS to Nicholas Schenck, Sept. 23, 1939 ("Gallup Poll 1939–1941–1942" file, box 3562, DOS Papers, HRHRC).

51. DOS to Howard Dietz, May 2, 1938 ("*GWTW* Distribution" file, box 182, DOS papers, HRHRC).

52. DOS to Wharton, Jan. 20, 1937 ("*GWTW* Distribution" file, box 183, DOS Papers, HRHRC).

53. "Jeff McCarthy, Pioneer Creator of the $2 Roadshow Film, Dies at 58," *Variety*, Mar. 3, 1937, 2; "Film Roadshows Drop," *MPH*, Aug. 20, 1938, 15–16.

54. DOS to Whitney, June 28, 1939 ("Gallup Poll 1939–1941–1942" file, box 3562, DOS Papers, HRHRC).

55. "Agreement regarding GWTW," Aug. 12, 1938 (file 8, box 159, DOS Papers, HRHRC); and also "Loew's Inc.," *Fortune* (Aug. 1939): 105–106.

56. DOS to Al Lichtman, MGM vice president, Oct. 20, 1939 ("Gallup Poll 1939–1941–1942" file, box 3562, DOS Papers, HRHRC).

57. Loew's Inc.," *Fortune* (Aug. 1939): 106, 110.

58. Preview Questionnairres, Oct. 10, 1939 ("*GWTW*—Distribution—Oct 1939" file); DOS to Rodgers, Nov. 22, 1939, and Rodgers' reply to DOS, Nov. 23, 1939 (in "*GWTW*—Distribution—Since Nov 1" file; all in box 182, DOS Papers, HRHRC).

59. DOS to Al Lichtman, Oct. 20, 1939 ("Gallup Poll 1939–1941 1942" file, box 3562, DOS Papers, HRHRC).

60. Calvert to DOS, July 7, 1939 ("*GWTW*—Distribution—Jan-Aug 1939" file, box 182, DOS Papers, HRHRC).

61. DOS to Calvert, July 17, 1939 (ibid., HRHRC).

62. DOS to Whitney, Sept. 5, 1939 (ibid., HRHRC).

63. DOS to Whitney, Oct. 2, 1939, and to William Rodgers, Oct. 14, 1939 (both in "*GWTW*-Distribution-October 1939" file, box 182, DOS Papers, HRHRC).

64. DOS to Schenck, Sept. 23, 1939 ("Gallup Poll 1939–1941–1942" file, box 3562, DOS Papers, HRHRC).

65. "Spotting *Wind* Again," *Variety*, Nov. 15, 1939, 7; "GWTW to Open Here Dec. 19," *NYT*, Nov. 22, 1939, 17; "MGM Pre Dates *Wind*," *MPH*, Nov. 25, 1939, 18; "Listen, the *Wind*!" *NYT*, Nov. 26, 1939, sec. 9, p. 4; "*Wind* Riding In," *MPH*, Dec. 2, 1939, 17–18; "Setting Final Policies on *Wind*," *MPH*, Dec. 9, 1939, 14.

66. W. R. Wilkerson, "Trade Views," *HR*, June 24, 1940, 1; "Repeat of *Gone*," *Variety*, Apr. 24, 1940, 23; "*Wind* Riding In," *MPH*, Dec. 2, 1939, 17.

67. DOS to JHW, June 28, 1939 ("Gallup Poll 1939–1941–1942," box 3562, DOS Papers, HRHRC).

68. Chester B. Bahn, "Metro Turns the Trick," *FD*, Dec. 12, 1939, 6.

69. "Most Costly Film," *WSJ*, Dec. 19, 1939, 1; "7-Week Gross," *FD*, Feb. 5, 1940, 1, 5; "Record Wind," *Time*, Feb. 19, 1940, 69; "*Wind* Gross Hits $17,250,000," *HR*, Apr. 9, 1940, 1; "London Sees 'The Wind,'" *NYT*, Apr. 19, 1940, 29; "*Gone with Wind* a London Success," *NYT*, Apr. 20, 1940, 14; C.A. Lejeune, "Forever England," *NYT*, May 19, 1940, sec. 9, p. 3; "Largest Upturn in Years," *WSJ*, Apr. 3, 1941, 1.

70. AIPO Ballot 188, Form T, Mar. 27–Apr. 1, 1940 (RCPOR).

71. Raymond Klune to DOS, Apr. 6, 1940 ("*GWTW* Poll," box 186, DOS Papers, HRHRC).

72. "Special Admission Scale for 1941 Release," *FD*, Oct. 17, 1940, 1, 3; "Metro Testing How to Sell *Gone*," *Variety*, Oct. 23, 1940, 7.

73. Chester B. Bahn, "Very Smart," *FD*, Nov. 12, 1940, 1.

74. Lowell Calvert to Howard Dietz, June 14, 1940 ("*GWTW* Poll," box 186, DOS Papers, HRHRC).

75. *FD*, Dec. 12, 1940, 3 (emphasis in the original). Also see "*Wind* on Regular Run," *MPH*, Feb. 8, 1941, 40.

76. Lowell Calvert to DOS, Jan. 16, 22, and 28, 1941 ("*GWTW* Second Playoff," box 191, DOS Papers, HRHRC); "The *Wind* Returns," *Advertising Age*, Jan. 27, 1941, 8.

77. "Schenck's Statement on Selznick," *Variety*, Aug. 28, 1940, 5.

78. "Dissolution of S-I," *Variety*, Aug. 7, 1940, 5; "S-I Dissolved," *FD*, Aug. 23, 1940, 1, 11; "Old Selznick Company," *Washington Post*, Aug. 24, 1940, 3; "Selznick International to Liquidate," *WSJ*, Aug. 24, 1940, 4; "Selznick International Dissolved," *MPH*, Aug. 31, 1940, 36; "Over $1,000,000 Dividends to S-I Partners," *Variety*, Sept. 4, 1940, 7; O'Shea to DOS, Aug. 15, 1940 ("*GWTW*, Grosses, Estimates," box 158, DOS Papers, HRHRC).

79. David Thomson, *Showman: The Life of David O. Selznick* (New York: Knopf, 1992), 345–91.

80. Edwin Schallert, "Maugham Will Write Selznick Screen Play," *Los Angeles Times*, Mar. 11, 1941, 13; "Jane Wyatt Gets Break," *Los Angeles Times*, May 15, 1941, A11; "D. O. Selznick Joins," *NYT*, Oct. 6, 1941, 12; "Financing Obtained," *FD*, Dec. 8, 1941, 1.

81. Edwin Schallert, "Broadway Sells," *Los Angeles Times*, Jan. 22, 1942, A10, and Schallert, "Super Tests," *Los Angeles Times*, Feb. 5, 1942, 8.

82. DOS to Rodgers and Dietz, Dec. 16, 1941, "John Hay Whitney" file, Box 331; Rodgers to DOS, Dec. 29, 1941 ("*GWTW* Third Playoff" file, box 193, both DOS Papers, HRHRC).

83. DOS to Calvert, Jan. 5, 1942 ("*GWTW* Third Playoff" file, box 193, DOS Papers, HRHRC).

84. DOS to Whitney, Jan. 5, 1942 (ibid., HRHRC).

85. Leonard Case to Whitney, Scanlon, and Alstock, Jan. 15, 1942 (ibid., HRHRC).

86. DOS to Dietz, Jan. 19, 1942 ("Gallup Poll 1939–1941–1942" file, box 3562, DOS Papers, HRHRC).

87. DOS to Calvert, Feb. 4, 1942 ("*GWTW* Third Playoff" file, box 193, DOS Papers, HRHRC).

88. Bosley Crowther, "Mr. Selznick and a Scarlett Future," *NYT*, Oct. 30, 1938, sec. 9, p. 5.

89. AIPO Survey 42–259, Forms K and T, Jan. 25–30, 1942 (RCPOR).

90. "*Gone with the Wind*," ARI Report 144, Feb. 19, 1942 (GLM).

91. Ibid.

92. Ads ran in the *New York Daily News*, Mar. 30, 1942, 24; the *Cleveland Press*, Feb. 6, 1942, and the *Cleveland News*, Feb. 6, 1942, 25; the *Times-Picayune* (New Orleans), Feb. 1, 1942; the *Sacramento Bee*, Feb. 9, 1942, 6; and the *New York Post*, May 1942, 31 (all in box 195, DOS Papers, HRHRC).

93. DOS to Calvert, May 30, 1942 ("*GWTW* Third Playoff," box 193, DOS Papers, HRHRC).

94. Calvert to DOS, Feb. 17, 1942 (ibid., HRHRC).

95. DOS to Calvert, May 30, 1942 (ibid., HRHRC).

96. In "*GWTW* Third Playoff" file (box 193, DOS Papers, HRHRC).

97. "*GWTW* $5,000,000 Gross Repeat," *HR*, Mar. 6, 1942, 1; and "$30,000,000 Gross for *Wind*," *MPH*, Mar. 28, 1942, 71.

98. "Gallup Survey for Selznick," *FD*, Apr. 16, 1942, 7.

99. Telegram to DOS, May 10, 1942 (in "Audience Research Institute (Gallup Poll)" file, box 842, DOS papers, HRHRC).

100. DOS to Ogilvy, May 11, 1942 ("Gallup Poll 1939–1941–1942" file, box 3562, DOS Papers, HRHRC).

101. DOS to Frank Freeman, vice president at Paramount Pictures and a member of the board, May 11, 1942 (ibid., HRHRC).

102. Ogilvy to DOS, May 15, 1942 (ibid., HRHRC).

9. Gallup Meets Goofy: Audience Research at the Walt Disney Studio

1. Bob Thomas, *The Art of Animation* (New York: Simon and Schuster, 1958), 32.

2. Bosley Crowther, "Cartoons on the Screen," *NYT*, Feb. 13, 1938, sec. 10, p. 4; Phil M. Daly, "Along the Rialto," *FD*, July 31, 1940, 3.

3. Richard Holliss and Brian Sibley, *The Disney Studio Story* (New York: Crown, 1988), 111–15.

4. "Radio Captures Disney," *Daily Variety*, Mar. 3, 1936, 1, cited in Betty Lasky, *RKO: The Biggest Little Major of Them All* (Santa Monica, Calif.: Roundtable, 1984), 137.

5. "President's Report of RKO Board Meeting, July 30, 1940" (Folder 681, box 90, Record Group III 2C, Nelson Rockefeller Papers, in the Rockefeller Archive Center; hereafter, RAC).

6. "Disney-RKO Deal," *Variety*, Mar. 4, 1936, 4; and Douglas Gomery, "Disney's Business History: A Reinterpretation," in Eric Smoodin, ed., *Disney Discourse: Producing the Magic Kingdom* (New York and London: Routledge, 1994), 72.

7. *Snow White* Seen Headed for Record," *MPH*, Oct. 15, 1938, 16; and Richard Jewell, "A History of RKO Radio Pictures, Incorporated, 1928–1942" (Ph.D. diss., University of Southern California, 1978), 400–402.

8. "Gross Rental from *Snow White*," *Variety*, July 19, 1939, 46.

9. "RCI-RKO Claim and Receivership, 1933–38" (folder 675, box 90, RG III 2C, Nelson Rockefeller Papers, RAC).

10. "*Snow White* Roadshow Tariff," *Variety*, May 11, 1938, 23; "*Snow White* Influ-

ence," *Variety*, July 13, 1938, 7; "Gross Rental from *Snow White*," 1, 46; "Disney Feature," *Variety*, May 29, 1940, 18.

11. "Disney's 800G Melon," *Variety*, June 29, 1938, 1, 52.

12. Jewell, "History of RKO," 422–30 and 480–81.

13. "RKO Radio Signs Pact," *FD*, June 20, 1939, 11.

14. "Disney and RKO Discuss," *MPH*, July 2, 1938, p. 22.

15. Ibid.

16. "Disney Feature," *Variety*, May 29, 1940, 18.

17. "President's Report of RKO Board Meeting" (RAC).

18. "Disney and RKO Discuss," 22.

19. "RKO's Budget," *Variety*, June 28, 1939, 6.

20. "*Pinocchio* Terms," *MPH*, Dec. 16, 1939, 29; "*Pinocchio*, Next 'Big' Arrivals," *MPH*, Feb. 3, 1940, 23; "*Pinocchio* Campaign," *MPH*, Dec. 9, 1939, 16; "Sales Strut," *Business Week*, Nov. 18, 1939, 4; "Disney's Deal," *Variety*, Feb. 21, 1940, 14; "*Pinocchio* to be Sold," *FD*, Dec. 11, 1939, 1, 7.

21. "*Pinocchio* Screen Triumph," *HR*, Jan. 30, 1940, 3; "*Pinocchio*," *Variety*, Jan. 31, 1940, 14.

22. "Loss for Walt Disney," *MPH*, Dec. 28, 1940, 40.

23. "President's Report of RKO Board Meeting" (RAC).

24. "Depinet Sees New Selling Plan," *FD*, Apr. 18, 1941, 1, 12.

25. "RKO Radio Flash," Mar.–June 1941, Louis B. Mayer Library, AFI; "No Gold-wyn-Disney-Welles in 'Fives'," *FD*, June 20, 1941, 1.

26. "Disney, RKO Renew," *MPH*, Sept. 28, 1940, 11.

27. Moya Luckett, "*Fantasia*: Cultural Constructions of Disney's 'Masterpiece,'" in Smoodin, ed., *Disney Discourse*, 214–36.

28. "Disney Distribution Setup," *FD*, Mar. 14, 1940, 1, 6.

29. Douglas W. Churchill, "Hollywood Gets Peek at *Fantasia*," *NYT*, Oct. 20, 1940, sec. 9, p. 5; and "Furore on *Fantasia*," *MPH*, Dec. 7, 1940, 1.

30. See "Mickey Mouse in Symphony," *Newsweek*, Nov. 25, 1940, 50–52; William Stull, "Fantasound," *American Cinematographer* (Feb. 1941): 58, 59, 80–81, and Stull, "*Fantasia* Sound" ("Better Theaters" section), *MPH*, Nov. 16, 1940, 7–8, 21; "Disney's 'Revolution,'" *MPH*, Mar. 16, 1940, 8.

31. "Distribution for *Fantasia*," *Variety*, Aug. 21, 1940, 6; "Stoki-Disney *Fantasia* Roadshow Plan," *Variety*, Mar. 20, 1940, 5, 20.

32. George Gallup to J. R. McDonough, Dec. 11, 1940 (ARI Correspondence File No. 1, RKO Papers, Culver City, California; hereafter, RKO Papers).

33. "Analysis of What Pix Scare Kids," *Variety*, Dec. 11, 1940, p. 27.

34. McDonough to Gallup, Jan. 9, 1941 (ARI Correspondence File No. 1, RKO Papers).

35. Gallup to McDonough, Apr. 9, 1941, and Schaefer to McDonough, May 12, 1941 (both in ARI Correspondence File No. 2, RKO Papers).

36. "RKO Releasing *Fantasia*," *FD*, Apr. 28, 1941, 1, 3; "*Fantasia* Under RKO Release," *FD*, May 6, 1941, 1, 8; "*Fantasia* Has Grossed," *Variety* Apr. 30, 1941, 7; "General Distribution for Disney *Fantasia*,'" *MPH*, May 3, 1941, 47.

37. The formula ARI developed involved taking the publicity penetration figure and twice the film's want-to-see score and multiplying this number by two-thirds to get the percentage of the box office return for the average RKO film. The number was meant to indicate whether the return for a new film would be generally above or below previous releases. See ARI's RKO Report 69, "When Should Publicity Start?" and Report No. 81, "Introduction to a New Index," in "Gallup Looks at the Movies: Audience Research Reports 1940–1950" (Princeton: American Institute of Public Opinion; Wilmington, Del.: Scholarly Resources, 1979); hereafter GLM.

38. David Ogilvy to McDonough, Jan. 1941 (ARI Correspondence File No. 1, RKO Papers).

39. Index of Publicity Penetration, for July 31 and Aug. 12, 1941, in "Increasing Profits through Continuous Audience Research" (GLM). A follow-up survey on January 17, 1942, confirmed these results.

40. "Unit Production Lags," *MPH*, Mar. 22, 1941, 14.

41. "Extend Disney-RKO Distribution," *FD*, Apr. 14, 1941, 1.

42. "Disney's Self-Trailer," *Variety*, Oct. 2, 1940, 2; and *"The Reluctant Dragon,"* *NYT*, July 25, 1941, 12.

43. Ned Depinet to Schaefer, Apr. 19, 1941; Schaefer to McDonough, Apr. 20, 1941; McDonough to Gallup, Apr. 21, 1941 (all in ARI Correspondence File No. 2, RKO Papers).

44. "RKO Radio Flash," Apr. 19, 1941 (AFI).

45. Ogilvy to McDonough, Apr. 19, 1941 (ARI Correspondence File No. 2, RKO Papers).

46. Index of Publicity Penetration, June 14–July 26, 1941, in "Increasing Profits" (GLM).

47. *"The Reluctant Dragon,"* *Time*, June 2, 1941, 83; and *MPH*, June 7, 1941, 38.

48. "Gross Rental from *Snow White*," 48.

49. Depinet to McDonough, June 3, 1941 (ARI Correspondence File No. 2, RKO Papers).

50. "Draggin' Disney's *Dragon* into N.Y.," *Variety*, July 23, 1941, 7.

51. "Mediators Hope," *Variety*, June 18, 1941, 22; "Labor Conciliator Steps In," *Variety*, July 9, 1941, 22; "Government Holds Off," *Variety*, July 16, 1941, 23; Anthony Bower, "Films: Snow White and the 1,200 Dwarves," *The Nation*, May 10, 1941, 565; "Disney Film Picketed," *NYT* July 25, 1941, 13. Harvey Deneroff has presented the most detailed analysis of the strike in "'Are We Mice or Men? The 1941 Disney Strike," paper presented at the annual conference of the Society for Animation Studies, Ottawa, Canada, 1991.

52. *"Dumbo* Gets Earlier Release," *Variety*, Dec. 11, 1940, 8.

53. "Disney Rides a Baby Elephant," *Newsweek*, Oct. 27, 1941, 61; "The New Pictures," *Time*, Oct. 27, 1941, 97–98, and "Mammal-of-the-Year," *Time*, Dec. 29, 1941, 27–28; *"Dumbo," Theatre Arts* (Dec. 1941): 907; Otis Ferguson, "Two for the Show," *New Republic*, Oct. 27, 1941, 537; *"Dumbo," FD*, Oct. 1, 1941, 4, and *Variety*, Oct. 1, 1941, 9.

54. Mark Langer, "Regionalism in Disney Animation," *Film History* 4 (1990): 305–321.

55. Index of Publicity Penetration, Oct. 11–Nov. 8, 1941 (GLM).

56. Gallup to McDonough, May 13, 1941; McDonough to Schaefer, May 20, 1941; McDonough to Gallup, May 20, 1941 (all in ARI Correspondence File No. 2, RKO Papers).

57. J. J. Aberdeen, *Hollywood Renegades: The Society of Independent Motion Picture Producers* (Los Angeles: Cobblestone Entertainment, 2000).

58. DOS to Gallup, Mar. 31, 1942 ("Gallup Poll 1939–1941–1942," box 3562, DOS Papers, HRHRC).

59. Eric Smoodin, *Animating Culture: Hollywood Cartoons from the Sound Era* (New Brunswick, N.J.: Rutgers University Press, 1993), 168–85.

60. George Gallup, interview by Thomas Simonet, Princeton, New Jersey, Sept. 21, 1977, transcript. Transcript courtesy of Thomas Simonet.

61. Ogilvy to DOS, Apr. 4, 1942 ("Gallup Poll 1939–1941–1942," box 3562, DOS Papers, HRHRC).

62. Ogilvy to DOS, June 9, 1942, and DOS to Ogilvy, July 25, 1942 (both in "Gallup Poll 1939–1941–1942," box 3562, DOS Papers, HRHRC).

63. Richard Shale, *Donald Duck Joins Up: The Walt Disney Studio During World War II* (Ann Arbor: UMI Research Press, 1982), 67–68.

64. ARI to Walt Disney, Sept. 2, 1942; Jack Sayers, ARI's Hollywood representative, to Disney executive Perce Pearce, Sept. 24, 1942; quoted in Shale, *Donald Duck Joins Up*, 69–70.

65. Shale, *Donald Duck Joins Up*, 76–77.

66. "Identification of Disney Characters" (Title Test Binder A-E, ARI box 10, The Walt Disney Studio Archive, Burbank, California; hereafter, WDSA).

67. "Cinderella" (Title Test Binder A-E, ARI box 10, WDSA).

68. "Cartoon Making Kicked Around," *Variety*, May 28, 1947, 6; and "Cut Cartoon Output," *Variety*, June 11, 1947, 5.

69. "The Walt Disney Studio Annual Report" for the fiscal year ending September 27, 1947 (WDSA).

70. "Net in 1946 for Disney," *Variety*, Jan. 15, 1947, 5; *Film Daily Yearbook* (1950), 1003.

71. Mark Kausler, John Cawley, and Jim Korkis, "Animated Oscars," *Cartoon Quarterly* 1 (1988): 15–18.

72. Arthur Knight, "Up from Disney," *Theatre Arts* (Aug. 1951): 34.

73. "Disney Preparing Eight New Features," *MPH*, June 1, 1946, 35.

74. Bill Peet, *An Autobiography* (Boston: Houghton Mifflin, 1989), 123.

75. Walt Disney, "Growing Pains," *Journal of the Society of Motion Picture Engineers* 36 (1941): 30–40.

76. W. E. Garity and J. L. Ledeen, "The New Walt Disney Studio," *Journal of the Society of Motion Picture Engineers* 36 (1941): 7, 8.

77. Jack Kinney, *Walt Disney and Other Assorted Characters* (New York: Harmony, 1988), 145.

78. Frank Thomas and Ollie Johnston, *Disney Animation: The Illusion of Life* (New York: Abbeville, 1984), 46–85.

79. "The Walt Disney Studio Annual Report" for the fiscal year ending September 27, 1947 (WDSA).

80. Several Disney animators discuss the studio's use of previews in their memoirs. See, for example, Kinney, *Walt Disney and Assorted Other Characters*, 46; Dave Hand, *Memoirs* (Cambria, Calif.: privately published, n.d.), 73–74; Shamus Culhane, *Talking Animals and Other People* (New York: St. Martin's, 1986). Also animation director and producer Ben Sharpsteen, interview by Dave Smith, Feb. 6, 1974, 5 (WDSA).

81. Culhane, *Talking Animals*, 113–14.

82. Walt Disney, Memo to art instructor Don Graham, Dec. 23, 1935, printed in Culhane, *Talking Animals*, 120.

83. William Weaver, "Studios Use Audience Research," *MPH*, July 20, 1946, 37.

84. Card Walker to Walt Disney, June 21, 1946 (*Casey Jones* file, ARI box 2, WDSA).

85. Walker to animator and director Charles Nichols, Mar. 9, 1950 (*Cold Turkey* non-critical rough file, ARI box 3, WDSA).

86. Walker to Walt Disney, Jan. 20, 1947 (*Pluto's Fledgling* rough preview file, ARI box 8, WDSA).

87. George Heinemann, conversation with the author, Aug. 3, 1995, Keene, New Hampshire.

88. Dallas Smythe, *Dependency Road: Communications, Capitalism, Consciousness, and Canada* (Norwood, N.J.: Ablex, 1981), 86.

89. Walker to Walt Disney, Oct. 31, 1946 (*Pluto's Blue Note* rough preview, ARI box 8, WDSA).

90. Walker to Harry Tytle, Nov. 5, 1948 (*Corn Chips* critical storyboard, ARI box 3, WDSA).

91. *Two Weeks Summer Vacation* file (ARI box 12, WDSA).

92. Walker to Disney, July 7, 1949 (*Pluto's White Elephant* storyboard, ARI box 8, WDSA).

93. Walker to Disney, Dec. 6, 1950 (*Two Gun Goofy* critical and non-critical storyboards, ARI box 12, WDSA).

94. This is illustrated in the numerous studies for *How to Sleep* (ARI box 5, WDSA).

95. *Grand Canyon Scope* file (ARI Box 4, WDSA).

96. Walt Disney, interview by Pete Martin, c. 1956 (WDSA).

97. Card Walker, telephone interview with the author, Feb. 23, 1992.

98. Maurice Rapf, conversation with the author, Aug. 3, 1995, Keene, New Hampshire.

99. For illustration of how these conferences could affect the animators, see Leo Salkin, "Disney's *Pigs Is Pigs*: Notes from a Journal, 1949–1953," in John Canemaker, ed., *Storytelling in Animation*, vol. 2 of *The Art of the Animated Image* (Los Angeles: American Film Institute, 1988): 11–20.

10. Like, Dislike, Like Very Much

1. Don Cahalan, interview by author, February 20, 1992, tape recording, Berkeley, California; *NORC [National Opinion Research Center] Report, 1985–86* (Chicago: University of Chicago, 1987): 73; Barbara Benson to David Selznick, December 8, 1943 ("Since You Went Away" previews, box 199, DOS Papers, HRHRC); "Al Sindlinger Joins Gallup," *FD*, January 20, 1943, 1, 3; "Audience Research in Expansion Move," *FD*, August 6, 1946, 3; "Sindlinger Resigns," *NYT*, September 1946, 48.

2. Sheatsley to Ogilvy, "Report of Field Trips," November 18, 1941 (ARI Correspondence File No. 3, RKO Papers).

3. Jean Converse, *Survey Research in the United States: Roots and Emergence, 1890–1960* (Berkeley: University of California Press, 1987), 186–236.

4. Robert P. Brundage, "Dr. Gallup Polls Public," *WSJ*, Oct. 23, 1946, 1.

5. "Problems Face Movie Makers," *Business Week*, December 6, 1947, 94–98; "Worries of Movie Makers," *U.S. News & World Report*, June 25, 1948, 31; "Hollywood Is a Little Better Off," *Business Week*, July 23, 1949, 61–64.

6. Leo Handel, *Hollywood Looks at Its Audience* (Urbana: University of Illinois Press, 1950; rpt., New York: Arno Press, 1976), 7.

7. "Science, Teamwork Needed in Pix," *HR*, May 7, 1946, 18.

8. "A.P. and Want-to-See," *Time* , July 22, 1946, 94–96.

9. George Gallup to publicity agent Robert Taplinger, Aug. 10, 1942 (*The More the Merrier*, George Stevens Collection, General Production Material, The Margaret Herrick Library, AMPAS).

10. William Weaver, "Audience Research Answers Question," *MPH*, July 27, 1946, 39.

11. Paul K. Perry, "Marketing and Attitude Research Applied to Motion Pictures," 5 (paper presented at the International Gallup Conference, New Delhi, India, Mar. 26, 1968; given to the author by Thomas Simonet).

12. "Gallup Poll Finds How to Sell a Movie," *Look*, October 26, 1948, 53–55.

13. Brundage, "Dr. Gallup Polls Public," 1.

14. ARI Report 108, "Carmen," October 14, 1941, in "Gallup Looks at the Movies: Audience Research Reports 1940–1950" (Princeton: American Institute of Public Opinion; Wilmington, Del.: Scholarly Resources, 1979).

15. "Gallup Poll Finds How to Sell a Movie," 55.

16. "How Gallup Poll Samples Public Opinion," *Business Week*, June 19, 1948, 39–53.

17. Bosley Crowther, "It's the Fans," *NYT Magazine*, June 24, 1945, 29–30.

18. Robert Shaw, "A Package Deal in Film Opinions," *The Screen Writer* 2 (March 1947): 35.

19. Red Kann, "On the March," *MPH*, July 29, 1944, 32.

20. *ARI Case Histories*, vol. 1: *The Jolson Story* (The Margaret Herrick Library, AMPAS).

21. Shaw, "A Package Deal," 33.

22. Handel, *Hollywood Looks at Its Audience*, 8–10.

23. William Weaver, "Studios Use Audience Research," *MPH*, July 20, 1946, 37; and Harold Wolff, "Pre-Testing Movies," *Science Illustrated*, Feb. 1947, 115.

24. Shaw, "A Package Deal," 28–29; Brundage, "Dr. Gallup Polls Public," 4; William Lydgate, "Audience Pre-Testing," *Sales Management*, Mar. 15, 1944, 98.

25. Marjorie Fiske and Leo Handel, "New Techniques for Studying the Effectiveness of Films," *Journal of Marketing* 11 (1947): 393–95; and Tore Hollonquist and Edward A. Suchman, "Listening to the Listeners: Experiences with the Stanton-Lazarsfeld Program Analyzer," in Paul F. Lazarsfeld and Frank N. Stanton, eds., *Radio Research 1942–1943* (New York: Duell, Sloan, and Pierce, 1941; rpt., New York: Arno Press, 1979), 266–76.

26. "Gallup Gadget," *Business Week*, February 3, 1945, 80; "Electric Movie 'Reviewers' Record Reaction," *Popular Mechanics* (May 1947): 149; Weaver, "Studios Use Audience Research"; Wolff, "Pre-Testing Movies," 44–45, 115.

27. Wolff, "Pre-Testing Movies," 44.

28. "Gallup Poll Finds How to Sell a Movie," 53–55.

29. Handel, *Hollywood Looks at Its Audience*, 53–56.

30. Kann, "On the March"; Crowther, "It's the Fans," 29; "A.P. & Want to See," 96; William Weaver, "Audience Research to Key Services," *MPH*, Aug. 17, 1946, 28–29; "New Gallup Preview Check," *HR*, Mar. 14, 1945, 6.

31. George Gallup, interview by Thomas Simonet, Princeton, New Jersey, Sept. 21, 1977, transcript (transcript courtesy of Thomas Simonet), 4; Phil Gustafson, "They Know What You Like," *Nation's Business* (November 1948): 80.

32. "Goldwyn Wants Ad Agency," *Variety*, June 19, 1946, 7.

33. "How's Your 'Audience Penetration'?" *Variety*, April 17, 1946, 32.

34. "Rathvon Outlines RKO Coordination," *Variety*, July 10, 1946, 21.

35. Brundage, "Dr. Gallup Polls Public," 1; Kann, "On the March"; "How Gallup Poll Samples," 49.

36. Gallup, interview by Simonet, 5. A detailed discussion of ARI's postwar work for Selznick can be found in Shannon Kelley, "Gallup Goes Hollywood: Motion Picture Audience Research in the 1940s," master's thesis, University of Texas at Austin, 1989.

37. Ernest Bornemann, "The Public Opinion Myth," *Harper's*, July 1947, 30–33. For another essay in a similar vein, see Gilbert Seldes, "How Dense Is the Mass?" *Atlantic*, Nov. 1948, 24–25.

38. Shaw, "A Package Deal," 34.

39. Thomas F. Brady, "Hollywood Augury," *NYT*, Nov. 7, 1948, sec. 10, p. 5.

40. "Korda Begins Fourth Film Phase," *NYT*, Apr. 14, 1946, sec. 2, p. 3.

41. Ranald [sic] MacDougall, "Reactions to Audience Research," *The Screen Writer* 2 (Apr. 1947): 30.

42. Ibid., 31.

43. "Audience Research Blues," *Variety*, May 8, 1946, 5.

44. "Gallup Rates '43 Pictures," *HR*, March 16, 1944, 1, 2.

45. "Photoplay" ad, *FD*, Feb. 1945, 11.

46. "Continuing Gallup Poll," *FD*, April 23, 1945, 2.

47. "Audience Research Blues," 25.

48. Gorham Kindem, "Hollywood's Movie Star System During the Studio Era," *Film Reader* 6 (1985): 18.

49. George Gallup, interview with Paul Sheatsley, Mar. 22, 1978, NORC, University of Chicago, transcript, 14.

50. "Irate Exhibs Sing 'Don't Blame Me," *Variety*, July 17, 1946, 20; Thomas M. Pryor, "Theatre Owners Sound Off on Ills of Movies," *NYT*, Feb. 27, 1949, sec 10, p. 5.

51. "Detroit Exhibitors' Poll," Jan. 24, 1951 (source not indicated, "Audience Research" clippings file, The Margaret Herrick Library, AMPAS).

52. Eliot L. Friedson, "Communications Research and the Concept of the Mass," *American Sociological Review* 18 (1953): 315–17; Seldes, "How Dense Is the Mass?" 25–27.

53. Dallas W. Smythe, Parker B. Lusk, and Charles A. Lewis, "Portrait of an Art-Theater Audience," *Quarterly of Film, Radio, and Television* 8 (1953): 28–50; Geoffrey Wagner, "The Lost Audience," *Quarterly of Film, Radio, and Television* 6 (1952): 338–50.

54. "For Whom Are We Making Pix?" *Variety*, September 27, 1950, 3; "Customers Down Three Million (Gallup)," *Variety*, February 23, 1949, 5.

55. Bernard Cirlin and Jack Peterman, "Pre-testing a Motion Picture: A Case History," *Journal of Social Issues* 3 (Summer 1947): 39–41; Handel, *Hollywood Looks at its Audience*, 49–55.

56. Leo Salkin, "Disney's *Pigs Is Pigs*: Notes from a Journal, 1949–1953," in John Canemaker, ed., *Storytelling in Animation*, vol. 1 of *The Art of the Animated Image* (Los Angeles: American Film Institute, 1988), 13–14.

57. See, for example, Olen J. Earnest, "*Star Wars*: A Case Study of Motion Picture Marketing," in Bruce Austin, ed., *Current Research in Film: Audiences, Economics, and the Law*, vol. 1 (Norwood, N.J.: Ablex, 1985), 1–18; Thomas Simonet, "Market Research: Beyond the Fanny of the Cohn," *Film Comment* (Jan.–Feb. 1980): 66–69.

58. "Gallup Seeks Comeback in Movie World," *Advertising Age*, Apr. 15, 1944, 30.

Index

Abe Lincoln in Illinois (1940), 137
Academy Awards, 157
adaptations, 94, 137–38
advertising, 16–17, 27–29, 29 (photo), 32–36, 39–44, 180 (photo), 183–88, 186 (photo), 217–20, 222
American College Testing Program (ACT), 20
American Institute of Public Opinion (AIPO), 53–56, 63–75, 82–83, 91, 243n8
Anderson, Harold, 53
Ang, Ien, 6–8
applied psychology, 17 20
Army Surgeon (1942), 155–56
Arnaz, Desi, 148–49, 150 (photo)
Astaire, Fred, 141–42
attendance surveys, 84–86, 88–89
audience research and efficiency, 206–13, 216
Audience Research Institute (ARI), 4, 12, 77–90, 94–101, 128, 215, 227
audience research today, 2–3, 228–29

Baker, M. Joyce, 134
Ball, Lucille, 149, 150 (photo)
Bambi (1942), 204
Baritz, Loren, 22
behaviorism, 20
Benamou, Catherine, 158
Benchley, Robert, 201
Beninger, James, 7
Benny, Jack, 39, 43
Benson, Barbara Miller, 82, 215
Benson, Susan Porter, 20–21
Bentham, Jeremy, 67
Bernstein, Matthew, 164
The Best Years of Our Lives (1946), 222
blind bidding, 93, 217
block booking, 93, 217
Bogart, Leo, 72
Bogeaus, Benedict, 217
Bornemann, Ernest, 224
Bourdieu, Pierre, 8, 74
Boyce, James, 72

Cahalan, Don, 77, 82, 215

Cantril, Hadley, 60, 66, 73
Carmen (1946), 219
casting tests, 141–46
Cattell, James McKeen, 18–19
Chase, Stuart, 32
Cherington, Paul, 51, 55
Cinderella (1950), 205–206, 212
class differences, 111–14, 113 (photo),
    128–31, 134–37, 185–87
Cohen, Patricia Cline, 7
coincidental method, 44–47
Colman, Ronald, 143–44
comic strips, 25–29
consent decree, 92–93,158
Continuing Audit of Marquee Values,
    145–46
Converse, Jean, 216
Cooperative Analysis of Broadcasting
    (CAB), 44–45
Cowles, Gardner, Jr., 25, 27, 56
Cowles, Gardner, Sr., 25
critical and noncritical tests (Disney),
    210–11
Crossley, Archibald, 4, 44, 51, 62, 90, 145
Crowther, Bosley, 113
Culhane, Shamus, 208
Custen, George, 253n34

Daily Iowan, 15–18, 53
dark horse surveys, 144–45
Depinet, Ned, 159, 201, 203
Des Moines Register & Tribune, 25–27
Dewey, John, 20, 67
Dies Committee, 139
Dietz, Howard, 180
Disney and RKO, 194–203
Disney studio, 207–208
Disney, Roy, 199, 207
Disney, Walt, 10–11, 86, 193–213
Doane, Mary Ann, 134
double features, 102–19, 107 (photo)
Duel in the Sun (1946), 223
Dumbo (1941), 202–203
Dunne, Irene, 133

Editor & Publisher, 36
ethnicity, 24, 147–49
expertise, concept of, 22

Fantasia (1940), 197–200, 199 (photo)
filter questions, 87–90
Fortune magazine polls, 55, 62, 84, 93
Foucault, Michel, 6, 8
Fox, Stephen, 32
Fuller, Kathryn, 113
Funk, Wilfred J., 60, 63

Gaines, Jane, 240n30
Gallup, George, Sr., 14–15
gender issues, 128, 133–34, 147, 239n24
Gilda (1946), 222
Gill, Sam, 114
Goldwyn, Samuel, 81, 101–103, 112–13,
    116, 199, 222
Gone with the Wind, 94, 95 (photo),
    168–91, 179 (photo), 180 (photo), 186
    (photo), 265n20
Grape-Nuts, 27–28, 29 (photo)

Hall, G. Stanley, 18
Handel, Leo, 11
Harrisburg Pennsylvanian, 57
Hays Office, 110, 138–39
Hearst, William Randolph, 27, 33, 62,
    68
Heinemann, George, 210
Herbst, Susan, 6–7, 72–73, 74
Hilmes, Michele, 79, 241n58
Hollywood Looks at Its Audience (Han-
    del), 11
Hopkins Televoting Machine, 221–22,
    225, 228
Hower, Ralph, 33–34
Hurja, Emil, 66
Hurwitz, Donald, 48

independent producers, 137–38, 163–64,
    166, 193

integrated commercials, 42–43
interviewers, 70, 82, 128, 216
Iowa, University of, 15–23, 237n44

J. Walter Thompson agency, 35–39
James, William, 19–20
Jefferson, Iowa (Gallup's hometown),
     13–15. See also Moraine, Thomas
Jell-O ads, 39, 43, 79
Jewell, Richard, 123, 158
The Jolson Story (1946), 220–22
Jones, Bob, 215

Katz, Daniel, 70
Killian Graphic Scale, 20–22
Killian's Department store, 16, 20–21
Kimball, Ward, 212
Kindem, Gorham, 226
Kitty Foyle (1940), 142, 151, 155, 156
     (photo)
Koerner, Charles, 159–60
Korda, Alexander, 225
Kornhauser, Arthur, 70
Koszarski, Richard, 235n15
Kuhn, Annette, 5
Kyser, Kay, 132

Lambert, Gerald, 90
Langer, Mark, 202
Larmon, Sigurd, 47, 79–80
Lazarsfeld, Paul, 73
Lever Brothers, 36–37
Liberty magazine study, 34–36, 37
     (photo), 39–40, 240n33
Literary Digest, 51–52, 57–63, 73, 82
Lloyd, Harold, 144
Loew's/MGM, 96, 100, 125, 165, 171–88,
     207, 217
lost audience, 111
Loy, Myrna, 154–55
Luce, Henry R., 62
Luckett, Moya, 198
Lux soap, 36–38, 240n30
Lydgate, William, 134

MacDougall, Ranald, 225
Macfadden, Bernarr, 34
Maltby, Richard, 99–100
Marchand, Roland, 26
mass vs. class debate, 111–14
Mayer, Louis B., 96, 99–100
McDonough, J. R., 126, 135–36, 145,
     151–54, 159, 161, 200–201
Meier, Norman, 82
Meyer, Eugene, 56–57, 65, 71, 96
MGM. See Loew's/MGM
Morain, Thomas, 14, 17
"Most interesting book" survey, 94
Motion Picture Producers Association
     (MPPA), 188–91
Mr. Lucky (1943), 218
Mrs. Miniver (1942), 160
Muni, Paul, 131
Münsterberg, Hugo, 18, 21

Napoli, Donald, 19, 22
The New Spirit (1942), 204
Nichols, Dudley, 225
Nightingale, Virginia, 5
Notorious (1946), 220
Notre Dame, University of, 79, 149
Nugent, Frank, 118
Nye, Senator Gerald, 140

"An Objective Method for Determin-
     ing Reader Interest in the Content
     of a Newspaper" (Gallup's doctoral
     thesis), 23–26
Odlum, Floyd, 123–24, 158–59
Ogilvy, David, 10, 79, 81–83, 97, 110,
     122, 128–34, 136–37, 146–49, 152–56,
     160–61, 200, 204, 215

Palladino, Grace, 132
Paramount, 96, 99–100, 125
Patrick, George, 19
Peter Pan (1953), 204–205, 212
Peters, John Durham, 73, 74
Photoplay, 36–37, 79, 226

Pinocchio (1940), 196–97
polling methods, 53–56, 59–60, 62–63, 71–75, 89–90, 96, 108–109, 243*n*14
Poovey, Mary, 7
Powell, William, 154–55
Prairie Grass Roots (Morain), 14
preview screenings, 177, 208–12, 217, 220–22, 225–28
Production Code, 138–39
Program Analyzer, 46–47, 221
The Psychological Corporation 51
The Public Is Never Wrong (Zukor), 1
Public Opinion Quarterly, 70, 89
public opinion theory, 6–12, 67–75, 247*n*87
publicity penetration, 200–202, 223, 271*n*37
Publisher's Syndicate, 53
The Pulse of Democracy (1940), 66–69

Quigley, Martin, 140

radio, 4, 42–49, 51, 62, 90, 145
The Ramparts We Watch (1940), 130
Rank, J. Arthur, 218–19
Rapf, Maurice, 213
Rathvon, N. Peter, 124, 149, 151, 158–59
The Reluctant Dragon (1941), 200–202
Renov, Michael, 134
response bias, 63–64
RKO Radio Pictures, 10, 121–61, 218, 226, 257*n*2
roadshows, 176–79
Robinson, Claude, 57, 59
Robinson, Daniel, 244*n*20
Rockefeller, Nelson, 121–25, 257*n*8
Rogers, Ginger, 141–42, 151
Roosevelt, Franklin, 37 (photo), 52, 59–66, 90
Roper, Elmo, 4, 51, 55, 62, 84, 90
Rorty, James, 33
Ross, Dorothy, 22
Rosten, Leo, 100–101, 110, 253*n*35
rough cuts (Disney), 211–12

Rousseau, Jean-Jacques, 67
Rubicam, Raymond, 31, 38–39, 47, 79

sample bias, 63
sampling, 54–56, 64–65, 152
Sarnoff, David, 123
Sayers, Jack, 215
Schaefer, George, 121, 124, 126–27, 135–37, 140–42, 158–59, 161, 201
Schiller, Herbert, 78, 90
Schlink, Frederick, 32
scientism, 22
Scott, Walter Dill, 18–19, 21, 40–42
Seashore, Carl, 19–20
Selznick, David O., 10–11, 80–81, 83, 87, 89, 124, 163–91, 204
Selznick, Lewis, 164
Selznick, Myron, 146, 164
Seversky, Alexander, 205
Shales, Richard, 205
Shaw, Robert, 225
Sheatsley, Paul, 82, 128, 215
Simonet, Thomas, 79
Sindlinger, Albert, 215
Small, Edward, 217
Smoodin, Eric, 204
Smulyan, Susan, 42
Smythe, Dallas, 210
Snow White and the Seven Dwarfs (1937), 195–96
Society of Independent Motion Picture Producers (SIMPP), 204
Song of the South (1946), 213, 219
A Song to Remember (1945), 220
Squire, Peverill, 63
Staiger, Janet, 164
star studies, 84, 125–26, 141–49, 154–55, 167–68, 226
Steele, Richard, 66
story tests, 125–26, 135–38, 149–53, 219–20, 224–25
storyboard tests (Disney), 211–12
studio ARI's (Disney), 209–12
Studlar, Gaylyn, 17

Sunset Boulevard (1950), 228
Susman, Warren, 7–8
Swanson, Gloria, 133

Taylor, Frederick Winslow, 19, 21
Technicolor surveys, 84–90
teenagers, 86, 106–108, 114, 131–33, 185–87, 219–20, 225–26
tel-auto lists, 58–59
Thomson, David, 182
Thorp, Margaret, 115
Through Many Windows (1926), 32–33
title tests, 218–19
Too Many Girls (1940), 149, 150 (photo)
Turner, Hawley, 27
Twentieth Century-Fox, 96, 99–100, 125

Victory Through Air Power (1943), 205

Walker, Card, 209–10
Waller, Gregory, 113, 223
Wanger, Walter, 81, 114, 140
war films, 139–41, 160

Warner Bros., 99, 207, 211
Washington Post, 56–57, 61, 64, 71, 73
Watson, John Broadus, 20
Wayne, John, 144
Wechsler, James, 69
Welles, Orson, 73, 127, 142, 143 (photo)
Whitney, Jock. *See* Whitney, John Hay
Whitney, John Hay, 80, 86–90, 124, 165, 167–68, 171–72, 175, 182
Wolcott, James, 215
Woodward, Helen, 32–33
World War II, impact on Hollywood, 93–94, 125, 139–41, 160, 178, 182, 206, 215–17
Wundt, Wilhelm, 18–19

Young & Rubicam agency, 27, 31–32, 39–48, 78–82, 210
Your Money's Worth (1927), 32

Zanuck, Darryl F., 96, 100, 127
Zukor, Adolph, 1–2

FILM AND CULTURE

A series of Columbia University Press

EDITED BY JOHN BELTON

What Made Pistachio Nuts? Early Sound Comedy and the Vaudeville Aesthetic
HENRY JENKINS

Showstoppers: Busby Berkeley and the Tradition of Spectacle
MARTIN RUBIN

Projections of War: Hollywood, American Culture, and World War II
THOMAS DOHERTY

Laughing Screaming: Modern Hollywood Horror and Comedy
WILLIAM PAUL

Laughing Hysterically: American Screen Comedy of the 1950s
ED SIKOV

Primitive Passions: Visuality, Sexuality, Ethnography, and Contemporary Chinese Cinema
REY CHOW

The Cinema of Max Ophuls: Magisterial Vision and the figure of Woman
SUSAN M. WHITE

Black Women as Cultural Readers
JACQUELINE BOBO

Picturing Japaneseness: Monumental Style, National Identity, Japanese Film
DARRELL WILLIAM DAVIS

Attack of the Leading Ladies: Gender, Sexuality, and Spectatorship in Classic Horror Cinema
RHONA J. BERENSTEIN

This Mad Masquerade: Stardom and Masculinity in the Jazz Age
GAYLYN STUDLAR

Sexual Politics and Narrative Film: Hollywood and Beyond
ROBIN WOOD

The Sounds of Commerce: Marketing Popular Film Music
JEFF SMITH

Orson Welles, Shakespeare, and Popular Culture
MICHAEL ANDEREGG

Pre-Code Hollywood: Sex, Immorality, and Insurrection in American Cinema, 1930–1934
THOMAS DOHERTY

Sound Technology and the American Cinema: Perception, Representation, Modernity
JAMES LASTRA

Melodrama and Modernity: Early Sensational Cinema and Its Contexts
BEN SINGER

Wondrous Difference: Cinema, Anthropology, and Turn-of-the-Century Visual Culture
ALISON GRIFFITHS

Hearst Over Hollywood: Power, Passion, and Propaganda in the Movies
LOUIS PIZZITOLA

Masculine Interests: Homoerotics in Hollywood Film
ROBERT LANG

Special Effects: Still in Search of Wonder
MICHELE PIERSON

Designing Women: Cinema, Art Deco, and the Female Form
LUCY FISCHER

Cold War, Cool Medium: Television, McCarthyism, and American Culture
THOMAS DOHERTY

Katharine Hepburn: Star as Feminist
ANDREW BRITTON

Silent Film Sound
RICK ALTMAN

*Home in Hollywood: The Imaginary
Geography of Hollywood*
ELISABETH BRONFEN

*Hollywood and the Culture Elite: How
the Movies Became American*
PETER DECHERNEY

Taiwan Film Directors: A Treasure Island
EMILIE YUEH-YU YEH AND
DARRELL WILLIAM DAVIS

*Shocking Representation: Historical
Trauma, National Cinema, and the Modern
Horror Film*
ADAM LOWENSTEIN

China on Screen: Cinema and Nation
CHRIS BERRY AND MARY FARQUHAR

*The New European Cinema: Redrawing
the Map*
ROSALIND GALT